Immigration and Asylum Handbook

This book supports the re-accreditation process of the Immigration and Asylum Accreditation Scheme (IAAS) and is written in conjunction with three online learning courses (see **www.lawsociety.org.uk/cpdcentre**):

Asylum Claims and Procedures
Mark Symes, HJT Training

Deportation and Detention
David Jones, HJT Training

Trafficking and Domestic Violence
Mark Symes, HJT Training

A range of other books from Law Society Publishing can be ordered from all good bookshops or direct (telephone 0870 850 1422, email **lawsociety@prolog.uk.com** or visit our online shop at **www.lawsociety.org.uk/bookshop**).

IMMIGRATION AND ASYLUM HANDBOOK

A Guide to Publicly Funded Legal Work under the
Immigration and Asylum Accreditation Scheme

General Editor: Mark Symes

The Law Society

Crown copyright material is reproduced with the permission of the Controller of Her Majesty's Stationery Office

ISBN-13: 978-1-78446-066-2

Published in 2016 by the Law Society
113 Chancery Lane, London WC2A 1PL

Reprinted in 2017

Typeset by Columns Design XML Ltd, Reading
Printed by Hobbs the Printers Ltd, Totton, Hants

The paper used for the text pages of this book is FSC® certified. FSC (the Forest Stewardship Council®) is an international network to promote responsible management of the world's forests.

Contents

Preface   ix
Notes on contributors   x
Table of cases   xiii
Table of statutes   xxii
Table of statutory instruments   xxiv
Table of international instruments   xxix
Abbreviations   xxxiii

1   Refugee claims   1

    1.1   Introduction: a reminder of the basics   1
    1.2   Asylum seekers   2
    1.3   Well-founded fear   3
    1.4   Evidence from victims of trauma   14
    1.5   Assessing risk: country evidence   18
    1.6   Activities in the UK   23
    1.7   Activities conducted in bad faith   25
    1.8   UNHCR mandated grants of status   26
    1.9   Risks arising from mode and reality of return   27
    1.10   Acts of persecution   28
    1.11   The 'Convention reasons'   34
    1.12   State protection   38
    1.13   Internal relocation   39
    1.14   Multiple countries of nationality or returnability 42
    1.15   Exclusion clauses   43
    1.16   Humanitarian protection   51

2   Asylum process and practice   56

    2.1   Claiming asylum   56
    2.2   Children as asylum seekers   61
    2.3   Gender and asylum   70
    2.4   Fast-track appeals   73
    2.5   Detained asylum casework   75
    2.6   Third country cases   76

2.7	'Clearly unfounded' certificates	81
2.8	Asylum claims from EU nationals	84
2.9	Fresh claims	84
2.10	Benefits of recognition as a refugee	94
2.11	Refugees and work, benefits and education	98
2.12	Benefits of humanitarian protection	98
3	**Human rights law and asylum appeals**	**100**
3.1	Human Rights Act 1998	100
3.2	European Convention on Human Rights	102
3.3	Discretionary leave	124
3.4	The Charter of Fundamental Rights of the European Union	128
3.5	Asylum appeals	131
3.6	Expert evidence	149
3.7	Fee exemptions	156
4	**Deportation**	**158**
4.1	Statutory framework	158
4.2	The deportation regimes	158
4.3	The procedure for deportation	160
4.4	Appeal rights under the 2014 Act	164
4.5	Nexus cases: a special deportation category	170
4.6	Leave to remain granted where deportation is resisted	172
4.7	Revocation of deportation order	172
4.8	Public policy removals and exclusions	173
4.9	EEA deportation appeals	177
5	**Detention**	**179**
5.1	Statutory framework and the power to detain	179
5.2	Detention processes	179
5.3	The exercise of the power to detain	181
5.4	Release and bail	183
5.5	Detention remedies summary	189
6	**Victims of trafficking**	**191**
6.1	The needs of victims	191
6.2	The Convention on Action against Trafficking in Human Beings	191
6.3	Assessing the claim	192
6.4	Definition of trafficking	196
6.5	Historic trafficking	197
6.6	Referral process	198

6.7	Decision-making process	199
6.8	Identification of victims and Article 4 duties	202
6.9	Challenging trafficking decisions	204
6.10	Support beyond assistance with immigration status	206

7 Victims of domestic violence **208**

7.1	Introduction	208
7.2	Immigration Rules: domestic violence route	208
7.3	Definition of domestic violence	210
7.4	Evidencing the claim	212
7.5	Right of appeal/review	214
7.6	'Destitution – domestic violence' (DDV) concession	215
7.7	EEA nationals and their family members	216

8 Public funding **217**

8.1	Legal Aid, Sentencing and Punishment of Offenders Act 2012	217
8.2	What remains in scope of legal aid	217
8.3	What is 'out of scope' under LASPO 2012	219
8.4	Exceptional case funding	220
8.5	Merits Criteria Regulations	221
8.6	Immigration and Asylum Specification of the 2013 Standard Civil Contract	225
8.7	For the future: a residence test for legal aid	226

APPENDICES

A Statutes **229**

A1	Immigration Act 1971 (extracts) [ss.3, 3C, 24, 24A, 25, 25A, 25B, 26]	231
A2	Immigration and Asylum Act 1999 (extracts) [ss.10, 31, 94, 95]	236
A3	Nationality, Immigration and Asylum Act 2002 (extracts) [ss.72, 76, 78, 78A, 82–86, 92, 94, 94A, 94B, 96, 97, 104, 113, 117A, 117B, 117C, 117D, 120]	241
A4	Asylum and Immigration (Treatment of Claimants, etc.) Act 2004 (extracts) [ss.1, 2, 4, 8; Sched.3, Part 2]	256
A5	UK Borders Act 2007 (extracts) [ss.32, 33, 34, 35, 36, 37, 38]	265
A6	Borders, Citizenship and Immigration Act 2009 (extract) [s.55]	270
A7	Identity Documents Act 2010 (extracts) [ss.4, 7]	272

B   Court procedure rules   **275**

B1   Tribunal Procedure (First-tier Tribunal) (Immigration and
      Asylum Chamber) Rules 2014   277
B2   Tribunal Procedure (Upper Tribunal) Rules 2008 (extracts)
      [rules 2, 5, 6, 12, 13, 15, 17, 17A, 21, 22A, 24, 25,
      36A, 44, 45, 46]   299
B3   Practice Directions: Immigration and Asylum Chambers of
      the First-tier Tribunal and the Upper Tribunal (extracts)
      [paras. 3, 4, 7, 9–13]   309
B4   Practice Statements: Immigration and Asylum Chambers of
      the First-tier Tribunal and the Upper Tribunal (extracts)
      [paras.3, 5, 7]   316

C   International conventions and EU-derived statutory instruments   **319**

C1   Immigration (European Economic Area) Regulations 2006
      (extracts) [regs.10, 19, 20, 20A, 20B, 21, 21A, 21B, 25,
      26, 27, 29AA, 29A]   321
C2   Refugee or Person in Need of International Protection
      (Qualification) Regulations 2006   331
C3   European Convention on Human Rights (extracts) [Articles
      1–15]   334
C4   UNHCR 1951 Refugee Convention (extracts) [Articles 1,
      31, 32, 33]   339
C5   Council of Europe Convention on Action against Trafficking
      in Human Beings (extracts) [Articles 1–4, 10, 12–14]   342

D   Immigration Rules (extracts)   **347**

D1   Part 11 – Asylum (paragraphs 326A to 352H)   349
D2   Part 11B – Asylum (paragraphs 357 to 361)   369
D3   Part 12 – Procedure and rights of appeal (paragraphs 353
      to 353B)   372
D4   Part 13 – Deportation (paragraphs A362 to 400)   373
D5   Appendix FM – Family members (extracts) [sections DVILR,
      E-DVILR, D-DVILR]   379

E   Home Office guidance and policy   **381**

E1   Asylum Policy Instruction: Discretionary Leave (extracts)   383
E2   Victims of Modern Slavery – Competent Authority Guidance
      (extracts)   384
E3   Victims of Domestic Violence (extracts)   393

Index   **405**

Preface

Law Society accreditation under the Immigration and Asylum Accreditation Scheme is a standard to which immigration practitioners aspire and which is compulsory for individuals conducting immigration and asylum work under a legal aid contract. Re-accreditation is a mechanism to ensure that accredited practitioners maintain standards, competence and knowledge of immigration and asylum law and practice.

The *Immigration and Asylum Handbook* has been designed to support candidates undertaking the re-accreditation course and in the assessments that follow. It will also be a resource for individuals accrediting at Levels 1 and 2.

The Handbook is practical in nature and will be a useful resource to practitioners in their day-to-day casework. It contains updates on core areas of legal aid practice including asylum, human rights, family reunion, domestic violence, human trafficking, detention, deportation and appeals. There is also guidance on legal aid as it applies in immigration and asylum casework. Further guidance for both accreditation and re-accreditation candidates can be found on the Law Society website.

We hope that practitioners will find the *Immigration and Asylum Handbook* to be a valuable guide through accreditation and re-accreditation and a practical resource in day-to-day casework.

The Handbook was compiled by Mark Symes of HJT Training with guidance from Kamla Adiseshiah, Chief Assessor of the Immigration and Asylum Accreditation Scheme.

The Law Society
May 2016

Notes on contributors

Julian Bild is a trainer and consultant in immigration and asylum law and practice. Before becoming a trainer, Julian had a 15-year career as a solicitor specialising in this area of work. Julian trained as a solicitor at Wilsons LLP, and has additional experience from working for the Refugee Legal Centre, as a solicitor in private practice, and as a senior lawyer and training manager for the Immigration Advisory Service. He has had conduct of many important reported and Country Guidance cases before the Tribunal and higher courts.

David Jones is a practising barrister at Garden Court Chambers. He specialises in human rights, European Union (EU) free movement and personal injury litigation. David has developed an expertise in deportation proceedings and civil litigation in relation to false imprisonment and unlawful detention cases, and has been at the vanguard of proceedings seeking to attain equality of treatment for foreign national prisoners. He has delivered legal training to numerous agencies, including the UNHCR, the Legal Services Commission, the Office of the Immigration Services Commissioner (OISC), Treasury Solicitor and the UK Border Agency and has participated in development and delivery of HJT core training courses for OISC assessments at all levels, particularly advocacy training. A contributor to academic works published by Liberty, LexisNexis and HJT, David is the co-founder of HJT Research which provides online country information on human rights conditions in over 80 countries.

Mark Symes provides advice and representation in all areas of immigration, asylum and human rights law, including EU free movement law. He has represented clients in every forum from the Tribunal to the Supreme Court, and the European Court of Human Rights. He has long specialised in asylum law generally, including all aspects of international protection, having originally worked for many years at the Refugee Legal Centre where he ultimately was the Tribunal team leader in charge of national legal strategy. He is also a deputy judge of the Upper Tribunal and a fellow of the Institute of Advanced Legal Studies, as well as being a founder director of HJT Training.

Colin Yeo is a director of HJT Training, a tenant at Garden Court Chambers and specialises in immigration law and family law. Colin is renowned for his free movement blog **www.freemovement.org.uk** and he has a great deal of training experience, having designed and delivered the Immigration Advisory Service's comprehensive two-week knowledge and skills course. He has substantially contributed to similar training programmes for Refugee and Migrant Justice and HJT.

Table of cases

A *v.* London Borough of Croydon [2009] EWHC 939 (Admin)......................... 2.2.3

A *v.* Staatssecretaris van Veiligheid en Justitie (United Nations High
Commissioner for Refugees (UNHCR) intervening) (Judgment) [2014]
EUECJ C-148/13 (02 December 2014) (C-148/13 to C-150/13) 1.3.11

A, R (on the application of) *v.* London Borough of Croydon [2009] UKSC 8........ 2.2.3

A, B, and C *see* A *v.* Staatssecretaris van Veiligheid en Justitie (United
Nations High Commissioner for Refugees (UNHCR) intervening)
(Judgment)

AA (Article 15(c)) Iraq CG [2015] UKUT 544 (IAC)................... 1.16.1.1, 2.9.5, 1.9

AA (risk for involuntary returnees) Zimbabwe CG [2006] UKAIT 61................. 1.6

AA (Uganda) *v.* Secretary of State for the Home Department [2008] EWCA
Civ 579 .... 1.13.1

AA (unattended children) Afghanistan CG [2012] UKUT 16 (IAC).................... 2.2.1

AB *v.* Secretary of State for the Home Department [2015] EWHC 1490
(Admin) 6.8

Abdullahi *v.* Bundesasylamt (C-394/12) [2014] 1 WLR 1895.......................... 2.6.2

Adam, R (on the application of) *v.* Secretary of State for the Home
Department; R (on the application of Limbuela) *v.* Secretary of State for
the Home Department; R (on the application of Tesema) *v.* Secretary of
State for the Home Department *(conjoined appeals)* [2005] UKHL 66 . 2.1.6, 3.2.6.5

Adan *see* R *v.* Secretary of State for the Home Department *ex p.* Adan

Adimi, R (on the application of) *v.* Uxbridge Magistrates' Court and another
[1999] Imm AR 560 (QB) 1.3.6, 1.3.10

AH (Algeria) *v.* Secretary of State for the Home Department [2012] EWCA
Civ 395 .... 1.16.2

AH (scope of s.103A reconsideration) Sudan [2006] UKAIT 38.................... 3.5.2.3

AH (Sudan) *see* Secretary of State for the Home Department *v.* AH (Sudan)
and others

AHK and others *v.* Secretary of State for the Home Department [2013]
EWHC 1426 (Admin) 3.7

Ahmed *v.* Secretary of State for the Home Department (Pakistan) (starred)
[2002] UKIAT 439 .... 1.3.7

AJ (Angola) *see* Secretary of State for the Home Department *v.* AJ (Angola)

Akhalu (health claim: ECHR Article 8) Nigeria [2013] UKUT 400 (IAC)........ 3.2.12.2

Akpinar, R (on the application of) *v.* Upper Tribunal (Immigration and
Asylum Chamber) [2014] EWCA Civ 937 .... 4.3.2.1

Alan *v.* Switzerland (UNCAT) [1997] INLR 29... 1.4

Alconbury Developments Ltd, R (on the application of) *v.* Secretary of State
for the Environment, Transport and the Regions [2001] UKHL 23, [2001]
2 WLR 1389 .... 3.1.1

Alladin, R (on the application of) *v.* Secretary of State for the Home
Department [2014] EWCA Civ 1334 .... 3.3.2
Al-Sirri *v.* Secretary of State for the Home Department [2012] UKSC 54.. 1.15.3, 1.15.5
AM (evidence – route of return) Somalia [2011] UKUT 54 (IAC)...................... 1.9
AM (s.117B) Malawi [2015] UKUT 260 (IAC)...................................... 3.2.11.1
AM, R (on the application of) *v.* Solihull Metropolitan Borough Council
(AAJR) [2012] UKUT 118 (IAC) 2.2.3
AMM and others (conflict; humanitarian crisis; returnees; FGM) Somalia CG
[2011] UKUT 445 (IAC) 1.16.1.1
AN and FA (children), R (on the application of) *v.* Secretary of State for the
Home Department [2012] EWCA Civ 1636 .... 2.2.1
Anufrijeva *v.* London Borough of Southwark [2003] EWCA Civ 1406............... 3.1.3
AO and another, R (on the application of) *v.* Secretary of State for the Home
Department [2011] EWHC 3088 (Admin) 3.3.3
AQ (Nigeria) *see* Secretary of State for the Home Department *v.* AQ
(Nigeria)
AS *v.* London Borough of Croydon [2011] EWHC 2091 (Admin)..................... 2.2.3
AS (Afghanistan) *v.* Secretary of State for the Home Department [2013]
EWCA Civ 1469 .... 6.9.1
AT and others (Article 15c; risk categories) Libya CG [2014] UKUT 318
(IAC) 1.16.1.1
Atamewan, R (on the application of) *v.* Secretary of State for the Home
Department [2013] EWHC 2727 (Admin) 6.5, 6.7.2, 6.8
Aydin *v.* Turkey (1998) 25 EHRR 251... 3.2.6.2
AZ, R (on the application of) *v.* Hampshire County Council (AAJR) [2013]
UKUT 87 (IAC) 2.2.3
B, R (on the application of) *v.* London Borough of Merton [2003] EWHC
1689 (Admin) 2.2.2
BA (demonstrators in Britain – risk on return) Iran CG [2011] UKUT 36
(IAC) 1.6, 1.7
Babar Ahmad and others *v.* UK [2012] ECHR 609...................................... 3.2.6.4
Bagdanavicius and another, R (on the application of) *v.* Secretary of State for
the Home Department [2005] UKHL 38 .... 3.2.6.5
Bah (EO (Turkey) – liability to deport) Sierra Leone [2012] UKUT 196
(IAC) 4.5
Bank Tejarat *v.* Council (Judgment) [2015] EUECJ T-176/12............................ 3.4
Batayav *v.* Secretary of State for the Home Department (No.1) [2003] EWCA
Civ 1489 .... 1.5.5
Batayav *v.* Secretary of State for the Home Department (No.2) [2005] EWCA
Civ 366 .... 1.5.5
Bensaid *v.* UK (2001) 33 EHRR 10, [2001] ECHR 82....................... 3.2.12, 3.2.12.2
BM and others (returnees – criminal and non-criminal) DRC CG [2015]
UKUT 293 (IAC) 1.5.1.1
BO and others (extension of time for appealing) Nigeria [2006] UKAIT 35 .... 3.5.1.5
Bouyid *v.* Belgium [2015] ECHR 819... 3.2.6.3
Brown (Jamaica), R (on the application of) *v.* Secretary of State for the Home
Department [2015] UKSC 8 .... 2.7
Bundesrepublik Deutschland *v.* Y and Z [2012] EUECJ C-71/11.................... 1.11.2
CA *v.* Secretary of State for the Home Department [2004] EWCA Civ 1165..... 3.2.12.1
Carter, R (on the application of) *v.* Secretary of State for the Home
Department [2014] EWHC 2603 (Admin) 3.7
Carvalho *v.* Secretary of State for the Home Department [2010] EWCA Civ
1406 .... 4.8.2

Chahal v. UK (1997) 23 EHRR 413 .... 3.2.4, 3.2.6.1, 3.2.6.5
Chiver (Asylum; Discrimination; Employment; Persecution) (Romania) [1994]
    UKIAT 10758 .... 1.4.3
CM (EM country guidance; disclosure) Zimbabwe CG [2013] UKUT 59
    (IAC) 1.5.1
Cvetkovs (visa – no file produced – directions) Latvia [2011] UKUT 212
    (IAC) 3.5.1.5
D v. Secretary of State for the Home Department [2012] EWCA Civ 39 .... 4.3.2.1
D v. UK (1997) 24 EHRR 423 .... 3.2.12
DA (unsigned interview notes) Turkey [2004] UKIAT 104 .... 1.3.11
Danian v. Secretary of State for the Home Department [1999] EWCA Civ
    3000, [2000] Imm AR 96 .... 1.7
De Souza Ribeiro v. France [2012] ECHR 2066 .... 4.4.2.1
Detention Action v. Secretary of State for the Home Department [2014]
    EWHC 2245 (Admin) 2.4
Detention Action, R (on the application of) v. Secretary of State for the Home
    Department [2014] EWCA Civ 1634 .... 2.4
Devaseelan see Secretary of State for the Home Department v. D (Tamil)
    (starred)
Dirshe, R (on the application of) v. Secretary of State for the Home
    Department [2005] EWCA Civ 421 .... 2.1.4
Dube (ss.117A–117D) [2015] UKUT 90 (IAC) 3.2.11.1; 4.4
E (a child), Re (Northern Ireland) [2009] 1 AC 536 (HL) 3.2.12.1
East African Asians v. UK (1981) 3 EHRR 76 .... 3.2.6.4
EK (Article 4 ECHR: Anti-Trafficking Convention) Tanzania [2013] UKUT
    313 (IAC) 6.7.4
El Kott, Abed El Karem and others v. Bevandorlasi es Allampolgarsagi Hivatal
    [2012] EUECJ C-364/11 .... 1.15.1
Elgafaji (Justice and Home Affairs) [2009] EUECJ C-465/07 .... 1.16.1.1
EM (Eritrea), R (on the application of) v. Secretary of State for the Home
    Department [2014] UKSC 12 .... 2.6.3
EM (Lebanon) v. Secretary of State for the Home Department [2008] UKHL
    64 .... 3.2.4, 3.2.8
EN (Serbia) v. Secretary of State for the Home Department and another
    [2009] EWCA Civ 630 .... 1.15.6
Essa v. Secretary of State for the Home Department (EEA:
    rehabilitation/integration) [2013] UKUT 316 (IAC) 4.8.2
Farquharson (removal – proof of conduct) Jamaica [2013] UKUT 146
    (IAC) 4.5
FK, R (on the application of) v. Secretary of State for the Home Department
    [2016] EWHC 56 (Admin) 6.9.2
FM, R (on the application of) v. Secretary of State for the Home Department
    [2015] EWHC 844 (Admin) 6.3, 6.7.3, 6.8, 6.9.2
FP (Iran) v. Secretary of State for the Home Department [2007] EWCA Civ
    13 .... 2.9.4
FV (Italy) see Secretary of State for the Home Department v. FV (Italy)
FZ, R (on the application of) v. London Borough of Croydon [2011] EWCA
    Civ 59 .... 2.2.3
Greenfield, R (on the application of) v. Secretary of State for the Home
    Department [2005] UKHL 14 .... 3.1.3
GS (Article 15(c): indiscriminate violence) Afghanistan CG [2009] UKAIT
    44 .... 1.16.1.1
GS (existence of internal armed conflict) Afghanistan CG [2009] UKAIT
    10 .... 1.16.1.1

GS (India) and others *v.* Secretary of State for the Home Department [2015]
EWCA Civ 40 .... 3.2.12.1
GS and EO (Article 3 – health cases) India [2012] UKUT 397 (IAC)............. 3.2.12.1
Gudanaviciene, R (on the application of) *v.* Director of Legal Aid Casework
[2014] EWCA Civ 1622 .... 3.2.10.1, 3.4, 8.4
Gungor, R (on the application of) *v.* Secretary of State for the Home
Department [2004] EWHC 2117 (Admin) 2.9.4
GW (EEA reg. 21: 'fundamental interests') Netherlands [2009] UKAIT 50.......... 4.8.4
HA (Article 24 QD) Palestinian Territories [2015] UKUT 465 (IAC)................. 1.14
Haile, R (on the application of) *v.* Secretary of State for the Home Department
[2015] EWHC 732 (Admin) 6.8
Hariri *v.* Secretary of State for the Home Department [2003] EWCA Civ
807 .... 1.5.5, 3.2.3
HC and RC (trafficked women) China CG [2009] UKAIT 27........................... 3.6.2
Heritage, R (on the application of) *v.* Secretary of State for the Home
Department and First-tier Tribunal (IJR) [2014] UKUT 441 (IAC) 3.2.11.1
HH (Somalia) and others *v.* Secretary of State for the Home Department
[2010] EWCA Civ 426 .... 1.9
HJ (Iran) *v.* Secretary of State for the Home Department [2010] UKSC 31
reversing [2009] EWCA Civ 172 .... 1.10.4
HK *v.* Secretary of State for the Home Department [2006] EWCA Civ 1037........ 1.4.2
HM and others (Article 15(c)) Iraq CG [2010] UKUT 331 (IAC)................. 1.16.1.1
HN *v.* Minister for Justice, Equality and Law Reform, Ireland (Judgment of
the Court) [2014] EUECJ C-604/12 .... 3.4
Horvath *v.* Secretary of State for the Home Department [1999] INLR 7
(IAT) 1.4.2
HSMP Forum Ltd, R (on the application of) *v.* Secretary of State for the
Home Department [2008] EWHC 664 (Admin) 3.2.11.1
Husan, R (on the application of) *v.* Secretary of State for the Home
Department [2005] EWHC 189 (Admin) 2.7
I, R (on the application of) *v.* Secretary of State for the Home Department
[2003] INLR 196 (CA) 5.3
IA *v.* Secretary of State for the Home Department (Scotland) [2014] UKSC
6 .... 1.8
Idira, R (on the application of) *v.* Secretary of State for the Home Department
[2015] EWCA Civ 1187 .... 3.2.9
IG (exclusion, risk, Maoists) Nepal (starred) [2002] UKIAT 4870................... 1.15.5
IK (returnees – records – IFA) Turkey CG [2004] UKIAT 312.......................... 1.6
Immigration Law Practitioners Association, R (on the application of) *v.*
Tribunal Procedure Committee and another [2016] EWHC 218 (Admin) 3.5.1.5
Ireland *v.* UK (1978) 2 EHRR 25... 3.2.6.1
IS *v.* Director of Legal Aid Casework and another [2015] EWHC 1965
(Admin) 8.4, 8.5.3
Is the draft EU agreement re: accession of the European Union to the
Convention for the Protection of Human Rights and Fundamental
Freedoms compatible with the Treaties? (Opinions of the Court) [2014]
EUECJ Avis-2/13 .... 3.4
Ishtiaq *v.* Secretary of State for the Home Department [2007] EWCA Civ
386 .... 7.4
Islam *v.* Secretary of State for the Home Department; R *v.* Immigration
Appeal Tribunal and another, *ex p.* Shah *(conjoined appeals)* [1999]
UKHL 20 .... 1.11.4
IY (Turkey) *v.* Secretary of State for the Home Department [2012] EWCA Civ
1560 .... 3.6.3

J *v.* Secretary of State for the Home Department [2005] EWCA Civ 629 .... 3.2.12.1

JA (Ivory Coast) and ES (Tanzania) *v.* Secretary of State for the Home
Department [2009] EWCA Civ 1353 .... 3.2.12.2

Januzi *v.* Secretary of State for the Home Department and others [2006]
UKHL 5 .... 1.13

JB (Jamaica), R (on the application of) *v.* Secretary of State for the Home
Department [2013] EWCA Civ 666 .... 2.4, 2.7

JL (medical reports – credibility) China [2013] UKUT 145 (IAC).................. 1.3.11

JO (qualified person – hospital order – effect) Slovakia [2012] UKUT 237
(IAC).. 4.8.2

JS (Sri Lanka), R (on the application of) *v.* Secretary of State for the Home
Department (Rev 1) [2010] UKSC 15 .... 1.15.4

JS and YK, R (on the application of) *v.* Birmingham City Council (AAJR)
[2011] UKUT 505 (IAC) 2.2.3

JT (Cameroon) *v.* Secretary of State for the Home Department [2008] EWCA
Civ 878 .... 1.3.6

K and Fornah *see* Secretary of State for the Home Department *v.* K; Fornah *v.*
Secretary of State for the Home Department

KA (Afghanistan) and others *v.* Secretary of State for the Home Department
[2012] EWCA Civ 1014 .... 2.2.1

Kalashnikov *v.* Russia [2002] ECHR 596, (2002) 36 EHRR 34 .... 3.2.6.4

Karanakaran *v.* Secretary of State for the Home Department [2000] EWCA
Civ 11, [2000] Imm AR 271 .... 1.3.3

Kardi, R (on the application of) *v.* Secretary of State for the Home
Department [2014] EWCA Civ 934 .... 3.3.4

KB (failed asylum seekers and forced returnees) Syria CG [2012] UKUT 426
(IAC) 1.3.1

KH (Article 15(c) Qualification Directive) Iraq CG [2008] UKAIT 23........... .1.16.1.1

KH (Afghanistan) *v.* Secretary of State for the Home Department [2009]
EWCA Civ 1354 .... 3.2.12

Kiarie, R (on the application of) *v.* Secretary of State for the Home
Department [2015] EWCA Civ 1020 .... 4.4.2

KJ (Sri Lanka) *v.* Secretary of State for the Home Department [2009] EWCA
Civ 292 .... 1.15.3, 1.15.4

KK and others (nationality: North Korea) Korea CG [2011] UKUT 92
(IAC) 1.14.1

Konan, R (on the application of) *v.* Secretary of State for the Home
Department [2004] EWHC 22 (Admin) 5.4.3

KS (benefit of the doubt) [2014] UKUT 552 (IAC)..................... 1.3.3, 1.3.8, 1.3.11

KS (Burma) and another *v.* Secretary of State for the Home Department
[2013] EWCA Civ 67 .... 1.7

KV (scarring – medical evidence) Sri Lanka [2014] UKUT 230 (IAC)........ 1.3.8, 3.6.3

L *v.* The Children's Commissioner for England *see* R *v.* L and others

LA (para 289A: causes of breakdown) Pakistan [2009] UKAIT 19................... 7.2.3

Ladd *v.* Marshall [1954] 1 WLR 1489 (CA)... 2.9.4

LG (Italy) *v.* Secretary of State for the Home Department [2008] EWCA Civ
190 .... 4.8.3

LH and IP (gay men: risk) Sri Lanka CG [2015] UKUT 73 (IAC).................. 1.10.4

Limbuela *see* Adam, R (on the application of) *v.* Secretary of State for the
Home Department

Lord Chancellor *v.* Detention Action [2015] EWCA Civ 840........................... 2.4

Lumba (WL) *v.* Secretary of State for the Home Department [2011] UKSC
12 .... 3.2.9, 5.2

M (Yugoslavia) *v.* Secretary of State for the Home Department [2003] UKIAT
4 .... 1.4.2
MA (Ethiopia) *v.* Secretary of State for the Home Department [2009] EWCA
Civ 289 .... 1.10, 1.14
MA (Somalia) *see* Secretary of State for the Home Department *v.* MA
(Somalia)
MA and AA (Afghanistan) *v.* Secretary of State for the Home Department
[2015] UKSC 40 .... 2.2.1
MA and others *v.* Secretary of State for the Home Department [2013] EUECJ
C-648/11 .... 2.6.1
Maaouia *v.* France (2001) 33 EHRR 42 .... 3.2.10.1
MAB (para 399; 'unduly harsh') [2015] UKUT 435 (IAC) 4.3.1
Mahad (previously referred to as AM) (Ethiopia) *v.* Entry Clearance Officer
[2009] UKSC 16 .... 3.1.1
Maslov *v.* Austria [2008] ECHR 546 .... 4.3.2.1
MD (same-sex oriented males: risk) India CG [2014] UKUT 65 (IAC) 2.7
MF (Nigeria) *v.* Secretary of State for the Home Department [2013] EWCA
Civ 1192 .... 3.2.11, 4.3.2
MG *see* Secretary of State for the Home Department *v.* MG
MG (prison – Article 28(3)(a) of Citizens Directive) [2014] UKUT 392
(IAC) 4.8.2
MG and VC (EEA Regulations 2006; 'conductive' deportation) Ireland [2006]
UKAIT 53 .... 4.8.3
Minani, R (on the application of) *v.* Immigration Appeal Tribunal [2004]
EWHC 582 (Admin) 3.6.3
Minh, R (on the application of) *v.* Secretary of State for the Home Department
[2015] EWHC 1725 (Admin) 6.2, 6.3, 6.7.1, 6.9.2
MK (documents – relocation) Iraq CG [2012] UKUT 126 (IAC) 2.9.5
MM (Zimbabwe) *v.* Secretary of State for the Home Department [2012]
EWCA Civ 279 .... 3.2.12.2
MM and others, R (on the application of) *v.* Secretary of State for the Home
Department [2014] EWCA Civ 985 .... 3.1.1
MN and KY *see* Secretary of State for Home Department *v.* MN and KY
(Scotland)
MNM (Surendran guidelines for Adjudicators) (Kenya) [2000] UKIAT 5 .... 3.2.10.1
MS (Somalia) and others *v.* Secretary of State for the Home Department
[2010] EWCA Civ 1236 .... 2.10.4
MSS *v.* Belgium and Greece [2011] ECHR 108 .... 2.6.3
Mutesi, R (on the application of) *v.* Secretary of State for the Home
Department [2015] EWHC 2467 (Admin) 6.3, 6.9.2
MVN *v.* London Borough of Greenwich [2015] EWHC 1942 (Admin) 2.2.3, 6.3
Myumyun *v.* Bulgaria [2015] ECHR 972 .... 3.2.6.2
N (Kenya) *v.* Secretary of State for the Home Department [2014] EWCA Civ
1094 .... 4.4.1
N *v.* Secretary of State for the Home Department [2005] UKHL 31 .... 3.2.12.1
N *v.* UK [2008] ECHR 453 .... 3.2.12.1
NA (UT rule 45: Singh *v.* Belgium) Iran [2014] UKUT 205 (IAC) 1.3.8
NA and VA (protection: Article 7(2) Qualification Directive) India [2015]
UKUT 432 (IAC) 1.12
NA *v.* UK [2008] ECHR 616 .... 1.16.1.1
Nare (evidence by electronic means) Zimbabwe [2011] UKUT 443 (IAC) 4.4.2
NS (European Union law) [2011] EUECJ C-411/10 .... 3.4
Ocalan *v.* Turkey (2003) 37 EHRR 10 .... 3.2.6.4

OD (Ivory Coast) *v.* Secretary of State for the Home Department [2008]
EWCA Civ 1299 .... 1.5.2
Omar, R (on the application of) *v.* Secretary of State for the Home
Department [2012] EWHC 3448 (Admin) 3.7
Opinions of the Court *see* Is the draft EU agreement re: accession of the
European Union to the Convention for the Protection of Human Rights and
Fundamental Freedoms compatible with the Treaties? (Opinions of the
Court)
PJ *v.* Secretary of State for the Home Department [2014] EWCA Civ 1011... 1.3.7, 1.3.8
PO (Nigeria) *v.* Secretary of State for the Home Department [2011] EWCA
Civ 132 .... 6.1
Poquiz, R (on the application of) *v.* Secretary of State for the Home
Department [2015] EWHC 1759 (Admin) 6.4
Pretty *v.* UK (2002) 35 EHRR 1 .... 3.2.4, 3.2.6.3
PS (prison conditions; military service) Ukraine CG [2006] UKAIT 16 .... 3.2.6.4
Public Law Project *v.* Lord Chancellor [2015] EWCA Civ 1193 .... 8.8
Quaquah *see* R *v.* Chief Immigration Officer *ex p.* Quaquah
QD (Iraq) *v.* Secretary of State for the Home Department [2009] EWCA Civ
620 .... 1.16.1.1
R *v.* Chief Immigration Officer *ex p.* Quaquah [2000] INLR 196 (QB) 3.2.10.1
R *v.* Immigration Appeal Tribunal and another *ex p.* Rajendrakumar [1995]
EWCA Civ 16; [1996] Imm AR 97 .... 1.3.3
R *v.* L and others *sub nom* L *v.* Children's Commissioner for England [2013]
EWCA Crim 991 .... 6.9.1
R *v.* Secretary of State for the Home Department *ex p.* Adan [1998] UKHL
15, [1998] Imm AR 338 .... 1.10.3
R (Iran) and others *v.* Secretary of State for the Home Department [2005]
EWCA Civ 982 .... 3.5.2.1
R, R (on the application of) *v.* London Borough of Croydon [2011] EWHC
1473 (Admin) 2.2.3
Rantsev *v.* Cyprus and Russia (2010) 51 EHRR 1 .... 3.2.7, 6.8
Ravichandran *see* R *v.* Immigration Appeal Tribunal and another *ex p.*
Rajendrakumar
Razgar, R (on the application of) *v.* Secretary of State for the Home
Department [2004] UKHL 27 .... 3.2.11, 7.5
RB (Algeria) *v.* Secretary of State for the Home Department [2009] UKHL
10 .... 3.2.10.2
RC *v.* Sweden [2010] ECHR 307 .... 1.3.8
RN (returnees) Zimbabwe [2008] UKAIT 83 .... 1.10.4
Robinson, R (on the application of) *v.* Secretary of State for the Home
Department (paragraph 353 – Waqar applied) (IJR) [2016] UKUT 133
(IAC) 2.9.1
RS (immigration and family court proceedings) India [2012] UKUT 218
(IAC) 3.5.1.5
RS (immigration/family court liaison: outcome) India [2013] UKUT 82
(IAC) 3.5.1.5
RS (Zimbabwe) *v.* Secretary of State for the Home Department [2008] EWCA
Civ 839 .... 3.2.12.1
RT (Zimbabwe) and others *v.* Secretary of State for the Home Department
[2012] UKSC 38 .... 1.10.4, 1.11.5
S and K *see* Secretary of State for the Home Department *v.* S and K Croatia CG
SA (Somalia) *v.* Secretary of State for the Home Department [2006] EWCA
Civ 1302 .... 3.6.3

Saadi *v.* UK [2008] ECHR 80 .... 3.2.9, 5.2

Said (Article 1D: meaning) Palestinian Territories [2012] UKUT 413 (IAC) 1.15.1

SB (PSG, Protection Regulations, Reg. 6) Moldova CG [2008] UKAIT 2 .... 1.11.4

SE (Zimbabwe) *v.* Secretary of State for the Home Department [2014] EWCA
    Civ 256 .... 4.4.1

Secretary of State for the Home Department *v.* AH (Sudan) and others [2007]
    UKHL 49 .... 1.13

Secretary of State for the Home Department *v.* AJ (Angola) [2014] EWCA
    Civ 1636 .... 4.4.1

Secretary of State for the Home Department *v.* AQ (Nigeria) [2015] EWCA
    Civ 250 .... 4.3.2.1, 4.3.1

Secretary of State for the Home Department *v.* D (Tamil) (starred) [2002]
    UKIAT 702 .... 3.2.4

Secretary of State for the Home Department *v.* FV (Italy) [2012] EWCA Civ
    1199 .... 4.8.2, 4.8.3

Secretary of State for the Home Department *v.* K; Fornah *v.* Secretary of State
    for the Home Department [2006] UKHL 46 .... 1.11.4

Secretary of State for the Home Department *v.* MA (Somalia) [2015] EWCA
    Civ 48 .... 4.4.1

Secretary of State for the Home Department *v.* MA (Somalia) [2010] UKSC
    49 .... 1.4.3

Secretary of State for the Home Department *v.* MG [2014] EUECJ
    C-400/12 .... 4.8.2

Secretary of State for Home Department *v.* MN and KY (Scotland) [2014]
    UKSC 30 .... 1.3.9

Secretary of State for the Home Department *v.* S and K Croatia CG (starred)
    [2002] UKIAT 5613 .... 3.2.6.4

Secretary of State for the Home Department *v.* SS (Congo) and others [2015]
    EWCA Civ 387 .... 3.2.11

Secretary of State for the Home Department *v.* TB (Jamaica) [2008] EWCA
    Civ 977 .... 1.15.5

Sepet and another, R (on the application of) *v.* Secretary of State for the Home
    Department [2003] UKHL 15 .... 1.10.2

SF, R (on the application of) *v.* Secretary of State for the Home Department
    [2015] EWHC 2705 (Admin) 6.3, 6.9.2

SG (Iraq) *v.* Secretary of State for the Home Department [2012] EWCA Civ
    940 .... 1.5.2

SH (Afghanistan) *v.* Secretary of State for the Home Department [2011]
    EWCA Civ 1284 .... 2.4

Shah and Islam *see* Islam *v.* Secretary of State for the Home Department; R *v.*
    Immigration Appeal Tribunal and another, *ex p.* Shah *(conjoined appeals)*

Shala *v.* Secretary of State for the Home Department [2003] EWCA Civ 233 .... 3.2.11.1

Sheikh *see* SS, R (on the application of) *v.* Secretary of State for the Home
    Department

Shepherd *v.* Germany [2015] EUECJ C-472/13 .... 1.10.2

Singh *v.* Belgium (application no. 33210/11) (2 October 2012) 1.3.8

Singh, R (on the application of) *v.* Governor of Durham Prison [1984] 1 WLR
    704 (QB) 5.3

Sivakumuran, R (on the application of) *v.* Secretary of State for the Home
    Department [1987] UKHL 1 .... 1.3.2

SK (Zimbabwe) *v.* Secretary of State for the Home Department [2011] UKSC
    23 .... 5.2

SM (Section 8: Judge's process) Iran [2005] UKAIT 116 .... 1.3.6

SO (imprisonment breaks continuity of residence) Nigeria [2011] UKUT 164
(IAC) 4.8.2
Soering v. UK (1989) 11 EHRR 439 .... 3.2.4, 3.2.6.3
SQ (Pakistan) and another, R (on the application of) v. Upper Tribunal
Immigration and Asylum Chamber and another [2013] EWCA Civ 1251 .... 3.2.12.2
SS (Congo) see Secretary of State for the Home Department v. SS (Congo)
and others
SS, R (on the application of) v. Secretary of State for the Home Department
[2011] EWHC 3390 (Admin) 3.7
Sufi and Elmi v. UK [2011] ECHR 1045 .... 1.5.1
Suleyman (application no. 16242) (11 February 1998) 1.4.2
T v. Secretary of State for the Home Department [1996] UKHL 8, [1996]
Imm AR 443 .... 1.15.2.2
T v. London Borough of Enfield [2004] EWHC 2297 (Admin) 2.2.2
Tarakhel v. Switzerland [2014] ECHR 1185 .... 2.6.3
TB (Jamaica) see Secretary of State for the Home Department v. TB
(Jamaica)
Thangarasa, R (on the application of) v. Secretary of State for the Home
Department; R (on the application of Yogathas) v. Secretary of State for
the Home Department [2002] UKHL 36 .... 2.7
Three Rivers DC v. Governor and Company of the Bank of England (No. 3)
[2003] 2 AC 1 (HL) 3.1.3
Tyrer v. UK (1978) 2 EHRR 1 .... 3.2.6.4
Ullah, R (on the application of) v. Special Adjudicator [2004] UKHL 26 ..... 3.2.4, 3.2.8
Üner v. The Netherlands [2006] ECHR 873 .... 4.3.2.1
V, R (on the application of) v. Asylum and Immigration Tribunal [2009]
EWHC 1902 (Admin) 4.5
Velasquez Taylor v. Secretary of State for the Home Department [2015]
EWCA Civ 845 .... 4.4.1
Williams, R (on the application of) v. Secretary of State for the Home
Department [2015] EWHC 1268 (Admin) 3.7
WM (DRC) v. Secretary of State for the Home Department [2006] EWCA Civ
1495 .... 2.9.2
X, Y and Z v. Minister voor Immigratie en Asiel [2013] EUECJ C-199/12.. 1.10, 1.10.4,
1.11.4
XB v. Secretary of State for the Home Department [2015] EWHC 2557
(Admin) 2.9.2, 6.9.1
Y v. Secretary of State for the Home Department [2006] EWCA Civ 1223 .... 1.4.2
Y and Z see Bundesrepublik Deutschland v. Y and Z
YB (Eritrea) v. Secretary of State for the Home Department [2008] EWCA
Civ 360 .... 1.6
YH, R (on the application of) v. Secretary of State for the Home Department
[2010] EWCA Civ 116 .... 2.9.2
Yogathas see Thangarasa, R (on the application of) v. Secretary of State for
the Home Department
ZH (Tanzania) v. Secretary of State for the Home Department [2011] UKSC
4 .... 3.2.11.1
ZL and another v. Secretary of State for the Home Department and Lord
Chancellor's Department [2003] EWCA Civ 25 .... 2.4, 2.7
ZT (Kosovo) v. Secretary of State for the Home Department [2009] UKHL
6 .... 2.9.2

Table of statutes

Asylum and Immigration
(Treatment of Claimants,
etc.) Act 2004 .... 1.3.6
s.1 .... **A4**
s.2 .... 2.1.1, **A4**
s.4 .... **A4**
s.8 .... 1.3.4, 1.3.6, 1.5.4, **A4**
Sched.3 .... 2.6.1, **A4**
Borders, Citizenship and
Immigration Act 2009
s.55 .... 7.4.1, **A6**
Children Act 1989
s.20 .... 2.1.6. 2.2.2, 2.2.3
Data Protection Act 1998 .... 5.2
Human Rights Act 1998 . 3.1, 3.2.5, 3.2.13
s.2(1) 3.1.1
s.6(1) 3.1.2
s.7(1) 3.1.2
(3) 3.1.2
s.8 .... 3.1.3
(2) 3.1.3
s.9(3) 3.1.3
Identity Documents Act 2010
s.4 .... **A7**
s.7 .... **A7**
Immigration Act 1971 .... 5.1
s.3 .... 4.1, **A1**
(5) 4.1, 4.2.2
(a) 4.2.1
(6) 4.2.2
s.3C 3.5.3, **A1**
s.5 .... 4.1
s.7 .... 4.1.1
s.24 .... **A.1**
s.24A **A1**
s.25 .... **A1**
s.25A **A1**
s.25B **A1**
s.26 .... **A1**
Sched.2 .... 5.1, 5.4.2.1
Sched.3 .... 5.1

Immigration Act 2014 ... 3.2.11.1, 3.5.1.1,
4.4, 4.4.2
Immigration and Asylum Act
1999
s.4 .... 2.1.6, 8.2.6
s.10 .... **A2**
s.31 .... **A2**
s.54 .... 5.4.2.1
s.94 .... **A2**
s.95 .... 2.1.6, 8.2.6, **A2**
Immigration, Asylum and
Nationality Act 2006
s.55 .... 1.15.5
Legal Aid, Sentencing and
Punishment of Offenders Act
2012 .... 8.1, 8.3, 8.8
s.9 .... 8.1
s.10 .... 8.1, 8.4
(3) 8.4
Sched.1, Part 1 .... 8.2, 8.3, 8.4
para.19(5) 8.2.1
(7) and (8) 8.2.1
paras.28 and 29 .... 8.2.4
para.30 .... 8.2.5
para.31 .... 8.2.6
para.32 .... 8.2.7
Part 3, para.13 .... 8.2.8
National Assistance Act 1948
s.21(1) 2.1.6
Nationality, Immigration and
Asylum Act 2002 .... 3.1.4, 3.2.13,
3.5.1.1
s.33 .... 4.4.2.1
s.55 .... 2.1.6
s.62 .... 5.1
s.72 .... 1.15, 1.15.6, **A3**
(4) 1.15.6
(5) 1.15.6
(6) 1.15.6
s.76 .... **A3**
s.77 .... 2.6

s.78 .... 2.7, **A3**
s.78A **A3**
s.79 .... 2.7
s.82 .... 2.15, 3.5.1.2, 4.4.2.1, 6.7.3,
                                      A3
  (1) 3.5.1.2, 4.4
    (a) 3.5.1.4
s.83 .... 6.7.3
s.84 .... 3.5.1.2, **A3**
s.85 .... 3.5.1.4, 3.5.1.5, **A3**
s.86 .... **A3**
s.92 .... 4.4.2, **A3**
s.94 .... 2.7, 2.9.2, 4.4.2, **A3**
s.94A **A3**
s.94B 4.4.2, 4.4.2.1, **A3**
  (1) 4.4.2
  (2) 4.4.2
  (3) 4.4.2
s.96 .... **A3**
s.97 .... **A3**
s.97A 4.2.3
s.104 .... **A3**
s.113 .... 2.1, **A3**
s.117 .... 3.2.11.1, 4.4.1
s.117A 3.2.11.1, 4.4, **A3**

s.117A(2) 3.2.11.1
s.117B 3.2.11.1, 4.4, **A3**
  (2) 3.2.11.1
  (3) 3.2.11.1
  (4) 3.2.11.1
s.117C 4.3.1, 4.4, **A3**
s.117D 3.2.11.1, 4.4, **A3**
  (1) 3.2.11.1
  (2) 4.4
  (6) 3.2.11.1
s.120 .. 2.1.5, 2.9.1, 3.5.1.1, 3.5.1.4,
                                 4.4, **A3**
Part 5A 3.2.11.1
Tribunals, Courts and
  Enforcement Act 2007
  s.25 .... 3.5.1.5
UK Borders Act 2007 .... 4.2.1, 4.3
  s.32 .... 4.2.1, 4.3.1, **A5**
    (4) 4.2.1
  s.33 .... 4.2.1, 4.3, **A5**
  s.35 .... **A5**
  s.36 .... **A5**
  s.37 .... **A5**
  s.38 .... **A5**

Table of statutory instruments

Asylum and Immigration Tribunal (Fast Track Procedure) Rules 2005, SI
 2005/560 .... 2.4
Asylum Seekers (Reception Conditions) Regulations 2005, SI 2005/7 .... 2.2.1
Civil Legal Aid (Merits Criteria) Regulations 2013, SI 2013/104 .... 8.5
 reg.5 .... 8.5.2
 reg.32(b) 8.5.1
 reg.40 .... 8.5.4
 reg.42 .... 8.5.5
 reg.60(3) 8.5.3
Civil Legal Aid (Merits Criteria) (Amendment) (No.2) Regulations 2015, SI
 2015/1571
 reg.2(2) 8.5.2
  (3) 8.5.5
  (4) 8.5.5
  (6) 8.5.3
Civil Legal Aid (Remuneration) Regulations 2013, SI 2013/422 .... 8.5.5
 reg.5A(1)(a)–(e) 8.5.5
  (2) 8.5.5
  (3)(c) 8.5.5
Civil Legal Aid (Remuneration) (Amendment) Regulations 2015, SI
 2015/898 .... 8.5.5
Detention Centre Rules 2001, SI 2001/238
 rule 35 .... 2.5
First-tier Tribunal (Immigration and Asylum Chamber) Fees Order 2011, SI
 2011/2841 .... 3.5.1.5
Human Rights Act 1998 (Amendment) Order 2004, SI 2004/1574 .... 3.2.5
Immigration (European Economic Area) Regulations 2006, SI 2006/1003 ...... 3.5.1, 4.8
 Part 1 (regs.1–10)
  reg.10(5) 7.7, **C1**
 Part 4 (regs.19–21)
  reg.19 .... **C1**
   (3)(b) 4.9
  reg.20 .... **C1**
  reg.20A **C1**
  reg.20B **C1**
  reg.21 .... 4.8.1, **C1**
  reg.21A **C1**
  reg.21B **C1**
 Part 6 (regs.25–29)
  reg.25 .... **C1**
  reg.26 .... **C1**

reg.27 .... **C1**
reg.29AA 4.9, **C1**
     (1)(c), (d) 4.9
     (2) 4.9
     (3) 4.9
     (4) 4.9
     (5) 4.9
     (6)–(7) 4.9
Immigration (Leave to Enter and Remain) Order 2000, SI 2000/1161
  art.13 .... 3.3.5
Immigration Rules 1.1
  Part 7 (paras.A246–276BVI)
    para.276 .... 3.2.11
    para.276ADE 3.2.11, 3.3.2
      (iii) 3.2.11
  Part 8 (paras.A277–319Y)
    para.289A 7.1
    para.319L 2.10.3.2
    para.319O 2.10.3.2
    para.319R 2.10.3.2
    para.319V 2.10.3.2
    para.319X 2.10.3.1
  Part 9 (paras.A320–324)
    para.320 .... 4.7
  Part 11 (paras.326A–352H) 1.1, **D1**
    para.326F 2.8
    para.334 .... 1.15
    para.339A 1.15, 2.10.2
    para.339C 1.16.1
      (ii) 1.16.1
    para.339D 1.16.2
      (i) 1.15.6
    para.339I 1.3.8
    para.339K 1.5.3
    para.339L 1.3.5
    para.339O 1.13
    para.339P 1.11.5
    para.339Q 2.10.2
      (i) 2.10.1, 2.10.2
    para.339R 2.10.2
      (iii) 2.10.2
    para.344A(ii) 2.12.2
      (iii) 2.12.2
    para.351 .... 2.2.1
    para.352A 2.10.3.1
    para.352AA 2.10.3.1
    para.352D 2.10.3.1
    para.352ZC 2.2.1, 3.3.2
    para.352ZD 2.2.1
  Part 11A (paras.354–356B) 2.1
  Part 11B (paras.357–361) 2.1, **D2**
    para.358 .... 2.1.1
    para.359 .... 2.1.1

Immigration Rules – *continued*
    Part 11B (paras.357–361) – *continued*
        para.360 .... 2.1.5
    Part 12 (paras.353–353B) **D3**
        para.353 .... 2.9.1, 3.3.2
    Part 13 (paras.A362–400) **D4**
        para.390 .... 4.7
        para.391 .... 4.7
            (a) 4.7
            (b) 4.7
        para.391A 4.7
        para.392 .... 4.7
        para.397 .... 4.3.1
        para.398 .... 4.7
            (a) 4.3.1
            (b)–(c) .... 4.3.
        para.399 .... 3.3.3
        para.399A 3.3.3, 4.3.1, 4.3.2
        para.399B 4.6
    Appendix AR 7.5
        para.AR3.2(c) 7.5
    Appendix FM 2.10.3.3, 3.2.11, 3.3.2, 7.1, 7.2
        Section S-ILR: Suitability for indefinite leave to remain
           para.S-ILR.1.4 .... 7.2.3
        Section EX: Exceptions to certain eligibility requirements for leave to remain
        as a partner or parent
           para.EX.1 .... 3.2.11
           para.EX.2 .... 4.3.1
        Section DVILR: Indefinite leave to remain (settlement) as a victim of
        domestic violence **D5**
           para.DVILR.1.1 .... 7.1, **D5**
        Section E-DVILR: Eligibility for indefinite leave to remain as a victim of
        domestic violence **D5**
           para.E-DVILR.1.3 .... 7.2.3
        Section D-DVILR: Decision on application for indefinite leave to remain as a
        victim of domestic violence **D5**
           para.D-DVILR.1.1 .... **D5**
           para.D-DVILR.1.2 .... **D5**
           para.D-DVILR.1.3 .... **D5**
    Appendix K 2.1.5
    Appendix KoLL 2.10.2
Nationality, Immigration and Asylum Act 2002 (Specification of Particularly
    Serious Crimes) Order 2004, SI 2004/1910 .... 1.15.6
Refugee or Person in Need of International Protection (Qualification)
    Regulations 2006, SI 2006/2525 .... 1.1, 2.10, **C2**
        reg.4(2) 1.12
        reg.5(1) **1.10**
            (2) 1.10
            (f) 1.10.2
        reg.6(1)(b) 1.11.2
            (d), (e) **1.11.4**
            (f) 1.11.5
            (2) 1.11.6

Tribunal Procedure (First-tier Tribunal) (Immigration and Asylum Chamber)
  Rules 2014, SI 2014/2604 (L 31) 2.4, 3.5.1.5
    Part 1 (rules 1–2) **B1**
      rule 2(1) 3.5.1.5
    Part 2 (rules 3–18)
      rules 4–18 .... **B1**
      rule 4 .... 3.5.1.5
        (3)(a) 3.5.1.5
          (c) 3.5.1.5
          (d) 4.5
          (h) 3.5.1.5
      rule 5 .... 3.5.1.5
      rule 6 .... 3.5.1.5
        (2)(a) 3.5.1.5
          (b) 3.5.1.5
        (3) 3.5.1.5
      rule 9 .... 3.5.1.5
      rule 11 .... 3.5.1.5
        (1) 3.5.1.5
        (2) 3.5.1.5
      rule 13 .... 3.5.1.5
      rule 14 .... 3.5.1.5
      rule 15 .... 3.5.1.5, 4.5
      rule 17 .... 3.5.1.5
    Part 3 (rules 19–29) **B1**
      rule 19 .... 3.5.1.5
        (2) 3.5.1.5
        (7) 3.5.1.5
      rule 20 .... 3.5.1.5
      rule 22 .... 3.5.1.5
      rule 23 .... 3.5.1.5
        (2)(b) 3.5.1.5
      rule 24 .... 3.5.1.5
        (2) 3.5.1.5
      rule 25 .... 3.5.1.5
      rule 27 .... 3.5.1.5
      rule 28 .... 3.5.1.5
    Part 4 (rules 30–36) **B1**
      rule 32 .... 2.4, 3.5.2.2
        (1) 2.4
          (a) 2.4
          (2)(d) 2.4
      rule 33(5)(c) 3.5.2.2
      rule 35 .... 3.5.2.2
    Part 5 (rules 37–44) **B1**
      rule 38 .... 5.4.2.2
      rule 39(3) 5.4.2.1
      rule 40(1) 5.4.2.2
    Schedule (The Fast Track Rules) 2.4
Tribunal Procedure (Upper Tribunal) Rules 2008, SI 2008/2698 (L 15)... 3.5.1.5, 3.5.2.3
    Part 1 (rules 1–3)
      rule 2 .... **B2**

Tribunal Procedure (Upper Tribunal) Rules 2008, SI 2008/2698 (L 15) – *continued*
    Part 2 (rules 4–20)
        rule 5 .... **B2**
            (3)(a) 3.5.2.3
        rule 6 .... **B2**
        rule 7 .... 3.5.2.3
        rule 8 .... 3.5.2.3
        rule 10 .... 3.5.2.3
        rule 12 .... **B2**
        rule 13 .... **B2**
        rule 15 .... **B2**
        rule 15(2A) 3.5.2.3
        rule 17 .... **B2**
        rule 17A 3.5.2.3, **B2**
    Part 3 (rules 21–26)
        rule 21 .... 3.5.2.3, **B2**
        rule 22A **B2**
        rule 24 .... **B2**
            (1A) 3.5.2.3
        rule 25 .... 3.5.2.3, **B2**
    Part 4 (rules 27–33)
        rule 31 .... 3.5.2.3
        rule 32 .... 3.5.2.3
    Part 5 (rules 34–38)
        rule 36A **B2**
    Part 6 (rules 39–40)
        rule 39 .... 3.5.2.3
    Part 7 (rules 41–48)
        rule 44 .... **B2**
        rule 45 .... **B2**
        rule 46 .... **B2**
Tribunals Judiciary, Practice Directions: Immigration and Asylum Chambers
    of the First-tier Tribunal and the Upper Tribunal
    Practice Direction 3 (procedure on appeal) 3.5.2.3, **B3**
        paragraph 3.1(c) 3.5.2.3
    Practice Direction 4 (evidence) **B3**
    Practice Direction 5 (pursuing appeal after grant of leave) 3.5.2.3
    Practice Direction 7 (case management review hearings and directions) **B3**
    Practice Direction 9 (adjournments) **B3**
    Practice Direction 10 (expert evidence) 3.6.1, **B3**
    Practice Direction 11 (citation of unreported determinations) **B3**
    Practice Direction 12 (Starred and Country Guidance determinations) **B3**
    Practice Direction 13 (bail applications) **B3**
Tribunals Judiciary, Practice Statements: Immigration and Asylum Chambers
    of the First-tier Tribunal and the Upper Tribunal
    Practice Statement 3 (where the Tribunal may not accept a notice of appeal) .. **B4**
    Practice Statement 5 (record of proceeding) **B4**
    Practice Statement 7 (disposal of appeals in Upper Tribunal) **B4**

Table of international instruments

Charter of Fundamental Rights of the European Union (OJ C 326, 26 October
2012) 3.4
    Article 1 (human dignity) 3.4
    Article 4 (prohibition of torture and inhuman or degrading treatment or
      punishment) 3.4
    Article 7 (respect for private and family life) 3.4
    Article 18 (right to asylum) 3.4
    Article 41 (right to good administration) 3.4
    Article 47 (right to an effective remedy and to a fair trial) 3.4, 4.9
    Article 52(1) (scope and interpretation of rights and principles) 3.4
        (3) 3.4
Council of Europe Convention on Action against Trafficking in Human Beings
2005 .... 6.2
    Article 1 (purposes of the Convention) **C5**
    Article 2 (scope) **C5**
    Article 3 (non-discrimination principle) **C5**
    Article 4 (definitions) 6.4, **C5**
    Article 10 (identification of the victims) 6.8, **C5**
        (3) 6.4
    Article 12 (assistance to victims) **C5**
        (1) 6.7.2, 6.7.3
    Article 13 (recovery and reflection period) **C5**
        (1) 6.7.2
    Article 14 (residence permit) **C5**
    Article 27 (ex parte and ex officio applications)
        (1) 6.7.2
EU Directive 2001/55/EC of 20 July 2001 on minimum standards for giving
    temporary protection in the event of a mass influx of displaced persons
    and on measures promoting a balance of efforts between Member States in
    receiving such persons and bearing the consequences thereof ('Temporary
    Protection Directive') 8.2.5
EU Directive 2004/38/EC of 29 April 2004 on the right of citizens of the
    Union and their family members to move and reside freely within the
    territory of the Member States ('Citizens' Directive') 4.8
EU Directive 2004/83/EC of 29 April 2004 on minimum standards for the
    qualification and status of third country nationals or stateless persons as
    refugees or as persons who otherwise need international protection and the
    content of the protection granted ('Qualification Directive') .. 1.1, 1.2, 1.10.1, 1.11.4,
                                1.13, 1.14, 1.15.5, 1.16, 2.12.1, 8.2.5
    Article 2(c) 1.3.2
    Article 4(1) 1.3.8

EU Directive 2004/83/EC of 29 April 2004 on minimum standards for the qualification and status of third country nationals or stateless persons as refugees or as persons who otherwise need international protection and the content of the protection granted ('Qualification Directive') – *continued*

Article 4(5) 1.3.2
Article 7(2) 1.12
Article 8(2) 1.13.2
Article 9 .... 1.10
Article 10(c) 1.11.3
Article 12(1)(a) 1,15.1
(2) 1.15.2
(b) 1.15.2.2
(3) 1.15.4
Article 15 .... 1.16.1
(a) 1.16.1.1
(b) 1.16.1.1
(c) 1.10.3, 1.16.1.1
Article 17 .... 1.16.2

EU Directive 2005/85/EC of 1 December 2005 on minimum standards on procedures in Member States for granting and withdrawing refugee status ('Procedures Directive') 2.1

EU Directive 2011/36/EU of 5 April 2011 on preventing and combating trafficking in human beings and protecting its victims, and replacing Council Framework Decision 2002/629/JHA 6.7.3, 6.7.5
Article 11(2), (3) 6.7.5
Recital 22 .... 6.7.5

EU European Commission Implementing Regulation 118/2014 of 30 January 2014 amending Regulation (EC) No 1560/2003 laying down detailed rules for the application of Council Regulation (EC) No 343/2003 establishing the criteria and mechanisms for determining the Member State responsible for examining an asylum application lodged in one of the Member States by a third-country national 2.6.1

EU Regulation 343/2003/EC of 18 February 2003 establishing the criteria and mechanisms for determining the Member State responsible for examining an asylum application lodged in one of the Member States by a third-country national ('Dublin II') 2.6.1

EU Regulation 604/2013 of 26 June 2013 establishing the criteria and mechanisms for determining the Member State responsible for examining an application for international protection lodged in one of the Member States by a third-country national or a stateless person (recast) ('Dublin III') 2.6.1
Recital 17 .... 2.6.2
Recital 35 .... 2.6.1
Article 3 (Access to the procedure for examining an application for international protection)
(2) 2.6.1
Article 4 (right to information) 2.6.1
Article 5 (personal interview) 2.6.1
Article 7 (hierarchy of criteria)
(2) 2.6.1
Article 10 (family members who are applicants for international protection) 2.6.1
Article 13 (entry and/or stay) 2.6.1

Article 16 (dependent persons) 2.6.2
Article 17 (discretionary clauses) 2.6.2
Article 19 (cessation of responsibilities) 2.6.2
     (1) 2.6.1
Article 20 (start of the procedure) 2.6.1
Article 21 (submitting a take charge request) 2.6.1
Article 22 (replying to a take charge request) 2.6.1
     (7) 2.6.1
Article 25(2) 2.6.1
Article 28 (detention) 2.6.2
Article 29 (modalities and time limits) 2.6.2
Article 31 (exchange of relevant information before a transfer is carried out) .....
    2.6.2
Article 49 (entry into force and applicability) 2.6.1
European Convention on Human Rights (Convention for the Protection of
   Human Rights and Fundamental Freedoms 1950 (ECHR)) 4.2.1
   Article 1 (obligation to respect human rights) 3.2.1, **C3**
   Article 2 (right to life) 1.16.1, 3.2.5, 3.2.6, 4.4.2, 8.2.5, **C3**
   Article 3 (prohibition of torture) 1.13, 1.15.5, 1.15.6, 1.16.1, 1.6.1.1, 2.1.6,
             2.6.3, 3.1.4, 3.2.1, 3.2.5, 3.2.6, 3.2.10, 3.2.12, 3.3.1, 3.6.3,
                                        4.4.2, 8.2.5, 8.3, **C3**
   Article 4 (prohibition of slavery and forced labour) 6.7.4, **C3**
     (1) 3.2.7
   Article 5 (right to liberty and security) **C3**
     (1)(f) 3.2.9
     (5) 3.1.3, 3.2.9
   Article 6 (right to a fair trial) 3.2.10, **C3**
   Article 7 (no punishment without law) **C3**
   Article 8 (right to respect for private and family life) . 3.2.1, 3.2.6, 3.2.10, 3.2.11,
             3.2.12.3.3.1, 3.3.3, 3.6.3, 4.3.1, 6.9.1, 7.5, **C3**
   Article 9 (freedom of thought, conscience and religion) **C3**
   Article 10 (freedom of expression) **C3**
   Article 11 (freedom of assembly and association) **C3**
   Article 12 (right to marry) **C3**
   Article 13 (right to an effective remedy) 3.2.1, 3.2.5, **C3**
   Article 14 (prohibition of discrimination) 3.2.13, **C3**
   Article 15 (derogation in time of emergency) **C3**
   Article 41 (just satisfaction) 3.1.3
   Protocol 13 (concerning the abolition of the death penalty in all circumstances),
     Article 1 .... 3.2.5
European Court of Human Rights, Rules of Court of the............................. 2.6.3
Istanbul Protocol: Manual on the Effective Investigation and Documentation
   of Torture and Other Cruel, Inhuman or Degrading Treatment or
   Punishment
     para.187 .... 3.6.3.1
     para.188 .... 3.6.3.1
Treaty on European Union... 4.2.1
   Article 6(2) 3.4
UN Convention on the Rights of the Child 1989................................ 2.2.11
UN Convention Relating to the Status of Refugees 1951 (Refugee
   Convention) 1.1, 1.10.3, 1.15.5, 1.15.6, 1.16.1, 2.2.1, 4.2.1, 4.3.1, 8.2.5
   Article 1 (definition of the term 'refugee') **C4**
   Article 1A(2) 1.1, 1.2, 1.15.1, 2.2.1

UN Convention Relating to the Status of Refugees 1951 (Refugee
    Convention) – *continued*
        Article 1D 1.15, 1.15.1
        Article 1E 1.15
        Article 1F 1.15, 1.15.2, 1.15.5, 2.2.1
            (b) 1.15.2.2, 1.15.6
        Article 28 (travel documents) 2.10.4
        Article 31 (refugees unlawfully in the country of refugee) **C4**
        Article 32 (expulsion) **C4**
        Article 33 (prohibition of expulsion or return 'refoulement') **C4**
            (2) 1.15, 1.15.6
        Protocol Relating to the Status of Refugees 1967 (New York) 1.1, 2.2.1

Abbreviations

AIDA	Asylum Information Database
AITCA 2004	Asylum and Immigration (Treatment of Claimants, etc.) Act 2004
ARC	application registration card
ART	asylum routing team
ASAP	Asylum Support Appeals Project
Bail Guidance	President of the Immigration and Asylum Chamber of the First-tier Tribunal, *Bail Guidance for Judges Presiding Over Immigration and Asylum Hearings*, July 2011, implemented June 2012
CAT	Council of Europe Convention on Action against Trafficking in Human Beings
CEOP	Child Exploitation and Online Protection Centre
CG	Country Guideline
CIG reports	Country Information and Guidance reports
CIO	Chief Immigration Officer
Citizen's Directive	EU Directive 2004/38/EC of 29 April 2004 on the right of citizens of the Union and their family members to move and reside freely within the territory of the Member States
CJEU	Court of Justice of the European Union
CLR	controlled legal representation
Competent Authority Guidance	*Victims of Modern Slavery – Competent Authority Guidance* (Home Office, version 3: 21 March 2016)
CPT	(Council of Europe) Committee for the Prevention of Torture
CRIS	Crime Reporting Information System
CSID	Civil Status Identity Document
CTD	Refugee Convention Travel Document
DDV	destitution – domestic violence
DFT	detained fast-track
DIRB	Documentation, Information and Research Branch of the Immigration and Refugee Board: Canadian independent documentation centre

DL	discretionary leave
DRC	Democratic Republic of Congo
Dublin III	EU Regulation 604/2013 of 26 June 2013 establishing the criteria and mechanisms for determining the Member State responsible for examining an application for international protection lodged in one of the Member States by a third-country national or a stateless person (recast)
ECHR	European Convention for the Protection of Human Rights and Fundamental Freedoms
ECO	entry clearance officer
ECRE	European Council on Refugees and Exiles
ECtHR	European Court of Human Rights
ECF	exceptional case funding
EEA	European Economic Area
EIN	Electronic Immigration Network
ELENA	European Legal Network on Asylum
ELR	exceptional leave to remain
EU	European Union
FGM	female genital mutilation
HP	humanitarian protection
HRA 1998	Human Rights Act 1998
IA 1971	Immigration Act 1971
IA 2014	Immigration Act 2014
IAA 1999	Immigration and Asylum Act 1999
IAAS	Immigration and Asylum Accreditation Scheme
IANA 2006	Immigration, Asylum and Nationality Act 2006
ILPA	Immigration Law Practitioners' Association
ILR	indefinite leave to remain
KoLL	knowledge of life and language in the UK
LASPO 2012	Legal Aid, Sentencing and Punishment of Offenders Act 2012
LTTE	Liberation Tigers of Tamil Eelam
Merits Criteria Regulations	Civil Legal Aid (Merits Criteria) Regulations 2013, SI 2013/104
NASS	National Asylum Support Service
NCA	National Crime Agency
NGOs	non-governmental organisations
NIAA 2002	Nationality, Immigration and Asylum Act 2002
NRM	National Referral Mechanism
Operational Guidance	UK Visas and Immigration Operational Guidance collection
PAP	Pre-Action Protocol

PNC	Police National Computer
Procedures Directive	Directive 2005/85/EC of 1 December 2005 on minimum standards on procedures in Member States for granting and withdrawing refugee status
Protection Regulations	Refugee or Person in Need of International Protection (Qualification) Regulations 2006, SI 2006/2525
PTSD	post-traumatic stress disorder
Qualification Directive	Directive 2004/83/EC of 29 April 2004 on minimum standards for the qualification and status of third country nationals or stateless persons as refugees or as persons who otherwise need international protection and the content of the protection granted
Refugee Convention	UN Convention Relating to the Status of Refugees 1951
RLG	Refugee Legal Group
SIAC	Special Immigration Appeals Commission
SIBP	self-infliction of injuries by proxy
SOAS	School of Oriental and African Studies
Temporary Protection Directive	Directive 2001/55/EC of 20 July 2001 on minimum standards for giving temporary protection in the event of a mass influx of displaced persons and on measures promoting a balance of efforts between Member States in receiving such persons and bearing the consequences thereof
UASC	unaccompanied asylum-seeking child
UK	United Kingdom
UKBA 2007	UK Borders Act 2007
UKVI	UK Visas and Immigration
UN	United Nations
UNCAT	United Nations Committee against Torture
UNHCR	United Nations High Commissioner for Refugees
UNODC	United Nations Office on Drugs and Crime
UNRWA	United Nations Relief and Works Agency for Palestine Refugees in the Near East
Upper Tribunal Rules	Tribunal Procedure (Upper Tribunal) Rules 2008, SI 2008/2698 (L 15)

CHAPTER 1

Refugee claims

1.1 INTRODUCTION: A REMINDER OF THE BASICS

The fundamental provision of the United Nations (UN) Convention Relating to the Status of Refugees 1951 (read with the 1967 New York Protocol), usually referred to as the Refugee Convention, is Article 1A(2). A refugee is defined therein as a person who:

> owing to well-founded fear of being persecuted for reasons of race, religion, nationality, membership of a particular social group or political opinion, is outside the country of his nationality and is unable or, owing to such fear, is unwilling to avail himself of the protection of that country; or who, not having a nationality and being outside the country of his former habitual residence … is unable or, owing to such fear, is unwilling to return to it.

This provision deals with the situation of both persons with a nationality and those without (i.e. the 'stateless'). The courts have interpreted the requirements of the definition to be the same in both cases.

The definition can be broken down into its constituent parts:

1. Possession of a well-founded fear.
2. Treatment that amounts to being persecuted.
3. One of the five reasons, referred to as the (Refugee) Convention reasons.
4. Being outside one's country.
5. Being unable or unwilling to obtain protection.

We can paraphrase the most relevant questions thus:

- Will it happen (credibility plus country evidence)?
- What will happen (persecution)?
- Why will it happen (Convention reason)?
- What might stop it happening (protection or internal relocation)?

Most of the relevant principles underlying these concepts were once found solely in domestic case law. Now they are conveniently defined in European Union (EU) Directive 2004/83/EC (the 'Qualification Directive'), transposed into United Kingdom (UK) law through the Refugee or Person in Need of International Protection

(Qualification) Regulations 2006, SI 2006/2525 (the 'Protection Regulations') (see **Appendix C2**) and modifications to the Asylum section of the Immigration Rules at Part 11 (see **Appendix D1**). For the purposes of accreditation, as well as one's own casework, those regulations often provide the easiest and most convenient solution to a question.

Practice point

We strongly recommend reading the following Immigration Law Practitioners' Association (ILPA) best practice guides, which are essentially asylum skills guides. They are written by skilled, experienced practitioners who have distilled their learning into readable and accessible form, and aspiring practitioners should not pass by the opportunity to learn from them. They are available for free download at **www.ilpa.org.uk/pages/publications.html**:

- Mark Henderson, *Best Practice Guide to Asylum and Human Rights Appeals* is an excellent practical guide to evidencing and running asylum claims. Updated versions can be found periodically, electronically via the Electronic Immigration Network (EIN) (**www.ein.org.uk**) and on paper, published by the Legal Action Group.
- Jane Coker, Garry Kelly and Martin Soorjoo (2002) *Making an Asylum Application: A Best Practice Guide* – while this is clearly out of date on substantive law and Home Office procedures, it is still very useful on issues such as taking instructions.

For current thinking on particular issues in asylum claims, country-based or otherwise, the Refugee Legal Group (RLG) is an essential forum. For details of how to join, find its page on the Asylum Aid website (**www.asylumaid.org.uk**).

If you are interested in reading further into the subject, the leading domestic textbook is *Asylum Law and Practice* by Mark Symes and Peter Jorro (Bloomsbury Professional, 2010).

1.2 ASYLUM SEEKERS

An asylum seeker is a person who has left his or her country of nationality or habitual residence, and has made a claim in a signatory country (i.e. an asylum claim or application) to the effect that he or she is entitled to protection there under the provisions of the Refugee Convention. The asylum seeker will hold that status until the asylum application is finally decided by that country.

If the asylum application is refused on the basis that the asylum seeker is not entitled to that protection, as the applicant does not meet the definition of a refugee in Article 1A(2), the Home Office (presuming the asylum claim is made in the UK) will then be obliged to consider whether that person is entitled to humanitarian protection under the Qualification Directive.

If the asylum seeker is refused under both protection regimes, and not entitled to stay in the UK on any other basis, that person will no longer be an asylum seeker. In some circumstances people may be able to make a further claim for asylum on human rights grounds under, what is called in the UK, the 'fresh claim' procedure. If they are not able to establish their claim for protection, they will generally be removable to their own country.

1.3 WELL-FOUNDED FEAR

There are two aspects to the possession of a well-founded fear: well-foundedness and fear. The 'fear' test is in practice something of a red herring. It is very hard to imagine an asylum seeker losing their appeal because they are accepted as being at risk of serious harm but are not frightened at the prospect. So really, from the perspective of the decision maker, the question of 'fear' collapses into the question of 'credibility', i.e. are they telling the truth?

1.3.1 Getting the story across: different types of asylum claim

Procedurally, asylum seekers will have an opportunity to establish that they do have a genuine fear of returning to their country in their asylum interview, with a detailed statement of their claim (if they are properly represented), and any corroborative evidence they may be able to submit to the Home Office. On the basis of this information, the Home Office will make an assessment of the truthfulness (or as the Home Office likes to call it 'credibility') of the asylum seeker. It will ask itself if the asylum seeker is telling the truth about his or her profile and about what happened to him or her in the past.

Asylum seekers may lie about some or all of their claim, or exaggerate their fear, but may still have a well-founded fear of persecution, e.g. establishing that they are a member of a class or group of persons who are at risk, even though they may not have a cogent case as to their own personal history:

- Members of Somali minority clans were at one time generally accepted as being at risk of persecution.
- Eritrean military service evaders have been accepted as a category (into which nearly everybody who left the country unlawfully fell).

A person may also be at risk if forced to return to a particular country, not because of anything they have said in their asylum claim, but because of the view taken by the authorities of that country of asylum seekers returning from abroad in general or from the UK in particular, as has been found from time to time regarding countries such as Sudan (where the security forces routinely imputed anti-regime political opinions to returnees), Zimbabwe (where roving gangs conducted political loyalty tests) or Syria (see e.g. *KB (Failed asylum seekers and forced returnees) Syria CG* [2012] UKUT 426 (IAC)).

Of course, it is easier for asylum seekers to succeed if they are accepted as telling the truth about the entirety of their account, but many asylum seekers do not tell the whole story, usually because they are poorly advised (not by inadequate lawyers so much as by agents, interpreters, members of their community or others they come across before or during the asylum process). But the examples given here show that claims can succeed notwithstanding that the individual's own story may be mostly rejected.

Practice point

Always look at the prevailing Country Guideline case law in relation to the country where your client is from to assess what 'target' you have to hit. Consider whether you can run the case in the alternative:

(a) 'my client can prove their account is true and so they face persecution as a political activist with a history of detention'; but
(b) 'whether or not you accept that, they are clearly shown by official records as family members of a political dissident who will be in danger because of their activities'; or
(c) 'even if you don't accept that, then they are members of a tribe of which bare membership creates a risk of serious harm'.

1.3.2 Well-foundedness

This is an objective test and concerns, in part, the claimant's account being looked at in the light of the conditions in the claimant's country of origin. It also requires a consideration of future risk. The claimant might not wish to return, but are their fears 'well founded' in the sense of there being a sufficient likelihood of their being realised?

The standard is that of 'well-founded fear', now found in the Qualification Directive at Article 2(c); the classic domestic expression of this was in the House of Lords decision of *R (on the application of Sivakumuran)* v. *Secretary of State for the Home Department* [1987] UKHL 1, which put the question as whether there was 'a reasonable degree of likelihood' of persecution.

- **Historic fact:**

    - standard of proof;
    - credibility/plausibility.

- **Future risk:**

    - country information;
    - past persecution;
    - specific or general risk;
    - activities in the UK;
    - future behaviour.

1.3.3 Standard of proof

The standard of proof for both aspects of well-founded fear is that of 'a reasonable degree of likelihood', which is lower than the civil standard of the balance of probabilities and is sometimes expressed as 'substantial grounds for believing' or 'real risk'. The leading case is *R* v. *Immigration Appeal Tribunal and another ex p. Rajendrakumar* [1996] Imm AR 97.

In *Karanakaran* v. *Secretary of State for the Home Department* [2000] Imm AR 271 the Court of Appeal found that an asylum claim could succeed even though the person assessing it (Home Office decision maker or immigration judge) might doubt parts of the account (whereas if the evidence was assessed on the traditional standard of proof in civil proceedings, the balance of probabilities, they would have to reject evidence that they doubted). The court held that the first three of the following four categories of evidence identified at [55] by a decision maker are relevant for this purpose:

(1) evidence they are certain about;
(2) evidence they think is probably true;
(3) evidence to which they are willing to attach some credence, even if they could not go so far as to say it is probably true;
(4) evidence to which they are not willing to attach any credence at all.

See also the comments of Brooke LJ in *Karanakaran* at [103]:

> when considering whether there is a serious possibility of persecution for a Convention reason if an asylum seeker is returned, it would be quite wrong to exclude matters totally from consideration in the balancing process simply because the decision-maker believes, on what may sometimes be somewhat fragile evidence, that they probably did not occur.

As it was put more recently in *KS (benefit of the doubt)* [2014] UKUT 552 (IAC) at [73]:

> in respect of every asserted fact when there is doubt, the lower standard entails that it should not be rejected and should rather continue to be kept in mind as a possibility at least until the end when the question or risk is posed in relation to the evidence considered in the round.

The requirement to give the benefit of the doubt applies only where the account is generally credible (United Nations High Commissioner for Refugees (UNHCR) Handbook, paragraphs 196, 204 and the Qualification Directive, Article 4(5)).

Example

A judge hears an asylum appeal involving a political dissident who claims to have suffered detention and torture. Reflecting on the evidence afterwards, he considers himself:

(a) certain the person was politically active;
(b) not sure whether they were detained;
(c) sure they were not tortured.

In going on from those credibility findings to determine whether the asylum seeker faces risk based on the country evidence, the judge has to take into account the facts at (a) and (b). In a civil case tried on the balance of probabilities, (b) would not be accepted as having been established.

1.3.4 Credibility

The assessment of past facts in asylum cases is a complex process. There are statutory provisions that have an impact on the assessment of credibility as well as Immigration Rules and case law. When seeking inspiration in relation to what credibility issues might arise, the Immigration Rules (see **Appendix D** for extracts) and the Asylum and Immigration (Treatment of Claimants, etc.) Act 2004 (AITCA 2004), s.8 (see **Appendix A4**) are a good source of inspiration: because if you can avoid the pitfalls therein, you are already off to a good start. However, beyond that, one of the most important modern authorities on the appropriate approach to take when assessing credibility is *Beyond Proof: Credibility Assessment in EU Asylum Systems* (UNHCR, May 2013). That is the best place to look for supportive propositions regarding many of the most commonly recurring criticisms of an asylum seeker's credibility. Relevant factors that need to be taken into account include:

(a)   the limits and variations of human memory, in particular the wide-ranging variability in people's ability to record, retain, and retrieve memories; in the accuracy of memories for dates, times, appearance of common objects, proper names, and verbatim verbal exchanges (the recall of all of which is nearly always reconstructed from inference, estimation and guesswork); directly relevant are also the impact of high levels of emotion on the encoding of any memory and the influence upon memory of the questioning and the way questions are asked;

(b)   the impact of trauma and other mental ill health on memory, behaviour and testimony;

(c)   the influence of factors such as disorientation, anxiety, fear, lack of trust in authorities or interpreters on the disclosure of material facts and submission of other evidence;

(d)   the influences of stigma, shame, fear of rejection by family and community, which may also inhibit disclosure. Stigma may also account for the lack of documentary or other evidence, including under-reporting of incidents of violence, and limits on their inclusion in country of origin information;

(e)   the influence on knowledge, memory, behaviour and testimony of aspects of the applicant's background, such as age, culture, education, gender, sexual orientation and/or gender identity, profession, socio-economic status, religion, values, and past experiences.

1.3.5 Immigration Rules

Paragraph 339L provides that when assessing credibility:

- the burden of proof is on the individual asylum seeker in general;
- however, where individuals have made every effort to substantiate their account, and provided a story which is coherent and plausible in the light of the country evidence, and explained any lack of corroboration, they should be given the benefit of the doubt.

This should be the starting point for the assessment of credibility. The rider that the applicant must be generally credible enables decision makers to attach appropriate weight to inconsistencies and other credibility issues, but this paragraph provides a useful reminder that corroborating evidence is not always required and that the benefit of the doubt should be given where it is not. But an asylum seeker must, where possible, corroborate a claim, and where attempts to do so have been made, but have failed, these should also be explained to the decision maker. It is not unreasonable for a decision maker to expect corroboration from sources that would appear to be available, particularly in this country, such as relatives or friends who have witnessed a particular event or heard about it from family or other sources.

Practice point

Judges, if not the Home Office, are usually impressed by a detailed account. Bringing a story alive with vivid detail will persuade many judges, and some primary decision makers, that the claim has the 'ring of truth'. So always probe your clients for the most detail they can come up with regarding:

- their political or other beliefs;
- examples of the problems they had in their country of origin;
- exactly what happened to them in detention; and
- how they left the country without being caught by the authorities.

Irene (Zimbabwe)

Irene was a journalist in Zimbabwe writing under a pseudonym. She cannot easily prove that it was she who wrote the articles in question, nor is it easy for her to obtain copies of the articles from Zimbabwe.

To an extent, she can address this in a witness statement and explain everything she remembers about the articles she wrote and the process of getting them published. However, her case would be much stronger if she could obtain copies of the articles or something that links her to the pseudonym she used, such as a letter from the publisher.

Failing that, most immigration judges would view her case more sympathetically if she could at least demonstrate that she has tried very hard to obtain the relevant evidence and show copies of letters written, calls made and so on, and explain in her statement what steps she has taken to try to obtain the evidence. This would distinguish her case from someone who

7

makes a claim but makes no attempt to substantiate it, at least as far as the decision maker or judge can see: see Immigration Rules, para.339L(i) and (ii) which authorise giving the benefit of the doubt where a genuine effort has been made to obtain supporting evidence and a satisfactory explanation has been provided for missing material.

1.3.6 Asylum and Immigration (Treatment of Claimants, etc.) Act 2004

Section 8 of AITCA 2004 introduced a mandatory requirement that specific types of 'behaviour' by asylum seekers after they left their own country be treated by decision makers, including judges, as damaging credibility:

* reliance on false documents and destruction of documents;
* claiming asylum after receiving an immigration decision or after arrest;
* not claiming asylum despite having had a reasonable opportunity to do so in a 'safe' third country (safe third countries for these purposes are the EU Member States).

In *SM (Section 8: Judge's process) Iran* [2005] UKAIT 116 the Tribunal found that even where s.8 applies, the evidence must be assessed as a whole: the provision in no way operated to deem evidence as lacking in credibility without a balanced assessment of the case as a whole.

Nevertheless, the types of behaviour falling within s.8 should as far as possible be addressed in individual claims. Both the Home Office and the Tribunal will be obliged to take them into account.

Regarding any failure to claim asylum in a 'safe' third country, bear in mind that this applies only to those countries defined as 'safe' in s.8(7) itself: i.e. EU countries. And remember that the courts accepted in *R (on the application of Adimi)* v. *Uxbridge Magistrates' Court and another* [1999] Imm AR 560 (QB) that there is some element of choice open to a refugee as to where they actually claim asylum.

However, an explanation should always be sought as to a failure to claim asylum abroad, particularly if there has been a lengthy stay in a country:

* a desire to join relatives in the UK, or a pre-arranged journey with only transit stops abroad, might be possible explanations;
* as might a wish to put one's case in a country where English is the predominantly spoken language;
* so might conditions in the third country (e.g. colonial or diplomatic relationships with the asylum seeker's country of origin might encourage or discourage an asylum claim).

Regarding delays in claiming asylum, much depends on the individual circumstances. Many asylum seekers who attempt to enter the country before making their claims will do so for the good reasons laid out by agencies such as the UNHCR, e.g. the effects of trauma, language problems, lack of information, previous experiences with authority and feelings of insecurity, rather than with a view to falsifying their claims with the assistance of contacts in this country.

Practice point

If an immigration judge relies heavily upon s.8 (or the Secretary of State does so in a fresh claim case), then make this a distinct point on which to appeal/judicially review the decision. Case law such as *JT (Cameroon)* v. *Secretary of State for the Home Department* [2008] EWCA Civ 878 is useful: therein treasury counsel endorsed the submission that s.8 should not be interpreted as affecting the normal standard of proof in an asylum/human rights appeal: it simply ensures that certain factors relating to personal credibility are taken into account when that standard of proof is applied, their weight and significance varying according to the context and the precise circumstances.

1.3.7 Approach to documents

Merely producing a document from the country of origin does not necessarily advance an asylum claim: its relevance needs to be carefully explained, as does its provenance, including how it was that it was brought to the UK (you might be surprised how often the account of how a document was obtained undermines some aspect of the client's account of being in fear of persecution). In *Ahmed* v. *Secretary of State for the Home Department (Pakistan)* (starred) [2002] UKIAT 439 we see the Tribunal setting down the relevant principles, which are essentially that:

- If an allegation of forgery of a document is made by the Home Office, then it bears the burden of proof in establishing that assertion. However, in most cases forgery is not the relevant issue, given that documents may be obtained through illicit means in many countries without actually being a forgery (i.e. a bribe might produce a 'valid' yet unreliable document).
- The general principle in asylum and human rights cases is that the applicant bears the burden of proof, which in turn requires that they establish the reliability of any particular document on which they seek to rely.
- The decision maker should consider whether a document is one on which reliance should properly be placed after looking at all the evidence in the round.

In practice this means that the general findings on a person's credibility are likely to be determinative of the approach taken to any particular document, unless its genuineness is supported by other evidence such as some form of verification report.

Farhan (Afghanistan)

Farhan is an asylum seeker from Afghanistan. He claims that the security forces murdered his father because of their suspicions that he was a Taliban activist. He lost touch with all his family members. Some time after arriving in the UK he obtains documents said to be genuinely from his village elder stating that he and his father were wanted for terrorist activities.

Think carefully about whether you should advise your client to submit these documents and about how you will seek to establish them as genuine. For example:

- Are they consistent with Farhan's account as to timing? (For example, when was his father killed and when are the documents dated?)
- How were they obtained in Afghanistan? (If wholly by postal connections is this consistent with the general account of not being in touch with any relatives; how were they fetched bearing in mind the dangers that might be involved in approaching his home village?)
- How and when were they brought to the UK? Did they come in an envelope and has that been retained?

Practice point

It is difficult for the Home Office to dispute the genuineness of documents that have entered legal proceedings not via an asylum seeker, whose own credibility may be in dispute, but from lawyers in the country of origin who have obtained them from a court and passed them directly to lawyers in the UK (see *PJ* v. *Secretary of State for the Home Department* [2014] EWCA Civ 1011 at [41]). This is particularly important in a 'fresh claim' case where the applicant's credibility may have already been rejected, at least partially, in earlier appeal proceedings.

1.3.8   Shared duty in establishing the facts

The burden of proof generally lies on the asylum seeker. However sometimes it may be that the government has access to information, or the potential to make enquiries, which means that there is effectively a 'shared duty' to build the case together. The Upper Tribunal addresses this in slightly fusty language in *KS (benefit of the doubt)* [2014] UKUT 552 (IAC) at [63]:

> the duty imposed on the Member State by Article 4(1) QD – and on decision makers in the UK by paragraph 339I of the Immigration Rules – to assess the relevant elements of an application '*[i]n cooperation with the applicant ...*' must at least have an ameliorative effect in respect of an applicant being able to discharge that burden.

An example of such a case is where documents emanate from the UNHCR abroad, because they are from an unimpeachable source whose verification should not be difficult: see e.g. the European Court of Human Rights (ECtHR) in *Singh* v. *Belgium* (application no. 33210/11) (2 October 2012).

Where the documents are of such a kind that the Home Office is under a duty to verify them, a failure to do so may prevent the Home Office challenging their authenticity on appeal (*PJ* v. *Secretary of State for the Home Department* [2014] EWCA Civ 1011 at [31]).

Another example of the principle is found in *RC* v. *Sweden* [2010] ECHR 307 where the Strasbourg Court found that where a medical report, albeit written by a non-expert, raised 'a rather strong indication' that the asylum seeker might be a torture victim, it was then for the government to dispel the ensuing doubts that their return might put them at risk of further serious harm. The Tribunal has not accepted that this necessarily means the burden shifts to the government in every case, but nevertheless has recognised the value of medical evidence in cases of this nature, see e.g. *KV (scarring – medical evidence) Sri Lanka* [2014] UKUT 230 (IAC) and *NA (UT rule 45: Singh* v. *Belgium) Iran* [2014] UKUT 205 (IAC) (which indicates that there is no duty on the Tribunal to commission medical evidence but leaves open whether it is the responsibility of the Home Office to do so before rejecting such evidence at the initial consideration stage).

1.3.9 Information and language analysis

One form of evidence relied upon by the Home Office in assessing asylum claims has been reports on an applicant's mode of speaking. For example, the organisation Sprakab, a privately owned company in Stockholm, Sweden, uses analysts and linguists working together to listen to recordings of an asylum seeker to seek out certain distinctive features of any particular language or dialect, with a view to identifying a person's place of origin or habitual residence.

The Supreme Court in *Secretary of State for Home Department* v. *MN and KY (Scotland)* [2014] UKSC 30 looked at the approach to be taken to Sprakab reports when assessing an asylum seeker's background. The court was critical of the approach of the Upper Tribunal which had previously ruled that such reports were highly expert in nature and should be departed from only with 'some very good reason'. Sprakab reports should, in fact, be approached as part of the evidence available to a decision maker as a whole rather than being given some special status meaning their conclusions should normally be accepted. Other points to note from *MN and KY* are:

- The comments in the Sprakab reports as to the asylum seeker's knowledge of country and culture were inadequately supported by any demonstrated expertise of the authors.
- There were valid reasons to take a less strict view than in the normal case as to granting anonymity regarding an institution such as Sprakab, subject to appropriate safeguards: the expertise claimed was on behalf of an organisation based on the collaborative work of individuals with different skills within it, and there was no doubt about its identity, working methods or the qualifications and experience of those involved in preparing its report.

Practice point

If your client's place of origin or habitual residence is disputed, think carefully about the available evidence.

- Are there relatives or friends who can describe their personal knowledge of your client's background? They are likely to be much more impressive witnesses if they attend court.
- Can you obtain expert evidence as to your client's knowledge of country and culture?

- If the Home Office has obtained a Sprakab report, has that report gone beyond linguistic analysis (where obviously it is owed some respect) and strayed into claims as to your client's knowledge of country and culture which are not backed up by proof of the report writer's own expertise?
- Is there an explanation for any Sprakab conclusions that count against your client's case, e.g. was the client raised by parents who did not speak the local language?

1.3.10   Entering the country

The capacity in which a person enters the country ought not to carry decisive weight in the analysis of that person's claim to need international protection. Someone might claim asylum having entered as a visitor: the UNHCR has warned that this will often arise out of an understandable desire to secure some form of temporary stay in a country, to avoid simply being returned home from the border.

Again, look at *Adimi* at [48]:

> Most asylum seekers who attempt to enter the country before making their claims will do so for the reasons suggested by UNHCR rather than with a view to falsifying their claims with the assistance of friends and contacts here.

1.3.11   Inconsistencies

Although there are lots of possible explanations for discrepancies, unexplained inconsistencies can properly justify rejection of a person's story – because if a person gives different versions of an event, this may well be because he or she is making it up rather than drawing on genuine recollections. For this reason one of the practitioner's most important functions is taking full and accurate instructions, in order to:

- avoid unnecessary discrepancies; and
- ensure that any existing inconsistencies are adequately explained.

In **2.2.1**, where we address the evidence of children, we mention the Joint Presidential Guidance Note No.2 of 2010, *Child, Vulnerable Adult and Sensitive Appellant Guidance*: the Upper Tribunal has stated that the approach therein (i.e. that a judge should bear in mind a person's vulnerability as a possible explanation for discrepancies) is important for vulnerable and sensitive appellants as well as children: *JL (medical reports – credibility) China* [2013] UKUT 145 (IAC).

Practice point

There is no such thing as perfect recall and no human being is capable of giving a completely consistent account of the same events on different occasions. The reasons for this lie in the way that memories are made:

- **Memories must be recorded.** Bystanders to the same events always perceive the same events differently and attach significance to different aspects of those events. The human brain searches for patterns and where information is absent (or even where it is present sometimes) the brain completes the 'picture' by filling in blanks.
- **Memories must be stored.** Sometimes memories are simply lost or partially lost and blanks filled in. Minor aspects of events, such as sensations, may be recalled long after the event even though major events are forgotten. The passage of time generally degrades memories.
- **Memories must then be recalled and recounted.** There is ample opportunity for memories to be recalled differently on different occasions. For example, the use of leading questions will often change the way that memories are recalled, particularly in children.

Despite this, the fact is that in many asylum cases the only evidence is the witness' own testimony. If it is perceived as flawed, it will be rejected.

Always consider possible explanations for discrepancies such a lack of formal education or a bad memory.

For a good source to read more, see Dr Juliet Cohen (2001) 'Errors of recall and credibility: can omissions and discrepancies in successive statements reasonably be said to undermine credibility of testimony?', *Medico-Legal Journal*, 69 (1): 25–34, The Medico-Legal Society (also reproduced at **www.medicaljustice.org.uk/medical-guidance/2285-errors-of-recall-and-credibility-2001.html**).

Due allowance must be made for the different stages of the asylum process, and the various ways in which information is elicited – the nature of the process is such that a single perfectly consistent telling of the story is unlikely. While the Tribunal has agreed that inconsistencies between accounts given at different times can properly be referred to for the purpose of assessing credibility, it will be necessary to consider all the circumstances of the interview process, including whether an explicit opportunity was given to add information in the context of the complexity of the questions and the scope for misunderstanding (*DA (unsigned interview notes) Turkey* [2004] UKIAT 104).

And in *KS (benefit of the doubt)* it was stated at [99]:

> a child-sensitive application of the lower standard of proof may still need to be given to persons if they are recounting relevant events that took place at a time when they were minors …

Practice point

Not all additional information is necessarily inconsistent with an earlier account. It is the very nature of the process that further questions are asked later on about an account that has already been given. Indeed, this is the whole purpose of a Home Office asylum interview. It would be truly absurd, then, to say that the provision of additional information is an elaboration of an account that is in some way not credible.

However, providing additional information is not the same as making changes to an account or adding new events, which are likely to cause significant credibility issues.

> Contemporaneous complaints about unsatisfactory interviews will be more telling than late challenges at appeal.

Failure to read back the contents of the interview to its subject may make the account unreliable and may be the basis for criticising an account, though see *DA (unsigned interview notes) Turkey* for the fact that an objection to an interview's conduct plus a mere failure to sign does not of itself mean an interview should be disregarded without analysing the circumstances of that interview. The screening interview is not intended to be a vehicle for exploring the substance of the asylum claim.

Another issue with interviews is the propriety of the questions actually asked: thus in *A, B, and C* [2014] EUECJ C-148/13 the Court of Justice of the European Union (CJEU) looked at the ways in which an asylum claim based on the individual's sexuality might be assessed, and stressed that the methods used to assess the case had to be consistent with the right to respect for human dignity and private and family life. This means:

- questions about sexual practices are a 'no go' area;
- stereotyped notions about how people behave should be avoided;
- 'testing' for sexuality is an unreliable process, and the filming of intimate acts is unlikely to take things further;
- reticence in revealing intimate aspects of one's life cannot be a factor counting against the acceptance of the claim's truthfulness.

1.4   EVIDENCE FROM VICTIMS OF TRAUMA

If you do have any inconsistencies in the case that cannot be otherwise explained, bear in mind that the client may be a victim of torture: the specialist international Tribunal regarding torture, the United Nations Committee against Torture (UNCAT), has warned that complete accuracy is seldom to be expected from victims of torture (*Alan* v. *Switzerland* (UNCAT) [1997] INLR 29).

1.4.1   Sexual and gender-based violence against males

The UNHCR guidelines *Working with Men and Boy Survivors of Sexual and Gender-based Violence in Forced Displacement* (2012) are essential reading for anyone working with such clients. They point out that sexual violence and rape can be used as a weapon of war against men as well as women and that these are inflicted on men as a means of disempowerment, dominance and undermining concepts of masculinity. The guidelines discuss triggers for survival sex and then go on to set out some indicators for the identification of survivors:

Male survivors rarely report sexual and gender-based violence incidents immediately, and frequently do so only when the physical effects of attacks require urgent intervention. Some men and boys only dare to seek assistance several years after the event.

The following behaviours are not always present; however, very frequently male survivors of sexual violence:

- cannot sit comfortably: they will often sit on the edge of a chair or request to stand during an interview or meeting;
- complain about lower back problems, signalling rectal problems;
- rarely make eye contact;
- show high levels of anger and irritability;
- show high levels of homophobia;
- show a strong gender preference in relation to who interviews them (sometimes male sometimes female);
- repeatedly discuss an apparently unrelated protection concern, even after this has been effectively addressed.

The UNHCR guidelines make recommendations for best casework practice in these cases, to:

- pay attention to these signs and respond to them;
- provide information about urgent medical services, if appropriate, and all other available services, confidentially and sensitively;
- convey the message that sensitive issues can be addressed confidentially when the survivor feels ready to talk about them;
- be alert to the possibility that sexual violence has occurred against a man if a woman who is counselled reports that her male partner:
    - has lost sexual interest and refuses intimacy;
    - is unable to relate to other persons, even their own children; or
    - has withdrawn from social or community activities and meeting spaces.

The guidelines go on to look at understanding the needs of men and boy survivors, make suggestions on building trust during interviews and urge us all to examine and challenge our own assumptions and stereotypes about gender, including male (in)vulnerability to sexual and gender-based violence and the harm it causes.

1.4.2 Plausibility

Asylum claims are often rejected because the story put forward is thought to be implausible. However, there are various caveats to be considered before a claim is so rejected.

Repressive regimes may act in a way that is unpredictable: see *Suleyman (16242; 11 February 1998)*:

It is clear to us that a repressive regime … may well act in ways which defy logical analysis. A person who is genuinely a victim of such a regime may well find that the partial account he is able to give of its activities as they have affected him is not something which will stand up to a strictly logical analysis. The regime may seem to govern by confusion; it may engage in other activities, of which the Appellant knows nothing; it may simply behave in a way which a person sitting in safety in the United Kingdom might regard as almost beyond belief.

Other considerations regarding plausibility are the need to assess the account in the light of the relevant country evidence, see e.g. *Horvath* [1999] INLR 7. Events in the kinds of countries that produce asylum seekers may well be rather more chaotic than the life experience of a decision maker in this country would lead them to expect: see *HK* v. *Secretary of State for the Home Department* [2006] EWCA Civ 1037 at [29]:

Inherent probability, which may be helpful in many domestic cases, can be a dangerous, even a wholly inappropriate, factor to rely on in some asylum cases. Much of the evidence will be referable to societies with customs and circumstances which are very different from those of which the members of the fact-finding tribunal have any (even second-hand) experience. Indeed, it is likely that the country which an asylum-seeker has left will be suffering from the sort of problems and dislocations with which the overwhelming majority of residents of this country will be wholly unfamiliar.

And again, see Sir Thomas Bingham quoted in *Y* v. *Secretary of State for the Home Department* [2006] EWCA Civ 1223 at [25]:

No judge worth his salt could possibl[y] assume that men of different nationalities, educations, trades, experience, creeds and temperaments would act as he might think he would have done or even – which may be quite different – in accordance with his concept of what a reasonable man would have done.

Another element of plausibility is demeanour – it would be wrong to presume that a witness would necessarily give evidence in a particular emotional state: see the findings of the Tribunal in *M (Yugoslavia)* v. *Secretary of State for the Home Department* [2003] UKIAT 4.

Practice point

None of this means that an account must be accepted at face value or that the decision maker must suspend their own judgment entirely if the story is fundamentally unlikely whether it is judged by European or local standards.

It will be for an adviser to anticipate and identify areas where an account may be found to be implausible and then take sufficient further instructions to show as far as possible how and why the events happened as claimed – detail may be the best response to an allegation of implausibility.

Where necessary country information can be found to help corroborate the account or at least show it is consistent with what happens in that country.

1.4.3 Dishonesty

Proven, or admitted, dishonesty inevitably counts against any person who seeks to demonstrate their story's truthfulness, but a lack of veracity on one issue does not necessarily disprove the remainder of the account. Any acts of dishonesty must be specifically explained (e.g. entering the country on false documents).

A famous case says that the core of an account may be credible even though some elements are not made out. See *Chiver (Asylum; Discrimination; Employment; Persecution) (Romania)* [1994] UKIAT 10758, a rather old authority now: the idea is more clearly expressed in *Secretary of State for the Home Department* v. *MA (Somalia)* [2010] UKSC 49 at [32]–[33]:

> People lie for many reasons ... So the significance of lies will vary from case to case.

Practice point

Asylum seekers are sometimes forced into illegal conduct because of the barriers put in their path during their journey to seek asylum. Think carefully about whether this explains any dishonesty in your particular case:

- Have they had adverse experiences with authority which mean they would be reluctant to rely on an asylum claim being vindicated or to tell their full story: and is this credible given the company they have kept in the UK (e.g. if various friends and relatives have had significant dealings with the Home Office immigration department it may be harder to sell this to a decision maker)?
- Were they mistreated in a third country en route here?
- Were they forced to travel on false documents and did they 'come clean' at the first reasonable opportunity?
- Were they simply traumatised by their experiences coming here?

1.4.4 Corroboration

While for understandable reasons there can be no absolute requirement of corroboration in an asylum case, one should always carefully consider what materials may be available. In general, the potential sources will be:

- witnesses by way of family members, friends or activists/office holders in groups sympathetic to the asylum seeker's situation (e.g. the UK branches of political parties or religious groups from their country of origin);
- documentary evidence particular to the asylum seeker and material to the case that they are putting (e.g. proof of nationality, proof of the asylum seeker's employment, political activities, indications of official interest in them by way of arrest warrants, etc.);
- media reports from the country of origin specific to the case mentioning the asylum seeker by name (though they are only of real use if they can be verified

as genuine, as may be the case if they can be seen online on the official website of the source in question);

- medical expert evidence going to the consistency of their state of mind with post-traumatic stress disorder (PTSD) or other mental health problems and their physical presentation with torture or other ill treatment;
- public domain country evidence;
- expert country evidence on both credibility (i.e. whether their account of past events is consistent with known conditions in the country) and risk (i.e. the likely consequences of the return to the country of origin of a person with their characteristics).

1.5   ASSESSING RISK: COUNTRY EVIDENCE

As already mentioned, asylum seekers need to demonstrate that they face an objective risk of their fears actually arising, i.e. they must show that there is a real chance that they will face serious harm if they return home.

Such risk needs to be shown by a combination of evidence:

- their own account which will show what individual factors are present in their case; and
- reports about circumstances in their country of origin.

1.5.1   Country information

Country information is an essential tool for demonstrating future risk. It is often referred to as 'objective' evidence. Given that most reporters write from one standpoint or another, absolute objectivity is difficult to demonstrate. However, some sources are more respected than others. The reliability of the evidence must be established by the party relying on it.

There are many different sources of country information, and each source has its advantages and disadvantages. A high quality source to which weight is likely to be attached would possess the following qualities:

- **Up to date:** the source would be a recent one, or failing that there would be information that suggested the situation or subject matter of the report was unlikely to have changed.
- **Objective:** there is no such thing as an entirely objective source, but clearly biased sources or sources more likely to have an agenda of some kind may be considered less reputable. However, even a biased source might include useful factual information: much depends on how the information is used and presented.
- **Origins:** the sources used by a report would be as well-informed as possible and their research methodology would be clear.

Common types of information source include:

- **Government reports:** e.g. the UK Visas and Immigration (UKVI) Country Information and Guidance (CIG) reports (used by UKVI officials to make decisions in asylum and human rights applications) or US Department of State reports (which may reflect the agenda of the government or government department concerned but subject to public review). Some governments sponsor fact-finding missions to particular countries: these have been criticised by the ECtHR where they rely on anonymous sources, see *Sufi and Elmi* v. *UK* [2011] ECHR 1045; the Upper Tribunal in *CM (EM country guidance; disclosure) Zimbabwe CG* [2013] UKUT 59 (IAC) decided that country evidence from unnamed non-governmental organisations (NGOs) would be allowed in certain circumstances.
- **Inter-governmental reports:** e.g. UNHCR, African Union. May be compromised by the agendas of different constituent governments or by the organisation's own agenda or remit. Tend to be infrequently updated.
- **Non-governmental reports:** e.g. Amnesty International, Human Rights Watch. May reflect campaigning agenda of the organisation concerned, but research methodology may be clear and the organisations have their reputations to protect. Annual reports are infrequent but updates are sometimes published.
- **Press:** e.g. national or international newspapers and websites. Some articles may be the product of good quality journalism, others less so. Tend to be very recent.

The suitability of a source depends on the context in which it is used. Normally, a blog post from an anonymous blogger in the country of origin would be given little weight. However, if the blog is long standing and appears unconnected personally to the asylum seeker, it might be useful corroboration of a claimed fact of some sort, particularly if backed up directly or indirectly by other sources.

An opposition newspaper might be expected by the reader to be highly critical of the government it opposes and to contain 'biased' information that suggests the opposition is badly treated. However, it may be corroborated by other sources and may contain specific facts or details that have a direct bearing on the account of a given asylum seeker.

Unusual sources should not be discarded merely because they can be said to be biased, but they should be used with care and further corroboration should always be sought.

Practice point

Use online sources to stay up to date with country evidence.

- If you are representing a person from a particular ethnicity or with particular religious beliefs or political affiliations, make sure you look up the best available country evidence, e.g. on the Electronic Immigration Network (**www.ein.org.uk**),

---

> UNHCR's Refworld (**www.refworld.org**) or European Country of Origin Information Network (**www.ecoi.net**).
> - Look to see what the most reputable country sources say first, then move on to media reports (e.g. you can search for all references to a political party known by an abbreviation).
> - Always make sure you identify your client's home area and show why it is they would face problems both there and elsewhere in their country.

1.5.1.1 Country evidence considerations

Note that Home Office sources will not necessarily be found reliable by the Tribunal: for example, the UK Borders Agency fact-finding mission report on the Democratic Republic of Congo (DRC) was considered at [73] of *BM and others (returnees – criminal and non-criminal) DRC CG* [2015] UKUT 293 (IAC): 'the material consists mainly of opinions and unsubstantiated assertions'.

On the other hand, a detailed survey by the British embassy was found impressive, albeit that it was appropriate to approach it with 'particular scrutiny' because of its institutional link to the Home Office.

The extent of monitoring of returnees may well be relevant, at least where there is evidence indicating that human rights abuses occur (*BM* at [82]).

1.5.2 Country Guidelines cases

Once it comes to assessing the country evidence, there are obvious advantages to achieving consistency of approach. For this reason the Tribunal has introduced a system of giving Country Guidelines, made in the context of particular asylum appeals which have reached what is now the Upper Tribunal. The higher courts have accepted the value of such a system and indeed the ECtHR itself often cites Upper Tribunal decisions.

It is essential to be familiar with any relevant Country Guideline (CG) case relating to your client's country of origin. A list of current CG cases is kept on the Courts and Tribunals Judiciary website page addressing Upper Tribunal (Immigration and Asylum Chamber) decisions and is regularly updated; you can also find a list of pending cases and the issues they aim to engage with there (**www.judiciary.gov.uk/about-the-judiciary/who-are-the-judiciary/judicial-roles/tribunals/tribunal-decisions/immigration-asylum-chamber**).

Most CG cases include clear pointers as to future risk for various categories of asylum claimants.

Hopefully you will find what you need from their headnotes, but do not forget that there may be a wealth of other information and further findings by the Upper Tribunal made within the decision itself – it is always worth looking up your client's home area and political affiliation using the 'Ctrl-F' search function.

They may also include other useful information, e.g. details of expert witnesses, opinion evidence by such experts which may be relevant to your particular case even though it did not find its way into the conclusions of the CG decision itself, or citations of country evidence which are, again, useful to you even though they may not have had a bearing on the outcome of the CG case.

First-tier Tribunal judges have to follow the findings in CG cases – a failure to do so is an error of law (see the Practice Directions of the Immigration and Asylum Chambers of the First-tier Tribunal and the Upper Tribunal, para.12.4, reproduced at **Appendix B3**).

You may be able to distinguish your client's case from unhelpful CG findings because of individual factors that are present in your case: CG cases are supposed to be guides rather than straitjackets. See e.g. *OD (Ivory Coast)* v. *Secretary of State for the Home Department* [2008] EWCA Civ 1299:

> The task of the immigration judge is not a simple tick box exercise. It should involve making an assessment of risk on the full evidence before the tribunal; that is why we have experienced immigration judges.

Alternatively, the country situation may have changed – the test to persuade a judge to depart from CG findings is to show that 'cogent evidence' has been provided justifying departure from the relevant guidance, see *SG Iraq* v. *Secretary of State for the Home Department* [2012] EWCA Civ 940.

Always bear in mind that CG cases can be a fabulous source of inspiration for issues that may be relevant in future asylum claims from other countries: so the cases on Zimbabwe and loyalty testing may give food for thought on relevant issues when other regimes freely attribute political opinions to opponents, and the approach to Ahmadi religious asylum claims from Pakistan may carry over to other stigmatised religions elsewhere.

1.5.2.1 *Considerations arising in Country Guidelines cases*

As always, CG cases often provide inspiration for running a particular kind of asylum claim, notwithstanding that it may arise against a different country back-drop.

Relevant considerations are:

- impartiality of experts, campaigning backgrounds;
- their precise expertise;
- the range of sources they have drawn upon;
- the currency of their expertise in the light of the durability of the country situation;
- their awareness and treatment of views contrary to their own (particularly, well-known views of government sources).

21

Practice point

Generally speaking, the most efficient way in which to research and present country evidence is this:

- Relevant CG findings (because if your client fits into a risk category as so identified, your country evidence work is done).
- A policy position struck by the Home Office (because if its own guidance suggests a class of person is at risk, it is very hard for it to argue against that position).
- The Home Office's own published country evidence compilations (which are found within its CIG reports: why repeat its work if it has made your case for you?).
- Other human rights reports (and then media reports, which are only necessary if the respected reporters like Amnesty have not covered the necessary ground, or where they post-date other evidence and show a worsening situation).

1.5.3 Relevance of past experiences to future risk

The past is always a useful guide to the future, and this common sense notion is adopted by Immigration Rules, para.339K:

> The fact that a person has already been subject to persecution or serious harm, or to direct threats of such persecution or such harm, will be regarded as a serious indication of the person's well-founded fear of persecution or real risk of suffering serious harm, unless there are good reasons to consider that such persecution or serious harm will not be repeated.

Past persecution is therefore useful as an indicator of future risk, so long as you have at least some evidence, by way of relevant CG findings or a recent country report, to demonstrate that the country situation remains the same.

Practice point

Where the country situation is the same as when your client left and shows a real risk of serious harm to people in their situation, press very hard to stress that they are still at risk and no detailed assessment of country evidence is necessary.

1.5.4 Specific individual risk

It is always important in an asylum case to look at individual risk factors thrown up in the individual case. These may be positive, such as:

- individual history and/or association with family members or political/religious figures who are themselves at risk;
- prominence locally and nationally, a record of detention by the security forces.

Or they may be negative, for example:

- leaving the country of origin on their own passport (which might imply that the authorities were not interested in them – but think about issues such as corruption, resources, access to information technology, or indeed whether the authorities are perfectly happy to be rid of some individuals);
- delaying in leaving the country ('if you were really in danger you would have left sooner');
- staying in the homes of relatives before departing ('if you were being sought you would have been found at these locations, which were an obvious place for the security forces to look');
- being of too low a profile to be at risk (either as shown by CG findings or based on the Home Office assessment of the country evidence generally);
- having been released from detention without suffering significant ill treatment which would not have happened if they were genuinely at risk (but think about whether, by their flight from their country, they have inevitably breached reporting conditions imposed on their release or shown their refusal to become informers or to co-operate with the authorities);
- any of the AITCA 2004, s.8 factors: while these are originally formulated as credibility points (i.e. 'you are not telling the truth because ...'), they may also crop up as risk points (i.e. 'if you were really at risk, whether you are telling the truth or not, you would claimed asylum sooner').

All of these points are better answered by country evidence than the citation of authority. It is very difficult to argue with recent authoritative statements of the position in a particular country.

1.5.5 Generic risk cases

Where an individual is relying for their claim of persecution not on a desire by officials or non-state actors to target them as an individual, but rather on general problems (e.g. poor prison conditions: see *Batayav* v. *Secretary of State for the Home Department* [2003] EWCA Civ 1489 and again at [2005] EWCA Civ 366), then it will be necessary to show that the matters complained of are truly endemic.

Thus the Tribunal may be right to look for a 'consistent pattern of gross and systematic violation of fundamental human rights' (*Hariri* v. *Secretary of State for the Home Department* [2003] EWCA Civ 807).

The correct test is whether there is a consistent pattern of serious ill treatment (*AA (risk for involuntary returnees) Zimbabwe CG* [2006] UKAIT 61).

1.6 ACTIVITIES IN THE UK

Refugees can base their claim for asylum on their own activities that post-date their departure from their country of origin, or on changes in the situation there (e.g. a coup that places all those holding their political affiliation at risk; or it may be that whereas they might not have been at risk had they never left the country, the increased attention they will attract on a return at the border will itself create a risk of persecution). These are known as *sur place* claims.

Immediate risk on return at an airport has been explored in considerable detail for some countries, such as Zimbabwe and Turkey, and is also argued for other countries, such as Eritrea and Sri Lanka. Compelling evidence is usually needed to succeed with such arguments as they affect a large number of asylum applicants. The latest CG cases should always be checked.

Returnees cannot be expected to lie about their beliefs or how they have spent their time in the UK (see *IK (returnees – records – IFA) Turkey CG* [2004] UKIAT 312 with regard to Turkey, but of interest in any 'questioning on return' case). And as we have just mentioned, if they have to act discreetly in relation to expressing their political opinions on a return, that in itself should be recognised as persecution if their discretion is caused by a desire to avoid serious harm (*RT (Zimbabwe) and others* v. *Secretary of State for the Home Department* [2012] UKSC 38).

If a claimant has engaged in activities directed against his or her own government while in the UK, it will be difficult to obtain evidence that the government in question:

(a)   monitors UK-based opposition activities;
(b)   communicates that information to the domestic authorities;

and that those authorities make use of that information to target the individuals concerned.

In *YB (Eritrea)* v. *Secretary of State for the Home Department* [2008] EWCA Civ 360 the Court of Appeal dealt with this question in the context of Eritrea and concluded that a common sense approach should be followed rather than an overly analytical approach which wrongly sought evidence of matters that could be readily inferred, such as the likelihood that repressive regimes probably monitor the internet for information about their political opposition or filmed nationals who demonstrated in front of their embassies. The real question was what would be the consequences for the asylum seeker in question of the information-gathering in question.

The most useful case in this line of authority for casework purposes is *BA (demonstrators in Britain – risk on return) Iran CG* [2011] UKUT 36 (IAC), cited below at [4]:

> The following are relevant factors to be considered when assessing risk on return having regard to sur place activities:
>
> **(i)   Nature of sur place activity**
>
> - Theme of demonstrations – what do the demonstrators want (e.g. reform of the regime through to its violent overthrow); how will they be characterised by the regime?
> - Role in demonstrations and political profile – can the person be described as a leader; mobiliser (e.g. addressing the crowd), organiser (e.g. leading the chanting); or simply a member of the crowd; if the latter is he active or passive (e.g. does he

carry a banner); what is his motive, and is this relevant to the profile he will have in the eyes of the regime?

- Extent of participation – has the person attended one or two demonstrations or is he a regular participant?
- Publicity attracted – has a demonstration attracted media coverage in the United Kingdom or the home country; nature of that publicity (quality of images; outlets where stories appear etc)?

(ii) Identification risk

- Surveillance of demonstrators – assuming the regime aims to identify demonstrators against it how does it do so, through, filming them, having agents who mingle in the crowd, reviewing images/recordings of demonstrations etc?
- Regime's capacity to identify individuals – does the regime have advanced technology (e.g. for facial recognition); does it allocate human resources to fit names to faces in the crowd?

(iii) Factors triggering inquiry/action on return

- Profile – is the person known as a committed opponent or someone with a significant political profile; does he fall within a category which the regime regards as especially objectionable?
- Immigration history – how did the person leave the country (illegally; type of visa); where has the person been when abroad; is the timing and method of return more likely to lead to inquiry and/or being detained for more than a short period and ill-treated (overstayer; forced return)?

(iv) Consequences of identification

- Is there differentiation between demonstrators depending on the level of their political profile adverse to the regime?

(v) Identification risk on return

- Matching identification to person – if a person is identified is that information systematically stored and used; are border posts geared to the task?

Practice point

Make sure you take instructions and identify sources of corroborative evidence against the list of factors identified in *BA (demonstrators in Britain – risk on return) Iran CG*. And, in submissions, always consider making the point that it may be debatable as to whether the security forces abroad will take the same view of someone's credibility that the asylum system has done in the UK.

1.7 ACTIVITIES CONDUCTED IN BAD FAITH

The issue of the wilful creation of an asylum claim through activities found to be conducted in 'bad faith' outside the country of origin (e.g. cynical attendance at demonstrations outside an embassy) has occasionally arisen. In *Danian v. Secretary of State for the Home Department* [2000] Imm AR 96 the Court of Appeal held that the motive behind activities is irrelevant, the only question is whether there is a well-founded fear of being persecuted for a Convention reason.

Immigration Rules, para.339J(iv) states that the Secretary of State must take into account in making an asylum decision:

> whether the person's activities since leaving the country of origin or country of return were engaged in for the sole or main purpose of creating the necessary conditions for making an asylum claim or establishing that he is a person eligible for humanitarian protection or a human rights claim, so as to assess whether these activities will expose the person to persecution or serious harm if he returned to that country …

This position was disapproved in *KS (Burma) and another* v. *Secretary of State for the Home Department* [2013] EWCA Civ 67, where the Court of Appeal found in a case concerning political 'hangers-on' from Burma (see [30]) that it would be wrong to presume that regimes with a record of persecution would make careful and rational assessments of which potential targets to pursue.

The Court of Appeal endorsed the approach taken in *BA (demonstrators in Britain – risk on return) Iran CG* [2011] UKUT 36 (IAC). *BA* pointed to a number of factors and 'a spectrum of risk'. The non-exhaustive list of factors in *BA* is grouped under a number of headings: nature of *sur place* activity; the chance of being identified as participating in such activities; factors triggering inquiry/action on return; the consequences if the asylum seeker is identified and thus associated with such activities, and the risk of that actually happening. Each heading is then illustrated and amplified.

1.8 UNHCR MANDATED GRANTS OF STATUS

From time to time an asylum seeker will arrive in the UK having been recognised as a refugee abroad. In many countries of the world the UNHCR is involved in that process. The Supreme Court in *IA* v. *Secretary of State for the Home Department (Scotland)* [2014] UKSC 6 looked at the approach to be taken to grants of refugee status under the UNHCR's mandate. It found:

- Such a grant did not bind decision makers elsewhere, nor did it create a presumption: however, it was a relevant factor.
- A national decision maker should have pause for thought before departing from the UNHCR assessment.
- There should be departure from the UNHCR view only for cogent reasons previously unavailable or where the decision maker has some new information which directly affects the assessment of the claim for refugee status and its credibility.
- A claim should not be rejected on credibility grounds unless the person's honesty is undermined by a source other than their own account (which will thus often be information which post-dates the UNHCR's decision).

Practice point

While it is disappointing that mandate status does not itself win the day for the client, it takes them a long way – really press their case hard on the absence of material from the Home Office that undermines the UNHCR assessment (by way of independent evidence of their claim being untrue or country evidence showing a change of circumstances).

1.9 RISKS ARISING FROM MODE AND REALITY OF RETURN

Some asylum claims may feature strong evidence of dangers posed by a journey through a dangerous part of the country. The Upper Tribunal held in *AM (evidence – route of return) Somalia* [2011] UKUT 54 (IAC) that when considering whether 'journey risks' could be assessed (which itself turns on whether the broad method of return is known, but does not require that every detail of return can be predicted: see *HH (Somalia) and others* v. *Secretary of State for the Home Department* [2010] EWCA Civ 426), there was no threshold requirement that the asylum seeker raise a 'cogent argument' but rather that 'the issue need only be considered if there was a proper evidential basis for doing so.'

Practice point

The issue of route of return has most frequently arisen with regard to countries such as Somalia and Iraq. It will not arise where the route of return is clear – e.g. over long periods of time, return routes have been readily apparent for the countries which involve the most asylum seekers: Afghans return via Kabul, Iraqis via Baghdad, Somalis via Mogadishu, and so on.

If the matter is less clear cut, look at Home Office UK Visas and Immigration Operational Guidance (**www.gov.uk/topic/immigration-operational-guidance**) or reported Tribunal cases where route of return is discussed (and judicial reviews of unlawful detention often raise issues of return, as the Secretary of State will often put forward evidence in those cases designed to show the ease with which returns can be made).

If the precise route of return is presently unknown, then risks arising from that route alone (as opposed to what would happen to the client once back in their home area) cannot be ruled upon in an appeal. Make sure you make a clear note on file about that situation though – because presumably once removal directions are set the route of return will become apparent, which may raise dangers not so far assessed by the Tribunal and which are therefore highly relevant to an application for judicial review of the removal directions.

Equally, if a person cannot be returned because of a lack of relevant identity documents, then he cannot rely on the risks that would ensue if he were returned and were unable to establish his own identity (such risks might include being forced into destitution without access to employment or welfare): see generally the headnote and discussion in *AA (Article 15(c)) Iraq CG* [2015] UKUT 544 (IAC).

Akram (Iraq)

Akram is from Iraq, from Kirkuk in the contested north. He has proven he has no living family members left in the country. He has never held a Civil Status Identity Document (CSID). When he claimed asylum he provided his own passport to the UK authorities. It has now expired.

When you read the CGs, you see that a person may be returned on their own expired passport but that they will have to be able to obtain a CSID to access services or employment: those can be obtained only from one's home area or with the help of relatives in Baghdad. In his appeal he can rely not only on the original dangers that led him to leave Iraq if they remain current, but additionally on risks arising from the lack of documentation, given he is returnable and lacks a CSID of his own and relatives to aid him in obtaining one.

1.10 ACTS OF PERSECUTION

The Qualification Directive sets out a minimum definition of what might constitute acts of persecution at Article 9, which has been transposed into the Protection Regulations, SI 2006/2525, reg.5 as follows:

(1) In deciding whether a person is a refugee an act of persecution must be:

    (a) sufficiently serious by its nature or repetition as to constitute a severe violation of a basic human right, in particular a right from which derogation cannot be made under Article 15 of the Convention for the Protection of Human Rights and Fundamental Freedoms; or

    (b) an accumulation of various measures, including a violation of a human right which is sufficiently severe as to affect an individual in a similar manner as specified in (a).

Key to this definition is a requirement that the act must be sufficiently serious to amount to a non-derogable right under the European Convention for the Protection of Human Rights and Fundamental Freedoms (ECHR). The non-derogable rights are Article 2 (right to life, except for deaths resulting from lawful acts of war), Article 3 (torture and inhuman or degrading treatment or punishment), Article 4(1) (slavery and servitude) and Article 7 (retrospective conviction).

Persecution has to constitute a serious violation of a basic human right or be an accumulation of equivalent measures.

Regulation 5(2) then goes on to give specific examples of persecution:

* physical/mental/sexual violence;
* discriminatory or disproportionate official measures, prosecution, punishment, and denial of judicial redress;
* prosecution or punishment for avoiding military service which would have involved conduct leading to exclusion from refugee status (i.e. committing war

crimes or crimes against humanity, or serious non-political crimes, or acts contrary to the purposes of the United Nations: all of which we address generally below).

In general, persecution must be assessed via its impact on the individual in question (see e.g. UNHCR Handbook, para.55). The Qualification Directive at Article 9 mentions that acts of a gender-specific or child-specific nature might constitute persecution.

In *X Y and Z* v. *Minister voor Immigratie en Asiel* [2013] EUECJ C-199/12 the CJEU looked at the state-sanctioned persecution of gay individuals, finding that:

- while the existence of laws that were not enforced was not necessarily persecutory, where terms of imprisonment were 'actually applied', that would represent a disproportionate or discriminatory punishment and would therefore be persecution;
- a person cannot reasonably be expected to exercise restraint in the expression of their sexual identity.

One particular class of serious harm is where someone is deprived of their nationality, as where a political activist or person of a particular ethnic origin is denied the opportunity to return home. It was recognised in *MA (Ethiopia)* v. *Secretary of State for the Home Department* [2009] EWCA Civ 289 that denying a person return to their country would deprive them of virtually all the rights attaching to citizenship and would thus amount to persecution: however, there has to be a link between the reasons why they left the country and their inability to return.

Practice point

Most asylum seekers base their claim on threats of truly serious harm, such as physical violence, torture or death, which means there can be no serious debates as to whether the risks they face amount to persecution. However, where a class of asylum seeker relies upon other forms of harm, then make sure you consider every aspect of their life in taking instructions to see whether their problems arguably amount to a fear of persecution. For example, think about risks of:

- forced labour;
- arbitrary detention and equality before the courts;
- interference with freedom of movement;
- interference with freedom of conscience, religion and expression;
- inability to sustain a livelihood compatible with human dignity.

A combination of these might arguably amount to 'an accumulation of various measures … sufficiently severe …' as to amount to 'a severe violation of a basic human right'.

1.10.1   Prosecution and persecution

Straightforward fugitives from justice are not refugees. However, to suggest that anyone who flees forms of harm that arise via prosecution is a criminal rather than a refugee is to over-simplify the question and it is clear from the Qualification Directive that there are circumstances where prosecution will amount to persecution: where it is disproportionate or discriminatory.

The Protection Regulations show that use of criminal justice powers such as prosecution may be persecutory where it is in itself discriminatory or implemented in a discriminatory way, be this in the original measures themselves, or via the prosecution or punishment that ensues, or because of a denial of judicial redress (reg.5(2)(a)–(d)).

1.10.2   Military service

It was found in *R (on the application of Sepet and another)* v. *Secretary of State for the Home Department* [2003] UKHL 15 that there is no international human right to conscientious objection. The necessary implication is that prosecution for refusal to perform military service will normally be a legitimate prosecution for breach of a state's criminal law. However, the situation will be different where (at [8]):

> such service would or might require him to commit atrocities or gross human rights abuses or participate in a conflict condemned by the international community, or where refusal to serve would earn grossly excessive or disproportionate punishment ...

Regulation 5(2)(e) of the Protection Regulations includes as persecution:

> prosecution or punishment for refusal to perform military service in a conflict, where performing military service would include crimes or acts falling under [the exclusion provisions at reg.7].

This provision was considered in *Shepherd* [2015] EUECJ C-472/13 where a helicopter engineer with the US army claimed asylum in Germany wishing to avoid involvement with the military conflict in Iraq, which he feared might involve the commission of war crimes. The CJEU set out the following principles at [37] onwards:

- Applicants providing logistical or technical support might qualify whether or not they would be involved personally in war crimes, and the fact that they might not be liable in criminal law did not undermine their asylum claims.
- They need not already have been involved in such crimes to have a viable asylum claim: the question was whether they faced a real risk of being involved in future.
- Military actions pursuant to UN Security Council resolutions or an international consensus offered a guarantee that war crimes would not ensue though the possibility of their occurrence cannot be ruled out by those mandates alone;

similarly, the fact that a state prosecuted war crimes strongly indicated that it would not be involved in them.

- The individual must show that desertion was the only way to have avoided committing the war crimes: enlisting, and re-enlisting, in the knowledge of the armed conflict in question, counted against such a conclusion.
- If the military service fell short of involvement in war crimes, then punishment for refusal to participate would need to be shown as disproportionate or discriminatory and the social ostracism and disadvantages associated therewith that might follow from desertion were not themselves sufficient to establish persecution.

Sergei (Russia)

Sergei is a Russian national and has received call-up papers to serve in the national army. He does not wish to serve because he is a conscientious objector in general and in particular because he does not want to support actions in Syria where he believes there is a probability of being associated with war crimes.

As to his claim to asylum on the grounds of being a conscientious objector, he will have serious difficulties: while he may well be able to show a Convention reason (e.g. political opinion opposed to his national authorities' policies), he would only be able to show that he faced a risk of persecution if he could show disproportionate or discriminatory consequences (five years' punishment was not thought excessive in *Shepherd*).

As to his claim on grounds of not wishing to support actions that might result in war crimes, he would have to show that:

- war crimes were being committed by Russian forces;
- there was a real risk that he would be supporting such actions (balanced against the probability of being involved in non-combat or combat roles in other Russian operations); and
- he had no choice other than to participate in these actions.

1.10.3 Civil war

In order to secure refugee status, the House of Lords in *R* v. *Secretary of State for the Home Department ex p. Adan* [1998] Imm AR 338 found that persons fleeing civil war must demonstrate that they face a differential impact over and above the general risks of a civil war in which law and order has broken down completely. The reasoning is essentially that of 'collateral damage': the ordinary victims of civil war are not being specifically targeted, rather they are simply in the way of the opposing factions and are accidentally caught in the crossfire.

Thus the Refugee Convention has not proven helpful to many victims of civil war: Article 15(c) of the Qualification Directive (see below) fills some of the resulting protection gap.

Civilians who can show that they are specifically targeted for a Convention reason or who suffer a differential impact in related activities such as looting and robbery following the breakdown of law and order can potentially make out a claim for refugee status.

In the case of *Adan*, it was found that there was a general state of civil war and lack of law and order in Somalia. All or many citizens of Somalia could be said to be victims of the civil war in a wide sense. In the leading judgment Lord Lloyd cited a number of authorities, including Hathaway: 'victims of war and conflict are not refugees unless they are subject to differential victimisation based on civil or political status.'

The same reasoning would not necessarily apply in a country such as 1994 Rwanda, where victims of genocide were being targeted for the very specific Convention reason of race. This went far beyond the normal threat from a general civil war.

1.10.4 Future activities

In the case of *HJ (Iran)* v. *Secretary of State for the Home Department* [2010] UKSC 31, the Supreme Court fundamentally changed the approach to the issue of how future behaviour will be considered relevant to the assessment of entitlement to refugee status. The previous legal analysis was a very British and pragmatic one. Essentially, whether future behaviour could make a person a refugee was a simple question of fact: would the person in question in fact, despite the dangers, behave in a way that would expose them to persecution?

HJ (Iran) establishes that where a person would in future refrain from behaving in a way that would expose them to danger because of the risk of persecution that behaviour brings, that person is a refugee.

The leading judgment in *HJ (Iran)* is that of Lord Rodger, who explains the series of issues that arise thus:

- Would the person be liable to persecution if they lived openly?
- If so, would this particular individual live openly on a return?
- If they would live openly on return, then they had a well-founded fear of persecution.
- If they would live discreetly on return, was this because of a risk of persecution?
- If so, then they also had a well-founded fear of persecution; however, if their discretion was merely due to social pressure or embarrassment, then they would not.

The context in *HJ (Iran)* is famously gender preference – would a gay man or lesbian woman have to conceal aspects of their sexuality in order to avoid persecution – but the legal principle is a wider one of profound significance. If a political or religious activist wants to continue their activities in future but would be prevented from so doing because of the risk of persecution, it is no answer to say that it would be reasonable for them to return to their country and just keep a low profile.

Following this approach, the Supreme Court held in the case of *RT (Zimbabwe) and others* v. *Secretary of State for the Home Department* [2012] UKSC 38 that asylum seekers cannot be expected to lie or dissemble about their political beliefs in order to achieve safety in their own country.

The issue arose from the old CG case of *RN (returnees) Zimbabwe* [2008] UKAIT 83, in which the Immigration Tribunal held that, in the febrile atmosphere before and following the 2008 elections, any Zimbabwean returned from the UK would have a well-founded fear of persecution unless he or she could prove loyalty to the ZANU-PF party. The Secretary of State had suggested in subsequent appeals that a person with no political allegiance could reasonably be expected to lie about being loyal to ZANU-PF to avoid persecution. However, this principle applies equally to a committed political activist and to a person with no political convictions: neither can be expected to lie.

It was recognised in *X, Y and Z* [2013] EUECJ C-199/12 that laws which mandated imprisonment for homosexual acts were themselves persecutory:

> such legislation must be regarded as being a punishment which is disproportionate or discriminatory and thus constitutes an act of persecution.

Relevant considerations will be:

- how widespread nationally are the reported problems;
- the extent to which lives are lived openly including at public events;
- whether or not it is culturally likely that two friends of the same gender might share a home without suspicion;
- the level of reporting of mistreatment;
- the likelihood of forced marriage and the availability of internal relocation against it;
- what is the reaction of the state authorities?

Many of these asylum claims also involve, as an alternative argument if the persecution claim fails, an allegation that it would be disproportionate to the couple's private life to expect them to return abroad. These claims must reach a high standard: the thinking of the Tribunal is seen repeatedly in cases such as *LH and IP (gay men: risk) Sri Lanka CG* [2015] UKUT 73 (IAC).

At [22]:

> the evidence before us is that the Sri Lankan state simply does not engage with the status of civil partner at all. Individuals in such relationships are not forced to renounce them: the status is ignored. There is no provision on official forms for it, but it continues to exist
> …

The court was therefore not satisfied that (at [25]):

> the Sri Lankan state's failure to recognise the appellants' status as civil partners has been shown to be sufficiently flagrant of itself to destroy or nullify their family life …

1.11   THE 'CONVENTION REASONS'

The Convention reasons are central to the Refugee Convention. A refugee is a person with a 'well-founded fear of being persecuted for reasons of …'. There must therefore be a causal link between the harm suffered and one of the five Convention reasons.

In addition, as described above, the Convention reasons can have a transformative effect on certain types of harm. For example, imprisonment as a result of criminal behaviour does not amount to persecution, whereas imprisonment for a Convention reason would amount to persecution.

The Convention reasons are outlined in more detail in this section.

1.11.1   Race

'Race' is interpreted to include '… all persons of identifiable ethnicity' (quote from Professor Hathaway's *The Law of Refugee Status*). The Qualification Directive states that 'the concept of race shall in particular include considerations of colour, descent, or membership of a particular ethnic group'.

1.11.2   Religion

The Protection Regulations, reg.6(1)(b) offer a very inclusive definition of religion:

> the concept of religion shall include, for example, the holding of theistic, non-theistic and atheistic beliefs, the participation in, or abstention from, formal worship in private or in public, either alone or in community with others, other religious acts or expressions of view, or forms of personal or communal conduct based on or mandated by any religious belief

Cases of religious conversion can be controversial, and are best prepared by anticipating possible Home Office objections to the credibility of any conversion. However, the depth of religious conviction of the apostate should not be permitted to obscure the fact that the agents of persecution may not be overly concerned about the theological commitment of the convert.

In its judgment in *Bundesrepublik Deutschland* v. *Y and Z* [2012] EUECJ C-71/11 the CJEU explained that this provision demonstrated that religious persecution encompassed serious acts that interfere with the applicant's freedom not only to practise his faith in private circles but also to live that faith publicly. It will be appreciated that the principles in *HJ (Iran)* set out above carry over to religious cases as much as gender preference and political opinion ones.

Abbas (Iran)

Abbas is an Iranian national who was born into a Muslim family. While at college he made friends with Afsar, a woman who introduced him to the Christian faith. Over time he began to accept the truth of her message and abandoned his Islamic faith. When the secret church meetings that he attended were discovered by the authorities during a crackdown on minority religions, he fled the country.

Credibility and factual basis for his claim:

- Can he provide a detailed account of the events that led to his problems and precisely what happened to him?
- Can he provide a detailed description of his religious identity and beliefs, and how these developed? However difficult this is, the burden of proof is on him.
- Does he understand the tenets of the Christian faith (he may be questioned on these at interview)? He need not be an expert and belief, of course, means different things for different people, but he should be ready for these questions, at any rate.
- Is he attending church in the UK and will he be vouched for as a committed Christian by a minister who will attend court – and does that church have links to where he practised his faith in the country of origin?
- Will other members of the congregation here support his claim?

Objective risk of persecution:

- Once you look at the country evidence, you will find that the Home Office's position from a recent CIG report on Iran is that the risk may exist for: 'Christians who can demonstrate that in Iran or in the UK they have and will continue to practise evangelical or proselytising activities because of their affiliation to evangelical churches or who would wear in public outward manifestations of their faith such as a visible crucifix' – so there are two routes by which religious belief itself may lead to persecution, either by public manifestations of faith such as wearing some religious symbol or by active evangelism, etc.
- Abbas may of course face persecution because of his individual history notwithstanding any public expression (or suppression) of his religious identity: so investigate what happened to his colleagues to see whether he might have an official record now that would be detected at the border on a return to the country.

Sahibzada (Pakistan)

Sahibzada is an Ahmadi from Pakistan; Ahmadis are forbidden from calling themselves Muslim or using any form of dress, other sign or symbol that might be interpreted as holding themselves out as such. He suffered numerous problems at the hands of local Islamic extremists including the destruction of his business. He fled the country.

You look up the relevant CGs decision and find that he will be recognised as a refugee if the anti-Ahmadi laws were genuinely an interference with his religious identity.

Credibility and factual basis for his claim:

- Identify what precisely happened to him and his family in Pakistan.
- Will the Ahmadi authorities vouch for him in the UK and can they confirm his history abroad?
- Identify whether any of the forms of open behaviour (identified in the CGs decision) are fundamental to his identity: preaching and other forms of proselytising; holding open discourse about religion with non-Ahmadis; openly referring to one's place of worship as a mosque and to one's religious leader as an imam; calling oneself Muslim or referring to one's faith as Islam; or referring to the call to prayer as azan.

Objective risk of persecution:

- Here the CGs case does the work for you: if he can prove that those forms of religious conduct are fundamental to his identity then he will be a refugee. In other kinds of religious asylum claim, those themes will hopefully provide inspiration.

1.11.3 Nationality

The Qualification Directive definition of nationality at Article 10(c) is an interesting one that extends conventional understanding of the concept:

> the concept of nationality shall not be confined to citizenship or lack thereof but shall in particular include membership of a group determined by its cultural, ethnic, or linguistic identity, common geographical or political origins or its relationship with the population of another State

1.11.4 Membership of a particular social group

Discrimination is central to determining whether a person is a member of a particular social group. Other relevant criteria are whether the discrimination is on the basis of an immutable characteristic of the individual: i.e. either one that is beyond the power of an individual to change (i.e. is innate) or one that it would be contrary to their fundamental human rights for them to forgo (i.e. is non-innate).

- **Innate characteristic:** e.g. gender, sexuality.
- **Common background that cannot be changed:** e.g. being a former teacher or policeman.
- **Fundamental belief or characteristic:** e.g. home schooling.

The House of Lords held in *Shah and Islam* [1999] UKHL 20 that women in Pakistan constituted a particular social group. This was because they share the common immutable characteristic of gender, they were discriminated against as a group in matters of fundamental human rights and the state gave them no adequate protection because they were perceived as not being entitled to the same human rights as men.

The Qualification Directive adopts the *Shah and Islam* approach but also elevates societal attitude to a strict requirement; both have to be shown to establish that there is a social group. This is also reflected in the Protection Regulations at reg.6(1)(d) and (e):

(d)   a group shall be considered to form a particular social group where, for example:

(i)   members of that group share an innate characteristic, or a common background that cannot be changed, or share a characteristic or belief that is so fundamental to identity or conscience that a person should not be forced to renounce it, and

(ii)   that group has a distinct identity in the relevant country, because it is perceived as being different by the surrounding society;

36

(e)   a particular social group might include a group based on a common characteristic of sexual orientation but sexual orientation cannot be understood to include acts considered to be criminal in accordance with national law of the United Kingdom;

The Qualification Directive therefore reads as more restrictive than the pre-existing position was thought to be. In *K and Fornah* [2006] UKHL 46 the House of Lords indicated that the Qualification Directive seemed out of line with the internationally understood interpretation of the Refugee Convention.

A social group cannot be defined by the persecution which a potential member is experiencing. It has to exist independently of the persecution, although the persecution may play a role in the group becoming identifiable. Potential future victims of female genital mutilation (FGM) may constitute a particular social group (*K and Fornah*).

Particular social groups that have been recognised include:

- 'Former victims of trafficking' and 'former victims of trafficking for sexual exploitation': because of their shared common background or past experience of having been trafficked (*SB (PSG, Protection Regulations, Regulation 6) Moldova CG* [2008] UKAIT 2).
- The family: this may enable individuals whose fears arise from family involvement in blood feuds to make good their claims for asylum (*K and Fornah*).
- Gender preference cases: the CJEU accepted in *X, Y and Z* [2013] EUECJ C-199/12 that a person's sexual orientation was a characteristic so fundamental to their identity that they could not be expected to renounce it – and the existence of criminal laws targeting gay individuals was strong evidence of their being seen as a particular social group.
- Victims of FGM (see *K and Fornah* at [31]):

    … FGM is an extreme expression of the discrimination to which all women in Sierra Leone are subject, as much those who have already undergone the process as those who have not. I find no difficulty in recognising women in Sierra Leone as a particular social group for purposes of article 1A(2) …

1.11.5   Political opinion

Expression of political opinion is perhaps the most often cited Convention reason. Most obviously it will reflect a political opinion against the interests of the state itself, but the Protection Regulations make it clear that it may equally well arise on the basis of political opposition to powerful non-state actors (reg.6(1)(f)):

the concept of political opinion shall include the holding of an opinion, thought or belief on a matter related to the potential actors of persecution … and to their policies or methods, whether or not that opinion, thought or belief has been acted upon by the person.

We have already seen above that a person who acts discreetly to avoid a risk of serious harm should nevertheless be accepted as facing persecution, and *RT*

(Zimbabwe) shows that this applies to a person holding political and religious opinions and beliefs as well as in gender preference cases.

Where a person claims asylum based partly on activities in the UK, Immigration Rules, para.339P warns that these cases may succeed:

> … in particular where it is established that the activities relied upon constitute the expression and continuation of convictions or orientations held in the country of origin or country of return.

So it will always be important to take careful instructions on the extent to which the expression of political opinions in this country are consistent with the person's history abroad.

1.11.6   Attributed Convention reasons

Regulation 6(2) of the Protection Regulations demonstrates that a characteristic may be externally ascribed (i.e. imputed or attributed) to an individual by the persecutor, even if it does not in fact exist. It states:

> In deciding whether a person has a well-founded fear of being persecuted, it is immaterial whether he actually possesses the racial, religious, national, social or political characteristic which attracts the persecution, provided that such a characteristic is attributed to him by the actor of persecution.

Attributed political opinion has traditionally been the best known possibility: but this provision shows that one could have a viable asylum claim based on an imputation of any other Refugee Convention characteristic too (a person wrongly thought to be gay might be attributed membership of a particular social group, or a person carrying out a particular trade might be presumed to be Christian).

1.12   STATE PROTECTION

The test for the level of protection afforded by the state against actions by third parties has often been discussed in the authorities. Now the real question is that set out in the Qualification Directive and transposed into the domestic Regulations (Protection Regulations, reg.4(2)):

> Protection shall be regarded as generally provided when the [national or powerful local authorities] take reasonable steps to prevent the persecution or suffering of serious harm by operating an effective legal system for the detection, prosecution and punishment of acts constituting persecution or serious harm, and the [asylum seeker] has access to such protection.

The Upper Tribunal looked at this test in *NA and VA (protection: Article 7(2) Qualification Directive) India* [2015] UKUT 432 (IAC), finding that protection could be provided by measures other than simply the detection, prosecution and punishment of relevant acts and might include witness protection schemes including a relocation package, home security or security advice. It followed that the mere availability of a system of detection, prosecution and punishment might not suffice, and that a judge would be wrong to only emphasise factors such as the political will to improve the security arrangements where the country evidence nevertheless showed deficiencies.

Besnik (Albania)

Besnik is a citizen from Albania. Following his father's death he became his family's sole breadwinner. Wishing to increase his earnings, he began to supplement his wages from a building site by running errands delivering packages for the boss. As time passed he began to have concerns about the lawfulness of this, as he was required to deliver them to increasingly shady locations. He told his boss he no longer wanted to help out, but was told that there was no way of stopping because he 'already knew too much'. He left his job and moved out of the family home; his mother subsequently received threats from armed men saying they had business with him and would find him wherever he went. He fled the country.

A case like this is very likely to be refused by the Home Office and certified as 'clearly unfounded', because, even accepting these facts, it will be presumed that both state protection and internal relocation would be available.

Essentially the case needs the provision of significant further information to be a runner. Always read the public domain country evidence first to see what themes are worth exploring. Relevant lines of enquiry would be:

- The identity of the boss and whether he might have powerful criminal or political associations.
- Information as to whether the threats have continued after Besnik left the country and some explanation as to why his relatively minor involvement is taken so seriously (which might need an expert report).
- Country evidence as to the failings in the domestic protection system:
    - Do the police carry out effective investigations?
    - Are prosecutions brought efficiently?
    - Are the courts impartial?
    - Are there any specific steps which would be necessary to protect the client, and would they be identified and implemented?
    - Overall, is the system effective?

1.13   INTERNAL RELOCATION

Situations arise where an individual may face persecution in a particular part of their country of origin but will be expected to relocate to a different part of their country where they can live in safety. This usually arises in non-state persecution cases, as it is difficult to imagine where a person might be able to relocate within the territory of a state while fearing persecution by that state. In *Januzi* v. *Secretary of State for the Home Department and others* [2006] UKHL 5, the House of Lords held that there is, however, no legal presumption that internal relocation is not viable in state persecution cases: so it all depends on the evidence.

The Immigration Rules refer to the concept of internal relocation and transpose the requirements of the Qualification Directive at para.339O. Essentially that paragraph sets out that:

- asylum or humanitarian protection will not be granted where there is a safe part of the country where a person can reasonably be expected to reside, taking account of the general circumstances prevailing in the safe part and the personal circumstances of the asylum seeker;
- technical obstacles to return are not relevant to the question (presumably this means that the fact that the Home Office cannot presently return a person to the safe part of the country, because of practical difficulties such as documentation or route of return, does not compel a five-year grant of refugee status).

The Immigration Rules at that paragraph (and the Directive) do not provide much practical guidance on approaching the question of whether internal relocation is applicable in a given case. Logically, there should be three stages of reasoning:

- Once risk is established in the home area, is there a safe haven elsewhere?
- Is that safe haven accessible?
- Would life there be unduly harsh or unreasonable?

Practice point

If the client is politically or religiously active in their home area, is internal relocation to a safe haven in truth exile from the only place where their beliefs can be meaningfully practised?

Ensure that the question of what their right to freedom of expression means to the individual is fully explained in their witness statement: a detailed statement can be expected from a person whose convictions are genuine.

In *AH Sudan* [2007] UKHL 49 the House of Lords upheld an Immigration Tribunal decision finding that relocation to refugee camps around Khartoum by Darfuri refugees was reasonable, nevertheless stressing that conditions might be unreasonable even though they fell short of violations of Article 3 of the ECHR; conditions in the home area and in the proposed area of relocation were relevant to the question. The approach was summarised thus by Lord Bingham who cites at [5] his opinion in *Januzi*:

'The decision-maker, taking account of all relevant circumstances pertaining to the claimant and his country of origin, must decide whether it is reasonable to expect the claimant to relocate or whether it would be unduly harsh to expect him to do so ... The decision-maker must do his best to decide, on such material as is available, where on the spectrum the particular case falls ... All must depend on a fair assessment of the relevant facts ...' [having regard to] the situation of the particular applicant, whose age, gender, experience, health, skills and family ties may all be very relevant ...

Baroness Hale alongside him helpfully placed weight at [20] on UNHCR's intervention in *Januzi*:

> 'the correct approach … is to assess all the circumstances of the individual's case holistically and with specific reference to the individual's personal circumstances (including past persecution or fear thereof, psychological and health condition, family and social situation, and survival capacities) … in the context of the conditions in the place of relocation (including basic human rights, security conditions, socio-economic conditions, accommodation, access to health care facilities), in order to determine the impact on that individual of settling in the proposed place of relocation and whether the individual could live a relatively normal life without undue hardship.'

Later the situation changed and the Home Office accepted that it was not reasonable to expect a Darfuri refugee to relocate to the refugee camps around Khartoum.

The UNHCR states in its valuable *Guidelines on International Protection: 'Internal Flight or Relocation Alternative' within the Context of Article 1A(2) of the 1951 Convention and/or 1967 Protocol relating to the Status of Refugees* (23 July 2003) at para.25:

> … Of relevance in making this assessment are factors such as age, sex, health, disability, family situation and relationships, social or other vulnerabilities, ethnic, cultural or religious considerations, political and social links and compatibility, language abilities, educational, professional and work background and opportunities, and any past persecution and its psychological effects. In particular, lack of ethnic or other cultural ties may result in isolation of the individual and even discrimination in communities where close ties of this kind are a dominant feature of daily life. Factors which may not on their own preclude relocation may do so when their cumulative effect is taken into account. Depending on individual circumstances, those factors capable of ensuring the material and psychological well-being of the person, such as the presence of family members or other close social links in the proposed area, may be more important than others.

1.13.1 Vulnerable relocators

AA (Uganda) v. *Secretary of State for the Home Department* [2008] EWCA Civ 579 held that it was unreasonable to expect a particularly vulnerable single young woman to relocate from her home area to the capital, where she had no connections and an expert had concluded she would be forced to make a living as a prostitute.

1.13.2 Fact-specific enquiries

In cases from Afghanistan, although there is plenty of evidence to suggest someone could be at risk from the Taliban in their home area, the prevailing thinking of the Tribunal is that most people – at least fit young men – can relocate to Kabul without difficulty, because there are documented job opportunities working with, or servicing, international organisations, or in labouring; and most ethnic groups are represented among those who have already internally migrated to the capital city. There are doubtless generic risks from Taliban attacks but these have never been

41

accepted as creating risks of sufficient severity to make good an international claim. So think carefully about evidencing whether or not the capital is truly a safe haven (e.g. because of having been found there in the past or due to the enquiries that might be made of someone's home area by landlords and employers wishing to confirm their reliability). On the other hand, where a man would be returning with, or to join, a wife and children, he might have to engage widely with the community and might find it much more difficult to live anonymously or to earn sufficient sums to support the family unit.

Practice points

Just as with every other aspect of a claim, you need evidence, beyond assertions by the client, to sustain an argument that internal relocation is unreasonable. Human rights reports read with the client's witness statement are likely to be useful in showing whether or not there is an extant safe haven, but only very focused reports (e.g. by UNHCR) or reports that are not necessarily addressing asylum issues (e.g. Red Cross or World Health Organization reports) are likely to discuss whether living conditions are unreasonable.

Consider the extent to which the client has attempted to find a safe haven, and whether they have already been pursued by their antagonists.

Bear in mind that cities all over the world tend to host large numbers of internal migrants who live in conditions that while not necessarily ideal will not necessarily be unduly harsh – you need to show that any expectation your client can join them is unrealistic.

Ensure the Secretary of State has clearly indicated where the safe havens are. This can be linked to a submission that under Article 8(2) of the Qualification Directive 'Member States shall at the time of taking the decision on the application have regard to the general circumstances prevailing in that part of the country and to the personal circumstances of the applicant.' This phrase, unique in Directive 2004/83, appears to require that the Secretary of State gives distinct and specific notice, as a matter of fairness, that she intends to argue that internal relocation is available and would not be unreasonable.

1.14   MULTIPLE COUNTRIES OF NATIONALITY OR RETURNABILITY

This has long been a vexed issue. In *HA (Article 24 QD) Palestinian Territories* [2015] UKUT 465 (IAC) the Upper Tribunal found that there was nothing in the Qualification Directive to change the long-held view that an asylum seeker had to establish a well-founded fear of persecution in each potential destination to succeed in their appeal on asylum grounds.

However, if a client cannot obtain entry to a country of nationality then they may be at risk of onwards *refoulement* to their country of origin (unless the evidence shows they would be returned to the UK).

Where a person may have an entitlement to a particular nationality, then they can be expected to make the appropriate application to their national authorities for that to be recognised. Thus, in *MA (Ethiopia)* v. *Secretary of State for the Home Department* [2009] EWCA Civ 289, it was held at [50] that:

> … where the essential issue before the AIT is whether someone will or will not be returned, the Tribunal should in the normal case require the applicant to act *bona fide* and take all reasonably practicable steps to seek to obtain the requisite documents to enable her to return …

1.14.1 Entitlements to nationality based on discretion rather than right

In *KK and others (nationality: North Korea) Korea CG* [2011] UKUT 92 (IAC) the Upper Tribunal ruled that where an asylum seeker could be shown to be entitled to a particular nationality as a matter of law, whether or not they held the relevant national passport, then they should be treated as a national of the country in question. However, where nationality would be granted only as a matter of discretion, they could not be treated as holding that nationality absent having made a successful application.

1.14.2 Stateless individuals

A stateless asylum seeker must show a well-founded fear of persecution for a Convention reason in their country of habitual residence. If they have multiple such countries, then their best argument may be that they are no longer admissible to any of them, save for the one where the country evidence shows them to be at risk.

Practice point

Work out exactly what category your client falls into – which will probably require expert evidence about, if not from, the country of origin. If an application needs to be made in order to demonstrate a lack of nationality, because the documentary evidence is not clear-cut, then ensure that it is adequately documented, by writing letters to the embassy yourself, attending an embassy appointment alongside the client or sending a clerk, or some reliable third party witness from the community, to record what happens – the bare word of the asylum seeker is unlikely to be accepted where reasonable steps have not been taken to corroborate their efforts.

1.15 EXCLUSION CLAUSES

The Refugee Convention has several forms of exclusion clause within it:

- Article 1D for, essentially, Palestinians and others who are assisted by the United Nations Relief and Works Agency for Palestine Refugees in the Near East (UNRWA);

- Article 1E, if there is a country beyond a person's country of nationality where he or she possesses rights akin to nationality: 'a person who is recognized by the competent authorities of the country in which he has taken residence as having the rights and obligations which are attached to the possession of the nationality of that country';
- the better known Article 1F which covers exclusions for crimes against international law and serious criminal activity of a non-political nature.

But even those accepted to be refugees may face limitations as to the duties owed to them, because of Article 33(2), which is the fundamental protection against *refoulement*:

> The benefit of the present provision may not, however, be claimed by a refugee whom there are reasonable grounds for regarding as a danger to the security of the country in which he is, or who, having been convicted by a final judgment of a particularly serious crime, constitutes a danger to the community of that country.

The UK has chosen to deem offences attracting particular periods of imprisonment as meeting these criteria under the Nationality, Immigration and Asylum Act 2002 (NIAA 2002), s.72 (see **1.15.6**).

Immigration Rules, paras.334 and 339A contain provisions which allow the Secretary of State to exclude a person from protection under the Refugee Convention, whether their case is being considered at the original application stage or whether the excludable activities are only identified subsequently.

1.15.1 Palestinians

The provision at Article 1D (replicated in the Qualification Directive at Article 12(1)(a)) is only applicable to Palestinian refugees receiving UNRWA assistance (because UNRWA's work in the Middle East represents the only current non-UNHCR protection work being carried out by the UN – it works in the Gaza Strip, the West Bank, Syria, Lebanon and Jordan, as its website explains). It states:

> This Convention shall not apply to persons who are at present receiving from organs or agencies of the United Nations other than the United Nations High Commissioner for Refugees protection or assistance.
>
> When such protection or assistance has ceased for any reason, without the position of such persons being definitively settled in accordance with the relevant resolutions adopted by the General Assembly of the United Nations, these persons shall *ipso facto* be entitled to the benefits of this Convention.

In *Said (Article 1D: meaning) Palestinian Territories* [2012] UKUT 413 (IAC) the Tribunal found that:

- A Palestinian forced out of the protection of the UNRWA region by virtue of circumstances beyond their control (as it was put in the slightly later CJEU decision to similar effect, *El Kott, Abed El Karem and others* v. *Bevandorlasi es*

Allampolgarsagi Hivatal [2012] EUECJ C-364/11, for reasons beyond their control and independent of their volition), such as armed conflict in their refugee camp, may well be entitled to the benefits of the Refugee Convention (because they are not presently receiving protection from a UN body, and given that the Palestinian question has not been finally resolved), regardless of whether or not they also possess a well-founded fear of persecution for a Convention reason under Article 1A(2) of the Refugee Convention.

- The right to protection under Article 1D applied to all those Palestinians who had received the protection of UNRWA, and not just those who were receiving it at the date the Refugee Convention was concluded in 1951.

Practice point

Remember – a Palestinian can be a refugee either because they have a routine claim for refugee status or because they were they forced out of the protection of UNRWA for reasons beyond their control.

1.15.2   Crimes against international law

The Refugee Convention, Article 1F (included in the Qualification Directive at Article 12(2)) excludes a person (who would otherwise be a refugee) when there are serious reasons for considering:

(a)   he has committed a crime against peace, a war crime, or a crime against humanity, as defined in the international instruments drawn up to make provision in respect of such crimes;

(b)   he has committed a serious non-political crime outside the country of refuge prior to his admission to that country as a refugee;

(c)   he has been guilty of acts contrary to the purposes and principles of the United Nations.

1.15.2.1   War crimes and crimes against humanity, etc.

The modern definition of these crimes is best found in the Rome Statute (of the International Criminal Court), representing as it does the considered view as to which crimes should be treated as the responsibility of the international community: crimes against humanity include murder, enslavement, forcible transfer of populations, torture, sexual violence and other inhumane acts; war crimes are more focused on grave attacks against the civilian population.

Ali (Tunisia)

Ali is a citizen of Tunisia who is accepted as being at risk of persecution for political reasons because he provided information to the government about the political opposition. A letter in support of his case indicates that some of the people on whom he informed were subsequently arrested, detained and tortured.

Arguably this is sufficient information to raise issues of exclusion (which the Tribunal may have to address as part of the refugee definition whether or not the Home Office raises the matter for itself). Torture is one of the specified crimes against humanity. One would need to look at the Rome Statute to see the definition: which one would then find includes a requirement for this to be part of an attack on a civilian population.

Relevant issues will be:

- whether he knew of the likely consequences of his informing, bearing in mind his level of education, political understanding and actual knowledge, and the extent to which torture was known to be prevalent in the criminal justice system;
- given he was not the actual perpetrator of torture, whether his actions had a substantial effect on the commission of torture (see **1.15.4** on 'guilt by association').

1.15.2.2   Serious non-political crimes

The Qualification Directive has added words to the Refugee Convention definitions, so that regarding Article 1F(b) 'serious non-political crime' cases, 'prior to his admission' is to be interpreted as prior to 'the time of issuing a residence permit based on the granting of refugee status' (see Qualification Directive, Article 12(2)(b)): so that it would seem that one could be excluded for a crime committed within the UK before refugee status was awarded, whereas Article 1F(b) looks only at crimes committed outside the country of asylum. Nevertheless, it will be the Qualification Directive interpretation that probably prevails if the matter is ever litigated, it being EU law that is directly effective in the UK.

Discussion of Article 1F(b) cases has often concentrated on whether a crime is political or non-political in nature. The House of Lords in *T* v. *Secretary of State for the Home Department* [1996] Imm AR 443 said that acts of terrorism, being incidents of depersonalised violence coldly indifferent to the human rights of the victims, were too distant from any meaningful political purpose.

1.15.3   Activities contrary to the purposes and principles of the United Nations

KJ (Sri Lanka) v. *Secretary of State for the Home Department* [2009] EWCA Civ 292 held that acts of a military nature committed by an independence movement (such as Sri Lanka's Liberation Tigers of Tamil Eelam (LTTE)) against the military forces of the government are not themselves acts contrary to the purposes and principles of the United Nations and suggested that an armed campaign against a government would not necessarily constitute an act contrary to the purposes and principles of the United Nations.

Al-Sirri v. *Secretary of State for the Home Department* [2012] UKSC 54 explained that such acts had to be of real severity (as was accepted in that case, carrying out military activities against the UN-mandated forces in Afghanistan), such as (at [13] and [40]):

> human rights violations and acts which have been clearly identified and accepted by the international community as being contrary to the purposes and principles of the United Nations … '… in extreme circumstances by activity which attacks the very basis of the international community's coexistence' [with] … the requisite serious effect upon international peace, security and peaceful relations between states.

The Supreme Court added at [16] that in general the article 'should be interpreted restrictively and applied with caution'.

1.15.4　Guilt by association

Article 12(3) of the Qualification Directive states that the exclusion:

> applies to persons who instigate or otherwise participate in the commission of the crimes or acts mentioned therein.

A number of cases have looked at the extent to which an asylum seeker has to be complicit in the activities that bring exclusion.

In *KJ (Sri Lanka)* v. *Secretary of State for the Home Department* [2009] EWCA Civ 292 it was accepted that mere membership of an organisation that, among other activities, commits acts of terrorism does not suffice to bring the exclusion into play – so whereas a foot soldier who has not participated in terrorist acts within an organisation that conducts both conventional military and terrorist activities would avoid exclusion, a person with a higher rank who might be expected to understand the overall picture might face exclusion, and any active member of an organisation which concentrates on terrorism is likely to be excluded.

In *R (on the application of JS) (Sri Lanka)* v. *Secretary of State for the Home Department* [2010] UKSC 15 the Supreme Court identifies at [30] the relevant factors:

(i)　the nature and (potentially of some importance) the size of the organisation and particularly that part of it with which the asylum-seeker was himself most directly concerned,

(ii)　whether and, if so, by whom the organisation was proscribed,

(iii)　how the asylum-seeker came to be recruited,

(iv)　the length of time he remained in the organisation and what, if any, opportunities he had to leave it,

(v)　his position, rank, standing and influence in the organisation,

(vi)　his knowledge of the organisation's war crimes activities, and

(vii)　his own personal involvement and role in the organisation including particularly whatever contribution he made towards the commission of war crimes.

This was the summary of liability given in *JS (Sri Lanka)* at [38]:

> Put simply, I would hold an accused disqualified under article 1F if there are serious reasons for considering him voluntarily to have contributed in a significant way to the

organisation's ability to pursue its purpose of committing war crimes, aware that his assistance will in fact further that purpose.

1.15.5 Evidence and procedure

Obviously exclusion is a serious issue and requires the most serious consideration. The decision maker needs to identify serious reasons for considering exclusion to be appropriate: this requires clear, credible and strong evidence, based on a considered judgment, albeit not requiring proof beyond reasonable doubt (*Al-Sirri* v. *Secretary of State for the Home Department* [2012] UKSC 54).

The exclusion clauses are part of the refugee definition, whether we take it from the Refugee Convention or from the Qualification Directive, and so can and indeed must be considered by the Tribunal even where the Secretary of State has not raised them, subject to giving an adequate opportunity to an appellant to deal with such issues – the foreseeability of the issue arising will be relevant to the need for an adjournment.

In *IG (exclusion, risk, Maoists) Nepal* (starred) [2002] UKIAT 4870, the Tribunal held that issues of exclusion may arise on appeal even though the point was not taken in the refusal letter.

The Secretary of State cannot raise such issues, though, after an appeal has been allowed, if she has forgone the opportunity to raise exclusion during the appeal process itself (*Secretary of State for the Home Department* v. *TB (Jamaica)* [2008] EWCA Civ 977).

As discussed in its guidance document *Asylum Instruction Exclusion: Article 1F of the Refugee Convention*, the Home Office may certify an appeal under Immigration, Asylum and Nationality Act 2006 (IANA 2006), s.55 on the grounds that the appellant is not entitled to the protection of the Refugee Convention because (in its view) Article 1F applies. The Tribunal (or Special Immigration Appeals Commission (SIAC)) is then required first to decide whether it agrees with the certificate. If it does, the appeal must be dismissed on asylum grounds (though the hearing will need to continue to consider whether removal will breach Article 3 of the ECHR) – however, in many cases issues of inclusion and exclusion will be bound together, as discussed in *IG (exclusion, risk, Maoists) Nepal*.

Practice points

No benefit of the doubt

Always remember that the benefit of the doubt principle does not apply in an exclusion case: if anything it applies adversely to the client, who can be excluded where there are 'serious reasons for considering' them to be guilty of the relevant crime. So witness statements which lack accuracy or detail are likely to count against an asylum seeker at risk of exclusion.

Defences to criminal responsibility

Make sure you know all the defences to criminal responsibility in the Rome Statute. These are found within the statute at Articles 30–33 and can be summarised as:

- coercion;
- obedience to superior orders (though not where they are manifestly illegal unless the person so ordered had no moral choice and were compelled to obey them);
- mental defect or disease that destroys an individual's capacity to appreciate the unlawfulness of their conduct, or to control their conduct;
- intoxication destroying their capacity to appreciate the unlawful nature of their conduct other than where the state was induced voluntarily without regard to the risk such conduct would bring;
- reasonable and proportionate actions in defence of themselves or (*vis-à-vis* war crimes) property;
- conduct caused by duress by way of imminent threat of death or serious injury, so long as no greater harm is caused than that sought to be avoided;
- a mistake of fact that negates the mental element of a crime.

1.15.6 Non-*refoulement*

Article 33(2) of the Refugee Convention lifts the ban on return to the frontiers of territories where they fear persecution ('non-*refoulement*') for refugees for whom there are reasonable grounds for regarding as a danger to the security of the country in which they are, or who have been convicted of a particularly serious crime. It is not limited to crimes committed outside the country of asylum, which is a difference between it and Article 1F(b)).

NIAA 2002, s.72, which brings Article 33(2) into domestic law, in effect excludes from refugee status those deemed to fall within the terms of that Article in advance of an immigration judge considering their asylum claim.

Note:

- The applicant retains the right to establish that his removal would be in breach of the ECHR, so this provision prevents people becoming refugees and (presently) obtaining indefinite leave to remain rather than condemning them to a return abroad to face torture or inhuman treatment, etc. Thus there would be no inhibition on their arguing that their removal would infringe their ECHR, Article 3 rights on appeal.
- They will presumably have no viable arguments on humanitarian protection (HP) grounds, because although there is no equivalent of s.72 for a HP claim, the exclusion grounds for HP are rather wider than under the Refugee Convention, including simply having committed a serious crime (Immigration Rules, para.339D(i)).

Section 72 creates a presumption that a person convicted of certain criminal offences for which he was sentenced to a period of imprisonment of two years either in or outside the UK:

- has committed a particularly serious crime; and
- represents a danger to the community.

Both those presumptions are rebuttable: the first under the principle recognised by *EN (Serbia)* v. *Secretary of State for the Home Department and another* [2009] EWCA Civ 630 (the argument against the presumption will depend on the severity of the offence taking account of all relevant circumstances such as desperation, social exclusion and mental health difficulties of the refugee), the second under the express words of s.72(6) (here the case against the presumption will concentrate on questions of reoffending risk).

Certificates mean that, unless the appellant persuades the immigration judge that the presumption should not apply to him, or it is rebutted, the Refugee Convention grounds of appeal must be dismissed. Given that Article 33(2) offending will normally have taken place after arrival in the UK, it is unlikely that there will be any connection between the claimed offending and the Refugee Convention case, and so it is more likely a judge will be able to rule on this at the outset of the appeal, though many will still prefer to consider the whole case after the hearing has finished.

The Secretary of State for the Home Department passed an order setting out certain offences, which, under s.72(4) and (5), gave rise to the presumption that the appellant is a danger to the community, regardless of the sentence (see the National-ity, Immigration and Asylum Act 2002 (Specification of Particularly Serious Crimes) Order 2004, SI 2004/1910). However, this order was declared unlawful by the Court of Appeal in the case of *EN (Serbia)* and at the time of writing the position remains that the entire order is *ultra vires* and therefore ineffective.

Farid (Iran)

Farid is a citizen of Iran. He came to the UK two years ago. He did not claim asylum on arrival. He has been convicted of two offences of theft and one of burglary for which he received sentences totalling 25 months' imprisonment. Once he did make a claim, the Secretary of State certified it under s.72 on the grounds that he represents a danger to the community having committed particularly serious crimes.

On taking instructions you learn that Farid has mental health problems caused by PTSD having been tortured in Iran which made him terrified of claiming asylum; accordingly, he lived for some time without support on the streets of London, and felt that he had had no alternative but to steal in order to survive.

Farid may well be able to mount an argument that:

- his crimes are not *particularly serious* ones because of the context in which they arose: expert evidence on his mental health will be essential;
- in any event, subject to obtaining good evidence of his reoffending risks, he will not be likely to reoffend now he is within the asylum system and receiving public funds (and will be similarly supported if he is granted status, if he does not find work) – so he poses no *danger to the community*.

1.16 HUMANITARIAN PROTECTION

Under the Refugee Convention, a person whose removal from the territory would threaten their life or freedom is entitled to remain in the country of asylum, and to various other rights to be enjoyed during their stay as a refugee (including non-discrimination). However, the ECHR, which has since 2 October 2000 been effective in domestic law to supplement the Refugee Convention as a way for a person to receive protection, did not give any rights to those who benefit from its provisions to the extent of removing return to their country of origin. In essence the only right provided is to be free from torture, etc., not other rights regarding the form of leave to remain, family reunion or travel documents.

From 10 October 2006 the Qualification Directive entered into force. It brought a new era of protection and includes both refugee status and HP under its wing.

It is important to realise that HP prior to that date was no more than a form of leave to remain given by virtue of Home Office policy – i.e. an administrative discretion.

HP after that date is a form of international protection given under directly effective EU law (in EU law it is known as 'subsidiary protection', but the UK has chosen to keep the name for the pre-existing form of leave). While the name may be the same, the legal basis is quite different.

1.16.1 Serious harm

The fundamental requirement for eligibility for HP is that a person faces a real risk of 'serious harm' in one of the following forms, see Article 15 of the Qualification Directive:

- death penalty or execution;
- torture or inhuman or degrading treatment or punishment of an applicant in the country of origin; or
- serious and individual threat to a civilian's life or person by reason of indiscriminate violence in situations of international or internal armed conflict.

This has been incorporated into the Immigration Rules (para.339C) thus:

Grant of humanitarian protection

339C. A person will be granted humanitarian protection in the United Kingdom if the Secretary of State is satisfied that:

...

(iii)   substantial grounds have been shown for believing that the person concerned, if he returned to the country of return, would face a real risk of suffering serious harm and is unable, or, owing to such risk, unwilling to avail himself of the protection of that country ...

Serious harm consists of:

(i)   the death penalty or execution;
(ii)   unlawful killing;

51

(iii)   torture or inhuman or degrading treatment or punishment of a person in the country of return; or

(iv)   serious and individual threat to a civilian's life or person by reason of indiscriminate violence in situations of international or internal armed conflict.

Basically, then, the question is whether the individual faces a real risk of 'serious harm' of one of the four defined species.

The forms of harm are reminiscent of the some of the more basic protections afforded by the ECHR (para.339C(ii) is based on the right to life protected by ECHR, Art.2; para.339C(iii) resembles ECHR, Art.3).

Note that unless a person is excluded from HP for wrongdoing, it will be wrong to say that one is relying on Article 3 of the ECHR as a fall-back if Refugee Convention arguments fail – because in fact one is relying on an EU species of international protection which is introduced into UK law by para.339C.

1.16.1.1   Article 15(c)

Article 15(a) and (b) of the Qualification Directive are relatively uncontroversial additions to the protection given to asylum seekers, as they flow so naturally from Article 3 of the ECHR. However, Article 15(c) (Immigration Rules, para.339C(iv)) finds no obvious reflection in pre-existing human rights law, and has sufficiently excited the courts to have inspired a whole string of cases ever since *KH (Article 15(c) Qualification Directive) Iraq CG* [2008] UKAIT 23. The challenge for judges and lawyers has been to find some protection therein which was not already recognised by Article 3 of the ECHR – after all, nobody would seriously dispute the possibility that civilians fearing serious injury or death in wartime would have an Article 3 claim if the risk was sufficiently severe. Indeed, the Strasbourg Court has recognised this in the context of Article 3 of the ECHR in cases such as *NA* v. *UK* [2008] ECHR 616.

This book is not the place to explore the learning on these differences. What we can say is this: in *QD (Iraq)* v. *Secretary of State for the Home Department* [2009] EWCA Civ 620 it was said at [27] that Article 15(c) 'seeks to cover … real risks and real threats presented by the kinds of endemic act of indiscriminate violence'. The conclusion of the Court of Appeal in *QD (Iraq)* at [40] was to put 'the critical question' in this way:

> Is there in Iraq or a material part of it such a high level of indiscriminate violence that substantial grounds exist for believing that an applicant … would, solely by being present there, face a real risk which threatens his life or person?

The European Court of Justice in *Elgafaji* [2009] EUECJ C-465/07 decided that 'indiscriminate violence' refers to a high intensity of violence: so high, in fact, that the side effects of armed conflict 'may extend to people irrespective of their personal circumstances'.

There may be classes of individual at enhanced risk due to personal factors (see *Elgafaji*). In UK case law, examples given in *GS (Article 15(c): indiscriminate violence) Afghanistan CG* [2009] UKAIT 44 were the disabled person who cannot flee shellfire as swiftly as the able-bodied civilians around them, and members of groups who might be sought out by parties to the conflict, or taking advantage of the conflict, for special attention; the Home Office instruction, *Humanitarian Protection* (part of the Asylum Decision-making Guidance (Asylum Instructions) collection at **www.gov.uk/government/collections/asylum-decision-making-guidance-asylum-instructions**) suggests a child or someone of advanced age, or a person in a group characterised by e.g. disability, gender, ill health, ethnicity or, for example, by virtue of being a perceived collaborator, medical professional, teacher or government official.

Past exposure to violence in a conflict might show a likelihood of a repetition of such experiences absent a change of circumstances.

In *GS Afghanistan CG* the Tribunal found that 'indiscriminate violence' would include that meted out by criminals taking advantage of the law and order vacuum created by the conflict.

The most useful consideration of Article 15(c) is now found in *HM and Others (Article 15(c)) Iraq CG* [2010] UKUT 331 (IAC). From it we can see the following key principles emerging:

- there must be a real risk of a relevant threat, threats being defined as the kinds of harm that flow from modern military conflict – 'it must extend to significant physical injuries, serious mental traumas and serious threats to bodily integrity' – including indirect harm for which the conflict was an operative cause (as where the harm is caused by a breakdown in law and order);
- it can be assumed that there will be a greater number of casualties than deaths, although the extrapolation from the latter to the former will depend on the forms of harm that prevail in the conflict in question.

At the time of writing internal armed conflicts had been found by the Tribunal to exist in Iraq (*QD Iraq*), Somalia (*AMM and others (conflict; humanitarian crisis; returnees; FGM) Somalia CG* [2011] UKUT 445 (IAC)) and Afghanistan (*GS (existence of internal armed conflict) Afghanistan CG* [2009] UKAIT 10). However, civilians in Afghanistan and Iraq were found not to be at sufficient risk to enliven Article 15(c) (so too in Libya in *AT and Others (Article 15c; risk categories) Libya CG* [2014] UKUT 318 (IAC)). The Upper Tribunal has found that Somalia is one of the few countries from where civilians would usually qualify for international protection due to conflict (though the CG cases have since moved on): parts of Iraq have been accepted as creating such risks in *AA (Article 15(c)) Iraq CG* [2015] UKUT 544 (IAC).

Practice point

When putting a case based on Article 15(c), investigate:

- the rate of civilian casualties of all kinds;

- the extent to which there is under-reporting of casualties;
- the geographical extent of the conflict and casualties;
- the indirect impact of the conflict on quality of life and the death rate because of interference with food and other vital supplies; and
- availability of humanitarian assistance (including access of NGOs and health professionals).

And always remember that if you can establish a local risk from the internal armed conflict in your client's home area, then all they have to show in the rest of the country is that return there would be unreasonable.

1.16.2 Exclusion and revocation of humanitarian protection

The Immigration Rules at para.339D substantially follow the wording of Article 17 of the Qualification Directive. To summarise, it excludes people in largely the same circumstances as does the Refugee Convention but with some extra ones added which make exclusion much more likely, i.e. where:

- there are serious reasons for considering a person has committed or instigated or otherwise participated in an international crime as per the Refugee Convention exclusion clauses – but also, beyond those offences, has had involvement in 'any other serious crime';
- there are serious reasons for considering a person has committed or been involved with acts contrary to UN purposes or principles;
- there are serious reasons for considering a person constitutes a danger to the community or to the security of the UK;
- the person has fled the country of origin solely to avoid sanctions from a crime other than those crimes just mentioned.

Exclusion should not be automatic and must be preceded by a fact-sensitive consideration of the case. In the Court of Appeal's judgment in *AH (Algeria)* v. *Secretary of State for the Home Department* [2012] EWCA Civ 395 we see at [54] that:

> Sentence is, of course, a material factor but it is not a benchmark. In deciding whether the crime is serious enough to justify his loss of protection, the Tribunal must take all facts and matters into account, with regard to the nature of the crime, the part played by the accused in its commission, any mitigating or aggravating features and the eventual penalty imposed.

Thus the Home Office guidance at para.5.1 of *Humanitarian Protection* is that:

> It is now accepted that a 12 month sentence (or more) should not alone determine the seriousness of the offence for exclusion purposes.

The Home Office policy also gives examples of those who are thought to constitute a danger to the community or to the security of the country: those on the Sex

Offenders Register; those whose character, conduct and associations threaten national security; and those who engage in unacceptable behaviours such as fomenting, justifying or glorifying terrorist acts, or fomenting hatred that may lead to inter-community violence.

Humanitarian protection may be revoked because facts that would have justified exclusion have come to light post-grant, and additionally where:

- there is a change of circumstances so that protection is no longer required though, as in refugee cases, in applying this test the question is whether the change is of a significant and non-temporary nature;
- there was misrepresentation or factual omission, including the use of false documents, which were decisive to the grant of HP.

Tanvir (Pakistan)

Tanvir, a citizen of Pakistan, claims to fear serious harm at the hands of criminals who tracked him down in Karachi because he had reported them to the police. Following his arrival in the UK and failure to declare that he was travelling on a false passport he was prosecuted for fraudulently possessing false identity documents and sentenced to two years' imprisonment.

Tanvir might in theory have a good claim for HP if the criminals are very powerful and have national influence. However he has been sentenced for a criminal offence. Bearing in mind the significant sentence imposed on him the Home Office might argue that he has committed a serious crime.

CHAPTER 2

Asylum process and practice

2.1 CLAIMING ASYLUM

An 'asylum claim' is legally defined at NIAA 2002, s.113:

> 'asylum claim' means a claim made by a person to the Secretary of State at a place designated by the Secretary of State that to remove the person from or require him to leave the United Kingdom would breach the United Kingdom's obligations under the Refugee Convention,

Asylum claims must be made in person at the port of entry or by appointment at the Asylum Screening Unit in Croydon.

From April 2013, the Home Office has been implementing its new Asylum Operating Model 'designed to deliver more conclusions, faster, at lower cost and higher quality than ever before'. Sadly, as stated by the Independent Chief Inspector of Borders and Immigration (**http://icinspector.independent.gov.uk**, News Archive) on 15 July 2014:

> A poorly managed change programme for asylum casework had resulted in the rapid loss of experienced staff, which led to a backlog of over 13,000 cases by the end of 2013.

Delays remain common within the asylum system.

Detailed guidance on asylum policies and processes is provided for Home Office staff, and is available as part of the UK Visas and Immigration Operational Guidance collection (Operational Guidance), under Asylum Policy, Asylum Decision-making Guidance (Asylum Instructions) at **www.gov.uk/government/ collections/asylum-decision-making-guidance-asylum-instructions**. These were previously known as asylum policy instructions (APIs). Other sources of law are the Immigration Rules (Parts 11, 11A and 11B: see **Appendices D1** and **D2**) and Directive 2005/85/EC of 1 December 2005 on minimum standards on procedures in Member States for granting and withdrawing refugee status (the 'Procedures Directive').

Simply put, the process for most asylum seekers, if their claim is refused, is broadly as follows:

- make asylum claim;

- screening interview;
- asylum interview;
- decision;
- further grounds;
- lodge appeal.

Excluded from this process, following the screening interview, will be those asylum seekers for whom the UK is not responsible for assessing their asylum claim, i.e. those who may be returned to another EU country which has that duty under EU law.

2.1.1 Screening interview and initial steps

Once a claim has been made, the next step is the screening process.

This includes fingerprinting of the applicant and the entry of those fingerprints into the EURODAC database to detect any multiple applications (including applications made in other EU countries).

Applicants are given a form of induction during which they receive an application registration card (ARC) which contains their personal details and acts as a form of identity. The Immigration Rules (para.359) require the Secretary of State to provide to an asylum seeker a document certifying their status as such, within three days of their arrival.

Under Immigration Rules, para.358, the Secretary of State must now inform asylum seekers, 'within a reasonable time not exceeding fifteen days after their claim for asylum has been recorded of the benefits and services that they may be eligible to receive and of the rules and procedures with which they must comply relating to them.'

A screening interview takes place which concentrates on obtaining personal details and mode of entry and travel to the UK, said by the Home Office to be intended to address identity and nationality and whether the applicant has potentially committed a passport offence under AITCA 2004, s.2. If the answers given by the applicant suggest an offence may have been committed, a referral to the police and Crown Prosecution Service will be considered by the Home Office.

2.1.2 Routing

Having been screened, usually the asylum seeker will be referred, via the asylum routing team (ART), to a regional asylum team where their case will be allocated to a case owner. The regional asylum teams are situated in Cardiff, Glasgow, Leeds, Liverpool, Central London, West London and Solihull.

Some classes of more specialist case are not immediately referred to the ART: those involving previous absconders, children, those convicted of a serious offence, those with damaged fingerprints, cases suitable for determination within detention, European Economic Area (EEA) nationals, medical cases, prosecution cases, repeat applications, Third Country Unit cases, and those who appear to be victims of trafficking. All of these will be dealt with in accordance with the relevant policies.

2.1.3 The role of the representative

Unless the asylum seeker is to be removed from the UK without a decision being made on their asylum application under the third country procedure, the asylum seeker will need help in preparing their asylum claim. Public funding remains available for this purpose. Where the asylum seeker is detained, a representative from a legal aid firm should be available on site. Otherwise, the asylum seeker will need to find their own representative.

The adviser will need to take instructions from the asylum seeker to establish the basis for and the merits of the asylum claim, and to give appropriate advice. The adviser will then take more detailed instructions with a view to drafting a statement of the claim and preparing the asylum seeker for their interview.

The process of taking a detailed statement from the asylum seeker should help prepare them for the asylum interview. An experienced adviser will closely question the asylum seeker, challenging them (in a friendly manner) where potential issues arise as to plausibility and consistency, and ensuring that the asylum seeker is aware of the level of detail they will need to provide as to their background and fears. The ILPA best practice guides on asylum applications and appeals remain essential reading for advisers on taking their clients' instructions and drafting representations.

A good statement will set out the asylum seeker's background, the events that led to her needing to leave to claim asylum, the process of leaving, arriving in the UK, activities and private/family life since arrival and comments on the screening interview. Many legal representatives prefer to serve the statement before the interview and update it afterwards to take the asylum seeker's comments on the interview into account. Alternatively, the statement can be completed post-interview and given to the case owner with detailed representations and any corroborative evidence available, before the asylum decision is made.

2.1.4 Asylum interview

Once an asylum seeker has been screened and accepted into the asylum procedure, the next big step in the decision-making process will be the substantive asylum interview. This differs from the screening interview in that it concentrates on the substance of the asylum claim. The Home Office has guidance on asylum interviews.

Representatives are not publicly funded to attend interviews unless the asylum seeker is a minor or particularly vulnerable. The Home Office should, on request, tape record the interview: see the case of *R (on the application of Dirshe)* v. *Secretary of State for the Home Department* [2005] EWCA Civ 421. It is strongly advisable that asylum applicants make use of this facility, which is available on demand but is not automatic, at least where there is a dispute as to credibility.

Practice point

If there is a dispute about whether or not questions were clearly put and understood at the interview, then the matter should be followed up in writing and if necessary a complaint should be made: this will encourage a judge on any subsequent appeal to take the matter seriously. Relevant steps when checking the fairness and adequacy of the interview process will be to:

- obtain the recording of the interview if there is one;
- check the recording and the transcript for accuracy against the asylum seeker's instructions;
- check not just for accuracy but for the interviewer's tone and whether they encouraged a full explanation to be given, and for corrections to be made;
- consider whether there was an interpreter present and their competence: did they appear to interpret everything or were things left out?

If there were any inadequacies, then a complaint should be made at once.

2.1.5 Decision

Decisions follow quite quickly from asylum interviews, although the time taken by individual case owners varies, depending on their working speed and whether they agree to wait for additional evidence or submissions. The Home Office published objective is to conclude new asylum claims within six months of the application being made, though its ability to do so ebbs and flows with its prioritisation of resources.

Asylum seekers can apply for permission to take up employment, although only in those occupations defined by Appendix K to the Immigration Rules, and excluding self-employment, if a decision at first instance has not been taken on their asylum application (or fresh asylum claim) within one year of the date on which it was recorded – so long as the delay is not attributable to them (para.360).

Upon a refusal of the claim, a NIAA 2002, s.120 'one stop' notice will be served, requiring notification of any grounds for remaining in the UK beyond asylum. Refusal of an asylum claim will carry the right of appeal (see NIAA 2002, s.82), subject to being certified as clearly unfounded.

2.1.6 Asylum support

Asylum support, often still referred to as 'NASS support' (a reference to the now defunct National Asylum Support Service), is available to asylum seekers (and those who have made a claim under Article 3 of the ECHR) aged over 18 and their dependants who would otherwise be homeless and/or destitute. Unaccompanied children will be supported by their local authority under Children Act 1989, s.20 and not by the Home Office.

Applicants are deemed to appear destitute if:

- they and their dependants do not have adequate accommodation or any means of obtaining it (irrespective of whether other essential living needs are met); or
- they and their dependants have adequate accommodation or the means of obtaining it, but cannot meet essential living needs.

Subsequently, support can be provided in three different ways under the Immigration and Asylum Act 1999 (IAA 1999), s.95 (see **Appendix A2**):

- accommodation only; or
- subsistence only (regular cash payments); or
- both accommodation and subsistence.

Asylum support can be claimed immediately on claiming asylum. The application will be processed by the same officials involved in considering the asylum application.

Information on asylum support can be found in the Home Office Operational Guidance, Asylum Support (Asylum Instructions) section at **www.gov.uk/ government/collections/asylum-support-asylum-instructions**. Very useful advice for advisers is provided by the Asylum Support Appeals Project (ASAP) (**www.asaproject.org/about-asap**).

Support is provided under IAA 1999, s.95. It is subject to a means assessment and takes the form of allocated accommodation, if the asylum seeker requires it, and a weekly income equivalent to approximately 70 per cent of income support. Emergency accommodation will be provided if necessary. The asylum seeker will then be dispersed somewhere outside London.

Asylum support can be denied to an asylum seeker who has not made a claim as soon as reasonably practicable after arriving in the UK, generally three days (a 'section 55 decision', i.e. NIAA 2002, s.55). An asylum seeker cannot though be left destitute as a result (see *Limbuela* [2005] UKHL 66). Compliance with the strict terms on which asylum support is granted is essential, as a failure to comply can lead to termination of support.

Where an asylum claim is finally determined, the asylum support will come to an end unless the asylum seeker has a dependent child. If the claim is successful, the asylum seeker (now a refugee) will be able to apply for mainstream benefits. Their asylum support will continue for four weeks to allow them to do so.

If an asylum seeker is refused asylum support, or support is withdrawn, they can appeal to the First-tier Tribunal (Asylum Support).

Those who are destitute and refused asylum can claim 'section 4 support' (i.e. IAA 1999, s.4) where there are practical obstacles to them returning home, e.g. an outstanding fresh claim, judicial review proceedings where permission has been granted, or in the absence of a viable route of return. Section 4 support consists of accommodation, and a weekly sum via a payment card.

Those asylum seekers who, because of age, mental or physical ill health, disability or any other circumstances, are in need of care and attention which they cannot access anywhere else (i.e. which cannot be met by the provision of IAA 1999, s.95 or s.4 support) may be entitled to support from a local authority under the National Assistance Act 1948, s.21(1). This is a complex area of law and advice should be sought from a community care specialist adviser or lawyer.

2.2 CHILDREN AS ASYLUM SEEKERS

2.2.1 Relevance of age

Being assessed as a child has multiple impacts for an asylum seeker – most importantly:

- how they are to be supported in the UK (e.g. they will be supported by social services, and may benefit from their support even after becoming an adult);
- how their asylum claim will be assessed.

There is a more generous approach to credibility for children (including procedural duties to help in establishing the claim recognised in *Processing an Asylum Application from a Child* (the Home Office Operational Guidance, Asylum Policy, Children (Asylum Instructions) at **www.gov.uk/government/publications/ processing-an-asylum-application-from-a-child-instruction**). It states at paragraph 16.1 that 'case owners may need to be proactive in their pursuit and consideration of objective factors and information relating to the child's claim), and thus, when assessing credibility, the guidance goes on to make clear the care that must be taken before discrepancies are held against a child asylum seeker:

> **16.4 Assessing credibility**
>
> A case owner must not draw an adverse credibility inference from omissions in the child's knowledge or account if it is likely that their age or maturity is [a] factor or if there are logical or other reasons for those omissions …
>
> Case owners must take account of what is 'reasonable' to expect a child to know in his/her given set of circumstances and in doing so taking account of his/her age, maturity, education and other relevant factors.
>
> Case owners should demonstrate explicit consideration of any mitigating circumstances … that should be taken into account when assessing credibility in a child's claim.
> …

Very little attention should be paid to interviews early in the process with asylum seeking children where no appropriate adult is present, and indeed it should be very difficult for the Home Office to persuade a judge to look at such interviews (e.g. *R (on the application of AN and FA (children))* v. *Secretary of State for the Home Department* [2012] EWCA Civ 1636).

Equally, breaches of the Home Office guidance on interviewing children (e.g. that a responsible adult should be present, that there should be a short informal conversation on a non-asylum topic to break the ice, that the interview should be conducted by a specially trained caseworker who makes clear their understanding that the child is giving information in an alien environment and may be distrustful, and that they 'put all inconsistencies in the child's subjective evidence or between the subjective and objective evidence to the child at the interview, to allow them an opportunity to explain further'), may well require that interviews, or aspects of them, are disregarded.

The Immigration Rules state:

> **352.** Any child over the age of 12 who has claimed asylum in his own right shall be interviewed about the substance of his claim unless the child is unfit or unable to be interviewed. When an interview takes place it shall be conducted in the presence of a parent, guardian, representative or another adult independent of the Secretary of State who has responsibility for the child. The interviewer shall have specialist training in the interviewing of children and have particular regard to the possibility that a child will feel inhibited or alarmed. The child shall be allowed to express himself in his own way and at his own speed. If he appears tired or distressed, the interview will be suspended. The interviewer should then consider whether it would be appropriate for the interview to be resumed the same day or on another day.

Breaks should be offered during interviews as often as required: interviewers should ensure they use appropriate language and pace of delivery. Information should be sought from other sources where possible: from parents, adults, or objective material regarding the country.

The UNHCR states in its *Guidelines on International Protection: Child Asylum Claims under Articles 1(A)2 and 1(F) of the 1951 Convention and/or 1967 Protocol relating to the Status of Refugees* ('Child Asylum Claims'):

> **72.** Children cannot be expected to provide adult-like accounts of their experiences. They may have difficulty articulating their fear for a range of reasons, including trauma, parental instructions, lack of education, fear of State authorities or persons in positions of power, use of ready-made testimony by smugglers, or fear of reprisals. They may be too young or immature to be able to evaluate what information is important or to interpret what they have witnessed or experienced in a manner that is easily understandable to an adult. Some children may omit or distort vital information or be unable to differentiate the imagined from reality. They also may experience difficulty relating to abstract notions, such as time or distance. Thus, what might constitute a lie in the case of an adult might not necessarily be a lie in the case of a child. It is, therefore, essential that examiners have the necessary training and skills to be able to evaluate accurately the reliability and significance of the child's account. This may require involving experts in interviewing children outside a formal setting or observing children and communicating with them in an environment where they feel safe, for example, in a reception centre.
>
> **73.** Although the burden of proof usually is shared between the examiner and the applicant in adult claims, it may be necessary for an examiner to assume a greater burden of proof in children's claims, especially if the child concerned is unaccompanied. If the facts of the case cannot be ascertained and/or the child is incapable of fully articulating

his/her claim, the examiner needs to make a decision on the basis of all known circumstances, which may call for a liberal application of the benefit of the doubt. Similarly, the child should be given the benefit of the doubt should there be some concern regarding the credibility of parts of his/her claim.

There is also a more liberal attitude to risk assessment which recognises that a broad array of harms may threaten the well-being of children (see *AA (unattended children) Afghanistan CG* [2012] UKUT 16 (IAC) for a good explanation of the difficulties that children may face by way of sexual exploitation and vulnerability to forced recruitment into the armed forces or militias, and to trafficking). In this regard there is no 'bright line' separating children aged under 18 from slightly older young adults (*KA (Afghanistan) and others* v. *Secretary of State for the Home Department* [2012] EWCA Civ 1014).

There are certain obligations as to tracing an unaccompanied minor's parents, stemming from EU law and found domestically in the Asylum Seekers (Reception Conditions) Regulations 2005, SI 2005/7, reg.6:

(1)   So as to protect an unaccompanied minor's best interests, the Secretary of State shall endeavour to trace the members of the minor's family as soon as possible after the minor makes his claim for asylum.

(2)   In cases where there may be a threat to the life or integrity of the minor or the minor's close family, the Secretary of State shall take care to ensure that the collection, processing and circulation of information concerning the minor or his close family is undertaken on a confidential basis so as not to jeopardise his or their safety.

These obligations have been found by the courts, in numerous cases culminating in *MA and AA (Afghanistan)* v. *Secretary of State for the Home Department* [2015] UKSC 40, to have a limited impact on Home Office decision making. A tracing failure may, however, be relevant to assessing an asylum seeker's claim where it has had ([53]) an 'effect on the nature and quality of the available evidence'; at [73]:

If the appellant has identified people who might be able to confirm his account, but the respondent has not pursued that lead, the tribunal might fairly regard the appellant's willingness to identify possible sources of corroboration as a mark of credibility, but this would be an evidential assessment for the tribunal.

Where a child's asylum claim is refused (if they are an unaccompanied asylum seeking child, i.e. one applying in their own right without a primary carer in this country – Immigration Rules, para.352ZD):

• they will receive leave to remain until the age of 17 and a half under para.352ZC;

• so long as there are no adequate reception arrangements in the country of return; and

• there are no public interest reasons to the contrary.

Representing asylum seeking children requires significant expertise, particularly where they are unaccompanied. For accreditation purposes, it is only really necessary to know the general principles, and to be keenly aware that there is much more information out there with which you should thoroughly acquaint yourself should you ever represent a child. Useful sources of information are:

- Coram Children's Legal Centre's immigration and asylum process guide, *Seeking Support* (**www.childrenslegalcentre.com**);
- ILPA's *Resources Guide for Practitioners Working with Refugee Children* (May 2011).

When representing children, make sure advisers working with children are appropriately accredited, suitably experienced, and have had enhanced criminal record checks undertaken.

If unaccompanied, children should be referred to the Refugee Council's Children's Panel of advisers. Bear in mind the possible need for counselling and a psychiatric report.

More attention should be afforded to objective indications of risk. Just because the child is too young to understand their situation does not mean they do not have a well-founded fear in the sense of an objective risk of persecution that a third party would be able to determine, whatever the child's own apprehension of future events (see Immigration Rules, para.351).

A decision on their claim should be made quickly, within a month if there is no good reason to delay it: there are repeated references to avoiding delay in the Home Office guidance, *Processing an Asylum Application from a Child*.

Remember, in making appointments for children, to ensure they attend with an appropriate adult who is responsible for the child's welfare (e.g. panel adviser, foster parent or social worker). Try to avoid appointments that will disrupt school.

Bear in mind social work records as a means of corroborating a child client's credibility. This is an essential source of information that is always worth examination, because it may record contemporaneous reactions to distressing news from abroad and extensively catalogue the child's behaviour in the light of their past experiences: indeed *Processing an Asylum Application from a Child* at paragraph 16.2 expressly notes that 'child psychological and physical health and development reports or information from welfare and health support professionals to whom the child may have disclosed relevant evidence' are a relevant source of supporting material.

On appeal, bear in mind Joint Presidential Guidance Note No.2 of 2010, *Child, Vulnerable Adult and Sensitive Appellant Guidance* (see also **1.3.11**):

10.3 Assessing evidence

Take account of potentially corroborative evidence

Be aware:

i. Children often do not provide as much detail as adults in recalling experiences and may often manifest their fears differently from adults …

Determination

…

14. Consider the evidence, allowing for possible different degrees of understanding by witnesses and appellant compared to those are not vulnerable, in the context of evidence from others associated with the appellant and the background evidence before you. Where there were clear discrepancies in the oral evidence, consider the extent to which the age, vulnerability or sensitivity of the witness was an element of that discrepancy or lack of clarity.

15. The decision should record whether the Tribunal has concluded the appellant (or a witness) is a child, vulnerable or sensitive, the effect the Tribunal considered the identified vulnerability had in assessing the evidence before it and thus whether the Tribunal was satisfied whether the appellant had established his or her case to the relevant standard of proof. In asylum appeals, weight should be given to objective indications of risk rather than necessarily to a state of mind.

Sources such as this are of particular importance because of the EU law duty (Procedures Directive, Recital 14) to lay down:

specific procedural guarantees for unaccompanied minors … on account of their vulnerability. In this context, the best interests of the child should be a primary consideration of Member States.

Ahmadullah (Afghanistan)

Ahmadullah is from Afghanistan. He is accepted as aged 16 at the date his asylum claim is assessed. His father was murdered by the Taliban because of the stance he took against them as the village headman. Ahmadullah was then expected to take his father's place when he was older; for now an older relative, Faizullah, would stand in for him. However, because of the threats that Ahmadullah received, his mother arranged for him to flee the country. He subsequently learned that Faizullah was murdered.

The Home Office refuses him asylum but grants him discretionary leave to remain for the next 18 months.

He has a right to recognition of his refugee status notwithstanding that he is not facing return, and it should be assessed at the present date.

Relevant considerations will be:

- Has the Home Office sought to trace his family members and has he provided sufficient information for it to be reasonably able to do so? If he has provided a detailed description of his home area which has not been acted upon, then this provides some measure of support for his story.
- Can he establish contact with his relatives via the Red Cross, and can further information be sought from them or the village authorities?

- If he is interviewed and discrepancies arise, read the interview carefully for compatibility with the various procedural requirements set out above.
- If his account is vague, is this explained by his age, education, trauma, or inability to identify what information he should provide to really help his case; and has he previously been let down by his own national or local authorities?
- If his account is discrepant, remember the Practice Direction on child witnesses.
- **Objective risk:** identify his home area and precisely what degree of risk he might face from the Taliban there – you might find sources beyond the standard human rights reports which mention problems if he can name his precise home area.
- **State protection:** will the authorities take the complaint of a young person seriously?
- **Internal relocation:** is he accepted to be at risk from the Taliban, or does he face dangers because of the likelihood of street homelessness if he returns home without having relatives to look after him?

Bear in mind the best interests of the child and the various rights found in the UN Convention on the Rights of the Child 1989 in assessing whether relocation (i.e. remaining in Kabul to where he would doubtless be returned) would be 'reasonable' for him: read the rights identified in the Convention's Articles against the country evidence.

2.2.2   Age assessment

There has been considerable litigation around disputed age assessments of young asylum seekers. Home Office policy is to treat a person claiming to be a minor as an adult only where their physical appearance/demeanour very strongly suggests that they are significantly over 18 years of age. The initial assessment process is often carried out by untrained and inexpert Home Office staff simply on the basis of a visual assessment.

If children are wrongly assumed to be adults, this will lead to their applications for asylum and other international protection being assessed by processes designed for adults rather than children.

- They might be detained, within the detained fast-track (DFT) process or otherwise, with adults (see **2.4**).
- Their vulnerability as a child may go unnoticed, which as just mentioned can be relevant both to the assessment of their credibility and to the forms of serious harm they may face abroad.
- Age is also a central part of children's identity and a failure to believe that they are children could lead to them losing all confidence in the decision-making system and failing to disclose further and necessary details about their past persecution and future fears.
- They will be refused accommodation under the Children Act 1989, s.20 and will be dispersed to NASS accommodation as adults.

Given the numerous benefits of a child being correctly treated as such, it is unsurprising that both Home Office guidance and a body of jurisprudence have developed in relation to challenges to age assessment.

The Home Office policy instruction, *Assessing Age* (Operational Guidance, Asylum Policy, Children (Asylum Instructions)) states:

2.1 Initial age assessment

Where there is little or no evidence to support the applicant's claimed age and their claim to be a child is doubted, the following policy should be applied:

1. The applicant should be treated as an adult if their physical appearance/demeanour **very strongly suggests that they are *significantly* over 18 years of age** …
2. **All other applicants should be afforded the benefit of the doubt and treated as children, in accordance with the 'Processing an asylum application from a child' AI [asylum instruction], until a careful assessment of their age has been completed.** This policy is designed to safeguard the welfare of children. It does not indicate final acceptance of the applicant's claimed age, which will be considered in the round when all relevant evidence has been considered, including the view of the local authority to whom unaccompanied children, or applicants who we are giving the benefit of the doubt and temporarily treating as unaccompanied children, should be referred …

Having been given the benefit of the doubt, an unaccompanied minor will be put under the care of a local authority which should then carry out a '*Merton* compliant' age assessment (i.e. one that complies with the procedural safeguards identified by Stanley Burnton J in *R (on the application of B)* v. *London Borough of Merton* [2003] EWHC 1689 (Admin)). The assessment carried out by the local authority will usually then be accepted by the Home Office.

Critical features of a *Merton* compliant assessment are:

- an assessment of age in the light of a person's general background including their personal circumstances and history, education and recent activities (and certainly not on appearance alone);
- having regard to procedural fairness which would require a provisional assessment of age to be put to the person in question;
- the benefit of the doubt should be given where there is uncertainty;
- trained social workers should make the evaluation.

In *T* v. *London Borough of Enfield* [2004] EWHC 2297 (Admin), the judge held in addition that it was necessary to ask the individual why they believed that they were a minor and take into account any evidence which indicates that they are suffering from trauma and/or have any special educational needs.

2.2.3 Challenging an age assessment

The sequence of challenges will normally be as follows:

1. Seek independent evidence or documents on age.
2. Check assessment is *Merton* compliant.
3. Seek independent paediatrician assessment.
4. Judicial review of social services department.

If the social services age assessment is unfavourable, there are different courses of action that can be pursued, including:

1. **Seeking alternative independent evidence of age.** Should new evidence become available social services will need to conduct a new age assessment.
2. **Seeking a paediatrician age assessment.** This is simply one form of independent evidence, but it is a controversial one because of the case of *A v. London Borough of Croydon* [2009] EWHC 939 (Admin). In this case Collins J held that paediatrician age assessments are unreliable and do not have to be given any particular weight by social services.

    Deciding someone's age is an extremely difficult exercise and it is not possible to be completely accurate. The most honest assessments include a margin of error of around two years either way. Any relevant evidence is therefore highly pertinent to the assessment.
3. **Judicial review of social services.** In the case of *R (on the application of A)* v. *London Borough of Croydon* [2009] UKSC 8 the Supreme Court held that an age assessment by social services for the purposes of the Children Act 1989, s.20 is not to be approached via the limited scope of a normal judicial review application: rather 'the question whether or not a person is a child is ... a question of fact which must ultimately be decided by the court'.

    This is very helpful when it comes to challenging a social services department. Judges on judicial review have to try the issues for themselves and to make a declaration as to the person's age when they come to make their judgment. The Supreme Court case came after the judgment of Mr Justice Collins (they are related but distinct cases) and undermines key parts of the reasoning of the earlier case, so it may prove to be the case that paediatrician assessments will be given more weight in the future – though the methods of some well-known experts have received damning criticism.

    As with asylum support issues, disputing age assessments has become a specialist area of the law, and advice should be sought from a community care specialist. Age assessment judicial reviews are usually heard now by the Upper Tribunal (and are routinely transferred there by the Administrative Court following *R (on the application of FZ)* v. *London Borough of Croydon* [2011] EWCA Civ 59 and *R (on the application of JS and YK)* v. *Birmingham City Council (AAJR)* [2011] UKUT 505 (IAC)) because Tribunal procedures are more appropriate to determining evidence-heavy issues than is the Administrative Court.

Practice point

Get inspiration on running an age assessment challenge by looking up other such cases. They are reported at **https://tribunalsdecisions.service.gov.uk/utiac/decisions** with an 'AAJR' prefix to the citation.

The courts have given useful bits of guidance in the course of those challenges: noting, for example, that it might be wrong to criticise foster parents on the grounds they might be compromised in their belief as to their charge's age by a lack of neutrality and objectivity, because it could be assumed that they would also wish to protect other children in their care from undue exposure to a person older than claimed (*MVN* v. *London Borough of Greenwich* [2015] EWHC 1942 (Admin) at [138]).

Practice point

Before seeking to challenge a Home Office age assessment it is important to obtain any independent evidence available as to a person's age. Any such evidence will carry weight with whoever conducts an age assessment. Relevant materials include the ADCS, *Age Assessment Guidance* (**http://adcs.org.uk/assets/documentation/ Age_Assessment_Guidance_2015_Final.pdf**). Relevant steps will be to:

- verify any documentation the child may have with them in the form of passports, national or school identity cards, family records or similar;
- chase schools, doctors, hospitals, local officials, NGOs in the field and other objective sources of data about age;
- obtain statements and affidavits from family and community members;
- ensure that a credible account has been provided of the child's background: their account of why they are present in this country, usually on asylum grounds, is an important part of this;
- ensure there is relevant country evidence that supports the child's account, e.g. with regard to the education system;
- ensure the interview process complied with best practice requirements.

Expert medical opinion, despite much criticism (e.g. *R (on the application of R)* v. *London Borough of Croydon* [2011] EWHC 1473 (Admin)), may be useful, particularly where it is linked to the more reputable methods of age assessment such as a sustained dropping off in height and weight gain, and the full emergence of the third molar (*R (on the application of AM)* v. *Solihull Metropolitan Borough Council (AAJR)* [2012] UKUT 118 (IAC)).

Possible flaws in age assessment decisions have been identified in the case law:

- failing to give a suitable margin for error;
- failing to disclose the age assessment reasons in good time;
- failing to give the subject an opportunity to comment on them;
- using obscure language which is difficult to understand;
- failing to follow best practice on building rapport;
- not paying attention to 'tiredness, trauma, bewilderment and anxiety', or ethnicity, culture, and customs of the person being assessed;
- automatically adopting a Home Office age assessment;
- making an unwarranted departure from a finding of age made on appeal by the Tribunal;
- not having an interpreter present consistently;

- having regard to physical appearance without taking account of relevant life history;
- holding the absence of corroborative documents against the subject without considering the kinds of difficulties in obtaining and carrying documents abroad which are well known to the immigration tribunals;
- failing to give an opportunity to comment on the provisional decision if minded to find the interviewee to be an adult;
- conducting an unduly confrontational interview;
- not properly explaining the nature and purpose of the process in advance.

See *AS* v. *London Borough of Croydon* [2011] EWHC 2091 (Admin); *R (on the application of AZ)* v. *Hampshire County Council (AAJR)* [2013] UKUT 87 (IAC); *R (on the application of AM)* v. *Solihull Metropolitan Borough Council (AAJR)* [2012] UKUT 118; and *R (on the application of B)* v. *London Borough of Merton* itself.

2.3 GENDER AND ASYLUM

The Home Office has now incorporated elements of the best practices contained in the old Immigration and Asylum Act 1999 Gender Guidelines and elsewhere, as *Gender Issues in the Asylum Claim* in its Operational Guidance, Asylum Policy, Asylum Decision Making Guidance (Asylum Instructions) section. Bear in mind persecution in the form of various sorts of ill treatment that may particularly affect women:

- marriage-related harm;
- violence within the family or community;
- domestic slavery;
- forced abortion;
- forced sterilisation;
- trafficking;
- female genital mutilation;
- sexual violence and abuse, and rape.

Women may be subjected to discriminatory treatment that is enforced through law or through the imposition of social or religious norms that restrict their opportunities and rights. Examples include:

- family and personal laws;
- dress codes;
- employment or education restrictions;
- restrictions on women's freedom of movement and/or activities; and
- political disenfranchisement.

There are cases where women are persecuted solely because of their family or kinship relationships, e.g. a woman may be persecuted as a means of demoralising or punishing members of her family or community, or in order to pressurise her into revealing information.

While women may be involved in conventional political activities and raise similar claims to men, this does not always correspond to the reality of the experiences of women in some societies, where gender roles mean they will more often be involved in low-level political activities, for instance hiding people, passing messages or providing community services, food, clothing or medical care. 'Low-level' political activity does not necessarily make it low-risk. The response of the state to such activity may be disproportionately persecutory because of the expectations held as to the boundaries of women's conduct.

In terms of establishing the facts of their cases, it should be remembered that women who have been sexually assaulted may suffer trauma. The symptoms of this include:

- persistent fear;
- a loss of self-confidence and self-esteem;
- difficulty in concentration;
- an attitude of self-blame, a pervasive loss of control; and
- memory loss or distortion.

Beware of inhibitors to taking instructions, e.g. the presence of family members.

Amina (Algeria)

Amina is from Algeria. She has been present in the UK as the spouse of a qualified person exercising EU Treaty rights; she had come here as a student, and has not told her family of her marriage. She recently learned that the man she thought of as her husband was in fact previously married and had not been lawfully entitled to marry her. A friend of hers told her family about her difficulties, and her sister rang her from Algeria to say there had been a conference at the local mosque about her: her father and brother had disowned her and other relatives had issued death threats against her because she was perceived as having brought disgrace on the family. She became fearful for her safety on a return abroad. She claims asylum.

The Home Office refuses her asylum claim, saying that it does not accept she would not have told her family about her problems therefore her story is not believed, and that honour crimes are rare in Algeria, a country which has a functioning police force, and anyway she could relocate to an urban centre where she could live and work without the need for family support.

She will need to take on the Home Office case on four issues: her credibility, the risks she actually faces, whether there is state protection or whether internal relocation is available.

Credibility: whenever a person claims asylum after being lawfully or otherwise resident here, there will be major questions asked by the Home Office. Consider:

- Does she have friends or relatives here who will support her claim and recount what they were told by her of her problems abroad and state how she has acted during their friendship if that shows she has been suffering stress due to events abroad, or an employer, tutor/lecturer or counsellor or similar person in a position of responsibility who can vouchsafe for her reaction to events abroad?

- Did they meet her former partner in the UK? Is there any relative abroad who will support her case by a letter?
- Can, at the very least, she give an account that is sufficiently vivid and detailed to have the 'ring of truth'?

Objective risks: is there country evidence to show that an educated woman will face a risk of domestic violence/honour crimes (there would be little difficulty in showing that physical threats of this kind were 'serious harm'), and that there are entrenched patriarchal attitudes in society?

Convention reason: do her problems have a religious dimension? If not, or alternatively, is she a member of a particular social group: look for evidence of:

(a)   a common background that cannot be changed (i.e. her past as a woman who has defied family expectations); and

(b)   societal recognition of a socially outcast woman as being different from other members of the community.

State protection:

- Are the police likely to leave these matters to families to sort out as they do not see it as falling within their crime prevention duties?
- Are women discriminated against in the access they have to the courts and in how their evidence would be received judicially?

Internal relocation: Would life alone for such a person without family to support her be unduly harsh?

Tahleel (Iran)

Tahleel is a citizen of Iran who is present in the UK as a student. She returned home to see her mother during a vacation and was arrested and detained by militia members for wearing clothes and make-up that they viewed as unduly provocative; she was raped in detention.

Her claim is refused – the Home Office disbelieves her account because:

- it thinks it unlikely that she would have taken the risk of so dressing given the serious consequences that can ensue;
- she did not dress extravagantly or wear cosmetics at her asylum interview.

Even if her story is true, the decision maker does not accept that her rapist was acting with the authority of the state, or that she was of real interest to the authorities given she was allowed to leave the country to return to the UK. When preparing her appeal, consider:

- Can medical evidence be obtained showing her distress following her rape?
- Are there witnesses to her emotional state before and after her return after the fateful trip back?
- Can evidence be obtained from family members in Iran? If not is there an explanation for this?
- Can she explain why she chose to dress inconsistently with Home Office expectations for her asylum interview?
- Did she claim asylum swiftly after her return to the UK and if not, is this explained?

Country evidence
- Is there evidence showing that women's attire is a battleground in Iran and that the reaction of state and non-state agents is arbitrary and unpredictable, and that exit bans are not automatic or are inefficient?
- Is there evidence showing that the dress restrictions are religious in motivation?

2.4   FAST-TRACK APPEALS

The 'detained fast-track' (DFT) procedure is one whereby the asylum decision and appeal take place in a very short timeframe. In order to ensure compliance with this process, the subject is detained throughout. In December 2014, the Court of Appeal in *R (on the application of Detention Action)* v. *Secretary of State for the Home Department* [2014] EWCA Civ 1634 found that the detention of asylum seekers in the DFT who were not at risk of absconding while their appeals are pending is unlawful, because the detention policy does not meet the required standards of clarity and transparency, and is arguably unjustified.

That was merely one of a series of blows struck against the fast track in litigation throughout 2014 and 2015. In *Detention Action* v. *Secretary of State for the Home Department* [2014] EWHC 2245 (Admin), Ouseley J found that the DFT system was unlawful as it was being operated, because lawyers were not involved at an early enough stage. The Court of Appeal decided though that measures the Home Office had put in place since the judgment – particularly the provision of a four-day period prior to the asylum interview for the asylum seeker to receive appropriate legal advice – were sufficient to ensure the system should in future operate lawfully.

However, ultimately the decision of the Court of Appeal in *Lord Chancellor* v. *Detention Action* [2015] EWCA Civ 840 had the consequence that the DFT has been suspended at the time of writing: though there is a consultation afoot that may well herald its return to action. There the court ruled that the DFT appeal system was systemically unfair. It noted the complex issues involved in many asylum claims and that instruction taking in the DFT was pressured because the client was in detention in circumstances where their lawyers had to investigate numerous issues at the same time. It found that the limited power to adjourn proceedings was not sufficient to ensure fairness.

The court was particularly concerned that it would be difficult to persuade the Tribunal that the appeal could not be justly determined within the prescribed timetable as there may not have been time to complete the relevant enquiries into the available corroborative evidence, and there was an inevitable tension between having to argue that the available evidence was insufficient while being aware that such evidence would be all that could be used to support the case if an adjournment was refused.

As of August 2015, asylum seekers whose cases have been heard in the DFT can apply for earlier decisions of the First-tier Tribunal to be set aside because of the lack of fairness. When making such an application, it would seem a good idea to highlight specific evidence which was not available because of the speed of the process, or point to some other unfairness.

The President of the First-tier Tribunal has clarified that rule 32 of the Tribunal Procedure (First-tier Tribunal) (Immigration and Asylum Chamber) Rules 2014, SI 2014/2604 (L 31) (see **Appendix B1**) can be relied on by the First-tier Tribunal to set aside a decision which disposes of proceedings (rule 32(1)) where it is in the interests of justice to do so (rule 32(1)(a)) because there has been a procedural irregularity in the proceedings (rule 32(2)(d)).

However, you should note that it is only the 2014 DFT rules that have been set aside, i.e. those that entered into force in October 2014 as the Schedule to the general Tribunal Procedure Rules 2014. Asylum seekers who fell foul of the DFT rules previously in force (the Asylum and Immigration Tribunal (Fast Track Procedure) Rules 2005, SI 2005/560) will have to show unfairness on the individual facts of their case.

The key features of fast-track appeals are as follows:

- low success rate;
- rapid interview and decision;
- foreshortened appeal time limits;
- tougher adjournment regime.

As can be seen, everything about the fast-track process points to the need to extract one's client from it if at all possible. The success rate of cases going through the fast-track process has consistently been very low indeed. One might wonder whether this is because the Home Office is spectacularly successful at selecting low merit cases for the process or whether any case that goes through the process thereby has a drastically reduced chance of success.

While the DFT process is presently in abeyance, there is already a consultation taking place as to the form that its successor might take. Given its possible resurrection, bear in mind the following:

- The time limit for serving notice of appeal and whether that is expressed in working days and the moment from which time runs (e.g. does it run only from receipt of the appealable decision). Usually there are provisions for extending time if it is in the interests of justice to do so.
- The Home Office must provide the Tribunal with specified documents within a period of receiving the notice of appeal from the Tribunal.
- The Tribunal must fix the date of hearing within a certain period after the day on which the documents are provided by the Home Office.
- The Tribunal must then provide notice of the date, time and place of the hearing to every party.
- There may be a target period within which the Tribunal must determine the appeal.
- There will be provisions for adjournment: the test can be expected to be the interests of justice.

There will probably be power for the First-tier Tribunal to order removal of the appeal from the DFT, as in the past:

- if all the parties consent; or
- if the Tribunal is satisfied that the case cannot justly be decided within the timescales provided for in the fast-track rules.

The historic criteria for inclusion, and the case law on fairness within the DFT, will be relevant to deciding which cases are appropriate for any future process. Cases suitable for the DFT were identified in the DFT policy instruction and included those where:

(a)   it appears that no further enquiries by the Home Office or the applicant are necessary in order to obtain clarification, complex legal advice or corroborative evidence;

(b)   it appears likely that any such enquiries can be concluded to allow a decision to take place within the normal indicative timescales;

(c)   it appears likely that it will be possible to fulfil and properly consider the claim within normal indicative timescales;

(d)   it appears likely that no translations are required in respect of documents presented by an applicant, or that translations can be obtained to allow a decision within normal indicative timescales; and

(e)   the case is one that is likely to be certified as 'clearly unfounded' under section 94 of the 2002 Act.

Examples of cases that were unsuitable for the DFT as shown by the case law are those:

- turning on authenticity of documents (see Lord Phillips MR in the Court of Appeal in *ZL and VL* v. *Secretary of State for the Home Department and Lord Chancellor's Department* [2003] EWCA Civ 25);
- where the Home Office had what amounted to expert evidence by way of a local authority age assessment which the appellant needs an opportunity to rebut (*SH (Afghanistan)* v. *Secretary of State for the Home Department* [2011] EWCA Civ 1284);
- where the basis for the case cannot 'be reliably established without evidence from sources external to the claimant himself' where further time is legitimately required to obtain that evidence (*R (on the application of JB) (Jamaica)* v. *Secretary of State for the Home Department* [2013] EWCA Civ 666: gender preference can only realistically be established by finding various witnesses from the community).

2.5   DETAINED ASYLUM CASEWORK

In July 2015, following the demise of the DFT, instruction policy guidance was published, addressing how the Home Office would henceforth deal with asylum claims from people in detention (*Detention: Interim Instruction for Cases in Detention Who Have Claimed Asylum, and for Entering Cases Who Have Claimed*

Asylum into Detention (Home Office, 16 July 2015) at **www.gov.uk/government/ publications/cases-in-detention-interim-instruction**).

A decision will normally be taken within 28 days of the initial asylum claim and continuous progression of the process needs to be shown. Detention must be reviewed regularly having particular regard to the applicant's need to obtain further evidence.

Key criteria will be:

- the ability to conclude the case within a reasonable timeframe, having particular regard to further information received which impacts on the complexity of the claim and thus on the likelihood of removal;
- any vulnerabilities, having particular regard to those identified in the *Enforcement Instructions and Guidance*, Chapter 55 on Detention and Temporary Release (Operational Guidance, Enforcement section).

Chapter 55 includes torture victims, whose cases will not normally be suitable for the detained asylum casework process if supported by independent evidence of torture via a (Detention Centre Rules 2001) rule 35 report, and those whose medical or mental health issues cannot be adequately managed in detention.

It is possible to bring a judicial review challenge against a person's continued detention and a judge may order suspension of the decision-making process to avoid the possibility of unfair prejudice resulting from unduly speedy consideration of a claim.

2.6 THIRD COUNTRY CASES

An asylum applicant cannot normally be removed from the UK without their claim being considered on its merits (NIAA 2002, s.77), i.e. considered substantively, as it is sometimes expressed. An exception to this is where the Home Office intends to remove the asylum applicant to a safe third country which is responsible under the EU law arrangements for allocating asylum seekers to particular countries depending on their place of arrival and their connections with individual Member States.

2.6.1 Dublin III

EU Regulation 604/2013 ('Dublin III') is the instrument which now generally governs the procedures by which one EU Member State only will be identified as responsible for a particular asylum claim. In practice this tends to be the State the asylum seeker was first detected as entering EU territory subject to having relatives or family members present in other countries, or other special circumstances such as having been granted a visa for another country.

Article 49 of Dublin III sets out that the Regulation applies where either:

- the asylum claim is made after 1 January 2014 (it is not yet clear whether this means the latest, or the first, asylum claim in the EU); or
- the 'take back' request is made after 1 January 2014.

Its predecessor, Dublin II, operates similarly to Dublin III in terms of the allocation of responsibility between Member States, but there are significantly greater procedural safeguards found in Dublin III.

Subsidiary EU legislation accompanies Dublin III, addressing the identification of relatives of an unaccompanied minor and their ability to care for the minor, establishing family links, dependency and care (Recital 35): see the Implementing Regulation 118/2014 of 30 January 2014.

Procedurally, the Dublin process is as follows:

- A EURODAC fingerprint database hit determines that the asylum seeker has already claimed asylum elsewhere in the EU.
- The Secretary of State will then tell the asylum seeker that he or she is suitable for the third country process, and will write to the third country to invite it to take responsibility (on the basis of the Home Office's understanding of the hierarchy of responsibility set out below).
- The third country will then accept responsibility. If it fails to do so, this is 'tantamount to accepting the request' and so it is deemed to have taken responsibility (see Articles 22(7) and 25(2) of Dublin III) where the requested Member State does not reply in time.
- The Secretary of State certifies that the asylum seeker's case is eligible for the third country process under Schedule 3 to AITCA 2004. That certificate has the consequence that the country in question is deemed to be a place where the asylum seeker will be safe from persecution in the Refugee Convention sense and will not be sent elsewhere incompatibly with the Refugee Convention.
- The only remedy at this stage will be for the asylum seeker to make a human rights claim. It is likely that the Secretary of State will then certify the human rights claim as 'clearly unfounded', meaning that the right of appeal against that refusal is out-of-country. Usually this will be based on the poor reception conditions there, perhaps combined with a low recognition of asylum claims generally or of a particular kind, or on the prospects of being sent onwards without the case being considered (which would breach the ECHR, and so is not ruled out as an argument by the deeming provision for Refugee Convention purposes).
- Absent an effective right of appeal, the assessment of the human rights claim as 'clearly unfounded' may only be challenged by way of judicial review.

Challenging certification of the human rights claim as 'clearly unfounded' is a tough job and it will only be in rare cases that such a challenge can succeed, because of the general presumption that EEA Member States take their fundamental rights obligations very seriously indeed and so would not fail to look after asylum seekers properly.

Chapter 3 of Dublin III sets out a hierarchy under which responsibility for an asylum claim is allocated to a particular Member State. Taking aside special cases such as minors, those where family members are present, and questions of visa requirements and issue, most asylum seekers will face return to the country where they first entered the EU. Cases are to be assessed 'on the basis of the situation obtaining when the applicant first lodged his or her application for international protection with a Member State' (Article 7(2)). The hierarchy for responsibility is essentially as follows:

Minors

1. Minors have their claim determined where they have a family member (spouse, unmarried partner, father, mother or guardian) provided this is in their best interests).
2. Unaccompanied minors should have their claim considered where they have a legally present 'relative' (who can care for them) – relatives are more broadly defined than family members to include adult aunts, uncles and grandparents.).
3. Unaccompanied minors without relatives have their claim determined in the State 'where the unaccompanied minor has lodged his or her application' – i.e. in the place they claim asylum – the CJEU in *MA and others* v. *Secretary of State for the Home Department* [2013] EUECJ C-648/11 explained that this meant the State where an asylum application was most recently lodged, i.e. usually their present location.

Adults

1. In the Member State where there is a family member (spouse, unmarried partner, minor unmarried dependent children):

    *   with international protection status, regardless of whether the family was previously formed in the country of origin, or
    *   with a pending claim for asylum that has so far not been the subject of a first decision (Article 10).

2. In the Member State which has issued a residence document or visa (even if it was 'issued on the basis of a false or assumed identity or on submission of forged, counterfeit or invalid documents'.
3. In the Member State into which an asylum seeker 'has irregularly crossed the border … by land, sea or air having come from a third country' as established on the basis of 'proof or circumstantial evidence' including EURODAC hits (Article 13).
4. Where no other Member State is responsible, the first country where an asylum claim has been lodged (Article 3(2)).

5.   If at any time a Member State issues a residence document to an asylum seeker, responsibility switches to that Member State (Article 19(1)).

There is a timescale for the various administrative actions to take place (see Articles 20 to 22). The request to take charge must be made within two months where there has been a EURODAC hit, and within three months in other cases. The reply must be made by the requested Member State within two months of receipt of the request. Where there is no reply, that state will be treated as having accepted the request. Timescales are reduced where the asylum seeker is detained.

2.6.2 Vulnerability

It is also possible that the client is vulnerable, or looking after somebody vulnerable. If this is:

- for reasons of pregnancy, a new-born child, serious illness, severe disability or old age; and
- the applicant is dependent on the assistance of his or her legally resident child, sibling or parent, or if they are dependent on the applicant; and
- the relationship existed in the country of origin,

then the UK should take responsibility for the asylum claim (Article 16).

For other humanitarian cases (presumably including other private and family life issues), Article 17 provides a general discretion.

Among the most important procedural developments in Dublin III:

- There is a general requirement for an effective remedy against transfer both because of conditions in the country of return, but also based on the allocation of responsibility (Recital 17, Article 27). Under previous third country regimes like Dublin II, the courts have generally ruled that individuals do not have any right to challenge the agreement between Member States as to which is responsible for a claim; see e.g. *Abdullahi* v. *Bundesasylamt (C-394/12)* [2014] 1 WLR 1895 in the CJEU.
- Authorities are required to inform an asylum seeker of the consequences of moving between Member States and to give a clear opportunity to submit information regarding the presence of family members and relatives at an early stage in the process (Articles 4–5).
- Detention may only take place where there is a significant risk of a person absconding, and not merely because a person is within the Dublin process (Article 28).
- Supervised and escorted transfers must take place humanely and in a manner reflecting the need to respect the person's dignity; and relevant medical information must be passed between states where the returnee has suffered torture, physical, psychological or sexual violence, and the receiving state must ensure these matters are adequately addressed (Articles 29, 31).

Practice point

Always check whether the UK is truly the responsible country, applying the hierarchy of responsibility, bearing in mind the age of the client and whether there are family members in this country. If this information has not been adequately communicated to the Home Office Third Country Unit before the removal process has begun, then consider carefully whether the client was given adequate information to understand the relevance of these factors.

Also investigate whether the responsibility of the third country has lapsed because of the length of the procedure, or because the client was removed from the EU following a prior asylum claim's rejection, or because the client has left the EU's territory for more than three months in any event (see Article 19 of Dublin III).

And remember the duty to assume responsibility for dependent relative cases under Article 16, and the residual Article 17 discretion.

2.6.3   Substance of third country challenges

Sometimes the challenge will be based on the reception conditions in the third country being inadequate such that there is a real risk of a violation of Article 3 of the ECHR – this may arise because of the individual circumstances of the returnee or because the system is in general inadequate.

However, the evidence must reach a high threshold before it will be accepted that a fellow EU Member State has a system which is that defective. The proper approach is explained in *R (on the application of EM (Eritrea))* v. *Secretary of State for the Home Department* [2014] UKSC 12, which shows that the relevant test is the usual one in Article 3 claims, i.e. whether there are substantial grounds for thinking there to be a real risk of the mistreatment occurring.

You can see the kinds of evidence that are necessary for a case to succeed in *MSS* v. *Belgium and Greece* [2011] ECHR 108, particularly at [249]–[264]. Aside from Greece, the courts have not accepted that other EU countries have inadequate systems, though in *Tarakhel* v. *Switzerland* [2014] ECHR 1185 the Strasbourg Court accepted that families with children could only be returned to Italy if specific assurances were obtained in advance.

Practice point

If running a challenge based on reception conditions regarding a country where there are not yet any clear judicial decisions on the compatibility of removal with human rights obligations, you must note the following actions:

*   Take a statement which clearly specifies the historic treatment of the asylum seeker in the third country, and establishes their vulnerability – read the statement against the known procedures in that country so that it makes sense in context.
*   Ensure you are aware whether your client was in the third country merely as an asylum seeker, a person recognised as needing international protection (of course if they were street homeless in the third country or left it very quickly after claiming asylum there, they may find this out only after leaving the country, e.g. when the

---

Home Office makes enquiries from here), or whether they are a failed asylum seeker there: it is very hard to see how the final class of applicant can benefit from challenges to reception conditions because the Strasbourg Court does not recognise any duty on states to alleviate poverty for persons not lawfully present in a country, so such an argument could only ever be run where you have very powerful evidence, not only of poor reception conditions, but of status determination procedures which are unreliable.

- Locate relevant country evidence from the European Council on Refugees and Exiles (ECRE) or European Legal Network on Asylum (ELENA), the Asylum Information Database (AIDA), UNHCR, local NGOs, etc., addressing both the adequacy of reception conditions and the availability of effective remedies in the third country both domestically and by way of application to Strasbourg (there are reports on the compliance of particular countries with Rule 39 obligations (Rules of Court of the ECtHR), for example, by ECRE and other NGOs).
- Argue by way of representations amounting to a human rights claim that personal facts plus country evidence equate to a viable Article 3 claim. See *MSS* reiterating the well-known case law of the ECtHR: 'to fall within the scope of Article 3 the ill-treatment must attain a minimum level of severity. The assessment of this minimum is relative; it depends on all the circumstances of the case, such as the duration of the treatment and its physical or mental effects and, in some instances, the sex, age and state of health of the victim' [219].

2.7 'CLEARLY UNFOUNDED' CERTIFICATES

An appellant cannot normally be removed from the UK whilst an asylum application or appeal is pending (NIAA 2002, ss.78 and 79). However, the Secretary of State has the power to certify asylum or human rights claims as clearly unfounded. If the Secretary of State issues such a certificate the applicant cannot appeal under NIAA 2002, s.82 while he is in the UK.

It will be appreciated that these certificates have very serious consequences for asylum seekers. Being returned to their own country may expose them to persecution if they are truly at risk of persecution. As the court put it in *ZL and another* v. *Secretary of State for the Home Department and Lord Chancellor's Department* [2003] EWCA Civ 25:

> If their fears are well-founded, the fact that they can appeal after they have been returned to the country where they fear persecution is scant consolation.

Under s.94, there are two classes of presumptively weak asylum claims:

- those where the asylum seeker comes from a country where it is generally thought there is no risk of persecution; and
- those where the substance of the claim regarding one of the key components is very weak – usually because the asserted objective risk of serious harm is not accepted, or any risk would have solutions by way of state protection or internal relocation, taking the case at its highest in credibility terms.

The section creates a presumption that all claims where the applicant is entitled to reside in listed countries are 'clearly unfounded' for reason that there was in general no serious risk of persecution there. The Home Office must certify such claims as clearly unfounded unless satisfied that they are not so. The list in the statute is frequently changed but at the time of writing includes:

Albania	Mali (men)
Bolivia	Mauritius
Bosnia Herzegovina	Moldova
Brazil	Mongolia
Ecuador	Montenegro
Gambia (men)	Nigeria (men)
Ghana (men)	Peru
India	Serbia
Kenya (men)	Sierra Leone (men)
Kosovo	South Africa
Liberia (men)	South Korea
Macedonia	Ukraine
Malawi (men)	

Bangladesh was added to the list but has been removed, as was Sri Lanka. In *R (on the application of Husan)* v. *Secretary of State for the Home Department* [2005] EWHC 189 (Admin), Wilson J concluded at [60] that the inclusion of Bangladesh on the list was unlawful:

> … whether in July 2003, when it was added to the list, or at any time since then, no rational decision-maker could have been satisfied that there was in general in Bangladesh no serious risk of persecution of persons entitled to reside there or that removal of such persons thither would not in general contravene the UK's obligations under the Human Rights Convention. The objective material drove and drives only one rational conclusion; and it is to the contrary.

In *R (on the application of JB (Jamaica))* v. *Secretary of State for the Home Department* [2013] EWCA Civ 666, the Court of Appeal found that the designation of Jamaica as a country in which there is, in general, no risk of persecution was unlawful. The Supreme Court subsequently upheld this decision in *R (on the application of Brown (Jamaica))* v. *Secretary of State for the Home Department* [2015] UKSC 8, holding that for a serious risk of persecution to exist in general, i.e. as a general feature of life in the relevant country, it must be possible to identify a recognisable section of the community to whom it applies, but to require it to be established also that the relevant minority exceeds any particular percentage of the population was objectionable.

As to cases where the claim is viewed by the Secretary of State as so hopeless as to merit certification even without the general presumption, i.e. cases that are weak on their own facts, it is of course not the designation of the country which is determinative. For example, Mr Husan, the claimant whose judicial review succeeded in establishing that Bangladesh should not have appeared on the list, still lost his case on its being clearly unfounded once it was analysed on its own merits.

A claim can be certified as clearly unfounded only if the Secretary of State is reasonably and conscientiously satisfied that the claim could not on any legitimate view of the relevant facts succeed (*Yogathas* [2003] 1 AC 920). Unfortunately, certificates under the post-April 2015 appeals regime can be made even after an appeal has been brought (hitherto, an appeal could not be stifled by certification once lodged).

Decision makers should be slow to find a claim to be clearly unfounded, especially on grounds of credibility. The appropriate test is in fact whether the case, taken at its highest for the purposes of considering whether it is unfounded, can succeed (i.e. an 'even if what you say is true' basis). In practice, in asylum cases the refusal will usually involve non-state actors, where the Home Office refusal turns on the availability of state protection and internal relocation.

Shakeel (Pakistan)

Shakeel is a citizen of Pakistan. He claims asylum four years after arriving in the UK as a student. His claim, based wholly on his own statement and interview and some letters from angry family members, is based on the disapproval that his family have shown for the 'love match' marriage he entered into just before arriving in this country which defied their wish that he enter into an arranged marriage.

The application is refused because the Home Office says that the timing of his asylum claim, only after his sponsor college lost its licence, suggests that it is not credible, while in any event both state protection and internal relocation should be available against risks from a family whose influence could only be limited and local. It additionally certifies his claim as 'clearly unfounded'.

The Home Office has a point here. Possibly its decision on credibility is vulnerable to challenge because it is inconsistent with taking his case at its highest; however, in its alternative reasoning it has assessed his case as if it is true so that is not a material error on its part. Where non-state actors whose influence is very unlikely to be national are the source of feared harm, only the strongest objective country evidence as to their possession of powerful contacts across the whole territory could establish an asylum claim (obviously there is a very significant difference between the capacity of aggrieved family members as opposed to organisations with national networks like the Taliban). There is no sign that such evidence was before the decision maker and so no judicial review could be brought until further representations had been made and refused (or ignored).

Sunil (India)

Sunil is a citizen of India. He is gay and fears social ostracism and physical violence if he returns there. He claimed asylum after studying in the UK for one year as a Tier 4 student. His claim is refused because of the possibility of state protection and internal relocation. The Home Office certifies it as clearly unfounded.

You review his claim against the CG decision of *MD (same-sex oriented males: risk) India CG* [2014] UKUT 65 (IAC). Whether or not the Home Office relies on this decision it will obviously be of central importance to your consideration of the viability of the claim. From the headnote you will see that there is no general risk of violence and that internal relocation to cities where same-sex relationships are tolerated is generally available: so the case against 'clearly unfounded' certification can only get off the ground if you can find evidence to counteract those general assumptions: relevant considerations may be the attitude of his family, his profile, and his ability to work in the self-employed sector.

2.8 ASYLUM CLAIMS FROM EU NATIONALS

It will never be an easy ride to establish an asylum claim from another EU Member State. Nationals of these countries will have a claim for international protection declared inadmissible (i.e. it will not simply be subject to a 'clearly unfounded' certificate; and thus it will not receive any further consideration from the Home Office) unless exceptional circumstances are present. Examples given by Immigration Rules, para.326F are:

- where their country of nationality has derogated from the ECHR;
- where the Council of Ministers has given a warning to a Member State that its conduct amounts to a clear risk of a serious breach of the EU values of respect for human dignity, freedom, democracy, equality, the rule of law and respect for human rights, including the rights of persons belonging to minorities; or
- where the Council has gone further and adopted a decision that the country is in fact in serious breach of those values.

Even if the asylum claim is considered substantively (because the Home Office has a discretion to depart from the Immigration Rules), there may not be an interview, this being one of the scenarios where the possibility of an interview is expressly excluded.

2.9 FRESH CLAIMS

It is possible to make further representations based on asylum grounds if a previous claim has failed (i.e. refugee or humanitarian protection grounds: fresh claims can also be pursued on other human rights grounds though that is beyond the scope of re-accreditation). A 'fresh claim' is essentially a new claim for protection that differs substantially from the previous claim such that it has a real prospect of success. It may also be a new claim based on human rights grounds relating to relationships established in this country.

Key information about fresh claims:

- They are made by way of 'further submissions', i.e. written representations accompanied by any documentary evidence available to support them.
- A form is available from the GOV.UK website, but its use is not mandatory.

- Immigration Rules, para.353A prevents a person being removed from the UK while the fresh claim is being considered.

The only remedy against rejection of further representations as a fresh claim is judicial review: these challenges are normally heard by the Upper Tribunal (Immigration and Asylum Chamber).

Further representations must be lodged in person in Liverpool. As can be seen in para.1.4 of the Home Office guidance, *Further Submissions* (from the Operational Guidance, Asylum Policy, Asylum Decision Making Guidance (Asylum Instructions), a strict line is taken on attendance:

> Whilst claimants are required to make an appointment to submit protection-based further submissions in person in Liverpool, they are not required to bring children with them. It is therefore unlikely that the requirement to lodge further submission in person would adversely impact on a child to such an extent that it would override the public interest in reducing the risk of fraud and maintaining effective immigration control. However, caseworkers should consider any exceptional arguments as to why someone cannot travel to Liverpool to attend in person on the basis of the interests of children, for example:
>
> - the claimant cannot make suitable childcare arrangements
> - travelling to Liverpool would force them to take the child out of school
>
> Any decision to allow a postal claim must be approved by a senior case worker.

The exceptions to a trip to Liverpool under the guidance are evidence-backed cases of disability or severe illness preventing travel, ongoing judicial review proceedings, imminent removal where the individual is detained, cases in the family returns process, and individuals who have come to light through enforcement action.

The main stages of the process are as below:

- Will the Home Office grant the application outright?
- If not, will the Home Office at least agree it is a fresh claim?

  - If yes, appeal.
  - If no, judicial review.

It is important to understand that in these cases, one is arguing that a fresh claim should be recognised. It is quite wrong to say that one has made a fresh claim, because that is not a correct statement of the legal position until the Home Office has accepted those representations as being such a claim.

2.9.1   Test under the Immigration Rules

The Immigration Rules set out the circumstances in which 'further submissions' will be accepted as constituting a fresh claim for asylum or human rights protection.

> **353.** When a human rights or asylum claim has been refused … and any appeal relating to that claim is no longer pending, the decision maker will consider any further submissions

and, if rejected, will then determine whether they amount to a fresh claim. The submissions will amount to a fresh claim if they are significantly different from the material that has previously been considered. The submissions will only be significantly different if the content:

(i) had not already been considered; and
(ii) taken together with the previously considered material, created a realistic prospect of success, notwithstanding its rejection. This paragraph does not apply to claims made overseas.

Rule 353 therefore requires the decision maker to consider:

• whether the material upon which the fresh claim is based has already been considered by the Home Office;
• whether that material is significantly different from anything previously evaluated;
• whether the new material, taken with all of the claims and decisions previously made, creates a realistic prospect of success on appeal.

To support the contention that the legal test has been met, it will usually be necessary to show one of the following:

• There is evidence of risk of serious harm that was not previously established, e.g. due to a change of government in the country of origin or a new CG decision shows that a person with your client's essential characteristics, as accepted by the Home Office or on appeal, is at risk of serious harm.
• The law has changed requiring, for instance, a different approach to be taken to the claim (e.g. the understanding of the approach to be taken to asylum claims based on suppression of fundamental rights to avoid persecution changed radically with *HJ (Iran)* v. *Secretary of State for the Home Department* [2010] UKSC 31).
• There is new evidence relating to the original claim that suggests that the previous decision and/or appeal was incorrectly decided.
• There is a different kind of claim altogether based on private and family life in the UK.

When the further submissions are considered by the Home Office, a decision maker must first decide whether or not to grant leave on the basis of the representations and new evidence. It is only on deciding not to do so that the decision maker must then go on to consider the fresh claim test in the Immigration Rules, para.353. The Home Office guidance *Further Submissions* addresses the relevant procedures.

Further submissions that meet these requirements will be treated as a fresh claim. The decision under para.353 is not therefore a substantive decision on whether leave is to be granted or not, as the Home Office will have refused to grant status before considering the fresh claim test – it is simply a decision as to whether the further submissions merit a further appeal. The appeal consequences vary depending whether the decision is before or after April 2015.

In the era of old style appeals, the Home Office had to make a fresh immigration decision to give effect to its conclusion that the claim was a fresh one which merited another appeal hearing – that immigration decision would then trigger a right of appeal to the Immigration Tribunal in accordance with NIAA 2002, s.82.

Under the post-April 2015 appeals system, the Home Office will in fact have arguably refused an asylum claim, and so the requirement for an appeal under s.82 is satisfied: it will have to be seen over time whether the courts accept this approach. For now they have taken the view that the para.353 procedure still acts as a gateway whereby the Home Office rather than the First-tier Tribunal determines access to the appeals system where further representations are lodged (see *R (on the application of Robinson)* v. *Secretary of State for the Home Department (paragraph 353 – Waqar applied) (IJR)* [2016] UKUT 133 (IAC)).

Whether the case arises under the saved or relevant provisions of NIAA 2002, the Home Office may be able to bar access to the First-tier Tribunal because the matters now sought to be raised could have been raised earlier – by issuing a certificate under NIAA 2002, s.96. This requires the Home Office to demonstrate that:

- the asylum seeker was previously notified of a right of appeal or received a section 120 notice, and did not raise the claim although it would have been possible to do so;
- there is no satisfactory reason for the claim not having been raised earlier;
- certification is appropriate as a matter of discretion, e.g. having regard to considerations such as the best interests of any dependent children.

2.9.2 Case law on fresh claims

In the case of *WM (DRC)* v. *Secretary of State for the Home Department* [2006] EWCA Civ 1495 the Court of Appeal gave guidance on the task of the Secretary of State when considering further representations and held that:

- the Secretary of State should consider whether an immigration judge on a future appeal would consider that the test was satisfied, bearing in mind that the test was a 'somewhat modest' one; and
- the reliability of any new material is an important consideration, as are any findings by a previous judge as to the claimant's honesty and reliability as a witness.

Although the test is in law a 'relatively modest' one, it can nevertheless be an uphill struggle to engage the interest of a judge in these challenges. This is particularly the case where the claimant was previously found to be dishonest. The challenge is therefore obtaining good quality evidence on which to base the claim.

Dinu (Sri Lanka)

Dinu is from Sri Lanka and made an unsuccessful claim for asylum in 2009 on the basis of his involvement with the Liberation Tigers of Tamil Eelam (LTTE). His claim was rejected at that time both on the basis that it was fabricated and on the basis that even if it was not, there was no risk on return because of the peace process.

Even at the height of the conflict between the Sri Lankan government and the LTTE it would have been very hard for Dinu to make out a successful fresh claim on the basis of his own evidence or deterioration in the country situation because of the earlier adverse credibility findings. He would have needed independent evidence to suggest that the credibility findings were in fact wrong, such as compelling documentary evidence, or evidence that notwithstanding his poor credibility, his profile is such that he would now be at risk (perhaps because of the regime's current attitude to failed asylum seekers).

In *ZT (Kosovo)* v. *Secretary of State for the Home Department* [2009] UKHL 6, the House of Lords considered the interaction of the tests for a fresh human rights claim and a clearly unfounded certificate imposed under NIAA 2002, s.94.

The two tests are similar sounding to the layman:

- Section 94: Does the claim exceed the relatively modest 'clearly unfounded' threshold?
- Rule 353: Does the claim have a realistic prospect of success?

There has been a certain amount of judicial musing over the potential differences between these two tests. Whatever else can be said, the basic difference for judicial reviews against the two kinds of decision is that:

- on a challenge to a 'clearly unfounded' decision, judges must take the case at its highest and essentially determine the strength of the case for themselves, albeit based on the evidence that was before the Home Office;
- in a fresh claim case, judges are more bound by the traditional limits of a public law challenge, i.e. they need to be persuaded that relevant evidence has been overlooked or that the conclusions on the evidence that has been assessed are irrational in the sense of being so unreasonable that no reasonable person could have come to them.

As discussed in *R (on the application of YH)* v. *Secretary of State for the Home Department* [2010] EWCA Civ 116 the critical question is whether anxious scrutiny has been given to the case, being:

the need for decisions to show by their reasoning that every factor which might tell in favour of an applicant has been properly taken into account.

88

Mirza

Mirza claims asylum and his claim is certified as 'clearly unfounded' under NIAA 2002, s.94. However, he is not immediately removed from the UK. In the meantime, he manages to acquire documentary evidence that assists his case.

Once this further material is put forward, the Home Office will either issue a further 'clearly unfounded' decision, or it may treat the new material as further representations which have to pass the test to be a fresh human rights claim.

If the further representations are assessed by the Home Office under Immigration Rules, para.353, applying the 'realistic prospect of success' test, and it decides that the test is not passed, then it will issue a new decision stating that the asylum claim is refused on its merits and that it does not merit recognition as a fresh claim. On that view there will be no right of appeal to the Tribunal. The only remedy would be an application for judicial review.

It may be that the new evidence is something which should have been disclosed by the Home Office during earlier appeal proceedings. Information that was not before the First-tier Tribunal when dismissing an appeal (such as the likelihood of officials in the country of origin discovering the individual's return because of Prison Service Order 4360 which requires prisons to inform the embassies of nationals of certain countries of the national's full name, date of birth, offence and, if available, sentence length) may bring alive a further asylum claim (*XB* v. *Secretary of State for the Home Department* [2015] EWHC 2557 (Admin)).

2.9.3   What makes a viable fresh claim?

Key issues are likely to be:

- whether evidence was previously available;
- whether the claim arises from a change of circumstances independent of the individual in question.

2.9.4   Previously unavailable evidence

The Home Office will always look carefully at whether material now provided could have been put forward on an earlier appeal. The old case of *Ladd* v. *Marshall* [1954] 1 WLR 1489 (CA) lays down the general test in English law for the approach to take in relation to admitting new material: its previous unavailability, significance and apparent credibility. Evidence is admissible where:

- the fresh evidence could not have been obtained with reasonable diligence for use at the trial;
- if given, it probably would have had an important influence on the result;
- it is apparently credible although not necessarily incontrovertible.

In asylum cases it is recognised that this test should not be operated too strictly because of the fundamental issues at stake: nevertheless, these three considerations are likely to be in the mind of any judge who considers a claim based on fresh evidence that might have been produced sooner, and common sense dictates that these considerations should be carefully addressed: very good reasons will need to be given as to why the material was not previously submitted.

However, even if evidence could have been reasonably obtained sooner, there may be a good explanation for a failure to do so, e.g. where the claimant was poorly represented by a previous adviser, who made highly prejudicial mistakes. A new adviser may be able to resurrect such a case, but unless the mistake is a very obvious one it will probably be necessary to pursue a complaint against the previous advisers via the appropriate complaints procedures and onwards to the relevant regulator. In *FP (Iran)* v. *Secretary of State for the Home Department* [2007] EWCA Civ 13 it was held at [46] that (particularly in asylum cases):

> there is no general principle of law which fixes a party with the procedural errors of his or her representative.

The case of *R (on the application of Gungor)* v. *Secretary of State for the Home Department* [2004] EWHC 2117 (Admin) shows the court accepting this possibility. Care needs to be taken in making allegations against a former representative, bearing in mind that the manner in which a case has been run may be down to tactical choice, not negligent error.

Decision makers sometimes reject newly submitted evidence that could have been obtained sooner (with appropriate diligence) by suggesting that it is not credible that such evidence would not have been produced sooner if the asylum seeker really believed that showed them to be at risk of serious harm.

It may be that the reason that evidence was not previously available is because the asylum seeker went through the DFT process so speedily that they lacked a fair opportunity to collect evidence in support of their case, so bear in mind the various flaws identified in that system discussed above: if the original appeal decision is set aside under the rule 32 procedure (see **2.4**), then the Home Office will be unable to rely on the findings of the appellate process and so the main barrier to further representations being accepted as a fresh claim will have been removed.

Sometimes an appeal fails because a judge takes a harsher line than was expected: the asylum seeker may be taken by surprise by the judge's findings in relation to an issue that had not been raised by the Home Office refusal letter, or evidence that the asylum seeker believed would be adequate to prove a particular point might nevertheless be rejected. In such cases the provision of further evidence may overcome the criticisms made of the case so far, particularly where it concretely establishes that the asylum seeker falls within a particular category, e.g. as a lawyer, teacher or political activist.

Many fresh claims rely on new evidence that has been obtained regarding the same risk on return as was previously relied upon. It may show that a claim that was previously disbelieved is in fact credible, or that a claim that was found credible, but not to demonstrate risk, is in fact well founded. Examples might include:

- new documents that post-date the previous case that have been obtained from the home country, such as an arrest warrant, a witness statement from an independent and objective source, particularly a figure of expertise or authority, or a newspaper article;
- new witness evidence from within the UK, e.g. members of the asylum seeker's political party based in this country or visiting here, or family members who have recently arrived.

The problem with producing new evidence is that if the claimant has already been found to be untruthful (and therefore capable of ongoing deceit), any new material that they want to put forward will be tainted by their own (lack of) credibility. Accordingly, it needs to come from an independent source to stand much chance of being accepted by the Home Office or a judge.

Carefully analyse the reasons why the claim was previously rejected in the last relevant decision, which will usually have been an appeal hearing.

- If the claim was rejected because of a lack of objective evidence showing the client to be at risk, then it may be sufficient to simply put forward further country reports or expert evidence.
- If the claim was rejected because the key parts of the account were not believed to be true, then work out the reasons for this – was it down to inconsistencies in the way the case was put across, or because it was viewed as implausible when read against the country evidence? Reasoning based on the latter thinking is more likely to be assailable via further representations.
- If there were significant discrepancies in the account as previously put, then an explanation needs to be found: medical evidence showing that the asylum seeker suffered from mental health or memory difficulties at the date of the last interview/appeal hearing is the most likely form of assistance.

In practical terms, it is important to be careful about how any new evidence is presented. For example, an original document with a professionally well-written and certified translation, backed up by an authentication report by an expert, is more likely to work than a badly faxed and poorly translated document.

Takunda

Takunda made a claim for asylum in 2008 and it was dismissed. He was found to have fabricated his account. Even his name and nationality were not accepted as genuine. At that time, he had no documentary evidence to support his claim.

He later makes a fresh claim, having in the meantime acquired some documentary evidence that supports important parts of his case, including his claimed identity. He did not seek to acquire this earlier because his representative did not suggest it and he had not realised it could be important.

> If this evidence is from an independent source and cannot be easily dismissed as itself being fabricated then he may well have a good case for why the evidence should be considered and a good fresh claim.

2.9.5 *Sur place* style arguments

As well as new evidence, there may well be new developments in the country of proposed removal that mean the case must be looked at afresh. These may be flagged up by news from the country or by a new CG case pointing to changes in the relevant risk factors.

One contemporary example is to be found with Sri Lanka. During the peace process many claims for asylum failed, but when that broke down and then ended, many Sri Lankans successfully put forward fresh claims. The situation changed again with the military defeat of the LTTE, potentially undermining those fresh claims. Subsequently new information came to light that notwithstanding the end of the civil war, the regime was continuing to torture those whom they saw as separatists.

These Sri Lankan claims often illustrate the potential problem with putting forward a new claim based on a change of circumstances (or on new evidence for that matter). If the claimant was previously found to be dishonest and, for example, was found not really to have been a member of the LTTE or not really to have been harassed and detained by the authorities, then a fresh claim is unlikely to get far. The Home Office and then a judge on judicial review are very likely to find that there is still no risk as there is no reason for the authorities to be interested in the claimant.

However, where there have been positive findings of fact, for example in a case where it was found that the claimant was detained and that there might be a record of that detention, but that there was no risk because of the peace process, then the claimant might have a sound fresh claim.

Iraq is another country where the CGs have ebbed and flowed over time. From around 2008 (when the run of test cases examining the internal armed conflict there were decided) until 2015, it was very difficult to succeed in an asylum claim because it was often presumed that even if there were fears of persecution that prevailed across the south and centre of the country, relocation would still be possible to the Kurdish north; in April 2012 with the ruling in *MK (documents – relocation) Iraq CG* [2012] UKUT 126 (IAC) this position hardened.

However, the decision in *AA (Article 15(c)) Iraq CG* [2015] UKUT 544 (IAC) on 30 October 2015 suddenly opened up the possibilities, because of a recognition that indiscriminate violence was now so serious that civilians would generally be at risk in the 'contested areas' and that relocation to the Kurdish north was possible only for those originating in those areas. So long as critical aspects of their claims were accepted such as their home area, many asylum seekers whose claims failed when measured against the CGs in force from 2008 to 2015 would have a viable claim applying the guidelines in *AA*.

Dinu (Sri Lanka)

In the earlier example of Dinu from Sri Lanka, his first asylum claim had been dismissed on both credibility and future risk grounds.

If it has been accepted that he had been telling the truth about several detentions he had suffered then his claim might still have been rejected at the time that the peace process was going on.

Assuming he was not removed in the meantime, the breakdown of the peace process might well have been a sufficient change of circumstances that a fresh claim could have succeeded.

Practice point

When preparing further representations arguing that a fresh asylum claim should be recognised you will need to analyse the issues that follow:

- The determination on any appeal is the factual basis for taking the case forwards. It is only facts which were accepted in that appeal which you can rely upon in the future, unless you have new independent evidence which undermines the rejection of aspects of the case.
- If there was no appeal, then the original asylum refusal stands as the starting point: do not presume that judges will not treat it as a lawful treatment of the claim just because it might have been appealed.
- There may be facts of the case which were accepted on appeal, or at least not rejected, which now have greater relevance due to fresh evidence, a new head of claim, or changing CGs (e.g. in an Iraqi case it might have been accepted that the client's father was in a pro-Saddam Hussein militia association, a factor that might not have assisted an asylum claim before the fall of that regime, but which in the modern era might prevent relocation to the Kurdish north).
- If there is new medical evidence, is it partially reliant on the doctor's acceptance of facts that were rejected on appeal? If so, it is seriously compromised.
- If there is new documentary evidence particular to the client (arrest warrants, confirmation of deaths in the family, letters from the community abroad):

    - Is it consistent with known facts in the case?
    - Does it meaningfully add to the case?
    - Is it genuinely independent of the client? If a client was found non-credible on appeal, then it is difficult to see that any document the client now brings forward carries much weight because it is not independent of that client: so can your firm carry out the enquiries directly in the country of origin, or via an agent, or expert, to remove the client from the chain of evidence gathering?

93

2.10   BENEFITS OF RECOGNITION AS A REFUGEE

2.10.1   Refugees and immigration status

When an asylum claim succeeds under the Refugee Convention, the applicant will be recognised as a refugee and five years' leave to remain will be granted (para.339Q(i)). Prior to 30 August 2005, indefinite leave to remain (ILR) was granted. The grant of refugee status will be made by way of a biometric residence permit. There will be no conditions on the grant of leave.

2.10.2   Settlement protection

Where the refugee reaches the end of the five-year period, the refugee can apply for settlement under the settlement protection route (Immigration Rules, para.339R).

Applications for settlement for refugees (and for those granted humanitarian protection) who have completed their five years of limited leave are made on Form SET(P). There are no requirements (e.g. under Immigration Rules, Appendix KoLL) to meet or fees to pay.

The Home Office will then consider whether there are any grounds to revoke or not renew the status under para.339A (i.e. the cessation provisions), and if not, any reasons to refuse or delay ILR for reasons of criminal conduct (para.339R(iii)).

There are criminality provisos similar to those elsewhere in the Immigration Rules (if any of these bars settlement, then there can be further grants of limited leave under para.339Q(i), until the relevant misdemeanour is sufficiently historic not to offend the bar on granting leave):

- having been sentenced to a term of imprisonment exceeding four years;
- having been sentenced to a term of imprisonment from one to four years unless a period of 15 years has passed;
- having been sentenced to a term of imprisonment of up to 12 months unless a period of seven years has passed since the end of the sentence;
- in the view of the Secretary of State caused serious harm by their offending or persistently offended and shown a particular disregard for the law;
- having received a non-custodial sentence or other out-of-court disposal recorded in their criminal record where they have been convicted of, or admitted, an offence in the last 24 months;
- presence not being conducive to the public good for reasons of character, conduct and associations for reasons falling short of those already identified.

If none of these bars to settlement applies, ILR will be granted without an active review of the applicant's circumstances or consideration of current risk.

If, during the five-year period, a Minister has issued a ministerial declaration that a particular country is now considered to be generally safe, all refugees of that nationality will have their cases individually reviewed, with a right of appeal against any decision to revoke refugee status. The burden will rest with the Home Office to establish that the individual is no longer a refugee. Assurances have been given that there will be few declarations, and there has been none to date. There have been ministerial suggestions that refugee status may be more aggressively reviewed in the future.

The asylum policy instruction, *Settlement Protection* (under the Operational Guidance, Asylum Policy collection, Asylum Decision Making Guidance (Asylum Instructions)) provides guidance on the practicalities.

Yasmine

Yasmine was recognised as a refugee by the Home Office in a decision made around five years ago. She comes to the office to request your help with a settlement application. She tells you that she was prosecuted successfully for benefits fraud three years ago and received a suspended sentence of two years' imprisonment about a year ago after a trial. She wants to make a settlement application given she has spent five years in the UK as a refugee.

You must advise Yasmine that as she has been convicted of an offence for which a 'non-custodial sentence' was imposed within the 24 months prior to her (proposed) application being decided, she has to wait until she can be confident that the application will not be determined within 24 months of her conviction. To avoid becoming an overstayer she needs to apply to extend her refugee leave under Immigration Rules, rule 339Q.

2.10.3 Refugee family reunion

The origin of the Home Office policy on family reunion lies in the Final Act of the United Nations Conference of Plenipotentiaries on the Status of Refugees and Stateless Persons. As set out at Annex I of the UNHCR Handbook, the Conference, considering that the family was 'the natural and fundamental group of society' and that unity of the family was 'an essential right of the refugee' recommended that 'Governments ... take the necessary measures for the protection of the refugee's family, especially with a view to ... ensuring that the unity of the refugee's family is maintained particularly in cases where the head of the family has fulfilled the necessary conditions for admission to a particular country'.

2.10.3.1 Pre-existing family

The refugee family reunion rules in Part 11 of the Immigration Rules promote the reunion of a recognised refugee (and those granted humanitarian protection) with family members that were left behind at the time that the refugee fled his or her country of origin (sometimes referred to as the 'pre-flight family'). The principal benefit of these rules is that there are no English language, maintenance and accommodation requirements to meet. There is no exemption however in respect of the general grounds of refusal.

The rules cover the following pre-flight family members:

- spouses or civil partners (para.352A);
- unmarried or same-sex partner (para.352AA);
- children (para.352D);
- child of a relative (para.319X).

There are various requirements:

- The applicant must not fall under the exclusion clauses.
- In partner cases, the relationship must be genuine and subsisting with an intention to live together permanently. Additionally, in unmarried partner cases the parties must have been 'living together in a relationship akin to either a marriage or a civil partnership which has subsisted for two years or more', i.e. a relationship of two years plus cohabitation, not two years of cohabitation.
- The family relationship must be 'pre-flight', i.e. the marriage or civil partnership must not have taken place after the person granted asylum left the country of his former habitual residence in order to seek asylum, or the relationship must have been extant at that time in unmarried partner cases, or, *vis-à-vis* children, they must have been part of the family unit of the refugee at the time that the refugee left.
- Children must be under 18, unmarried and without a new family unit, and not be leading an independent life.
- The sponsor must be someone 'who is currently a refugee', so they should not prematurely apply to naturalise, for British citizens and persons with ILR will have to satisfy the full rigours of the Immigration Rules for non-refugees.

These are not grants of leave to remain in line with the refugee such that the family member receives refugee status: their status is derivative from that of the refugee. Visas issued under these rules are often wrongly endorsed with a condition that the person has no recourse to public funds. The rules do not allow for such a prohibition. Errors can be corrected by writing to RCU EC Errors, 15th Floor, Apollo House, 36 Wellesley Road, Croydon CR9 3RR (see ECB19 in the Entry Clearance Guidance Correcting an incorrect endorsement).

The British Red Cross can assist where necessary with family tracing, and in making arrangements for the family to travel to the UK, including help with travel costs.

Practice point

In a family reunion case it may be necessary to provide the following:

- a detailed account of the family's migration movements over time;
- a history of financial support and the various means by which it has been given; explanation for any lack of evidence;
- where relevant, detailed information as to precisely how they regained contact with one another;
- an explanation of conditions in the host country;

- a clear explanation for any historic dishonesty regarding a family member's existence or of any failure to mention a particular family member earlier in the sponsor's dealings with the authorities in this country.

2.10.3.2 'Post-flight' and other family members

New and existing family members not entitled to family reunion, for example because they do not satisfy the 'pre-flight' relationship requirements, can be sponsored under other provisions of the Immigration Rules by refugees with limited leave as such:

- Spouses and civil partners can apply under para.319L.
- Same-sex partners can apply under para.319O.
- Children can apply under para.319R.
- Parents, grandparents and other dependent relatives can apply under para.319V.

These paragraphs contain requirements rather like those which preceded the introduction of Appendix FM for spouses and other family members. Their essential requirements are English language proficiency (subject to provisos if over 65 or having physical or mental conditions preventing them meeting the test), that the relationship is established as genuine, and that there will be adequate accommodation and maintenance available.

Adult dependent relatives have various possible routes under which to apply depending (mainly) on their marital status, with much more demanding requirements if they are aged under 65 years of age in which case they must be living alone outside the UK in the most exceptional compassionate circumstances.

2.10.3.3 Applications outside the rules

Where a family member cannot meet these requirements, it may be possible to make an application outside the rules, if family life can be shown to be established and that the decision interferes with it, if there are compelling circumstances that justify departure from the Immigration Rules.

2.10.4 Travel documents

Recognised refugees are entitled to a Refugee Convention Travel Document (CTD), under Article 28 of the Refugee Convention.

These CTDs are blue in colour and resemble a passport in appearance. They can be used for travel to any country that is a signatory to the Refugee Convention other than the country from which the holder is a refugee.

Applications, which now include an application for a biometric residence permit, are made on Form TD112. The cost is £72 (£46 for a child under 16). The document will be valid for the length of the refugee's leave, or for 10 years if the refugee is settled (five years for a child).

Pre-existing family members of refugees are often issued a CTD on request but this does not constitute recognition as a refugee and does not entitle the bearer to bring in other further family members under refugee family reunion rules (see *MS (Somalia) and others* v. *Secretary of State for the Home Department* [2010] EWCA Civ 1236).

2.11 REFUGEES AND WORK, BENEFITS AND EDUCATION

Any person with refugee status, indefinite leave to remain (ILR), exceptional leave to remain (ELR), humanitarian protection, or discretionary leave has the right to work in the UK and does not need to ask permission from, nor informs the Home Office before taking up employment or setting up a business.

A refugee or person granted humanitarian protection may apply for a loan to assist with their integration into the community; for a rent deposit, household items, or for education and training for work: see generally the government guidance on refugee integration loans (**www.gov.uk/refugee-integration-loan/overview**) for more details.

Refugees will be treated as home students for the purpose of tuition fees and student support, as will their dependants who were pre-flight family members. Those granted discretionary leave will be treated as overseas students. They will have to pay higher fees and will not be entitled to student support.

2.12 BENEFITS OF HUMANITARIAN PROTECTION

2.12.1 Immigration status

'Subsidiary protection' status (as it is called in the Qualification Directive) or humanitarian protection (HP) as it is called in the UK is in most practical respects equivalent to refugee status. A person who qualifies for HP will be granted leave for five years.

Holders of HP who have completed five years of leave will be eligible to apply for ILR under the settlement protection route as for refugees (see above). Individuals should apply for settlement shortly before the expiry of their HP leave.

2.12.2 Family reunion and travel documents

Those with subsidiary protection are entitled to family reunion on the same terms as refugees.

A person with HP can obtain travel documents (Immigration Rules, para.344A(ii)):

> ... where that person is unable to obtain a national passport or other identity documents which enable him to travel, unless compelling reasons of national security or public order otherwise require.

If such a person can theoretically obtain such documents but has not done so, then a travel document may be issued if (para.344A(iii)):

> ... he can show that he has made reasonable attempts to obtain a national passport or identity document and there are serious humanitarian reasons for travel.

The document issued will be a Certificate of Travel, which does not carry the weight of a CTD. A number of countries, currently including Austria, Belgium, Denmark, France, Germany, Greece, Iceland, Italy, Luxembourg, the Netherlands, Portugal, South Africa, Spain, Switzerland, do not accept Certificates of Travel.

CHAPTER 3

Human rights law and asylum appeals

We deal generally with the ECHR in this section. We do not aim to deal with private and family life claims in any great detail because these are outside the scope of publicly funded work.

3.1 HUMAN RIGHTS ACT 1998

The Human Rights Act 1998 (HRA 1998) came into force in the UK on 2 October 2000. It brought the ECHR into domestic law and made the rights protected by the ECHR directly enforceable in the British courts.

The Act has had a very important impact on immigration and asylum law.

3.1.1 Interpretation of statute

Decisions and other material emanating from the European Court of Human Rights (ECtHR, often referred to by the shorthand 'Strasbourg' as this is where the court sits) must be taken into account by judges here (HRA 1998, s.2(1)). The English judiciary has indicated that it will aim to follow the Strasbourg approach. This is what Lord Slynn said in *Alconbury* [2001] 2 WLR 1389 at [26]:

> In the absence of some special circumstances it seems to me that the court should follow any clear and constant jurisprudence of the European Court of Human Rights.

Section 3(1) of HRA 1998 is the key to the future interpretation of English statute:

> So far as it is possible to do so, primary legislation and subordinate legislation must be read and given effect in a way which is compatible with the Convention rights.

The system of immigration control as a whole is compatible with HRA 1998 so long as cases can succeed inside or outside the rules (i.e. the rules do not themselves have to recognise every kind of application that could succeed, so long as discretion will be exercised to make good any gaps outside the rules): see e.g. *Mahad (Ethiopia)* v. *Entry Clearance Officer* [2009] UKSC 16 and, in the era following the July 2012 changes to the Immigration Rules, *R (on the application of MM and others)* v.

Secretary of State for the Home Department [2014] EWCA Civ 985. At the time of writing that decision is on appeal to the Supreme Court so we must all await the last word from the domestic courts as to the relationship between the Immigration Rules and the ECHR itself.

3.1.2 Effect on public authorities

Section 6(1) of HRA 1998 demonstrates that the ambit of the Act is in no way limited to the review of statutory material – rather, any acts of a public authority may be challenged if they conflict with the fundamental rights and freedoms recognised in the ECHR:

> It is unlawful for a public authority to act in a way which is incompatible with a Convention right.

This includes the Home Office and also the courts and tribunals, including the Immigration Tribunal. Do note that the proper ground of appeal is not incompatibility with the ECHR, but incompatibility with HRA 1998.

Under HRA 1998 itself, a person who claims that a public authority has acted (or proposes to act) incompatibly with the ECHR brings proceedings against the authority under HRA 1998 in the appropriate court or tribunal, or may rely on the ECHR right or rights concerned in any legal proceedings (that is to say, the Immigration Tribunal will normally be the appropriate venue; otherwise the ECHR may be relied on in any judicial review proceedings) (s.7(1)). Such an individual has to demonstrate that they would be a victim of the act to have standing (s.7(3)).

Under the post-April 2015 appeals system, people will enjoy a right of appeal to the Tribunal, so long as they establish that the decision made against them amounts to the refusal of an international protection or human rights claim.

3.1.3 Damages and compensation

Under HRA 1998, s.8(2) damages may be awarded only by a court which has power to award damages, or to order the payment of compensation in civil proceedings. The Immigration Tribunal lacks powers of this kind: however, the High Court and the Court of Appeal do possess them.

Section 9(3) of HRA 1998 indicates that the opportunity to obtain damages for judicial errors regarding human rights will be limited, except, perhaps, in bail cases:

> In proceedings under this Act in respect of a judicial act done in good faith, damages may not be awarded otherwise than to compensate a person to the extent required by Article 5(5) of the Convention.

Section 8 of HRA 1998 authorises the payment of compensation where this is necessary to afford just satisfaction, taking into account the principles applied by the ECtHR in relation to the award of compensation under Article 41 of the ECHR. There are three preconditions to an award of just satisfaction:

1. A violation of a relevant human right.
2. Where there is no adequate remedy under domestic law (this can often be the case in public law proceedings, as discussed below).
3. 'Just satisfaction' to the injured party requires an award.

The issues are discussed in *R (on the application of Greenfield)* v. *Secretary of State for the Home Department* [2005] UKHL 14. Generally speaking, awards will be moderate, and more in line with those made in Strasbourg than in analogous domestic proceedings: *Anufrijeva* v. *London Borough of Southwark* [2003] EWCA Civ 1406.

The great value of HRA 1998 damages is that they may be available against a public authority which could not otherwise be realistically challenged for misconduct which is merely negligent. There is a potential action under the common law, for misfeasance in public office, but such an action has a very significant obstacle to surmount: the need to show targeted malice by a public officer, i.e. conduct specifically intended to injure a person or persons, or at least reckless conduct (*Three Rivers DC* v. *Governor and Company of the Bank of England (No 3)* [2003] 2 AC 1 (HL)).

3.1.4 Remedies and 'human rights' arguments

When a migrant is refused permission to enter or remain in the UK (including refusals of entry clearance) in circumstances where that decision involves the refusal of a human rights claim, there will be a right of appeal to the First-tier Tribunal under the relevant provisions of NIAA 2002.

Challenges to breaches of human rights in the UK (e.g. regarding conditions of detention in reception centres, withdrawal of support or accommodation leading to destitution sufficiently severe to raise Article 3 issues, etc.) will go via the judicial review route.

3.2 EUROPEAN CONVENTION ON HUMAN RIGHTS

The ECtHR has a very useful website with the full texts of the Convention and Protocols and the Rules of Court along with all of the judgments and admissibility decisions of the court and the old Commission. It is found at **www.echr.coe.int**. It includes a search engine, known as HUDOC.

3.2.1 Human Rights Act 1998 and Article 1

Section 1 of HRA 1998 explains which ECHR rights are incorporated. The rights and fundamental freedoms protected are summarised: Article 1 of the ECHR requires the contracting states to secure to everyone 'within their jurisdiction' the ECHR rights and freedoms. This was not actually incorporated into domestic law by HRA 1998 – nor was Article 13, the requirement to provide an 'effective remedy'.

Practice point

Although it is important to know about all the rights enshrined in the ECHR, the most useful and frequently relied on by immigration lawyers are Articles 3 and 8.
The other rights are frequently relied on but very rarely successfully so.

3.2.2 Categories of rights

The rights and freedoms dealt with by the ECHR can be categorised in three ways:

- torture;
- family life;
- degrading treatment.

3.2.3 Standard of proof: 'real risk'

The standard of proof for assessing whether the likelihood of a human rights breach is sufficient for the ECHR to be engaged is whether there is a 'real risk' of the claimed problem actually happening, or 'substantial grounds for believing' a breach will occur. The test is essentially the same as the 'reasonable degree of likelihood' test in refugee cases. Both can conveniently be summarised as asking whether there is a real risk of the feared event coming to pass.

However, in some cases, the claimant may assert that he will be subject to a generalised risk of a breach of his rights, e.g. by being exposed to poor conditions in a country's prisons system or generalised problems in military service in a given country. Then it is necessary to show that anyone in the applicant's circumstances would face a certain minimum level of risk. The relevant test has been expressed as asking whether there are gross, flagrant and systematic breaches of human rights extant: only then will it be established that all members of the relevant category are at risk (we revert to this theme when we consider degrading treatment/punishment in the context of prison conditions at **3.2.6.4**). The words of the judge in *Hariri* v. *Secretary of State for the Home Department* [2003] EWCA Civ 807 at [8], where that test was considered, may be thought more helpful to cite:

> the situation to which the appellant would be returning was one in which such violence was generally or consistently happening.

3.2.4 Applicability of the ECHR in immigration cases

The protected ECHR rights are universal and intended to apply to everyone within the United Kingdom's jurisdiction, not just to British nationals. Furthermore, the preamble of the ECHR describes the rights as having a universal quality – they apply to all persons regardless of nationality, race, sex or other 'status'.

There are two broad categories of case where the ECHR has an impact in the field of immigration and asylum law, identified by the House of Lords in *R (on the application of Ullah)* v. *Special Adjudicator* [2004] UKHL 26.

It was this case that established definitely in UK law that all of the Articles of the ECHR can potentially be relied on in foreign cases. The Strasbourg cases of *Soering* v. *UK* (1989) 11 EHRR 439 and *Chahal* v. *UK* (1997) 23 EHRR 413 had already established that Article 3 could operate to prevent removal where there was a real risk of a future breach of human rights. However, for Articles other than Article 3, it is necessary to show that there would be a 'flagrant breach' of the right or rights in question, or that the right or rights would be completely nullified. This is sometimes referred to as the *Devaseelan* test after the starred determination ([2002] UKIAT 702) that first set out this test, later approved by the House of Lords in *EM (Lebanon)* v. *Secretary of State for the Home Department* [2008] UKHL 64 (see the test's practical application at **1.10.4**).

There are some principles which are overarching and may be relevant in the interpretation of any of the ECHR rights. As the ECtHR said in *Pretty* v. *UK* (2002) 35 EHRR 1, para.65:

> The very essence of the Convention is respect for human dignity and human freedom.

This is worth bearing in mind whenever, for example, an old or vulnerable person faces living alone in circumstances that threaten their dignity.

3.2.5 Article 2: right to life

Article 2 of the ECHR is as follows:

1. Everyone's right to life shall be protected by law. No one shall be deprived of his life intentionally save in the execution of a sentence of a court following his conviction of a crime for which this penalty is provided by law.
2. Deprivation of life shall not be regarded as inflicted in contravention of this article when it results from the use of force which is no more than absolutely necessary:
   (a) in defence of any person from unlawful violence;
   (b) in order to effect a lawful arrest or to prevent the escape of a person lawfully detained;
   (c) in action lawfully taken for the purpose of quelling a riot or insurrection.

So far, in immigration cases, the Article tends to be argued in addition to Article 3, for the simple reason that death or execution would be rather likely to be considered in the modern world to cross the threshold for Article 3 ill treatment in any event.

There has not yet been a removal case in the UK or at Strasbourg that has succeeded on Article 2 but not on Article 3. It is worth remembering that in *Soering* the claimant feared execution and the experience of 'death row', and his case succeeded on the latter ground only.

Article 1 of Protocol No.13 contains an absolute prohibition on the death penalty. Following the UK's ratification of Protocol No.13, reference to it has been inserted into Part 3 of Schedule 1 to HRA 1998 (Human Rights Act 1998 (Amendment) Order 2004, SI 2004/1574). Thus, where there are 'substantial grounds for believing' that following a removal from this country a person will be condemned to death or executed, even if for murder, such removal would be to breach their human rights. The Article reads:

> The death penalty shall be abolished. No-one shall be condemned to such penalty or executed.

3.2.6 Article 3: prohibition of torture

The right is expressed in these terms, and is notably unqualified:

> No one shall be subjected to torture or to inhuman or degrading treatment or punishment.

There are therefore three forms of ill treatment, but each is afforded the same level of protection in immigration proceedings.

Outside an immigration context, these three forms of ill treatment can be seen as a spectrum, with torture at the most serious end, going through inhuman treatment and then degrading treatment. However, for ill treatment to amount to torture it would probably always have to be deliberately inflicted and intentional, whereas, as is discussed below, inhuman and degrading treatment can potentially be passive in nature.

3.2.6.1 Absolute nature of Article 3

Article 3 is absolute in nature, meaning that there are no circumstances in which it can be derogated from, nor can there be any justification for failure to observe it. This means that even very unpleasant individuals who have committed very serious crimes can benefit from its protection.

In *Soering*, the claimant was mentally ill and had horribly murdered two people in the United States. His extradition to stand trial there was being sought. Strasbourg held that he could not be extradited because of the real risk of exposure to the death row experience, which would breach Article 3.

In *Chahal* v. *UK* (1997) 23 EHRR 413, the claimant was accused of being a terrorist extremist and a danger to the national security of the UK, but the ECtHR found that because the Article 3 right is absolute his removal to India was not permitted because 'the activities of the individual in question, however undesirable or dangerous, cannot be a material consideration' (para.80).

Whether Article 3 is breached or not in an individual case is a question of fact, based on measuring up all the relevant considerations – so it is always necessary to examine the impact of the feared future treatment on this individual. The courts say that (e.g. *Ireland* v. *UK* (1978) 2 EHRR 25 at para.162):

> ill-treatment must attain a minimum level of severity if it is to fall within the scope of Article 3 (art.3). The assessment of this minimum is, in the nature of things, relative; it depends on all the circumstances of the case, such as the duration of the treatment, its physical or mental effects and, in some cases, the sex, age and state of health of the victim, etc.

The right operates so as to prevent removal of a person within a country's territory to another territory in which there would be a breach of Article 3 of the ECHR. It is, therefore, irrelevant from an immigration perspective whether the breach of which the claimant complains will be one that amounts to torture, inhuman treatment or degrading treatment. For the purposes of understanding Article 3 it is nevertheless important to explore the nature of each type of ill treatment.

Practice point

Always focus on the individual facts of the case – what is the impact of a particular kind of treatment on a particular individual?

Are there circumstances of their case making them particularly vulnerable, such as age, physical or mental health or life experiences?

3.2.6.2   Definition of torture

In *Ireland* v. *UK* (1978) 2 EHRR 25 torture was defined as 'deliberate inhuman treatment causing very serious and cruel suffering'. This was thought to be a very high threshold which could be reached by very few cases indeed.

More recent decisions such as *Myumyun* v. *Bulgaria* [2015] ECHR 972 have summarised the relevant considerations that might lead to a finding on torture:

> different factors – such as the gravity and duration of the treatment, the intention behind it, and the physical and psychological effects on the victim – had underpinned its findings in various cases.

In the case of *Aydin* v. *Turkey* (1998) 25 EHRR 251 the ECtHR found that rape amounted to torture.

3.2.6.3   Inhuman treatment or punishment

Modern thinking from the Strasbourg Court is shown by cases such as *Bouyid* v. *Belgium* [2015] ECHR 819 which at [87] states that an Article 3 violation:

usually involves actual bodily injury or intense physical or mental suffering. However, even in the absence of these aspects, where treatment humiliates or debases an individual, showing a lack of respect for or diminishing his or her human dignity, or arouses feelings of fear, anguish or inferiority capable of breaking an individual's moral and physical resistance, it may be characterised as degrading and also fall within the prohibition set forth in Article 3 …

Pretty v. *UK* (2002) 35 EHRR 1 at para. 52 shows that natural illness, if made worse by certain conditions, may cross the threshold:

> As regards the types of 'treatment' which fall within the scope of Article 3 of the Convention, the Court's case-law refers to 'ill-treatment' that attains a minimum level of severity and involves actual bodily injury or intense physical or mental suffering … Where treatment humiliates or debases an individual showing a lack of respect for, or diminishing, his or her human dignity, or arouses feelings of fear, anguish or inferiority capable of breaking an individual's moral and physical resistance, it may be characterised as degrading and also fall within the prohibition of Article 3 … The suffering which flows from naturally occurring illness, physical or mental, may be covered by Article 3, where it is, or risks being, exacerbated by the treatment, whether flowing from conditions of detention, expulsion or other measures, for which the authorities can be held responsible …

The death row phenomenon can constitute inhuman punishment, see *Soering* v. *UK* (1989) 11 EHRR 439.

3.2.6.4 Degrading treatment or punishment

In *Ireland* v. *UK* at [167] the court said the following about the nature of degrading treatment:

> The techniques were also degrading since they were such as to arouse in their victims feelings of fear, anguish and inferiority capable of humiliating and debasing them and possibly breaking their physical or moral resistance.

The ECtHR has held that prison conditions can amount to degrading treatment, and even inhuman treatment. See for example *Kalashnikov* v. *Russia* (2002) 36 EHRR 34 at [95]:

> … The suffering and humiliation involved must in any event go beyond that inevitable element of suffering or humiliation connected with a given form of legitimate treatment or punishment.
>
> Measures depriving a person of his liberty may often involve such an element. Yet it cannot be said that detention on remand in itself raises an issue under Article 3 of the Convention …
>
> Nevertheless, under this provision the State must ensure that a person is detained in conditions which are compatible with respect for his human dignity, that the manner and method of the execution of the measure do not subject him to distress or hardship of an intensity exceeding the unavoidable level of suffering inherent in detention and that, given the practical demands of imprisonment, his health and well-being are adequately secured …

107

> When assessing conditions of detention, account has to be taken of the cumulative effects of those conditions, as well as the specific allegations made by the applicant ...

However, on the presumption that this complaint is raised on the basis of general prison conditions in a country rather than any particular feature of the applicant's account, when considering this kind of case it is necessary for the individual to show a generic risk (in the sense of showing that all individuals in prisons face a real risk of human rights abuses). The Tribunal accordingly says that it is necessary to demonstrate a consistent pattern of gross and systematic violations of the human rights of those detained before it will be satisfied of the extent of the risk. Nevertheless, cases have been successful on this basis. See, for example, *PS (prison conditions; military service) Ukraine CG* [2006] UKAIT 16.

Life sentences with no prospect of parole can also amount to an Article 3 breach, where the sentence is grossly disproportionate to the offence in question or where it is no longer justified in penal terms and incapable of reduction: *Babar Ahmad and others* v. *UK* [2012] ECHR 609.

Practice point

While the law says that a person cannot be removed if he or she is going to be detained in conditions that would be contrary to Article 3 of the ECHR, it is not at all easy to prove that the conditions will in fact be so bad as to meet this threshold. A few critical words from a single human rights report will be unlikely to suffice.

Expert evidence will be needed, and/or specific reports on detention conditions in that country by a relevant international NGO or monitoring organisation of some sort, such as Penal Reform. ECHR signatories are monitored by the Committee for the Prevention of Torture (CPT), an official organ of the Council of Europe. The reports of the CPT were instrumental in the Ukrainian case. Unfortunately, such detailed and influential reports do not generally exist outside Council of Europe countries, so other forms of evidence must be sought. Always check HUDOC, the ECtHR's case database, for decisions involving the detention conditions in the country in question.

In *Tyrer* v. *UK* (1978) 2 EHRR 1 the ECtHR held that corporal punishment of a minor amounted to degrading treatment or punishment, but said that the punishment must exceed the usual element of humiliation involved in the criminal justice system, and at [31] that 'a punishment does not lose its degrading character just because it is believed to be, or actually is, an effective deterrent or aid to crime control':

> **30.** ... In the Court's view, in order for a punishment to be 'degrading' and in breach of Article 3 (art. 3), the humiliation or debasement involved must attain a particular level and must in any event be other than that usual element of humiliation referred to in the preceding subparagraph. The assessment is, in the nature of things, relative: it depends on all the circumstances of the case and, in particular, on the nature and context of the punishment itself and the manner and method of its execution.

31. ... As regards their belief that judicial corporal punishment deters criminals, it must be pointed out that a punishment does not lose its degrading character just because it is believed to be, or actually is, an effective deterrent or aid to crime control. Above all, as the Court must emphasise, it is never permissible to have recourse to punishments which are contrary to Article 3 (art. 3), whatever their deterrent effect may be ...

In *Ocalan* v. *Turkey* (2003) 37 EHRR 10 at para.220 the court looked at the actual intention of the treatment in question:

Furthermore, in considering whether a punishment or treatment is 'degrading' within the meaning of Article 3, the Court will have regard to whether its object is to humiliate and debase the person concerned and whether, as far as the consequences are concerned, it adversely affected his or her personality in a manner incompatible with Article 3 ...

In *East African Asians* v. *UK* (1981) 3 EHRR 76 the court concluded at [207] that:

... discrimination based on race could, in certain circumstances, of itself amount to degrading treatment within the meaning of Article 3 of the Convention.

The Commission recalls in this connection that, as generally recognised, a special importance should be attached to discrimination based on race; that publicly to single out a group of persons for differential treatment on the basis of race might, in certain circumstances, constitute a special form of affront to human dignity; and that differential treatment of a group of persons on the basis of race might therefore be capable of constituting degrading treatment when differential treatment on some other ground would raise no such question.

The Tribunal in *Secretary of State for the Home Department* v. *S and K Croatia CG* (starred) [2002] UKIAT 5613 at [17] found that racial motivation could cause the threshold to be crossed, e.g. where ill treatment is motivated by racial grounds:

We do not doubt that discrimination on the ground of race is a factor that should be taken into account in deciding whether a breach of Article 3 has been established. It may in some circumstances tip the balance.

3.2.6.5 Specific features of Article 3 cases

You might wonder, given the availability of international protection by way of refugee status and HP, quite what role Article 3 of the ECHR plays in the 'asylum' context. It mainly operates where a person is excluded from international protection: given that the thresholds for exclusion are relatively moderate (particularly for HP), and arise both in relation to international or other criminality abroad, and for offending in this country, an increasing number of people have to rely on the residual protection offered by Article 3.

ABSENCE OF EXCLUSION CLAUSES

Article 3 is subject to no limitation, and unlike the Refugee Convention, there are no exclusion clauses to deprive an individual of the rights which it recognises (*Chahal* v. *UK* (1997) 23 EHRR 413). Nevertheless, while the Secretary of State cannot remove some individuals, she can treat them differently *vis-à-vis* the form of leave to remain bestowed – so an individual who can establish a risk of a human rights breach on removal but who has committed serious criminal offences may well find that they receive a restricted form of leave rather than HP. Even a person who can establish the inclusion requirements for refugee status may suffer the same fate if they are excluded under the Refugee Convention.

In the most serious cases the Home Office policy is to grant periods of six months' discretionary leave at a time, and there is a review on each application until the individual has attained 10 years of residence.

ABSENCE OF CONVENTION REASONS

It will be obvious that, unlike the position under the Refugee Convention, there is no requirement under the ECHR that the harm feared be linked to the individual's race, religion, nationality, membership of a particular social group or political opinion. In cases where the individual faces serious ill treatment or harm on return but behind which there is no Convention reason, the individual may not be entitled to refugee status but may not nevertheless be removed. The availability of HP in a non-exclusion case means that this difference is not presently of significant importance.

SUFFICIENCY OF PROTECTION

R (on the application of Bagdanavicius and another) v. *Secretary of State for the Home Department* [2005] UKHL 38 shows that the test for the availability of protection in a human rights case is very similar to the question posited in an international protection one: either way, essentially one must show that there is not a reasonable level of protection available before the claim is made out.

It is therefore not possible to argue that the 'sufficiency of protection' test does not apply in human rights cases or that it is a different test to that which applies under the Refugee Convention. Basically, everybody has to show first, that they are at real risk of serious harm/persecution, and second, that there is no effective system (which they can access) capable of protecting them.

DESTITUTION IN THE UK

The positive withdrawal of welfare and support leading to an imminent prospect of street homelessness will amount to inhuman and degrading treatment following *Limbuela* [2005] UKHL 66.

UNAVAILABILITY OF MEDICAL TREATMENT ABROAD

It is argued in some cases that a difference in medical treatment between the UK and the country to which a person is to be removed will cause suffering or death and that removal would therefore breach the person's human rights and engage the UK's responsibilities. We deal with this further below as it crosses over between Articles 3 and 8.

SUCCESSFUL ARTICLE 2, 3 OR 8 CLAIMS AND LEAVE TO REMAIN

A person succeeding on the basis that their Article 2 or 3 rights would be breached in the country of return because of the actions of non-state actors against which no state protection was available would be entitled to humanitarian protection under Immigrations Rules, para.339C.

3.2.7 Article 4: prohibition of slavery and forced labour

Article 4(1) is the only absolute right among the parts of this Article, which could capture cases involving the future threat of trafficking, forced prostitution, or bonded labour:

1. No one shall be held in slavery or servitude.
2. No one shall be required to perform forced or compulsory labour.
3. For the purpose of this Article the term 'forced or compulsory labour' shall not include:
   (a) any work required to be done in the ordinary course of detention imposed according to the provisions of Article 5 of this Convention or during conditional release from such detention;
   (b) any service of a military character or, in case of conscientious objectors in countries where they are recognised, service exacted instead of compulsory military service;
   (c) any service exacted in case of an emergency or calamity threatening the life or well being of the community;
   (d) any work or service which forms part of normal civic obligations.

In *Rantsev* v. *Cyprus and Russia* (2010) 51 EHRR 1, the ECtHR held that trafficking falls within the scope of Article 4 of the ECHR and that there is a procedural obligation under Article 4 to investigate alleged trafficking.

3.2.8 Threshold for interference in foreign cases

The other Articles that we now address are all qualified and/or limited ones.

In 'foreign cases' (a term coined in *R (on the application of Ullah)* v. *Special Adjudicator* [2004] UKHL 26, i.e. cases where the alleged breach of rights will take place in the future, after removal, rather than arising inside the UK itself by the action or inaction of the UK authorities) it has to be shown that there will be a 'flagrant denial' of the right in question if it is not an absolute right.

The leading case is *EM (Lebanon)* v. *Secretary of State for the Home Department* [2008] UKHL 64, in which the House of Lords held that the 'complete nullification' and 'flagrant denial' tests, which seemed in the lower courts to have been understood to represent different thresholds, are simply reflections of the same test. *EM (Lebanon)* is believed to have made European legal history by being the first significant decision in which this very high test was made out. There the applicant had the advantage of uncontradicted expert evidence that her child would automatically be removed from her care should she be returned to the Lebanon and given into the care of the father or the father's family: it was accepted that this would wholly nullify the family life of mother and daughter.

3.2.9   Article 5: right to liberty and security

Article 5 of the ECHR is as follows:

1.   Everyone has the right to liberty and security of person. No one shall be deprived of his liberty save in the following cases and in accordance with a procedure prescribed by law:

   (a)   the lawful detention of a person after conviction by a competent court;
   (b)   the lawful arrest or detention of a person for noncompliance with the lawful order of a court or in order to secure the fulfilment of any obligation prescribed by law;
   (c)   the lawful arrest or detention of a person effected for the purpose of bringing him before the competent legal authority on reasonable suspicion of having committed an offence or when it is reasonably considered necessary to prevent his committing an offence or fleeing after having done so;
   (d)   the detention of a minor by lawful order for the purpose of educational supervision or his lawful detention for the purpose of bringing him before the competent legal authority;
   (e)   the lawful detention of persons for the prevention of the spreading of infectious diseases, of persons of unsound mind, alcoholics or drug addicts or vagrants;
   (f)   the lawful arrest or detention of a person to prevent his effecting an unauthorised entry into the country or of a person against whom action is being taken with a view to deportation or extradition.

2.   Everyone who is arrested shall be informed promptly, in a language which he understands, of the reasons for his arrest and of any charge against him.

3.   Everyone arrested or detained in accordance with the provisions of paragraph 1(c) of this Article shall be brought promptly before a judge or other officer authorised by law to exercise judicial power and shall be entitled to trial within a reasonable time or to release pending trial. Release may be conditioned by guarantees to appear for trial.

4.   Everyone who is deprived of his liberty by arrest or detention shall be entitled to take proceedings by which the lawfulness of his detention shall be decided speedily by a court and his release ordered if the detention is not lawful.

5.   Everyone who has been the victim of arrest or detention in contravention of the provisions of this Article shall have an enforceable right to compensation.

It will be seen that Article 5(1)(f) most obviously applies in the context of the detention of migrants.

In *Saadi* v. *UK* [2008] ECHR 80 (a case which made its way from the House of Lords and then on to Strasbourg), the Strasbourg Court accepted that short-term detention of asylum seekers is permissible, even absent any risk of their absconding, for the purposes of processing their asylum claims.

Detention will be arbitrary for the purposes of Article 5 if infected by bad faith or deception, if imposed for a purpose other than one of those specified in Article 5 of the ECHR, or where the detainee is held in an inappropriate place or conditions (*R (on the application of Idira)* v. *Secretary of State for the Home Department* [2015] EWCA Civ 1187).

As mentioned at **3.1.3**, damages are available under HRA 1998, s.9(3), even for judicial acts carried out in good faith. There have been a number of successful claims for damages in immigration detention cases: excellent reviews of the relevant considerations are found in Dunlop and Denholm, *Detention under the Immigration Acts: Law and Practice* (Oxford University Press, 2015) and Dubinsky with Arnott and Mackenzie *Foreign National Prisoners: Law and Practice* (Legal Action Group, 2012).

The requirement that liberty be lost only pursuant to 'a procedure prescribed by law' has the consequence that the Secretary of State must reveal any policies which underlie detention decisions. In *Lumba (WL)* v. *Secretary of State for the Home Department* [2011] UKSC 12 the Supreme Court made it clear at [38] that it was necessary to publish:

> that which a person who is affected by the operation of the policy needs to know in order to make informed and meaningful representations to the decision-maker before a decision is made.

The Article may also have extra-territorial application (which is why we cite all the sub-articles as they might be relevant to a 'foreign' case).

As discussed at **3.2.8**, the risk of a flagrant breach of qualified/limited Articles can inhibit removal to a country, in relation to Article 5 where a person's right to liberty and security of person might face nullification or flagrant breach – the more aspects of Article 5 are in play (a lack of prompt information as to the reasons for arrest, failure to move to speedy trial, etc.), the stronger the argument will be as to whether there is a flagrant breach of the Article.

Given that only the authorities of a country can lawfully deprive an individual of their liberty pursuant to law, there must be an argument that loss of liberty at the hands of non-state actors constitutes a fundamental breach of the Article.

3.2.10 Article 6: right to a fair trial

Article 6 of the ECHR reads as follows:

1. In the determination of his civil rights and obligations or of any criminal charge against him, everyone is entitled to a fair and public hearing within a reasonable time by an independent and impartial tribunal established by law. Judgment shall be pronounced publicly but the press and public may be excluded from all or part of

the trial in the interests of morals, public order or national security in a democratic society, where the interests of juveniles or the protection of the private life of the parties so require, or to the extent strictly necessary in the opinion of the court in special circumstances where publicity would prejudice the interests of justice.

2.   Everyone charged with a criminal offence shall be presumed innocent until proved guilty according to law.

3.   Everyone charged with a criminal offence has the following minimum rights:

(a)   to be informed promptly, in a language which he understands and in detail, of the nature and cause of the accusation against him;

(b)   to have adequate time and facilities for the preparation of his defence;

(c)   to defend himself in person or through legal assistance of his own choosing or, if he has not sufficient means to pay for legal assistance, to be given it free when the interests of justice so require;

(d)   to examine or have examined witnesses against him and to obtain the attendance and examination of witnesses on his behalf under the same conditions as witnesses against him;

(e)   to have the free assistance of an interpreter if he cannot understand or speak the language used in court.

3.2.10.1   Article 6 and its application in the course of legal proceedings in the United Kingdom

The Tribunal in *MNM (Surendran guidelines for Adjudicators) (Kenya)* (starred) [2000] UKIAT 5 (starred) confirms at [16] that, consistently with the decision of the ECtHR in *Maaouia* v. *France* (2001) 33 EHRR 42, Article 6 does not apply in immigration appeals in the UK because immigration rights are not 'private' in nature and therefore are not 'civil rights and obligations'. However, the Tribunal took the view that the common law would guarantee everything that Article 6 would provide (except possibly a speedy trial), so this should not matter very much:

> The fact is that the IAA provides an independent and impartial tribunal established by law. The hearing is in public and the procedures are designed to ensure that it is fair. If there is any unfairness, the tribunal or the Court of Appeal will correct it. Thus any complaints that the special adjudicator conducted an unfair hearing fall to be considered by us and we apply the same tests as would be applicable if Article 6(1) applied. The only advantage which Article 6(1) might confer is the requirement that the hearing be held within a reasonable time. That does not arise in this case and should not, unless some disaster occurs, arise in any case having regard to the timetables and procedures laid down by the adjudicators and the tribunal.

The impact of this restrictive interpretation of the ECHR is limited by the fact that Article 8 includes a procedural dimension which ensures the effective protection of the right to family and private life (see *Gudanaviciene* [2014] EWCA Civ 1622).

The Home Office does accept in its guidance *Considering Human Rights Claims in Visit Applications* (Operational Guidance, Asylum Policy, Asylum Decision Making Guidance (Asylum Instructions)), on the authority of the *Quaquah* case ([2000] INLR 196), that Article 6 may be engaged when the applicant is bringing legal proceedings against it, for example seeking damages for unlawful conduct, and was removed before the conclusion of those proceedings having made an allegation of bad faith as to the circumstances of that removal.

3.2.10.2   Article 6 and its extra-territorial application to resist removal

Article 6 may also have some limited applicability in preventing removal if a lack of fair trial would be the gateway to Article 3 breaches. As discussed at **3.2.8**, authorities such as *Ullah* show that a flagrant denial of justice abroad may prevent removal.

The issue was revisited in practice in *RB (Algeria)* v. *Secretary of State for the Home Department* [2009] UKHL 10. Lord Phillips in the House of Lords held that the Court of Appeal's statement of the test for a flagrant breach of Article 6 was the correct one – i.e. the test was whether there was a real risk of a total denial of the right to a fair trial – but went on at [136] to say that:

> A trial that is fair in part may be no more acceptable than the curate's egg. What is required is that the deficiency or deficiencies in the trial process should be such as fundamentally to destroy the fairness of the prospective trial.

The important question was the potential consequences of unfairness by way of further human rights violations.

3.2.11   Article 8: right to respect for private and family life

Article 8 provides as follows:

1. Everyone has the right to respect for his private and family life, his home and his correspondence.
2. There shall be no interference by a public authority with the exercise of this right except such as is in accordance with the law and is necessary in a democratic society in the interests of national security, public safety or the economic well-being of the country, for the prevention of disorder or crime, for the protection of health or morals, or for the protection of the rights and freedoms of others.

Private and family life applications, as seen by the Home Office, are now addressed within the Immigration Rules (at para.276, particularly para.276ADE, and within Appendix FM). These areas will only rarely fall within the scope of publicly funded work and we do not address them here in any detail.

There are a series of questions arising in an Appendix FM or para.276ADE case. Taking the example of the in-country parent or partner:

(a)   Does the case succeed under the Immigration Rules, i.e. have the suitability, eligibility, immigration and financial requirements been satisfied, in which case the appeal succeeds under the Immigration Rules without regard to the exception at para.EX.1?
(b)   If not (a), is the exception within the rules at EX.1 in play?
(c)   If not (a) or (b), does nevertheless Article 8 of the ECHR, taking into account

whether there are particularly compelling or exceptional circumstances present leading to unjustifiably harsh consequences, render the immigration decision disproportionate?

Regarding the consideration outside the Immigration Rules, in *R (on the application of Razgar)* v. *Secretary of State for the Home Department* [2004] UKHL 27 at [17], the court explained that:

> ... In a case where removal is resisted in reliance on article 8, these questions are likely to be:
>
> (1) Will the proposed removal be an interference by a public authority with the exercise of the applicant's right to respect for his private or (as the case may be) family life?
>
> (2) If so, will such interference have consequences of such gravity as potentially to engage the operation of article 8?
>
> (3) If so, is such interference in accordance with the law?
>
> (4) If so, is such interference necessary in a democratic society in the interests of national security, public safety or the economic well-being of the country, for the prevention of disorder or crime, for the protection of health or morals, or for the protection of the rights and freedoms of others?
>
> (5) If so, is such interference proportionate to the legitimate public end sought to be achieved?

The test for whether a claim should succeed outside the Immigration Rules is essentially whether it is a 'compelling one'.

The balance between private right and public interest struck under the Immigration Rules retains relevance to the consideration of Article 8 outside the rules: as it was put in *Secretary of State for the Home Department* v. *SS (Congo) and others* [2015] EWCA Civ 387 at [48]:

> What *does* matter, however – whether one is dealing with a section of the Rules which constitutes a 'complete code' (as in *MF (Nigeria)*) or with a section of the Rules which is not a 'complete code' (as in *Nagre* and the present appeals) – is to identify, for the purposes of application of Article 8, the degree of weight to be attached to the expression of public policy in the substantive part of the Rules in the particular context in question (which will not always be the same: hence the guidance we seek to give in this judgment), as well as the other factors relevant to the Article 8 balancing exercise in the particular case (which, again, may well vary from context to context and from case to case).

3.2.11.1 *Nationality, Immigration and Asylum Act 2002, Part 5A considerations*

When considering the last of the questions set out above (*Razgar*), i.e. (5): 'proportionality', the starting point for the courts and tribunals is to 'have regard' to the considerations laid out under Part 5A of NIAA 2002, inserted as from 28 July 2014 by the Immigration Act 2014 (IA 2014).

117A   Application of this Part

...

(2)   In considering the public interest question, the court or tribunal must (in particular) have regard -

  (a)   in all cases, to the considerations listed in section 117B, and

  (b)   in cases concerning the deportation of foreign criminals, to the considerations listed in section 117C.

(3)   In subsection (2), 'the public interest question' means the question of whether an interference with a person's right to respect for private and family life is justified under Article 8(2).

117B   Article 8: public interest considerations applicable in all cases

(1)   The maintenance of effective immigration controls is in the public interest.

(2)   It is in the public interest, and in particular in the interests of the economic well-being of the United Kingdom, that persons who seek to enter or remain in the United Kingdom are able to speak English, because persons who can speak English –

  (a)   are less of a burden on taxpayers, and

  (b)   are better able to integrate into society.

(3)   It is in the public interest, and in particular in the interests of the economic well-being of the United Kingdom, that persons who seek to enter or remain in the United Kingdom are financially independent, because such persons –

  (a)   are not a burden on taxpayers, and

  (b)   are better able to integrate into society.

(4)   Little weight should be given to –

  (a)   a private life, or

  (b)   a relationship formed with a qualifying partner,

that is established by a person at a time when the person is in the United Kingdom unlawfully.

(5)   Little weight should be given to a private life established by a person at a time when the person's immigration status is precarious.

(6)   In the case of a person who is not liable to deportation, the public interest does not require the person's removal where –

  (a)   the person has a genuine and subsisting parental relationship with a qualifying child, and

  (b)   it would not be reasonable to expect the child to leave the United Kingdom.

These considerations are only part of the assessment. Given the words of s.117A(2), there is no suggestion in the statute that other factors should be excluded, even though the statutory ones should be evaluated 'in particular', so the existing case law on Article 8 of the ECHR remains relevant (see *Dube (ss.117A–117D)* [2015] UKUT 90 (IAC)).

There is no obligation on the Home Office to have regard to these factors in its own decision making: s.117 is aimed at 'a court or tribunal'.

It can be seen that the factors at s.117B(2) and (3) may count in favour of many migrants, where they are economically self-sufficient and speak English: though according to *AM (s.117B) Malawi* [2015] UKUT 260 (IAC), self-sufficiency and language skills merely mean that this aspect of the public interest weighs less heavily against an applicant, rather than actively counting in the applicant's favour.

At s.117B(4) little weight is to be given to 'a relationship with a qualifying partner' (i.e. a British citizen or settled sponsor): s.117D(1)) established on the basis of unlawful residence – but this does not bite on broader Article 8 relationships beyond partnership, including those with children.

At s.117B(6) the 'seven-year rule', based on a qualifying (i.e. seven-year resident or British citizen: s.117D(1)) child's lengthy residence where it would be unreasonable to expect their carer to leave, is now enshrined in statute: indeed s.117B(6) amounts to a straightforward statement of the public interest rendering other considerations largely irrelevant, so long as no issue of deportation arises, that in such cases, removal would be disproportionate. This also seems to answer the question left open by rule 276ADE(iii), which addresses the child rather than the parent, by stating the consequence for the caring parent of a child whose own removal would be unreasonable under that sub-rule.

It is clear that the notion of 'precarious' immigration status is wider than being 'in the United Kingdom unlawfully'. In *AM (s.117B) Malawi* [2015] UKUT 260 (IAC) the Upper Tribunal found that immigration status is 'precarious' if a migrant's continued presence in the UK will be dependent upon their obtaining a further grant of leave; it may even be the case that a person with indefinite leave to remain, or a person who has obtained citizenship, enjoys a status that is 'precarious' either because that status is revocable by the Secretary of State as a result of their deception, or because of their criminal conduct. In such circumstances the person will be well aware that he has imperilled his status and cannot viably claim thereafter that his status is other than precarious. Nevertheless, in determining whether the public interest in enforcing immigration control trumps the private life in question, think carefully about the circumstances that made immigration status 'precarious', and when a migrant might be present, with or without leave to remain, without it being necessarily being fairly described as 'precarious':

- A person may have been in an immigration route that would have led to indefinite leave to remain subject to circumstances outside their control, directly (because the rule itself permitted a settlement application to be made), or because case law recognised that it should do so as in the HSMP litigation (e.g. *R (on the application of HSMP Forum Ltd)* v. *Secretary of State for the Home Department* [2008] EWHC 664 (Admin)).
- A person may have been exercising European Treaty rights in the past (e.g. *R (on the application of Heritage)* v. *Secretary of State for the Home Department and First-tier Tribunal (IJR)* [2014] UKUT 441 (IAC)).
- A person may have come here for reasons outside their control, ranging from historic trafficking to an asylum claim that was undermined by a post-departure

change of circumstances by which time they had put down roots in this country (e.g. *Shala* v. *Secretary of State for the Home Department* [2003] EWCA Civ 233, where it was accepted that the applicant's family unit originally had a strong claim to enter this country because of the dangers they had faced at the time they arrived here).

- A person may have come here as a minor at a time when decisions as to their future were made on their behalf (as is accepted, in a different context, in *ZH Tanzania* v. *Secretary of State for the Home Department* [2011] UKSC 4) and when they could not reasonably be expected to do anything else than make a life for themselves here as best they could, such that it might be thought unfair for the precariousness of their position to count strongly against them.

3.2.12 Unavailability of medical treatment abroad

It is argued in some cases that a difference in medical treatment between the UK and the country to which a person is to be removed will cause suffering or death and that removal would therefore breach the person's human rights and engage the UK's responsibilities. This raises issues under both Article 3 and Article 8, but because they often overlap, it is convenient to deal with everything together.

Under Article 3 of the ECHR it may be argued that the suffering will be so serious as to amount to a breach of Article 3, relying on a principle established in the case of *D* v. *UK* (1997) 24 EHRR 423, subsequently developed in the case of *N* v. *UK* [2008] ECHR 453. In *KH (Afghanistan)* v. *Secretary of State for the Home Department* [2009] EWCA Civ 1354 the Court of Appeal held that the *N* threshold is also to be applied in cases of mental illness considered under Article 3.

The other argument is that although the suffering would not be so serious as to engage Article 3, the suffering allied to other issues may engage Article 8, relying on the case of *Bensaid* v. *UK* (2001) 33 EHRR 10. This is not a soft option.

3.2.12.1 The Article 3 line of authority

In *N* v. *UK* [2008] ECHR 453 Strasbourg examined the case of a Ugandan woman known as N who had contracted HIV/AIDS and was receiving treatment in the UK. The case had previously been considered by the House of Lords in *N* v. *Secretary of State for the Home Department* [2005] UKHL 31 who had examined N's case and rejected it. The Strasbourg Court rejected it too.

It is worth examining the House of Lords judgment to see how unwavering it is. For example, it was accepted that the claimant would die in unpleasant circumstances within approximately one year if removed, as Lord Hope made abundantly clear at [20]:

> The decision which your Lordships have been asked to take in this case will have profound consequences for the appellant. The prospects of her surviving for more than a year or two if she is returned to Uganda are bleak. It is highly likely that the advanced medical care which has stabilised her condition by suppressing the HIV virus and would

sustain her in good health were she to remain in this country for decades will no longer be available to her. If it is not, her condition is likely to reactivate and to deteriorate rapidly. There is no doubt that if that happens she will face an early death after a period of acute physical and mental suffering. It is easy to sympathise with her in this predicament.

At [50] Lord Hope outlines the test for a successful claim:

> For the circumstances to be ... 'very exceptional' it would need to be shown that the applicant's medical condition had reached such a critical stage that there were compelling humanitarian grounds for not removing him to a place which lacked the medical and social services which he would need to prevent acute suffering while he is dying.

So dying in unpleasant circumstances within approximately one year if removed did not make for a very exceptional case, but allowing someone to stay here to die to prevent acute suffering while dying does. It is a thin line.

A number of scenarios have been accepted as meeting the high threshold, or departing from it.

In *CA* v. *Secretary of State for the Home Department* [2004] EWCA Civ 1165 the return of sick mother and child where the mother would have to watch her child suffer and die was considered exceptional, as Laws LJ put it at [26]:

> It seems to me obvious simply as a matter of humanity that for a mother to witness the collapse of her new-born child's health and perhaps its death may be a kind of suffering far greater than might arise by the mother's confronting the self-same fate herself.

A claim might succeed where there is discrimination in the healthcare available to the sick (e.g. *RS (Zimbabwe)* [2008] EWCA Civ 839 discussing the possibility that there might be a deliberate withholding of medical care or food).

In *GS and EO (Article 3 – health cases) India* [2012] UKUT 397 (IAC), the Tribunal recognised that a claim might succeed where there was an absence of resources through civil war or similar human agency.

Laws LJ in *GS (India) and others* v. *Secretary of State for the Home Department* [2015] EWCA Civ 40 at [70] recognised another possibility where treatment of critical value is imminently due and would be lost if removal proceeds:

> If there is a real possibility of this transplant in the near future ... there may be a question whether GM's removal from the United Kingdom before it is carried out would violate Article 3 on the specific footing that to deprive him of such an imminent and transformative medical recourse amounts to inhuman treatment.

Medical problems may ensue other than from a want of resources, e.g. where the human rights interference is caused not by the difference in treatment between here and abroad and the repercussions of that difference, but where the act of removal actually causes a deterioration in physical or mental health. See *J* v. *Secretary of State for the Home Department* [2005] EWCA Civ 629 where it was the trauma of removal bringing with it an enhanced risk of suicide rather than any 'want of resources' that led to the human rights interference.

A lower threshold of suffering should apply to children than to adults. There is considerable authority behind the proposition that treatment or punishment that would not breach the rights of an adult may nevertheless breach the rights of a child. See *Re E (a child) (Northern Ireland)* [2009] 1 AC 536 (HL) at [9]:

> The special vulnerability of children is also relevant to the scope of the obligations of the state to protect them from such treatment.

3.2.12.2 The Article 8 line of authority

Bensaid v. *UK* [2001] ECHR 82 shows that mental health must also be regarded as a crucial part of private life associated with the aspect of moral integrity.

In *JA (Ivory Coast)* [2009] EWCA Civ 1353 at [25] the court accepted that lawful residence where leave to remain was granted in the context of full knowledge of a person's health situation might differentiate the case from the norm:

> JA's is a markedly different case. Her position as a continuously lawful entrant places her in a different legal class from N, so that she is not called upon to demonstrate exceptional circumstances as compelling as those in *D* v. *United Kingdom*. There is no finding by the AIT that she has much if any hope of securing treatment if returned to Ivory Coast, or therefore as to the severity and consequences of removal (see *Razgar* [2004] UKHL 27). Depending on these, the potential discontinuance of years of life-saving NHS treatment, albeit made available out of compassion and not out of obligation, is in our judgment capable of tipping the balance of proportionality in her favour.

This approach is exemplified in *Akhalu (health claim: ECHR Article 8) Nigeria* [2013] UKUT 400 (IAC). Here, the appellant had arrived in the UK legally in 2004 to study, but was then diagnosed in the UK as suffering from end stage kidney failure. It was accepted that she was not aware of the illness prior to arriving in the UK. After successfully completing her studies, she received a kidney transplant and thereafter required carefully monitored medication to ensure that the transplanted organ is not rejected. It was accepted that she could not afford such treatment in Nigeria and would therefore die soon after returning there. In upholding the allowed appeal, the Upper Tribunal concluded:

> **49.** It cannot be said that this was an appeal allowed simply because of a disparity in the treatment available. That is to misrepresent what the judge has said. He plainly concluded that this was one of the 'very rare cases' contemplated by the Tribunal in *GS and EO (India)* that could succeed under article 8 where the claim relies in part upon the need to continue with medical treatment being received here.

> **50.** Correctly understood, in our judgement, the judge did not allow the appeal simply because the claimant could continue to receive medical treatment here that she would not have access to in Nigeria. His was a holistic assessment, drawing on the truly exceptional level of engagement with her local community that was disclosed by the evidence he alluded to and which he did not need to set out extensively in his determination and a comparison of her ability to enjoy any private life at all in Nigeria, as well as the foreseeable consequences for her health should she be removed to Nigeria.

In *R (on the application of SQ (Pakistan) and another)* v. *Upper Tribunal Immigration and Asylum Chamber and another* [2013] EWCA Civ 1251 the Court of Appeal showed that health cases involving children, where Article 8 is raised, should be assessed via a balancing exercise (and certainly could not be dismissed out of hand); at [27]:

> On the one hand, MQ can pray in aid his lawful entry and his status as a child with the protection of the *ZH* approach. On the other hand, he arrived with his serious medical conditions at an advanced stage and, although not an unlawful entrant, it will be relevant to consider whether his arrival here was a manifestation of 'health tourism'. If it was, that would fall to be weighed in the balance.

However, *Akhalu* in the headnote also shows that a person whose healthcare must come from the state will have an uphill struggle to show their removal is disproportionate.

> The consequences of removal for the health of a claimant who would not be able to access equivalent health care in their country of nationality as was available in this country are plainly relevant to the question of proportionality. But, when weighed against the public interest in ensuring that the limited resources of this country's health service are used to the best effect for the benefit of those for whom they are intended, those consequences do not weigh heavily in the claimant's favour but speak cogently in support of the public interests in removal.

A case might be rather stronger where the critical factor is the need for personal care from a close friend or family member resident in the UK.

While, as can be seen, it is very difficult for a health case to succeed, the situation may be different where questions of health and dependency arise in a context where other Article 8 rights are established: as was noted in *MM (Zimbabwe)* v. *Secretary of State for the Home Department* [2012] EWCA Civ 279 at [23]:

> Suppose, in this case, the appellant had established firm family ties in this country, then the availability of continuing medical treatment here, coupled with his dependence on the family here for support, together establish 'private life' under Article 8 ... Such a finding would not offend the principle ... that the United Kingdom is under no Convention obligation to provide medical treatment here when it is not available in the country to which the appellant is to be deported.

However the case is argued, clear medical evidence must be provided, and the UKVI guidance sets out requirements that it must satisfy: it must be dated within three months of receipt.

Jamil (Pakistan)

Jamil is a citizen of Pakistan aged seven. He entered this country with his mother as a visitor. He has always suffered from a serious bone disease. It has been treated with only moderate success abroad and his life expectancy is shorter by some years if he cannot find anything better. He and his mother visit your office and ask about the prospects of staying here because of his health. They do not have the money to qualify under the medical visitor route in the future.

It is very difficult to see an Article 3 case succeeding in these circumstances. There is not a complete absence of medical care abroad and he has his mother to look after him.

Nor is an Article 8 case likely to succeed: first because it suffers from the same problems as the Article 3 case, second because, unless there has been some significant recent change of circumstances, it would seem that Jamil's mother has deliberately entered the country in full knowledge that an application to remain longer than the permitted visit would be inconsistent with the intention to leave the country at the end of the stay which is a condition of the visa being granted.

The situation might be different had Jamil entered school and established a healthcare regime in this country. He could not be blamed for taking advantage of the opportunities: indeed Lord Hope in *ZH (Tanzania)* emphasised that the sins of parents should not be held against their children.

Practice point

Health cases are not necessarily all doom and gloom. In an Article 3 case look for:

- individual factors in a case which amount to compelling humanitarian grounds;
- an absence of social and family support;
- whether or not medical treatment is in practice available;
- imminence of death if adequate treatment is not received; the expelled person's degree of decline and the consequent indignity;
- a mother's natural distress at seeing her child's decline and death;
- the greater impact of suffering upon a child than on an adult;
- whether there is any discrimination in government provision of healthcare services;
- removal at a critical moment in transformative treatment.

In an Article 8 case look for, in addition to the factors above:

- a combination of established family/private life in the UK, and health issues (see *MM (Zimbabwe)* – discussed further above);
- a lack of treatment abroad compared to an established treatment regime here;
- lawful residence in this country – of particular relevance are grants of leave in the knowledge of the applicant's health situation;
- private health insurance which would reduce the public interest in restricting access to the limited resources of the NHS.

3.2.12.3 Health claims and leave to remain

Applications on health grounds (e.g. due to suicide risks or to the applicant's inability to access suitable treatment) must be made on Forms FLR(O) and SET(O). They are free of charge if made solely, or predominantly, relying on Article 3. Leave is granted by way of 30 months' rolling grants, on a 10-year route to settlement;

though if leave was first granted under this route before 9 July 2012, the old DLR policy will be honoured so that indefinite leave to remain is granted after six years.

See the Home Office guidance, *Human Rights Claims on Medical Grounds* (**www.gov.uk/government/publications/human-rights-claims-on-medical-grounds**).

3.2.13   Article 14: prohibition of discrimination

Article 14 prohibits discrimination only when it can be linked with a lack of respect for one or more of the rights otherwise set out in the ECHR – it is the enjoyment of those rights which must be secured without discrimination. The restriction on grounds of appeal for new-style appeals under the relevant provisions of NIAA 2002 to HRA 1998 grounds (and thus the substantive Articles of the ECHR) means that Article 14 continues to be available – indeed, it will be the vehicle by which complaints of race discrimination in the course of immigration decision making may be litigated.

3.3   DISCRETIONARY LEAVE

This is a residual form of leave to remain given to some individuals who do not qualify for other forms of leave to remain.

Following July 2012's landmark changes, the *Discretionary Leave* policy (in the Operational Guidance, Asylum Policy, Asylum Decision Making Guidance (Asylum Instructions) and reproduced at **Appendix E1**) explains how leave will be granted outside the rules. It significantly narrows the group to whom discretionary leave (DL) would have hitherto been granted, but saves the position of those granted DL before that date.

Applications are free of charge if made solely, or predominantly, relying on Article 3. Leave is granted by way of 30 months' rolling grants, on a 10-year route to settlement; though if leave was first granted under this route before 9 July 2012, the old DLR policy will be honoured so that indefinite leave to remain is granted after six years.

There are three different types of leave granted in similar but slightly different circumstances.

- Discretionary leave.
- Restricted leave – essentially, DL for domestic and international law criminals.
- Leave outside the Immigration Rules – apparently intended by the Home Office for cases that raise compelling reasons falling outside ECHR issues.

3.3.1   Pre-July 2012 discretionary leave

The most common situation where you would, pre-9 July 2012, have expected to see a grant of discretionary leave to remain was in Article 8 cases where removal would breach the person's or their family's right to a private and family life in the UK, or where a person's medical condition would render their removal in breach of Articles 3 or 8.

In those circumstances, a person would normally have been granted three years' DL, followed by an active review, a further three years' DL if successful, and then ILR. Those on that route under the old policy will continue upon it towards settlement so long as they do not fall foul of the criminality thresholds.

3.3.2 Modern discretionary leave

Those who would once have been granted DL on Article 8 grounds will now be granted 30 months' leave to remain on a 10-year route to settlement. Such grants are not discretionary, being awarded under Immigration Rules, para.276ADE or Appendix FM.

So the modern form of DL has a very restricted ambit: it essentially arises only for 'other cases where return would breach the ECHR':

- medical cases which would not give rise to a grant of humanitarian protection;
- where there is a flagrant breach of a qualified or limited right;
- in cases where it is thought appropriate to grant residence to a person accepted as a victim of trafficking.

Unaccompanied minors refused asylum used to be granted DL until they were aged 17 and half years, but that policy was incorporated into the rules from 6 April 2013, so they will now be granted leave under the rules (para.352ZC).

Discretionary leave may also be granted where further submissions are considered under rule 353, where, having considered the factors set out and the guidance in Chapter 55, para.53.1 of the *Enforcement Instructions and Guidance* (Operational Guidance collection, Enforcement), removal is no longer considered appropriate. Some applicants in this category will be entitled to an immediate grant of ILR under the pre-9 July 2012 policy.

Grants of DL will usually be for 30 months. An application for an extension can be made where there is a continued need for such leave. A person with DL under the new policy will not usually be able to apply for ILR until they have had DL for 10 years. As each application for an extension will be subject to an active review, the course to settlement will be uncertain.

Some challenges have been brought to the policy of granting limited rather than indefinite leave to remain on the basis of the best interests of the child. Following decisions such as *R (on the application of Alladin)* v. *Secretary of State for the Home Department* [2014] EWCA Civ 1334 it is clear that a strong evidence-backed case needs to be put as to why the 'staged' approach to settlement should not be followed.

The asylum policy instruction of the Operational Guidance, *Discretionary Leave*, states as follows (para.3.7):

> There are likely to be very few other cases in which it would be appropriate to grant DL to a failed asylum seeker. However, it is not possible to anticipate every eventuality that may arise, so there remains scope to grant DL where individual circumstances, although not falling within the broad categories listed above, are so compelling that it is considered appropriate to grant leave.

There are provisions for revocation of DL. However, given that discretionary leave to remain does not normally result from any 'protection' need but rather is based on relationships or care in the UK, travel to the country of origin and use of the person's own national passport do not bring the same negative connotations as in asylum and humanitarian protection cases.

There are no provisions which entitle a person with DL to sponsor family members to join them in the UK. They can of course rely on Article 8 to make an application outside the Immigration Rules.

3.3.3 Discretionary leave for criminals

A person with a criminal record may be excluded from the usual 30-month slices of leave that may lead to settlement. Where such persons do not fall into the ambit of the restricted leave policy (which we deal with next: see **3.3.4**), they will be granted six-month rolling grants of leave to remain under para.2.5 of the DL guidance.

They can apply for ILR only after 10 years. In *R (on the application of AO and another)* v. *Secretary of State for the Home Department* [2011] EWHC 3088 (Admin) the High Court found that the 10-year policy for exclusion cases was an unlawful fettering of the Secretary of State's discretion. In an exceptional case, it will therefore be possible to argue that a person should not have to wait 10 years before ILR will be considered.

Those liable to deportation but who have made out a successful claim under Article 8 (as transposed into Immigration Rules, paras.399–399A) will be entitled to 30 months' leave within the Immigration Rules.

3.3.4 Restricted leave

Individuals who would have qualified for refugee status or HP but for committing international crimes that have caused their exclusion or otherwise behaving such as to be deemed a danger to the public will usually receive leave for periods of six months at a time. The policy is subject to its own distinct regime as governed by the relevant asylum policy instruction, *Restricted Leave* (Operational Guidance, Asylum Policy, Asylum Decision Making Guidance (Asylum Instructions)):

- Cases will be reviewed regularly with a view to removal of individuals as soon as possible and only in exceptional circumstances will individuals on restricted leave ever become eligible for settlement or citizenship.

- There will be restrictions on the right to work, which may be limited to voluntary work, or imposed so as to avoid exposure to vulnerable individuals – and a restriction on study, to emphasise the impermanence of stay and preserve public funds.
- There will be a condition as to residence: any change of address will have to be notified to the Home Office (possibly in advance), and individuals may be required to live in a specified area if their accommodation is publicly provided.
- There will be regular reporting restrictions.

Numerous challenges to the regimes for granting limited periods of leave to persons excluded from more generous residence regimes have been brought, and have largely failed, e.g. in *R (on the application of Kardi)* v. *Secretary of State for the Home Department* [2014] EWCA Civ 934, the short grants of leave and reporting requirements (there, monthly ones), restriction on working (to general trader only) and residence (to notify changes of address) were all found proportionate on the facts of that case. However, the court was concerned as to the reasonableness of restricting the claimant's studies where this prevented him from taking up a short English language course where removal was not imminent.

The policy instruction states at para.1.2.5 that:

> only in exceptional circumstances will individuals on restricted leave ever become eligible for settlement or citizenship. Such exceptional circumstances are likely to be very rare.

3.3.5 Travel documents

A person granted DL will be expected to travel on their national passport (on the basis that the grant is not normally based on any lack of protection by their national authorities). They can apply to the Home Office for a certificate of travel, but only if they have been unreasonably and formally (i.e. by letter) refused a national passport.

A refusal of a national passport will not be accepted as unreasonable where motivated by a person's failure to complete military service, failure to provide evidence to confirm identity or due to a person having a criminal record in their country.

Children need to apply for their own travel documents. All applicants will now have to enrol their biometrics with the Home Office.

The GOV.UK website sets out the requirements for amendments to applications and travel documents. In virtually all cases a full further application form (and full fee) needs to be sent together with extrinsic evidence (e.g. on a change of name, the relevant legal documentation must be produced; if documents are lost or stolen, a police report must be provided). If details on the travel document that is issued are incorrect, and the Home Office is at fault, then there will be no further fee. The documents are not extendable, and if they expire while the holder is abroad, then it will be necessary to apply to the nearest British Embassy or High Commission for advice.

There will be an investigation into the loss and so the Home Office warns that applications to replace lost documents can take considerably longer than the usual period.

A person with DL should ensure they do not travel at a time when their leave is due to expire. They will not have any right of re-entry if they return after their leave has expired, as they will no longer benefit from Article 13 of the Immigration (Leave to Enter and Remain) Order 2000, SI 2000/1161 which permits travel and return while one holds current leave.

3.4   THE CHARTER OF FUNDAMENTAL RIGHTS OF THE EUROPEAN UNION

The Charter of Fundamental Rights of the European Union became binding across the EU with the entry into force of the Treaty of Lisbon in December 2009. It operates only (but always) when a Member State is applying EU law, as was discussed in *NS (European Union law)* [2011] EUECJ C-411/10 (including cases when a discretion is exercised within the context of EU law) – in the immigration context, this applies most obviously in the field of free movement and international protection law (i.e. in the UK – in all EEA, asylum and HP cases).

It contains many rights similar or identical to those in the ECHR, and also some additional ones, which are understood to be derived from general principles of EU law. It is the central plank of the European policy to clarify and make accessible EU law's adherence to fundamental rights principles, a programme which includes an ambition for the EU itself to sign up to the ECHR, albeit one that may now be a long way off following the *Opinions of the Court* [2014] EUECJ Avis-2/13 that the agreement to pursue this is incompatible with Article 6(2) of the Treaty on European Union. A useful guide to its rather controversial history in this country is found in the House of Commons European Scrutiny Committee report, *The Application of the EU Charter of Fundamental Rights in the UK: A State of Confusion* (March 2014).

It has the greatest legal force, akin to the Treaties themselves. Article 6(1) of the Treaty on European Union provides:

> The Union recognises the rights, freedoms and principles set out in the Charter of Fundamental Rights of the European Union of 7 December 2000, as adapted at Strasbourg, on 12 December 2007, which shall have the same legal value as the Treaties.

A general principle of proportionality is found in Article 52(1):

> Any limitation on the exercise of the rights and freedoms recognised by this Charter must be provided for by law and respect the essence of those rights and freedoms. Subject to the principle of proportionality, limitations may be made only if they are necessary and

genuinely meet objectives of general interest recognised by the Union or the need to protect the rights and freedoms of others.

EU law will reflect the meaning and scope of fundamental rights found in the ECHR where they correspond to Charter rights (Article 52(3)), though:

This provision shall not prevent Union law providing more extensive protection.

It is to be interpreted with regard to a published series of Explanations.

Some rights familiar to immigration lawyers are found in terms similar to those in the Charter as they are in the ECHR. For example, the rights to family life, and to be free from inhuman and degrading treatment, are found at Articles 4 and 7. In an EU free movement case, one should be referring to Article 7 of the Charter rather than to the ECHR, at least until it is clear that the case has moved beyond the scope of EU law altogether.

The rights likely to be of the greatest interest in the immigration context are these:

Article 1 Human dignity

Human dignity is inviolable. It must be respected and protected.

Article 18 Right to asylum

The right to asylum shall be guaranteed with due respect for the rules of the Geneva Convention of 28 July 1951 and the Protocol of 31 January 1967 relating to the status of refugees and in accordance with the Treaty on European Union and the Treaty on the Functioning of the European Union (hereinafter referred to as 'the Treaties').

Article 47 Right to an effective remedy and to a fair trial

Everyone whose rights and freedoms guaranteed by the law of the Union are violated has the right to an effective remedy before a tribunal in compliance with the conditions laid down in this Article.

Everyone is entitled to a fair and public hearing within a reasonable time by an independent and impartial tribunal previously established by law. Everyone shall have the possibility of being advised, defended and represented.

Legal aid shall be made available to those who lack sufficient resources in so far as such aid is necessary to ensure effective access to justice.

The right to good administration at Article 41 seemed originally to be of interest (particularly in cases involving delay or other maladministration). However, it has been interpreted as only binding the EU institutions themselves, albeit that Member State authorities may nevertheless be bound by the same right as a general principle of EU law, albeit not in the form of a Charter right – see *HN* v. *Minister for Justice, Equality and Law Reform, Ireland (Judgment of the Court)* [2014] EUECJ C-604/ 12.

Abdulla (Eritrea)

Abdullah, a citizen of Eritrea, claimed asylum 18 months ago. The claim has not been determined. His wife is stranded in Libya unable to apply to join him here absent a positive result on his application.

Abdullah could argue that good administration requires reasonably efficient determination of his asylum claim.

Article 1 may offer support to arguments that seekers and beneficiaries of asylum (and HP) status should be treated at a minimum level of decency and may be similarly applicable to removees in cases with an EU dimension.

Article 18 bestows a 'right' to refugee status – notoriously the Refugee Convention gives no more than a right not to be removed to territories where one's life or freedom would be threatened, not a right to status.

Article 47 has both a procedural and a substantive dimension. Procedurally it requires:

- an effective remedy before a tribunal;
- within a reasonable time;
- with the possibility of legal representation;
- legal aid where effective access to justice would otherwise be threatened.

See *Gudanaviciene* [2014] EWCA Civ 1622, holding at [32] that:

> if the Director concludes that a denial of [funding] would be a breach of an individual's Convention or EU rights, he must make an exceptional funding determination. But as we shall see, the application of the ECtHR and CJEU case-law is not hard-edged. It requires an assessment of the likely shape of the proposed litigation and the individual's ability to have effective access to justice in relation to it.

Substantively, it requires effective review of government decisions: see *Bank Tejarat* v. *Council (Judgment)* [2015] EUECJ T-176/12 at [37]:

> The effectiveness of the judicial review guaranteed by Article 47 of the Charter of Fundamental Rights of the European Union requires in particular that the Courts of the European Union ensure that the measure at issue, which affects the person or entity concerned individually, is taken on a sufficiently solid factual basis. That entails a verification of the facts alleged in the summary of reasons underpinning that measure, with the consequence that judicial review cannot be restricted to an assessment of the cogency in the abstract of the reasons relied on, but must concern whether those reasons, or, at the very least, one of those reasons, deemed sufficient in itself to support that decision, is substantiated ...

3.5   ASYLUM APPEALS

3.5.1   Appeals in the First-tier Tribunal

3.5.1.1   Introduction

Under NIAA 2002, certain decisions of the Home Office give rise to an independent right of appeal before a judge of the First-tier Tribunal (Immigration and Asylum Chamber). The First-tier Tribunal judge has the power to allow or dismiss an appeal, subject only to a further challenge on points of law to the Upper Tribunal (Immigration and Asylum Chamber).

The appeals system created by the extensive amendment of NIAA 2002 by IA 2014 entered into full effect on 6 April 2015, although there will be a lengthy transitional period while cases under the old appeals system are listed and heard. The new appeals provisions are known as the 'relevant provisions' because that is how they are described in the commencement orders that introduce IA 2014 (whereas the old appeals system is known as the 'saved provisions'). Key features are:

(a)   new removal powers under the 'single decision' process, empowering removal via a single step for anyone who needs leave to enter/remain but does not have it, under which the Home Office says it will give only limited notice of removal beyond the provision of a 'one stop' notice when the last application is refused;

(b)   a clear ongoing duty to appraise the Home Office of any changes to one's circumstances under NIAA 2002, s.120;

(c)   no right of appeal unless the present immigration decision relates to a claim on human rights or asylum grounds;

(d)   no grounds of appeal other than human rights or asylum, preventing a review of the decision's correctness by reference to the Immigration Rules or on the basis that it is otherwise not in accordance with the law;

(e)   for those cases that lack a right of appeal, a potential remedy by way of administrative review, and a potential further remedy by way of judicial review;

(f)   appeals against EEA decisions survive the changes (as they arise not from NIAA 2002 but from the Immigration (European Economic Area) Regulations 2006, SI 2006/1003), but themselves become subject to the one stop regime, so that human rights can be raised only if a one stop notice is served on the applicant and returned to the Home Office.

3.5.1.2   Rights of appeal

The immigration appeals system radically changed from 6 April 2015 (for our purposes: migrants under the points-based system entered the new system earlier;

131

deportees entered it from autumn 2015). The practical operation of the appeals system, from the Home Office perspective, is explained in a series of guidance documents within the Operational Guidance collection (Modernised Guidance, Appeals at **www.gov.uk/government/publications/appeals**).

Under the system with which immigration practitioners were long familiar, a right of appeal arose with respect to an immigration decision (e.g. to refuse entry clearance, leave to enter or leave to remain, in the latter case only where current leave was held at the date of decision; to make removal directions against illegal entrants and overstayers; to cancel leave to enter; and so forth); then various grounds of appeal were available. The immigration decisions were set out in NIAA 2002, s.82; the grounds of appeal in s.84.

Sections 82 and 84 still exist, but they have different content. Now a refusal of a protection or human rights claim gives rise to a right of appeal; other encounters with the authorities do not do so.

Section 82(1) now reads:

82 Right of appeal to the Tribunal

(1)   A person ('P') may appeal to the Tribunal where –

    (a)   the Secretary of State has decided to refuse a protection claim made by P,

    (b)   the Secretary of State has decided to refuse a human rights claim made by P, or

    (c)   the Secretary of State has decided to revoke P's protection status.

3.5.1.3   Protection claims

A protection claim is one where a person alleges their removal would contravene the Refugee Convention or the UK's obligations in relation to HP. Such a claim is refused where the Home Office decides that removal would not breach the relevant Convention.

3.5.1.4   Grounds of appeal

Section 84 of NIAA 2002, which provides the grounds (or legal reasons or basis) for an appeal, now provides:

84 Grounds of appeal

(1)   An appeal under section 82(1)(a) (refusal of protection claim) must be brought on one or more of the following grounds –

    (a)   that removal of the appellant from the United Kingdom would breach the United Kingdom's obligations under the Refugee Convention;

    (b)   that removal of the appellant from the United Kingdom would breach the United Kingdom's obligations in relation to persons eligible for a grant of humanitarian protection;

The new system has a number of implications as to the way that immigration lawyers think about appeals:

- Encounters with the immigration authorities no longer generate a right of appeal absent an asylum/human rights application (so decisions to issue removal directions or cancel leave to enter or remain will no longer carry the right of appeal until the relevant application has been made and refused: section 120 notices should be issued when such encounters occur, so nobody should face removal before they have had the opportunity to respond to those notices).
- There will still be upgrading appeals against refusal of refugee status or HP notwithstanding the grant of discretionary leave to remain: because the grant of any form of leave to remain is irrelevant to the existence of a right of appeal, and the refusal of international protection itself generates a right of appeal.
- It seems that post-decision evidence can be introduced in new-style appeals generally, i.e. there is no longer a distinction between entry clearance appeals and in-country ones.
- The Home Office may control the raising of new arguments on appeal, via granting/withholding consent regarding matters sought to be raised late – in particular under NIAA 2002, s.85 it has to give its consent for a matter to be admitted on appeal where it has not been previously considered either in the decision appealed against or in a decision on grounds raised in a response to a 'one stop' notice.
- Post-decision evidence can be taken into account in all kinds of immigration appeals under NIAA 2002, s.85.

3.5.1.5   First-tier Tribunal Procedure Rules

Immigration appeals in the First-tier Tribunal are, as from 20 October 2014, governed by the Tribunal Procedure (First-tier Tribunal) (Immigration and Asylum Chamber) Rules 2014, SI 2014/2604 ('the Rules').

Immigration appeals to the Immigration and Asylum Chamber of the Upper Tribunal are governed by the amended Tribunal Procedure (Upper Tribunal) Rules 2008, SI 2008/2698, addressed at **3.5.2**.

The procedure rules are supplemented by Practice Directions (**Appendix B3**), Practice Statements (**Appendix B4**) and Guidance Notes.

The current rules are drafted by an independent panel of lawyers (not simply by the Home Office, as were their predecessors). Their features include:

- new and significantly longer deadlines for lodging appeals (rule 19);
- the possibility of an award of 'wasted' costs, where a party has acted improperly, unreasonably or negligently (rule 9);
- some measure of judicial control over attempts by the Home Office to vary refusal letters because of the need for consent to vary a document and to alert the Tribunal of the basis for defending a case 28 days before the hearing (rules 23 and 24);

- some measure of judicial control over withdrawal of Home Office decisions, because an appeal can be heard notwithstanding the withdrawal of the underlying decision where there is 'good reason' (rule 17).

OVERRIDING OBJECTIVE

The overriding objective of the Rules, and therefore the Tribunal, is to deal with cases fairly and justly (rule 2(1)). This replaces the old maxim of 'fairly, quickly and efficiently as possible'. Gone too is a reference to 'the public interest'. This all sounds good, particularly for appellants seeking directions against the Home Office, or adjournments. Rule 2(1) interprets 'fairly and justly' as including:

(a) dealing with the case in ways which are proportionate to the importance of the case, the complexity of the issues, the anticipated costs and the resources of the parties and of the Tribunal;

(b) avoiding unnecessary formality and seeking flexibility in the proceedings;

(c) ensuring, so far as practicable, that the parties are able to participate fully in the proceedings;

(d) using any special expertise of the Tribunal effectively; and

(e) avoiding delay, so far as compatible with proper consideration of the issues.

These considerations should be borne in mind whenever a judge is making any decision under the Rules, from extending time to considering the consequences of breach of directions.

LODGING APPEALS

The notice of appeal must be sent, faxed, or submitted online to the First-tier Tribunal (Immigration and Asylum Chamber) itself, though detainees can serve their notice of appeal on their custodian if in detention.

Information about submitting appeals including online lodging is online headed 'Appeal against a visa or immigration decision'.

The notice of appeal must, if reasonably practicable, be accompanied by the notice of decision, and the reasons for that decision, against which the appellant is appealing (rule 19).

Rule 19 also requires the notice of appeal to set out the grounds of appeal (but not, as under the old rules, the reasons), and lists the additional information that must be provided with the notice.

A fee is payable for appeals before the Tribunal, under the provisions of the First-tier Tribunal (Immigration and Asylum Chamber) Fees Order 2011, SI 2011/2841, unless the appellant is exempt. Those exempt include those appealing a removal decision, those in receipt of legal aid, and minors being cared for by a local authority. The fee is £140 for an oral hearing and £80 for the appeal to be decided on the papers.

Detailed guidance on fees is available in the guidance including assistance on applying for a fee remission if there are exceptional circumstances (i.e. you cannot afford to pay the fee): it makes the point that as most immigration routes require self-sufficiency it is hard to imagine grounds for fee exemption in any of those cases.

As well as filling out the information on the form, an appellant should provide:

- the notice of decision against which the appeal is brought, or an explanation as to why it is not practicable to do so;
- any statement of reasons for that decision;
- all documents not already supplied to the respondent;
- an application to the Lord Chancellor to issue a certificate of fee satisfaction;
- any further documents or information required by any relevant practice direction.

DEADLINE FOR APPEAL

The deadlines for receipt by the Tribunal of the notice of appeal are specified at rule 19:

- 14 days after being sent the notice of decision if appellant is in the UK;
- 28 days after departure where appellant was in the UK when decision made, but appeal is out of country;
- 28 days from receipt of the decision in other cases.

The distinction between business and calendar days has largely disappeared, as have the deemed receipt provisions; there is no longer any difference between deadlines for those detained as opposed to those at liberty. Days are calendar days, finishing at midnight; but where a deadline falls on a day other than a working day, the act is done in time if it is done on the next working day (rule 11).

Rahul

Rahul comes to your office having received a decision from the Home Office on Tuesday 12 May; the notice of decision is dated Friday 8 May. He wishes to identify the deadline to appeal.

He is in the UK so the relevant provision is rule 19(2): 'the notice of appeal must be received not later than 14 days after they are sent the notice of the decision'.

These are 'days' not 'working days'. Sometimes the rules do refer to working days, but not here. So the primary focus is on when he was sent the decision (thus prudent legal offices always keep copies of the envelopes in which decisions are sent on file where there is a difference between the stamped date of posting and the date on the notice of decision itself).

If the refusal letter was sent on Friday 8 May, the notice of appeal must be sent not later than 14 calendar days later: so he has until Friday 22 May, until midnight that day (rule 11(1)). If the refusal letter was sent on Saturday 9 May, while the calculation would initially produce the date of Saturday 23 May, rule 11(2) allows the application to be treated as in time when done on the next working day, i.e. Monday 25 May.

EXTENSION OF TIME FOR LODGING NOTICE OF APPEAL

There is provision at rule 20 for lodging an appeal outside the time limit in rule 19. The notice of appeal must include an application for such an extension of time and the reason why the notice of appeal was not provided in time.

Where the Tribunal believes that an appeal has not been lodged in time, but there has been no application for an extension, the Tribunal must notify the person in writing to give them an opportunity to either contend that it was lodged in time or apply to extend time.

There is no independent legal test in rule 20 to govern the exercise of the Tribunal's discretion (under rule 4(3)(a)) to extend time. The Tribunal must make a decision that is fair and just as per its overriding objective.

Any application for an extension should therefore give reasons why it is fair and just in the particular case to extend time – explaining, with evidence, the reason for the delay, and showing why justice requires a hearing. The interests of justice will usually depend on the importance of the issues being litigated and the merits of the client's case. If there is some real purpose to the hearing, justice suggests it should be allowed to go ahead. There is a significant amount of guidance given in *BO and others (extension of time for appealing) Nigeria* [2006] UKAIT 35, which identifies five principal themes likely to arise:

- Strength of the grounds of appeal (strong grounds may compensate for a poor excuse).
- The consequences of the decision (removal from the UK is a more pressing consequence than the refusal of leave where another application can be made).
- Length of delay (shortness of delay is not in itself a reason to extend time; a good excuse can explain even the longest of delays).
- Prejudice to the respondent (unlikely to be relevant in individual cases).
- Mistakes, delays and breaches of rules by the respondent (if the Home Office has delayed in the case's consideration or issued misleading information, this may mitigate a putative appellant's own delays).

Practice point

Always back applications for the exercise of discretion, such as seeking an extension of time, by a reasoned explanation supported by evidence.

Critically interrogate any documents you are provided with before submitting them – a doctor's note that is equivocal, uses language such as 'I am told ...' or 'I have no reason to doubt' is not persuasive.

And never let the deadline expire once you are instructed. It is better to stay in the office late and get something submitted in time, or instruct counsel to do the drafting if you have no time, even if you may then need to apply to vary the grounds of appeal later when you have more information. This applies however late in the relevant window for appealing the document was received by you or your client.

> If the error truly lies in your office, then admit it: it is difficult for the Tribunal to let a migrant suffer because of the errors of their legal representatives.

REJECTING INVALID NOTICE OF APPEAL

The First-tier Tribunal has specific powers to reject an invalid notice of appeal under rule 22. These operate where a person has given a notice of appeal to the Tribunal and there is no appealable decision (i.e. no 'decision from which there is a right of appeal to the Immigration and Asylum Chamber of the First-tier Tribunal' or where the Lord Chancellor has not issued a certificate of fee satisfaction.

In these circumstances the Tribunal must decline to accept the notice of appeal, notify the person giving the notice of appeal and the respondent, and then take no further action. The Tribunal aims to scrutinise all notices of appeal for validity and identify the problems early on, though the Practice Statement explains that the point may nevertheless only be noticed at the hearing stage in which case it will have to be dealt with there and then. In the former case the Tribunal will rule on the question as a preliminary issue so there will be no right of appeal and judicial review will be the only remedy; if the matter arises at a hearing then the Tribunal will issue a decision and there will be a right of onwards appeal: see Practice Statement 3.2–3.3 and *BO and others (extension of time for appealing) Nigeria* [2006] UKAIT 35.

Example

In a new-style appeal, the Home Office has refused further representations claiming to be a fresh human rights claim, concluding that they are not sufficiently different from the claim as previously put to have any prospect of success. You disagree. You lodge an appeal to the First-tier Tribunal arguing that as, properly evaluated, there was a fresh human rights claim present, and that therefore the Tribunal's jurisdiction is engaged.

The First-tier Tribunal responds by issuing a notice that in its view there is no appealable immigration decision.

If you want to take the matter further, you must now issue judicial review proceedings: in the Administrative Court, as the Upper Tribunal does not deal with judicial reviews within the Tribunal system itself.

If, on the other hand, the First-tier Tribunal decided to hold a hearing for the matter of jurisdiction to be argued, then the remedy would be a right of appeal to the Upper Tribunal.

CASE MANAGEMENT POWERS

Under the new Rules, at rules 4 and 14 particularly, the Tribunal has wide-ranging case management powers.

Under rule 4, the Tribunal may give a direction in relation to the conduct or disposal of proceedings at any time, including a direction amending, suspending or setting aside an earlier direction. A party can request or challenge a direction under rule 5.

Among other things, the Tribunal may:

- extend or shorten time limits;
- consolidate (join) proceedings (e.g. where family members or business partners have similar claims);
- permit or require a party to or another person to provide documents, information, evidence or submissions;
- permit matters to be decided as preliminary issues.

There is no longer a specific provision relating to the holding of case management review hearings, but the Tribunal can hold a hearing on a case management issue if it so directs.

Directions as to issues, evidence, expert evidence, and witnesses can be given under rule 14. Witnesses can be summoned to attend, or answer questions or produce documents on application of either party or on the Tribunal's own volition under rule 15.

Rule 6 allows the Tribunal to take such action as it considers just where there has been non-compliance with a rule or direction, including referring the matter to the Upper Tribunal to exercise its powers under s.25 of the Tribunals, Courts and Enforcement Act 2007 (which are the same as those exercised by the High Court – i.e. scary ones which include powers to punish breach of an order to attend court by witness summons, or to produce documents, via contempt proceedings).

Example

You have failed to comply with a direction to produce witness statements for every witness you wish to call. The judge has a choice of action under rule 6 (though the draconian option of referral to the Upper Tribunal for contempt proceedings under rule 6(3) is not available as this does not involve a witness summons or production of a document):

- waiving the requirement under rule 6(2)(a) (i.e. proceeding to hear oral evidence without a witness statement);
- requiring the failure to be remedied under rule 6(2)(b) (i.e. ordering a witness statement be drafted there and then); and
- thinking up another appropriate option given that the possibilities mentioned in the Rules are not exhaustive: so other options may be relevant, including adjournment if the evidence of the witness is something that demands sufficient notice to the Home Office for it to make its own enquiries into the person's assertions or immigration history.

In practice, standard directions issued with the notice of hearing sent to the parties will include a date by which directions must be complied with, and require the appellant to produce:

- witness statements of the evidence to be called at the hearing, such statements to stand as evidence in chief at the hearing;
- a paginated and indexed bundle of all the documents to be relied on at the hearing with a schedule identifying the essential passages (where an essential reading list is provided, it should never simply mirror the index to the bundle: the essential reading list refers to those passages that the advocate will actually be taking the judge to in court);
- a skeleton argument, identifying all relevant issues including human rights claims and citing all the authorities relied upon; and
- a chronology of events.

A witness statement should confirm that it has been read back and understood by its author, and that it represents a true account of the relevant facts, with a separate clause signed by the interpreter (if one was used) confirming that the author understood the read-back.

FAMILY LAW PROCEEDINGS

There is specific guidance as to liaison between the immigration and family courts where there are extant family law proceedings. Where this situation arises, it is necessary to consider whether one court would benefit from findings made in the other. You can see the issues described in the case law, particularly *RS (immigration and family court proceedings) India* [2012] UKUT 218 (IAC) and *RS (immigration/family court liaison: outcome) India* [2013] UKUT 82 which recognise that:

- The two legal systems are likely to benefit from one another's findings, i.e. the family court will be assisted by knowing whether a particular individual will be remaining in this country, and the immigration court will be interested to know where the best interests of any children actually lie.
- The First-tier Tribunal lacks some of the facilities available in family proceedings such as qualified independent guardians and social workers, which means that the latter's informed view on best interests is very likely to be valuable to the Tribunal's decision making.

Relevant questions as set out in *RS India* will be:

i)   Does the claimant have at least an Article 8 right to remain until the conclusion of the family proceedings?

ii) If so, should the appeal be allowed to a limited extent and a discretionary leave be directed …?

iii) Alternatively, is it more appropriate for a short period of an adjournment to be granted to enable the core decision to be made in the family proceedings?

iv) Is it likely that the family court would be assisted by a view on the present state of knowledge of whether the appellant would be allowed to remain in the event that the outcome of the family proceedings is the maintenance of family contact between him or her and a child resident here?

Further considerations will arise in a criminal deportation case, such as whether there is reason to think the family proceedings amount to an attempt to stave off removal without there being any genuine underlying family life and whether realistically any such proceedings will make any difference to the appeal's outcome.

Vikram and Manjit

Vikram has three children by different mothers. Throughout their lives he has rarely seen them and has taken little interest in their upbringing. The records held by social services about the family do not mention him as playing any significant part in their lives in the past. It is difficult to see that there is any need for adjournment of the immigration proceedings if family proceedings are now commenced because of the relatively low chance that there will be a family order that changes the status quo.

Manjit has two children with whom he lived until he separated from his wife two years ago in acrimonious circumstances with mutual accusations of unreasonable behaviour. His wife was awarded custody of the children in the short term pending further family proceedings and he has had limited access rights so far. Manjit would seem to have quite a strong chance of improving his access rights in family law proceedings and his attempts to engage with historic proceedings suggest he is serious in his wish to play a part in litigation for which he needs to be present in order to participate in best interests assessments by social services and so forth.

DOCUMENTS TO BE SENT TO TRIBUNAL BY THE HOME OFFICE

When the notice of appeal is sent to the Home Office, rules 23 (for entry clearance cases) and 24 (for other cases) require the Home Office to provide to the Tribunal:

- the notices of decision to which the appeal relates;
- any document giving reasons for the decisions;
- any statement or application form;
- interview records relevant to the decisions;
- any other unpublished documents referred to in the decision or reasons for refusal (which could range from interview records to the evidence backing up assertions about the situation in a particular country or about an individual's immigration history);
- the notice of any other appealable decision made in relation to the appellant.

This gives some power to the Tribunal to extract documents from the Home Office. If the Home Office or entry clearance officer (ECO) fails to produce the materials set out above, then they may well have failed to discharge the burden of proof that lies on them in a general refusal reasons case (see *Cvetkovs (visa – no file produced – directions) Latvia* [2011] UKUT 212 (IAC)).

The appellant can additionally request directions and/or the issue of a witness summons to get further disclosure, as dealt with above under directions under rule 4.

Interview records should be disclosed, as should any adverse related comments by the interviewing officer that are passed on to the decision maker.

OTHER IMPORTANT PROCEDURE RULES

There are a few other procedure rules that it is worth being familiar with, although this accreditation course is very much intended to be a brief overview – do consider one of our other HJT courses, such as Appeals for Experts, if you want to know more.

Evidence has to be disclosed to all parties in general, though there are some powers under rule 13 to withhold disclosure if otherwise a person might be caused serious harm and where it is proportionate to the interests of justice to do so – in *R (on the application of Immigration Law Practitioners Association)* v. *Tribunal Procedure Committee and another* [2016] EWHC 218 (Admin), the court found that were this rule ever to be used, the judge must act judicially and apply the overriding objective of the Immigration Rules to achieve fairness: its use would have to be proportionate, and it was improbable that a judge properly directing himself would in fact invoke it so as to exclude an appellant and their representative from relevant parts of the proceedings.

Grounds of appeal can be varied with the First-tier Tribunal's permission (rule 19(7)) (subject to the need for Home Office consent under NIAA 2002, s.85).

The ECO's or Home Office's refusal letter can be amended but this requires permission (rule 4(3)(c)) and the making of a formal application 28 days before the hearing (rules 23(2)(b) and 24(2)).

Adjournments are addressed at rule 4(3)(h) and must be applied for not later than 5 pm a full working day before the hearing, otherwise there must be representation at the hearing to pursue the application.

Good grounds for adjournment will include illness or other compelling reasons preventing attendance, late changes to the circumstances of the appellant or to the refusal reasons, or a need for further time to collect evidence for reasons outside the requesting party's control. Reasons to refuse adjournments will be late applications, speculative ones which do not evidence a reliable source or timetable for the evidence to be obtained, or which have not identified a relevant issue to which such evidence relates, or where the party or representative has not been duly diligent in pursuing lines of enquiry – see generally Presidential Guidance Note No.1 of 2014.

Hearings generally take place in public (rule 27) subject to powers to exclude a disruptive person or one who might inhibit the giving of evidence or making of submissions, and to exclude a person where material that might cause serious harm is involved, or where the purpose of the hearing would be defeated by their attendance (anonymity might be ordered in the last scenario). The Guidance Note on Anonymity Directions in the First-tier Tribunal highlights cases involving children or vulnerable persons where the appeal may involve their personal infor-mation and their welfare may be injured by undue disclosure, and any cases where there is highly personal evidence that should remain confidential or might risk harm to individuals if disclosed.

An appeal may be heard in the absence of a party where due notice of the hearing has been given and it is in the interests of justice to do so (rule 28); and may be considered without a hearing (i.e. on the papers in the absence of both parties) by consent, or where the interests of justice or serious non-compliance with the procedure rules or directions make this a proportionate response to the situation, both sides having been given the opportunity to make representations (rule 25).

3.5.2   Onwards appeals to the Upper Tribunal

3.5.2.1   Basis of application

Applications for permission to appeal are made only on the basis of an error of law, which basically requires the First-tier Tribunal to have:

- made a misdirection of law (e.g. about the meaning of the Immigration Rules, or the definition of persecution or state protection in an asylum claim);
- (much more commonly) overlooked evidence;
- conducted the proceedings unfairly; or
- made an error of fact to which the appellant did not contribute.

These were the errors as identified in *R (Iran) and others* v. *Secretary of State for the Home Department* [2005] EWCA Civ 982 which went on to consider in detail what amounts to 'an error of law'.

3.5.2.2   Seeking permission to appeal to the Upper Tribunal from the First-tier Tribunal

A decision of the First-tier Tribunal can be challenged by either party on a point of law. To do so the complaining party must make an application to the First-tier Tribunal for permission to appeal to the Upper Tribunal. If permission is refused, the application for permission to appeal can be made directly to the Upper Tribunal. The practice point at **3.5.2.3** above sets out the various stages in applying for permission to appeal and pursuing such an application further.

APPLICATION TO THE FIRST-TIER TRIBUNAL

An application form is provided on the HM Courts and Tribunals Form Finder website, IAFT-4: Application to the First-tier Tribunal for permission to appeal to the Upper Tribunal (**http://hmctsformfinder.justice.gov.uk**).

The deadline for receipt of the application by the First-tier Tribunal is 14 days after the date on which the party making the application was provided with written reasons for the decision and 28 days where the appellant is outside the UK.

The application must:

(a)   identify the decision of the Tribunal to which it relates;
(b)   identify the alleged error or errors of law in the decision; and
(c)   state the result that the party seeks.

An application for an extension of time can be made if necessary (rule 33(5)(c) – the touchstone for decisions generally in the First-tier Tribunal is dealing with cases fairly and justly).

Under the Rules, there are several possible routes to a First-tier Tribunal decision being overturned: self-review (rule 35), 'set aside' where a document was over-looked or a hearing not attended or some other procedural irregularity took place (rule 32), as well as the much more common grant of permission to appeal to the Upper Tribunal. If the party does have a preference, submissions could be made on this point in the grounds of appeal.

Decisions made in the First-tier Tribunal on review and permission to appeal are made by a select band of experienced First-tier Tribunal judges. Those made in the Upper Tribunal are made by Upper Tribunal judges or deputy judges.

The first thing the First-tier Tribunal has to do on receipt of an application for permission to appeal is decide whether it should itself review the decision against which an appeal is sought. This is very rare.

3.5.2.3   Seeking permission to appeal from the Upper Tribunal

If the First-tier Tribunal refuses permission, or refuses to extend time for the application for permission, a further application can be made directly to the Upper Tribunal. Applications to the Upper Tribunal are governed by the Tribunal Proce-dure (Upper Tribunal) Rules 2008 (Upper Tribunal Rules) (see **Appendix B2**).

The application to the Upper Tribunal must be received no later than 14 days after the date on which notice of the First-tier Tribunal's refusal of permission was sent to the appellant (or four less in fast-track cases). The time limit is one month where the appellant is outside the UK (see Upper Tribunal Rules, rule 21). Rule 5(3)(a) imparts the Upper Tribunal with discretion to vary any time limits, so if an application is made late reasons should be included.

The form provided (although not specified as compulsory in the rules) for applications to the Upper Tribunal for permission to appeal to the Upper Tribunal is IAUT–1: Application to the Upper Tribunal for permission to appeal to the Upper Tribunal.

If permission to appeal to the Upper Tribunal is granted by the Upper Tribunal, written notice must be given to both parties.

STATUS AND RACE RELATIONS APPEALS

There is a specific procedure laid out at Upper Tribunal Rules, rule 17A and Practice Direction 5 for pursuing an appeal where leave has been granted and the appeal would otherwise be treated as abandoned, i.e. where refugee status is sought or the appellant wants a finding made on race discrimination grounds.

PURSUING AN UPPER TRIBUNAL APPEAL

Procedure in the Upper Tribunal is dictated by the amended Tribunal Procedure (Upper Tribunal) Rules 2008 in combination with the joint Practice Directions and Practice Statements of the First-tier Tribunal and Upper Tribunal Immigration and Asylum Chambers. Because the Immigration and Asylum Chamber joined the unified tribunal structure fairly late in its procedural development, very often the immigration-specific rules are made by way of amendments, so always read through a particular rule carefully to ensure that you are actually reading about immigration rather than general Upper Tribunal procedure.

NON-COMPLIANCE IN THE UPPER TRIBUNAL

Non-compliance with Upper Tribunal Rules is explicitly dealt with at rule 7 and also rule 8 (strike out of case), rule 10 (wasted costs) and rule 5 (case management). However, rules 8 and 10 do not apply in immigration and asylum cases, leaving the Upper Tribunal with very limited powers.

RESPONDENT'S RESPONSE TO APPEAL

Rule 24(1A) states that, subject to any directions from the Tribunal, the respondent 'may' (not 'must') lodge a response to a notice of appeal. However, it is always open to the Upper Tribunal to consider the response to be an important stage of the process and failure to lodge one may have consequences so it is a good idea to always give brief reasons for defending the appeal against the arguments made by the appellant Secretary of State or ECO. The response should state:

- the respondent's name and address for service purposes;
- whether they oppose the appeal;
- their grounds for doing so; and
- whether they seek an oral hearing.

If the appellant to the Upper Tribunal wishes to take issue with something said in the response, they may lodge a reply – on the earlier date of either a month of being sent the response, or five days before the hearing (Upper Tribunal Rules, rule 25).

FURTHER EVIDENCE

The Upper Tribunal may consider fresh evidence not previously relied on in the First-tier Tribunal. A specific provision was inserted into the general Upper Tribunal Rules to deal specifically with immigration and asylum appeals, however; see rule 15(2A):

> (2A) In an asylum case or an immigration case –
>
>> (a) if a party wishes the Upper Tribunal to consider evidence that was not before the First-tier Tribunal, that party must send or deliver a notice to the Upper Tribunal and any other party –
>>
>>> (i) indicating the nature of the evidence; and
>>> (ii) explaining why it was not submitted to the First-tier Tribunal; and
>>
>> (b) when considering whether to admit evidence that was not before the First-tier Tribunal, the Upper Tribunal must have regard to whether there has been unreasonable delay in producing that evidence.

Practice Direction 4 emphasises that rule 15(2A) must be complied with in every case where a party wishes to rely on further evidence. In addition, a party seeking to adduce new evidence must make it clear in the rule 15(2A) notice whether the evidence is (para.4.2):

> (a) in connection with the issue of whether the First-tier Tribunal made an error of law, requiring its decision to be set aside; or
> (b) in connection with the re-making of the decision by the Upper Tribunal, in the event of the First-tier Tribunal being found to have made such an error.

In asylum and human rights cases where the facts have to be decided at the date of hearing, it will be normal for fresh country information evidence to be admitted.

INITIAL HEARING

The first issue to be decided in the Upper Tribunal will be whether there was in fact an error of law in the decision of the First-tier Tribunal. This test is a prerequisite to an appeal to the Upper Tribunal and must be satisfied in all cases, whether permission was granted by the First-tier Tribunal or the Upper Tribunal. The possible grounds for asserting that there is an error of law are addressed briefly above.

It will be unusual for new evidence to be relied on at this stage in the proceedings (unless it goes to procedural unfairness which actually took place at the hearing) because the focus must be the material that was before the decision maker who it is contended committed an error of law.

The procedure to be followed on appeal is set out in Practice Direction 3. There is a clear steer towards the Upper Tribunal retaining cases for final decision rather than remitting them to the First-tier Tribunal, though in practice there appears to be a shift more towards remittal.

145

A choice has to be made as to whether the appeal should be prepared for full re-hearing in advance of an initial error of law hearing: if the preparation is done it may be wasted as no error of law may be established; if it is not done, then a Upper Tribunal judge may wish to proceed to the second stage of re-determining the appeal in any event.

Practice Direction 3 provides as follows:

> 3.2 The parties should be aware that, in the circumstances described in paragraph 3.1(c), the Upper Tribunal will generally expect to proceed, without any further hearing, to re-make the decision, where this can be undertaken without having to hear oral evidence ...
>
> 3.3 In a case where no oral evidence is likely to be required in order for the Upper Tribunal to re-make the decision, the Upper Tribunal will therefore expect any documentary evidence relevant to the re-making of the decision to be adduced in accordance with Practice Direction 4 so that it may be considered at the relevant hearing; and, accordingly, the party seeking to rely on such documentary evidence will be expected to show good reason why it is not reasonably practicable to adduce the same in order for it to be considered at that hearing.

It therefore seems safe to assume that where the error of law asserted is such that oral evidence would be necessary for a re-decision, witnesses need not attend the initial Upper Tribunal hearing and full up-to-date evidence need not be prepared. In all other cases, representatives have to assess whether it is 'reasonably practicable' to prepare and adduce any necessary further evidence.

It is impossible to give firm guidance. Common sense and experience will be required in assessing whether to prepare on the basis that the Upper Tribunal may immediately re-hear the case. Consider the examples which follow:

- **Credibility challenge in an asylum case:** it is unlikely that the case can be redecided without oral evidence – adjournment very likely.
- **Failure to consider relevant evidence:** oral evidence may not be needed – adjournment unlikely.
- **Legal error such as Convention reason:** oral evidence is unlikely to be needed – adjournment very unlikely. In *AH (scope of s.103A reconsideration) Sudan* [2006] UKAIT 38, under the old regime but with clear analogies to the new, the Tribunal said that on reconsideration the Tribunal should adopt any parts of the earlier determination that are not vitiated by error of law.

It should be noted that consent orders are now specifically provided for, at Upper Tribunal Rules, rule 39. This would obviate the need for an error of law hearing where the error is clear though this process would require that the Home Office respond to correspondence.

Practice point

It can be seen that the main stages in the Upper Tribunal (Immigration and Asylum Chamber) procedure, from the grant of permission to the hearing should be that:

---

1. The appellant considers, if granted permission by the First-tier Tribunal (Immigration and Asylum Chamber) whether there are any grounds on which they have been refused permission that they wish to pursue, via an application direct to the Upper Tribunal.
2. The appellant and respondent have regard to the terms of the permission granted for any directions relevant to future conduct of the case.
3. The respondent considers whether to file and serve a response under rule 31, within one month (though two weeks is the target set in the Practice Directions) of the Upper Tribunal sending them the permission grant, or whether there is any aspect of the determination below, not appropriate for a response, against which they should seek permission to appeal.
4. The appellant considers whether to file and serve a reply to any respondent's response under rule 32 (within one month, or sooner).
5. The parties consider whether they wish to submit any further evidence, and if doing so should supply a rule 15(2A) notice (in line with directions or otherwise as 'soon as is practicable') indicating its nature (i.e. whether it is oral or documentary, and addressing whether it is necessary for it to be considered in relation to establishing error of law or only in the event the decision must be remade) and why it was not submitted to the First-tier Tribunal, as soon as practicable after permission to appeal is granted subject to other direction of the Upper Tribunal.
6. Any skeleton argument is provided, five working days before the hearing under the generic standard directions or as otherwise directed.
7. At the first hearing, the Upper Tribunal will consider whether an error of law has been established. If it has not, the appeal will be dismissed, orally at the hearing or subsequently in writing.
8. If an error of law has been established, the Upper Tribunal will proceed to remake the decision. In general, the expectation should be that the decision is remade there and then, subject to the need to make further findings of fact which, if a significant amount of oral evidence is required, is likely to require an adjournment or transfer in the Upper Tribunal or remittal to the First-tier Tribunal, subject to directions having been given prior to the first hearing for the taking of such evidence.

Remittal to the First-tier Tribunal is appropriate where either:

• there was not a fair hearing below, or one party lost the opportunity to put their case fully to the First-tier Tribunal;
• the extent of future fact finding demands this, i.e. a full re-hearing (necessitated because all findings in the decision are contaminated by the error(s) of law identified) is more likely to require remittal than an appeal where there is an extant platform of findings on which to build.

3.5.3 Judicial review

Unlike with modern appeals, there is no limit on the scope or the breadth of the arguments you can put: so you can challenge the decision on the basis that the Immigration Rules or Guidance have not been understood, or that evidence has been overlooked, or that the process was unfair. The most difficult kind of challenge is where the decision maker has looked at the evidence, and made a decision which you do not like, without overlooking anything – then you have to pass the highest of all public law thresholds, and establish that the decision is irrational or perverse, i.e. that no reasonable person could have come to it.

As judicial review is a 'discretionary' remedy, it may be refused where another avenue of challenge was open to you.

Damages may be available, but absent some EU or human rights law point, it will be very difficult to obtain them: in general, merely showing even serious administrative error by the Home Office is not sufficient, because you need to demonstrate malfeasance in public office which requires overt evidence of intentional or reckless mistreatment of a client, and even the most gross incompetence is unlikely to reach this threshold.

You have three months to lodge your challenge. That is a 'long stop' not a time limit. So get on with it. You need to write a Pre-Action Protocol (PAP) letter first, normally providing 21 days for reply: this in itself requires action to be taken well before the three months are up. The greater the correlation between the PAP letter and the grounds on which the judicial review ultimately succeeds, the more chance you have of recovering costs against the other side. And vice versa. The less time you give them to change their minds before lodging, the more difficult it may be to recover costs.

An elementary point but worth stressing: the PAP letter and the response to it in no way reset the clock. The whole point of the Protocol is to ensure that timely challenges are brought against original decisions. So it is not realistic to argue that a response to a PAP letter means that time starts to run again.

Normally judicial review will be brought in the Upper Tribunal. There are limited classes of case (cases with an unlawful detention dimension, declarations of incompatibility with HRA 1998) that are still lodged in the Administrative Court. You are the claimant in the Administrative Court, the applicant in the Upper Tribunal. The other side is respectively the defendant and respondent.

Judicial review is not an appeal. It is restricted to the evidence that was before the original decision maker. It causes needless confusion to mingle pre- and post-decision evidence in a judicial review bundle.

Further evidence can be admitted on judicial review proceedings only where either:

(a)   the court/Tribunal directs its admission, which might happen if permission is granted; or

(b)   where post-decision representations have been made relying on that evidence and a new decision is made.

That might happen before or after a decision on permission. At that point it is open to the applicant to apply to amend their grounds to assault the new decision. The Home Office is allowed to move the goalposts: although it is vulnerable to paying costs of the action so far if it does so (costs liability will depend on whether the reconsideration is due to an admission of inadequacy in the original decision, or has taken place wholly in response to new evidence).

148

An application for judicial review does not bring the protection of section 3C leave under IA 1971, unlike appeals and administrative review applications. So a person seeking judicial review has to recognise that unless and until he or she overturns the Home Office decision, which may be a lengthy process because of the huge numbers of challenges lodged in the Upper Tribunal, he or she will be treated as an overstayer.

Once the application for judicial review has been lodged, the Home Office will have to lodge an Acknowledgment of Service including its summary grounds of defence. That gives you a chance to see how strong its case is: it may well reveal information that you did not previously know. Then a judge will consider the application on the papers and grant or refuse permission; if the latter, you have the right to renew the application to an oral hearing.

If permission is granted, there will be a full 'substantive' hearing of the application some months after the permission decision.

If the claim fails, at either the permission or substantive stage, then the applicant is liable to pay the legal costs of the respondent, normally limited to the costs of preparing the Acknowledgment of Service if permission was refused.

3.6 EXPERT EVIDENCE

3.6.1 Instructing experts

The instruction of experts is regulated by paragraph 10 of the Practice Direction of Immigration and Asylum Chambers of the First-tier Tribunal and the Upper Tribunal.

- A party who instructs an expert must provide clear and precise instructions, together with all relevant information concerning the nature of the appellant's case, including their immigration history, the refusal reasons leading to the appeal, and copies of any relevant previous reports.
- It is the duty of experts to help the Tribunal on matters within their own expertise; this duty is paramount and overrides any obligation to the person from whom they have received instructions or by whom they are paid.
- Expert evidence should be the independent product of the expert uninfluenced by the pressures of litigation, assisting the Tribunal by providing objective, unbiased opinion on matters within the author's expertise, and should not assume the role of an advocate.

Experts should:

- consider all material facts, including those which might detract from their opinion;
- make it clear when a question or issue falls outside their expertise; and
- state when they are unable to reach a definite opinion, for example because of insufficient information.

If, after producing a report, an expert changes his or her view on any material matter, that change of view should be communicated to the parties without delay, and when appropriate to the Tribunal. An expert's report should be addressed to the Tribunal and not to those instructing the expert.

Additionally, an expert's report must:

(a) give details of the expert's qualifications;

(b) give details of any literature or other material which the expert has relied on in making the report;

(c) contain a statement setting out the substance of all facts and instructions given to the expert which are material to the opinions expressed in the report or upon which those opinions are based;

(d) make clear which of the facts stated in the report are within the expert's own knowledge;

(e) say who carried out any examination, measurement or other procedure which the expert has used for the report, give the qualifications of that person, and say whether or not the procedure has been carried out under the expert's supervision;

(f) where there is a range of opinion on the matters dealt with in the report:

(i) summarise the range of opinion, so far as reasonably practicable, and

(ii) give reasons for the expert's own opinion;

(g) contain a summary of the conclusions reached;

(h) if the expert is not able to give an opinion without qualification, state the qualification; and

(i) contain a statement that the expert understands his or her duty to the Tribunal, and has complied and will continue to comply with that duty.

A suitable Statement of Truth would take the form:

> I confirm that insofar as the facts stated in my report are within my own knowledge I have made clear which they are and I believe them to be true, and that the opinions I have expressed represent my true and complete professional opinion.

It is advisable to submit your letter of instructions together with the report, because then the immigration judge can be certain of what the expert was asked to do; and it avoids any chance that the report will be given diminished weight on account of a lack of clarity over precisely what instructions were given to the expert.

Practice point

Always check the following when instructing experts:

- fees (clarify with the expert);
- timing of report (almost inevitably there is a degree of urgency, and in any event you should agree a timetable);
- availability for giving oral evidence.

And ensure that you:

- enclose all relevant documentation (a schedule is advisable for clarity);
- explain the purpose of the report, succinctly and without legalese;
- have asked all relevant questions with regard to medical reports, psychiatric and physical (including the impact of each on the other), dealing with future prognosis, present diagnosis, present and future treatment.

3.6.2 Country expert reports

Relevant considerations in assessing such evidence (*HC and RC (trafficked women) China CG* [2009] UKAIT 27 at [50]) are:

> the authority and reputation of the author, the seriousness of the investigation by means of which they were compiled, the consistency of their conclusions and their corroboration by other sources ...

3.6.2.1 Examples of the assistance that country experts can give

While expert evidence is often provided in asylum appeals, it is seldom relied on in other kinds of immigration case, even though many would benefit from it (e.g. in assessing whether conditions abroad would be unduly harsh or would be such as to prevent integration in an Article 8 case under the Immigration Rules). In short, expert evidence will potentially be available to prove any aspect of the case, such as:

- the likely reaction of the authorities or other agencies to any aspect of your client's circumstances (including whether your client is 'low-level' and whether this matters) including whatever activities they have undertaken, and whether her sexuality or ethnicity will place her at risk;
- whether the criminal offence for which she is wanted may put her at risk of ill treatment during interrogation, detention conditions that will be inhuman or degrading, or an unfair trial;
- the consequences of future actions that the client proposes on a return;
- whether she will be at risk of ill treatment as an expelled asylum seeker;
- whether dissident activities abroad are monitored, and whether your client's activities in the UK may place her at risk;
- any aspect of the case as to which evidence that you have to hand is lacking – e.g. parties or groups unmentioned in the country evidence;
- questions of protection – whether the government's statements on human rights are contradicted by its deeds and how effective are its investigations into human rights abuses by its security forces;
- whether the relevant tests for the availability of internal location are met:

  (a) accessibility of safe haven;
  (b) safety in reaching the safe haven, or living there;
  (c) undue harshness in reaching the safe area, or living there;

(d)   discriminatory breaches of socio-economic rights;

- where such matters are in dispute, expert evidence on whether language and accent/dialect, behaviour, knowledge of local areas, are consistent with the client's account of their own background;
- the likelihood of destitution (availability of social services, family networks, discrimination in access to human rights);
- the availability of medical treatment: remember, there is little reason to suppose that most doctors have knowledge of the state of medical care abroad, as opposed to the consequences of removal on health;
- the level of stigma nationally and in local communities, e.g. regarding rape or HIV victims.

You might also wish for expert evidence as to the situation if family members were to relocate – medical treatment, discrimination or dangers aimed against westerners, health and educational facilities for children.

3.6.2.2   Finding an expert witness

The ILPA Directory of Expert Witnesses, now available on the EIN, is one source. The School of Oriental and African Studies (SOAS) is also a useful resource, and the searchable RLG website can be very helpful (contact **rlg@asylumaid.org.uk** for details).

3.6.2.3   Testing the expert witness

A guide for experts, the *Best Practice Guide for Country Evidence Experts in UK Immigration and Asylum Appeals*, is available on the EIN website. You should ensure that the expert is not partisan so as to give the appearance of a lack of objectiveness. Bear in mind the possibility for the expert to give evidence in private if there are issues of confidentiality or safety involved. Obtain a CV, bearing in mind the following indicia of expertise:

- publications, especially recent and relevant ones;
- journalism, particularly for media with a reputation for impartiality;
- advising national or international bodies, and reputable NGOs. Obviously if an expert has at any stage advised the Foreign Office, or if the Home Office has relied upon their work, that will be of particular interest. The Canadian independent documentation centre (Documentation, Information and Research Branch of the Immigration and Refugee Board (DIRB)), is among foreign organisations perceived by the Tribunal as reliable;
- academic discipline, postings and research, and work with research organisations and think tanks;

- relevant work with reputable NGOs, particularly human rights monitoring but also in the aid and development fields;
- time spent in the country.

Determine whether the expert has given evidence in legal proceedings previously – and specifically whether he or she has done so in the immigration courts.

It is advisable for the expert to avoid stepping on the toes of the judicial decision maker by expressing conclusions on 'ultimate issues' – i.e. by stating a fear of persecution is 'well founded'; by saying that a particular form of harm is 'persecution' or 'inhuman or degrading treatment or punishment'; or by stating that protection is not satisfactory to the standard required by international law. It is preferable for experts to give their opinion in their own words without using legal terms of art.

Experts should steer clear of stating that a claim is credible, although it is not inappropriate for them to comment on its consistency with country conditions, i.e. its plausibility, or to note that discrepancies involving dates are not surprising in the context of a particular culture.

Although the expert report is legally privileged, a judge may often be impressed by seeing the letter of instructions, to ensure there was no slant in the questions posed.

3.6.3 Medical evidence

Medical evidence can be of use in a number of scenarios:

- In establishing the facts of the case independently of the client's oral evidence, e.g. by showing that there is scarring present, and perhaps also that it does not have any obvious explanation other than that offered by the appellant (e.g. bullet wounds, blade wounds to the back).
- In showing physical evidence of past problems that might exacerbate risk on return to the country of origin, or in showing that present health questions may attract discrimination (e.g. HIV in some countries).
- In establishing why the client cannot themselves give a coherent account, e.g. because they have mental health problems following serious ill treatment, or because it would be unusual for a victim of trauma to be able to give details of certain episodes in their life.
- In establishing that the client has health problems counting against their return to their country of origin, where this would amount to a breach of Article 3 or Article 8 of the ECHR – this will be particularly relevant where they cannot access healthcare at all there.

Before setting out to write your letter of instructions, you should determine which of these functions you hope that the evidence will serve. While there is no absolute requirement for corroboration, bear in mind that a lack of medical evidence that is in principle capable of being obtained is sure to raise doubts in the mind of a decision maker: so always think carefully about the possibilities of obtaining a report.

Sometimes the doctor recites the asylum seeker's own account. Remember to check this for consistency with any other version provided elsewhere – there are lots of reasons why they may differ (the doctor may have less time than the solicitor to go into the story, and may have less experience of the pitfalls of working through interpreters, or may not attach quite the same weight to accuracy).

Bear in mind the chance that the witness will be found to lack credibility by the immigration judge who hears oral evidence. In such a case, the value of the report may be significantly diminished. Consider if it is possible to preserve some aspects of its value, e.g. comments on the impact of return on a traumatised individual may retain relevance even if the reasons for the trauma are rejected.

It may be that an expert's conclusion that an individual suffers PTSD is effectively decisive of the individual's claim to have suffered torture, abuse or mistreatment; or it may be that the evidence as a whole may require the appellant's account to be rejected, notwithstanding a supportive medical report: see Davis LJ in *IY (Turkey)* v. *Secretary of State for the Home Department* [2012] EWCA Civ 1560.

Equally, as was said in *KV (scarring – medical evidence) Sri Lanka* [2014] UKUT 230 (IAC) at [295]:

> In the context of a holistic assessment, where for example a claimant has given a strongly consistent and plausible account of his claim to have been tortured, but the medical evidence points against this, a decision maker might properly conclude that the claimant has nevertheless made out his claim to the lower standard.

Good reasons need to be provided before finding that an appellant has connived to mislead an expert – see Moses J in *R (on the application of Minani)* v. *Immigration Appeal Tribunal* [2004] EWHC 582 (Admin) at [26]:

> to say that it is not the duty of a doctor to disbelieve the account given by a patient may be correct but takes one absolutely nowhere. It is plain that a psychiatrist does exercise his critical facilities and experience in deciding whether he is being spun a yarn or not, and all of us sitting in these courts in different jurisdictions from time to time have heard psychiatrists saying that they do believe an account or that they do not believe an account.

3.6.3.1 Corroboration of physical injuries and scarring – the Istanbul Protocol

The UN Istanbul Protocol (*Manual on the Effective Investigation and Documentation of Torture and Other Cruel, Inhuman or Degrading Treatment or Punishment*, 2004) sets out, under Chapter V, section D, 'Examination and evaluation following specific forms of torture':

> **187.** … For each lesion and for the overall pattern of lesions, the physician should indicate the degree of consistency between it and the attribution given by the patient. The following terms are generally used:

(a)   Not consistent: the lesion could not have been caused by the trauma described;

(b)   Consistent with: the lesion could have been caused by the trauma described, but it is non-specific and there are many other possible causes;

(c)   Highly consistent: the lesion could have been caused by the trauma described, and there are few other possible causes;

(d)   Typical of: this is an appearance that is usually found with this type of trauma, but there are other possible causes;

(e)   Diagnostic of: this appearance could not have been caused in any way other than that described.

188. Ultimately, it is the overall evaluation of all lesions and not the consistency of each lesion with a particular form of torture that is important in assessing the torture story …

The Istanbul methodology was approved in *SA (Somalia)* v. *Secretary of State for the Home Department* [2006] EWCA Civ 1302. The Tribunal will often say that the existence of an injury is not probative of its alleged causation. But the more particular the injury, the greater the argument for saying that it could not have an alternative history (contrast cigarette burns on the back with scarring on the knee).

In *KV (scarring – medical evidence) Sri Lanka* the Upper Tribunal considers the question of self-infliction of injuries by proxy (SIBP). It concludes that, given it was not beyond human experience that people might voluntarily undergo SIBP, an expert should engage with the possibility where there is 'some presenting feature about the state of the evidence'.

Practice point

It is important that a medical expert's report:

- shows the doctor has read all relevant evidence including adverse assessments of the account by decision makers, resisting any temptation to conduct a running commentary on the approach of a judge;
- shows precisely what expertise is held and deployed including assessing whether a story is true (e.g. all doctors are likely to have some expertise at identifying malingerers);
- explains the extent to which their belief in an account is based on medical indicia independent of the patient's word; and
- addresses the possibility of self-infliction of scars by the appellant or by proxy where there is some presenting feature that enlivens this possibility (though this possibility should not be considered unless an appellant has had the opportunity to deal with such a suggestion).

Additionally, consider:

- Has the doctor made judgments based on the truthfulness of the appellant's account? If so, does this mean the value of the report will be wholly lost if an adverse credibility finding is made based on the evidence 'in the round', and is there anything that can be done about this (e.g. is it possible to isolate some elements of the report from the acceptance of the story)? Have they made it clear that they are aware of criticisms of the client's account (e.g. it is unhelpful to say 'I have no reason to disbelieve …' in the context of a case where there is a detailed refusal letter criticising a person's credibility)?

- Has the doctor commented on the possible causes of the client's physical and mental presentation, if it is realistic to do so, and have they given the basis for their expertise in determining causation?
- Is there any reason to make the doctor available for cross-examination, so as to be able to answer specific questions from an immigration judge?
- Has the doctor provided their methodology including any relevant diagnostic criteria?
- Has the doctor explained the reasons for their diagnosis and prognosis and any other conclusions, and is it clear how their conclusions are reached based on the presentation of the patient to them?
- Is the doctor liable to criticism from an immigration judge for not having spent sufficient time with the patient to justify their conclusions?

3.7 FEE EXEMPTIONS

There are no fees for asylum claims. Many applications do however require fees to be paid. An application may be made for a fee exemption in such cases. There are various relevant authorities.

As to applications for leave to remain, *R (on the application of Omar)* v. *Secretary of State for the Home Department* [2012] EWHC 3448 (Admin) finds at [82] that:

> The Secretary of State, as a public official, is under a duty to make and interpret rules in the light of section 3 of the Human Rights Act. The requirement in regulations 6 and 30 of the 2010 Fees Regulations that, in this class of case, a fee must be paid, there is no provision for waiver and an application without a fee 'is not validly made' must, in the light of section 3, be read subject to a qualification that the specified fee is not due where to require it to be paid would be incompatible with a person's Convention rights.

The guidance on leave to remain exemptions was ruled to be unlawful (though is not to be overturned until appeal to the Court of Appeal is resolved) because of a failure to be 'clear and objective' with respect to its treatment of a person who was on NASS or destitute *vis-à-vis* one who could objectively show themselves unable to pay a fee by cogent evidence (*R (on the application of Carter)* v. *Secretary of State for the Home Department* [2014] EWHC 2603 (Admin)).

In entry clearance cases, the relevant question is not simply whether Article 8 rights may be in play, see *Sheikh* [2011] EWHC 3390 (Admin) at [74(10)]:

> But in a case where the claimant, sponsor and family can show that they have no ability to pay the fee, it will in my view be necessary to assess in broad terms the strength and force of the underlying claim which is to be made. If, upon undertaking such an exercise, it can be seen that the claimant may well have a strong claim under Article 8 involving an aspect of the interests protected by that provision of particularly compelling force ... and that insistence on payment of the fee will set that claim at nought, then in my view an obligation may arise under Article 8 for the Secretary of State to waive the fee ... the Secretary of State and the court ... are entitled to subject the case to critical evaluation to determine its true underlying strength ...

There is no automatic duty to exempt fees in a nationality application, as found (at least for now) in *R (on the application of Williams)* v. *Secretary of State for the Home Department* [2015] EWHC 1268 (Admin) and *AHK* [2013] EWHC 1426 (Admin).

The statutory instrument requiring fees is not *ultra vires* for incompatibility with fundamental rights because most children will eventually clock up sufficient residence to make immigration applications that will bring leave to remain for them and their parents who will then be able to earn the funds to pay for such applications, and Parliament has endorsed the present strict regime.

The lack of British nationality may bring disadvantages but does not represent a material interference with someone's private life akin to a lack of leave to remain because life can go on much as before with access to travel and family life, the status quo therefore continuing.

CHAPTER 4

Deportation

4.1 STATUTORY FRAMEWORK

Section 3 of the Immigration Act 1971 (IA 1971), reproduced at **Appendix A1**, sets out that a non-British citizen is liable to deportation if:

- this is thought conducive to the public good, or he or she is a family member of such a person (s.3(5));.
- he or she is convicted of an imprisonable offence and recommended by a criminal court for deportation (s.3(6)).

Section 5 of IA 1971 describes the effect of a deportation order. It requires the person to depart, invalidates any leave that he holds, and prohibits his return while the order is extant, with the effect that those deported must first apply for the deportation order to be revoked before attempting to apply to return to the UK.

4.1.1 Exempted persons

Section 7 of IA 1971 does provide limited exemptions from deportation for long-term residents.

Persons will be exempt if they:

- are Commonwealth or Irish citizens and were such on 1 January 1971 when the 1971 Act came into force;
- were ordinarily resident in the UK on 1 January 1973 ('ordinarily resident' has no statutory meaning but has been held to exclude unlawful residence);
- have been resident in the UK for five years at the time of either a court or the Secretary of State considering whether to make a deportation order.

4.2 THE DEPORTATION REGIMES

There are currently three regimes for deportation:

- automatic;
- discretionary;
- national security.

Inclusion in a particular category is determined ordinarily by the nature of an offending act, and/or the duration of any prison sentence imposed following a conviction.

4.2.1 Automatic deportation

Automatic deportation was introduced by s.32 of the UK Borders Act 2007 (UKBA 2007) (see **Appendix A5**).

That section places a duty on the Secretary of State to make a deportation order in respect of a person who is not a British citizen and who has been convicted in the UK of an offence and sentenced to a period of imprisonment of at least 12 months (Condition 1). A second condition (Condition 2), for serious criminals not imprisoned for 12 months or more, has not yet been brought into force.

Imprisonment for 12 months or more does not include suspended sentences, or shorter consecutive sentences which only meet the test when aggregated (see definitions in s.38).

Section 32(4) introduces a statutory presumption that a deportation to which s.32 applies is conducive to the public good for the purpose of IA 1971, s.3(5)(a).

There are a series of specific exceptions to automatic deportation which are set down in UKBA 2007, s.33, as follows:

- breach of the ECHR, or Refugee Convention;
- age (under 18 at date of conviction);
- breach of EU Treaty rights;
- extradition – where the person is the subject of extradition proceedings;
- mental health grounds – but only where specific sections of the Mental Health Act 1983 apply to the person;
- recognised victim of trafficking – it is acceptance by the competent authority, rather than the making of a claim, that is critical.

The burden is on the applicant to raise the operation of an exception and to evidence the application.

Where one of these exceptions is held to be operative, either by the Secretary of State on receipt of representations or by a judge on appeal, the deportation order against an applicant will be revoked.

4.2.2 Discretionary deportation

Deportation decisions can also be made on discretionary grounds based either on a decision of the Secretary of State or on recommendation of a criminal court judge (IA 1971, s.3(5) and (6) respectively).

There is fairly limited scope for discretionary deportation now given the relatively low sentencing threshold that operates to attract automatic deportation.

However, it can be utilised in instances where one of the exceptions to automatic deportation applies.

It is also the mechanism used to effect deportation in instances where an individual presents as a persistent offender, but where sentencing does not reach the automatic deportation threshold.

4.2.3 National security cases

Where the Secretary of State certifies that the decision to make a deportation order was taken on the grounds that the person's removal from the UK would be in the interests of national security (NIAA 2002, s.97A), a person may not appeal to the Tribunal. Such a person will be able to appeal only to the Special Immigration Appeals Commission (SIAC), and only from outside the country.

If the person then makes a human rights claim, he or she can appeal in country unless the Secretary of State certifies that removal would not breach the person's human rights. In such a case, the person can appeal, in country, to SIAC against that certificate.

Given the narrow band of persons affected by this process, we will not explore this category further in this book.

4.3 THE PROCEDURE FOR DEPORTATION

There are slightly different processes in the procedures for discretionary and automatic deportation decisions, though with few practical implications. See **Table 4.1** for a comparison.

Table 4.1 Comparison of discretionary and automatic deportation

Discretionary deportation	Automatic deportation
Secretary of State identifies a person subject to deportation	Secretary of State identifies a person subject to deportation
Notice of liability to deportation is issued and an opportunity is afforded to make representations	An order is made upon identification of offending falling within the statutory scheme of UKBA 2007
Secretary of State determines whether to proceed with enforcement action, and if it is decided to proceed, notice of intention to deport is issued	An opportunity is afforded to make representations for inclusion within the statutory exceptions contained in UKBA 2007, s.33
No deportation order is made unless and until any application/appeal is finally determined	If inclusion within the exceptions is demonstrated, on application or appeal, the deportation order is revoked

4.3.1 Deportation criteria inside the Immigration Rules

The Secretary of State undertakes an assessment of whether to proceed with deportation where there are human rights considerations at play, protected by

Article 8 of the ECHR by reference to the Immigration Rules. The critical aspects of the rules in this regard are set down in paras.398 to 399C (see **Appendix D4**). As the courts have made increasingly clear, the considerations under the Immigration Rules and outside them (when they must be considered with reference to NIAA 2002, s.117C) are effectively the same.

The court in *Secretary of State for the Home Department* v. *AQ (Nigeria)* [2015] EWCA Civ 250 from [66] described the operation of the rules in an accessible manner. Paragraph 398(b) or (c) applies where either:

- criminality was punished by imprisonment of between one and four years; or
- the Secretary of State thinks the offender caused serious harm or was a persistent offender showing particular disregard for the law.

In such cases the public interest in deportation will be outweighed only where family life is established via:

- a genuine and subsisting parental relationship with a British citizen or seven-year resident child where it would be unduly harsh for the child to live with the deportee abroad or without them in the UK (para.399(a)); or
- a genuine and subsisting relationship with a British citizen or settled partner (para.399(b)) where:

  - the relationship was formed at a time when the deportee was in the UK lawfully and when his immigration status was not precarious; or
  - it would be unduly harsh for the partner to live with the deportee abroad, or in the UK without the deportee, because of compelling circumstances over and above the level as expressed in the Immigration Rules, Appendix FM, para.EX.2, i.e. exceeding 'very significant difficulties'/'very serious hardship'.

As to the meaning of 'unduly harsh', the Upper Tribunal in *MAB (para 399; 'unduly harsh')* [2015] UKUT 435 (IAC) held *inter alia* that:

> the consequences for an individual will be 'harsh' if they are 'severe' or 'bleak' and they will be 'unduly' so if they are 'inordinately' or 'excessively' harsh taking into account of all the circumstances of the individual.

Private life is established (para.399A) via:

- lawful residence in the UK for most of the deportee's life;
- social and cultural integration here;
- significant obstacles to integration into the country of return.

Paragraph 398(a) applies where criminality was punished by imprisonment exceeding four years or more.

In such cases the public interest in deportation will only be outweighed where there are very compelling circumstances over and above the private and family life routes just described.

If a person does not fall within the above thresholds, his case will be considered by reference to para.397 which states that a deportation order will not be made if the person's removal pursuant to the order would be contrary to the UK's obligations under the Refugee Convention or the ECHR.

Yumi (Thailand)

Yumi is a Thai national. She is present in the UK with limited leave having entered as the spouse of a British citizen in 2012. The couple have one child born in the UK in 2013.

In 2015 Yumi is convicted of importing class A drugs and sentenced to 54 months' imprisonment. Yumi is susceptible to automatic deportation under UKBA 2007, s.32. She can invoke the human rights exception specified in s.33(1) given her family life ties to the UK.

That deportation process is assessed against the criteria laid down in para.398(a) of the Immigration Rules, however: the fact of her marriage and the birth of her British child will not suffice to prevent removal even if it could be shown that it would be unduly harsh for them to relocate or be left without her. Rather, Yumi will have to show very compelling circumstances above and beyond obstacles to relocation by her family members, and/or the severance of family life in order to defeat deportation.

Gregor (Ukraine)

Gregor is Ukrainian. He has resided in the UK since 1994 having entered age 17. He has no family in the UK but has developed strong friendships over time.

Over the course of his residence he has committed more than 20 offences of petty crime including shoplifting and criminal damage. None of his offending has led to the imposition of a custodial sentence until 2015 when he was convicted of two counts of theft from a domestic dwelling, each of which attracted a six-month custodial sentence to run consecutively.

Gregor is not amenable to automatic deportation which is triggered only where the 12-month custody threshold is imposed in respect of a single offence. He can be deported on *discretionary* grounds as a persistent and serious offender, but may be able to resist deportation by relying upon his long residence which exceeds half his life. He will, however, need to demonstrate that he has strong attachments to the UK and is integrated here, and that there are very significant obstacles to his integration in Ukraine.

William (Jamaica)

William is a Jamaican national. He is 26 years of age. He has been present in the UK for 12 years and has been living in Brixton for most of that time. William had been admitted as a visitor but had become an overstayer failing to depart within the currency of his original leave.

In 2013, William was granted 30 months' limited leave having established on application that he had enjoyed a lengthy cohabiting relationship with Sheila, a British national, with whom he had a child. In February 2015, however, William was arrested and charged with breach of the peace and threatening behaviour following a routine stop and search during which he became agitated and remonstrated with the police. He was sentenced to 12 months in prison suspended for two years. The sentencing judge also recommended deportation.

Automatic deportation is precluded as the custodial sentence was suspended. The Secretary of State may, on the other hand, institute *discretionary* deportation proceedings against William, by reason of the recommendation for deportation. Since he is not a serious or persistent offender, he would fall within Immigration Rules, para.397, and so by reference will be subject to the generally applicable approach to the assessment of Article 8 claims.

4.3.2 Deportation criteria outside the Immigration Rules

There is potential for consideration both inside and outside the Immigration Rules.

In *MF (Nigeria)* v. *Secretary of State for the Home Department* [2013] EWCA Civ 1192, the Court of Appeal in the context of the Immigration Rules in 2012 (amended June 2014) held that the deportation rules 'provide a complete code', but indicated at [44] that 'the exceptional circumstances to be considered in the balancing exercise involve the application of a proportionality test as required by the Strasbourg jurisprudence'. This was because those rules expressly stated that 'it will only be in exceptional circumstances that the public interest in deportation will be outweighed by other factors', where the private and family life criteria as set out in those rules were not met.

4.3.2.1 'Very compelling circumstances'

The phrase 'exceptional circumstances' has been replaced in the current rules. Instead they say that where the rules are not met: 'the public interest in deportation will only be outweighed by other factors where there are very compelling circumstances over and above those described'. That change did not alter the fact that there remains a two-stage test:

- **Stage 1:** Consider the case against the benchmark of the Immigration Rules.
- **Stage 2:** If there are compelling factors falling outside the three examples of private family life given in para.399, these must be considered outside the rules.

Pitchford LJ in *Secretary of State for the Home Department* v. *AQ (Nigeria)* [2015] EWCA Civ 250 explained, however, that the second stage fell to be assessed through the 'lens of the Act and rules', so as to give the public interest proper weight.

For matters impacting on an assessment outside the Immigration Rules, there is guidance from the ECtHR in cases such as *Üner* v. *The Netherlands* [2006] ECHR 873 and *Maslov* v. *Austria* [2008] ECHR 546, the court in *Maslov* emphasising *inter alia* the following factors as material:

- the special situation of aliens who have spent most, if not all, their childhood in the host country, were brought up there and received their education there;
- the nature and seriousness of the offence committed by the applicant;

- the length of the applicant's stay in the country from which he or she is to be expelled;
- the time elapsed since the offence was committed and the applicant's conduct during that period;
- the nationalities of the various persons concerned;
- the solidity of social, cultural and family ties with the host country and with the country of destination.

Note: the Court of Appeal in *R (on the application of Akpinar)* v. *Upper Tribunal (Immigration and Asylum Chamber)* [2014] EWCA Civ 937 and *D* v. *Secretary of State for the Home Department* [2012] EWCA Civ 39 emphasised that unlawful long residence, even from childhood, does not necessarily make deportation for criminal offending disproportionate, though it may be a weighty factor in the balancing exercise.

Raymond (Togo)

Raymond is a Togolese national. He entered the UK in 2006 aged 10 years. His only surviving family member, a sister, is in the UK and is a naturalised British citizen. In 2015 Raymond was convicted of assault and was sentenced to 18 months in prison. He has now been made the subject of an automatic deportation order.

While the duration of his sentence would enable him to fall within the auspices of Immigration Rules, paras.398(b)–(c) and 399A his particular facts do not:

(a)   he has neither a wife nor children in the UK; and
(b)   he has not been present for more than half his life.

He may, however, advance a case outside the rules. His long residence, prolonged cohabitation with his sister and lack of ties to Togo may enable a contention that it would be disproportionate to deport him.

4.4   APPEAL RIGHTS UNDER THE 2014 ACT

With the commencement of parts of the Immigration Act 2014 on 20 October 2014, those defined under NIAA 2002, s.117D(2) as a foreign criminal will no longer have an automatic right of appeal.

They will be served with a s.120 notice giving them an opportunity to raise a human rights or asylum claim.

The refusal of the asylum or human rights claim will give rise to a right of appeal under NIAA 2002, s.82(1).

If one manages to obtain an effective right of appeal against deportation, whether 'in-country' or 'out-of-country', the battle is by no means over.

This is because of the very high thresholds set out in the Immigration Rules. Additionally, we now have the statutory public interest considerations set out in the new s.117C of NIAA 2002. Section 117C is for the consideration of 'courts and tribunals' and largely replicates the public policy position struck by the Immigration Rules themselves:

117C Article 8: additional considerations in cases involving foreign criminals

(1) The deportation of foreign criminals is in the public interest.

(2) The more serious the offence committed by a foreign criminal, the greater is the public interest in deportation of the criminal.

(3) In the case of a foreign criminal ('C') who has not been sentenced to a period of imprisonment of four years or more, the public interest requires C's deportation unless Exception 1 or Exception 2 applies.

(4) Exception 1 applies where –

   (a) C has been lawfully resident in the United Kingdom for most of C's life,

   (b) C is socially and culturally integrated in the United Kingdom, and

   (c) there would be very significant obstacles to C's integration into the country to which C is proposed to be deported.

(5) Exception 2 applies where C has a genuine and subsisting relationship with a qualifying partner, or a genuine and subsisting parental relationship with a qualifying child, and the effect of C's deportation on the partner or child would be unduly harsh.

(6) In the case of a foreign criminal who has been sentenced to a period of imprisonment of at least four years, the public interest requires deportation unless there are very compelling circumstances, over and above those described in Exceptions 1 and 2.

(7) The considerations in subsections (1) to (6) are to be taken into account where a court or tribunal is considering a decision to deport a foreign criminal only to the extent that the reason for the decision was the offence or offences for which the criminal has been convicted.

As to the proper approach to the interpretation and application of ss.117A–117D, the Tribunal in *Dube (ss.117A–117D)* [2015] UKUT 90 (IAC) furnished the following guidance:

- 'Judges are duty-bound to "have regard" to the specified considerations.'
- The provisions are only expressed as being binding on a 'court or tribunal' so that the Secretary of State 'is not directly bound' to consider them.
- The considerations specified 'are not expressed as being exhaustive'.
- Section 117B lists considerations that are 'applicable "in all cases", which must include foreign criminal cases', so that 'when s.117C (which deals with foreign criminals) states that it sets out "additional" considerations that must mean considerations *in addition to* those set out in s.117B'.
- Sections 117A–117D 'do not represent any kind of radical departure from or "override" of previous case law on Article 8'.
- 'It is not an error of law to fail to refer to sections 117A–117D considerations if the judge has applied the test he or she was supposed to apply according to its terms; what matters is substance, not form'.

4.4.1 Assessing the public interest on appeal

Whether or not an appeal is being considered inside or outside the rules, the public interest must be accorded substantial weight.

It is material that, in the context of deportation, as the Court of Appeal observed in *SE Zimbabwe* v. *Secretary of State for the Home Department* [2014] EWCA Civ 256, the public interest has multiple facets each of which the decision maker must consider. Those facets may be detailed as follows:

- the need to prevent the foreign national reoffending;
- the need to deter others from offending;
- the need to express society's revulsion at the criminality.

While no one of those considerations takes precedence, showing a low risk – or even no risk – of recidivism may not be decisive in cases of serious offending (see *N (Kenya)* v. *Secretary of State for the Home Department* [2014] EWCA Civ 1094).

A judge determining a deportation appeal must consider the case having regard not only to the statutory considerations set out in NIAA 2002, s.117, but also to the public policy considerations identified in the Immigration Rules (*Secretary of State for the Home Department* v. *AJ (Angola)* [2014] EWCA Civ 1636).

Further, in any determination the extent of the public interest as described in statute and rules must be expressly recognised. The Court of Appeal in *Secretary of State for the Home Department* v. *MA (Somalia)* [2015] EWCA Civ 48 observed that: 'great weight [was] to be attached to [the] public interest [and] that something very compelling is required to outweigh that public interest'.

In *Velasquez Taylor* v. *Secretary of State for the Home Department* [2015] EWCA Civ 845 the Court of Appeal found that it was an error of law to allow a deportation appeal without giving sufficient weight to the requirements of the Immigration Rules and thus the public interest in the deportation of foreign criminals. Before finding the removal of foreign criminals disproportionate to their rights in respect of private and family life, it is necessary to discuss and attribute appropriate importance to the public interest in expulsion.

Practice point

It is important to consider what arguments and evidence might be available. It is not easy to acquire good evidence in deportation cases but this will be decisive on appeal. Of course getting detailed testimony from your clients and expert evidence will be far more difficult if they are to be outside the UK when preparing their appeal.

Evidence to seek might include:

- **Sentencing judge remarks.** Ensure a complete copy is obtained and do not leave it to the Home Office to do so. The Home Office often quotes very selectively and a full copy may be helpful to the client.
- **Up-to-date probation report.** Some probation officers are helpful, some are not. Whether an up-to-date report on risk of reoffending can be obtained might be critical.

- **Copies of all pre-sentence reports.** There may have been a psychological or psychiatric assessment as well as a pre-sentence probation report.
- **Solid and incontrovertible evidence of family life.** The Home Office will question everything in a deportation case, including even the existence of children or a partner. A critical factor can be whether the client can get out on bail and therefore re-establish a current and strong family life before the appeal hearing.

4.4.2 Non-suspensive appeals

We have seen that winning a deportation appeal is difficult because of the high hurdles now posed by the Immigration Rules, and by the weight afforded to public policy even outside the rules. But that is not an end to the difficulties faced by deportees.

Section 94 of NIAA 2002 has been substantially modified (with effect from 28 July 2014) so as to enable the Secretary of State to require any appeal advanced on Article 8 human rights grounds against deportation to be brought from abroad.

To create this new power, a new s.94B was inserted into NIAA 2002 by the Immigration Act 2014. Under that provision an appeal will be certified:

- in any case where deportation is considered conducive to the public good by the Secretary of State or where a court has ordered deportation: this effectively catches all deportation cases (s.94B(1));
- where the provisional Home Office view is that removal would not breach HRA 1998, and therefore the ECHR (s.94B(2));
- where the Secretary of State considers that the deportee would not, before the appeals process is exhausted, face a real risk of serious irreversible harm if removed to the proposed destination (s.94B(3)).

The effect of the certificate is described in an amended s.92 of NIAA 2002 which states that where the appeal: 'has been brought from within the United Kingdom … the appeal must be continued from outside the United Kingdom'.

4.4.2.1 'Without serious irreversible harm'

The Home Office Guidance, *Section 94B of the Nationality, Immigration and Asylum Act 2002* (**www.gov.uk/government/publications/certification-guidance-for-non-eea-deportation-cases-section-94b**), shows that it will seek to use these s.94B powers in all cases:

> The Government's policy is that the deportation process should be as efficient and effective as possible. Case owners must therefore consider whether section 94B certification is appropriate in all deportation cases where a human rights claim has been made and falls for refusal …

The idea of non-suspensive appeals in private and family life cases does not contravene fundamental rights in and of itself.

Indeed the Strasbourg Court in *De Souza Ribeiro* v. *France* [2012] ECHR 2066 expressly states that a remedy with suspensive effect, while essential in Article 3 cases, is not necessarily required in Article 8 proceedings.

Pursuant to the above the power will not be used in protection cases at least, a fact confirmed by the Home Office guidance, para.2.5, because:

> removal is likely to give rise to a real risk of serious irreversible harm such that deportation pending the outcome of an appeal may breach human rights.

As to the criteria against which serious and irreversible harm will be assessed the following considerations are material:

- the test relates to the period between deportation and the conclusion of any appeal, after which the person will return to the UK if successful;
- the test requires that the harm be serious *and* irreversible;
- while the legal burden of proof may be on the Home Office, once it makes a certificate to such effect, the evidential burden is firmly on the deportee, and only independent objective evidence will suffice.

The guidance suggests situations that in its view would not meet the test, i.e. where:

- a person will be separated from his or her child/partner for several months while the individual appeals against a human rights decision;
- a family court case is in progress;
- a child/partner is undergoing treatment for a temporary or chronic medical condition that is under control and can be satisfactorily managed through medication or other treatment and does not require the person liable to deportation to act as a full-time carer;
- the foreign national offender has a medical issue where removal would not breach Article 3 of the ECHR;
- a person has strong private life ties to a community that will be disrupted by deportation (e.g. a job, a mortgage, a prominent role in a community organisation, etc.).

The guidance offers examples of what might cross the threshold:

- where there is a genuine and subsisting parental relationship with a child or partner who is seriously ill, requires full-time care, and there is no one else who can provide that care;
- where a British citizen child's enforced departure to accompany the deportee (being his or her sole carer) would cause significant disruption to the child's education;
- where expulsion would interfere with court ordered contact with a child;
- a serious medical condition regarding which medical treatment would be unavailable or inaccessible such as to risk a significant deterioration in their health;
- where an effective appeal would be compromised.

Alexander (Russia)

Alexander, a Russian national, has been residing in the UK for more than eight years with leave as a student. In January 2015 he was convicted of a serious offence and sentenced to 20 months' imprisonment.

The sentence triggered automatic deportation and the Home Office took the view, having considered Alexander's representations, that none of the s.33 exceptions applied. Alexander was then served with a deportation order shortly before he was eligible for release in October 2015.

While a right of appeal arose under NIAA 2002, s.82, on the grounds that his deportation would breach private life ties he had established over the course of his residence (through social ties, education and the acquisition of property, i.e. a car and house), because the deportation decision post-dated 28 July 2014, the decision contained a s.94B certificate with the effect that the right of appeal was not suspensive (i.e. Alexander will have to await deportation before the appeal hearing can go ahead).

Alexander's human rights claim will not help to bring the appeal back in-country unless he is able to show that he faces a real risk of serious irreversible harm if removed to Russia. Any challenge to the certificate would have to be by way of judicial review. Given the nature of the issues invoked in support of his human rights claim, however, it is highly improbable he would displace the certificate.

If on being deported he appeals and is successful, the deportation order will be revoked and he will be able to return to the UK upon obtaining leave to do so. If the appeal is dismissed, the order will remain in force and he will not be able to return to the UK, subject to a successful future application for its revocation.

It had been thought that it may be possible to contend that procedural difficulties in pursuing an appeal from abroad might present powerful reasons for showing that expulsion pre-deportation would cause 'serious irreversible harm'. However, *R (on the application of Kiarie)* v. *Secretary of State for the Home Department* [2015] EWCA Civ 1020 finds that in general out-of-country appeals could be expected to secure people's interests, subject to evidence to the contrary in an individual case. In the appropriate case the First-tier Tribunal could make a witness summons demanding the appellant's presence.

Practice point

In a s.94B case, think carefully about the impact that removal will have both on the client's private and family life and on his prospects of winning the appeal, and about the kinds of evidence you might obtain to support each contention:

- indicators as to the likely processing time for an appeal;
- disruption of the family at a critical stage of a child's education;
- disruption of family law proceedings leading to a result that may be contrary to a child's best interests;

- instruction and evidence on the mental and physical health of the deportee and/or family members, describing too the impact of any enforced removal on conditions and care;
- concrete evidence demonstrating the existence of obstacles to the preparation of the appeal from abroad;
- inability to access/afford video link facilities from abroad;
- whether video evidence can be given in conditions that ensure the remedy is effective (see e.g. *Nare (evidence by electronic means) Zimbabwe* [2011] UKUT 443 (IAC) on the appropriate minimum level of formality and witness supervision for giving video evidence);
- damage to businesses that employ British citizens.

4.5 NEXUS CASES: A SPECIAL DEPORTATION CATEGORY

Operation Nexus is a joint initiative between immigration enforcement and the police, which commenced in the Metropolitan Police area in October 2012 and has now been implemented nationwide. Cases brought under it are increasingly common.

The Home Office describes the aim as: 'to more effectively tackle offending by foreign nationals, through close working and smarter use of police and immigration interventions'.

Benefits of the scheme (from the Home Office perspective) have been noted to include:

- linking police and Home Office fingerprint databases so that arrested individuals are automatically checked to determine if they were a foreign national, resulting in status checks being made with the Home Office;
- allowing the Home Office to refer Criminal Casework cases to the police to facilitate tracing of absconders and re-documentation; and
- the police referring to the Home Office cases which met its definition of 'high harm', resulting in 85 removals or deportations in 2013/14.

For the purposes of deportation proceedings, in Nexus cases the Home Office will then seek to rely on evidence from police intelligence which has not been subjected to a court process leading to the appellant's conviction.

The forms of evidence relied upon are diverse, varying from reports from police officers to evidence from informants, and although the content and origin of the evidence are often vague or controversial, the evidence still has some weight. As one judge put it in *R (on the application of V)* v. *Asylum and Immigration Tribunal* [2009] EWHC 1902 (Admin) at [46]:

> whilst I see that this evidence inevitably loses considerable weight by being anonymous and (in part) hearsay, thereby preventing any direct challenge to the relevant witnesses, I cannot say that this evidence must inevitably be given no weight by the tribunal – or that to admit the evidence at all will inevitably deny the claimant a fair hearing.

The two lead cases concerned with the processing of Nexus cases, *Bah (EO (Turkey) – liability to deport) Sierra Leone* [2012] UKUT 196 (IAC) and *Farquharson (removal – proof of conduct) Jamaica* [2013] UKUT 146 (IAC) establish that:

- acts that lead to a charge, but not a conviction, may be established by the Secretary of State as 'conduct' capable of justifying a public interest in removal/deportation;
- the standard of proof applied by the Tribunal when assessing alleged offending/conduct which has not resulted in conviction remains the balance of probabilities.

Thus the Secretary of State and the police can enforce deportation of those they suspect of criminality by advancing evidence, intelligence and opinion which would not enable a prosecution before the criminal courts, and can do so against a much more attainable threshold from their perspective.

The Tribunals in *Bah* and *Farquharson* do constrain the potential arbitrariness of the process somewhat, although the extent is modest, observing that:

- evidence is more likely to be impressive when allegations from informants are corroborated;
- suspicion should not replace proof;
- the gist of how evidence was obtained must be disclosed and if that is too sensitive to disclose, then the information should not be relied upon;
- if the Secretary of State seeks to establish the conduct by relying upon the contents of police Crime Reporting Information System (CRIS) reports, the relevant documents should be produced rather than bare witness statements referring to CRIS reports.

Practice point

Preparation of Nexus appeals requires particular care. The evidence presented by the police and Home Office alleging criminal acts and associations should be robustly challenged where unsubstantiated by actual convictions. When preparing a case for hearing, consider the following:

- Take thorough instructions on each assertion of alleged criminality raised in the police evidence and produce a detailed statement.
- Further disclosure may be required with regard to incidents described in the police evidence.
- Directions requiring third parties, including the police, to produce additional documents may be sought from the Tribunal in reliance upon rule 4(3)(d) of the Tribunal Procedure (First-tier Tribunal) (Immigration and Asylum Chamber) Rules 2014.
- Where the police or other sources provide statements consider requesting that the author attends as a witness, and in the event the Secretary of State declines to produce them, then a witness summons may be sought under rule 15.
- Nexus inclusion will frequently be founded on alleged gang associations. Bear in mind that gang membership is often alleged based on nothing more than the client

---

being seen with individuals in the client's neighbourhood, and these may often be people with whom the client has gone to school, or who are from the same estate.

- Police officers should be challenged in cross-examination with regard to the actual evidence of association with and identification of known gang members.
- Enquiry should be made about the nature of surveillance that led to sighting so as to ascertain its reliability: e.g. was it prolonged or simply done on a 'drive-by' basis?
- If the context/purpose of contact leading to observation was not dedicated surveillance challenge the reliability of any identification.
- The gang statement analysis is rarely produced by the officers who allegedly sight the client, and those officers rarely appear to give evidence. You should consider requiring that they be produced, and challenge their credentials (e.g. they may be civilian analysts who lack field experience and merely collate reports and give undue weight to hearsay).
- Also look for evidence of actual arrests arising out of gang activity or with known gang members, without which there will be no clear link to criminality regardless of links to gang members.
- Challenge general assertions as to the criminal history of alleged 'gang members' with whom the client associated.

4.6 LEAVE TO REMAIN GRANTED WHERE DEPORTATION IS RESISTED

In the event that the deportation process is successfully resisted either through representations or on appeal, the form of leave an individual obtains is addressed at para.399B of the Immigration Rules, the rule describing the process for acquisition of leave as follows:

- **Leave granted:** successful applicants will be granted 30 months' leave, regardless of the leave they had (or lack of it) prior to the deportation proceedings.
- **Previous leave:** will be granted 30 months' leave, regardless of the leave they had (or lack of it) prior to the deportation proceedings.
- **Loss of settlement:** those possessed of indefinite leave to remain will be faced with revocation of the same and its replacement with a 30-month grant.

4.7 REVOCATION OF DEPORTATION ORDER

Where deportation cannot be resisted and/or removal is effected, para.390 of the Immigration Rules outlines the circumstances in which an order may be revoked, requiring an assessment of:

- the grounds on which the order was made;
- the interests of the community including maintaining effective immigration control;
- the applicant's interests including compassionate circumstances.

The test is whether, where para.398 applies (i.e. criminality was punished by imprisonment exceeding a year, or where the Secretary of State thinks the offending caused serious harm or considers the person to be a persistent offender showing particular disregard for the law), there is:

- a breach of the right to private and family life to the high standards already identified; or
- otherwise exceptional circumstances showing the public interest is outweighed by other factors.

Paragraphs 391–392 then go on to repeat the private and family life/exceptional circumstances test that we just summarised, adding that:

- where the sentence of imprisonment exceeded four years there will be an indefinite ban on return (para.391(a));
- where the sentence of imprisonment was between one and four years, there will be a 10-year ban on return (para.391(b));
- in other cases, there will be a revocation normally only where there has been a material change of circumstances or material fresh information has come to light not previously before the Home Office or Tribunal: the passage of time may itself constitute a change of circumstance (para.391A);
- revocation of an order does not itself entitle a person to return: it simply opens the gateway to applying under an appropriate category of the rules (para.392).

Note that applications for revocation may be made from inside or outside the UK.

The general grounds for refusal contained in the Immigration Rules (para.320 onwards) are often invoked even after revocation is required in order to decline leave to enter, based on the same criminality that caused deportation.

4.8 PUBLIC POLICY REMOVALS AND EXCLUSIONS

The Immigration (European Economic Area) Regulations 2006 (which implemented Directive 2004/38/EC, the 'Citizens' Directive'; see **Appendix C1**) enhanced the protection afforded to EEA citizens and their family members.

The Secretary of State may refuse to issue, revoke or refuse to renew a registration certificate, a residence card, and a document certifying permanent residence or a permanent residence card if the refusal or revocation is justified on grounds of public policy, public security or public health. Similarly, an Immigration Officer may revoke a family permit on a person's arrival in the UK on the same grounds.

4.8.1 Different levels of protection against expulsion

Under reg.21 of the Immigration (European Economic Area) Regulations 2006, different periods of residence are rewarded with different levels of protection against expulsion. See **Table 4.2** below.

Table 4.2 Decisions taken on public policy, public security and public health grounds

Age/period of residence	Expulsion grounds
Children under 18	Imperative grounds of public security The decision must be in child's best interests
Aged 10 years or over	EEA nationals only Imperative grounds of public security
Permanent residence	Serious grounds of public policy or public security
First five years or on initial entry	Grounds of public policy, public security, public health

Note that there are two ways in which the protection given by EEA law is enhanced with the length of stay in the UK:

1.   There is a narrowing of the grounds, from 'public policy, public security or public health', to 'public policy and public security', to 'public security' alone.
2.   There is a raising of the threshold, from bare 'grounds', to 'serious grounds', to 'imperative grounds'.

4.8.2   The impact of imprisonment

Identifying the level of residence in, and attachment to, the UK will clearly be crucial in identifying the appropriate level of protection in a particular case.

A person who has misbehaved seriously enough to warrant exclusion from the UK will often be someone who has spent a significant period in prison. Such periods of imprisonment may well occur over a period which is potentially relevant to the acquisition of the higher levels of protection. The thorny question as to what extent residence in prison counts as residence for the purposes of determining which of the reg.21 legal tests applies continues to be batted around the courts with none coming up with an authoritative conclusion.

In *Secretary of State for the Home Department* v. *FV (Italy)* [2012] EWCA Civ 1199 it was held that in determining whether accrued residence rights are lost by virtue of a period of absence from the UK or imprisonment, the question is one of *integration*. A period of imprisonment does not of itself prevent a person accruing 10 years' residence and therefore benefiting from the higher protection provided by the 'imperative grounds' threshold.

Similarly, once 10 years of residence has been acquired, a period of imprisonment does not necessarily cause the person to lose the safeguard against deportation.

The court opined that a period of imprisonment would disrupt the acquisition of permanent residence, but makes clear that once permanent residence is acquired it will not be lost through a period of imprisonment. This view was upheld by the Tribunal in *Essa* v. *Secretary of State for the Home Department (EEA: rehabilitation/integration)* [2013] UKUT 316 (IAC).

When the CJEU looked at this question in *Secretary of State for the Home Department* v. *MG* [2014] EUECJ C-400/12 it held that the 10-year period of residence must be continuous and was to be calculated by counting back from the date of the decision ordering expulsion.

It then rather muddied the waters by saying at [38]:

a period of imprisonment is, in principle, capable both of interrupting the continuity of the period of residence for the purposes of that provision and of affecting the decision regarding the grant of the enhanced protection provided for thereunder, even where the person concerned resided in the host Member State for the 10 years prior to imprisonment. However, the fact that that person resided in the host Member State for the 10 years prior to imprisonment may be taken into consideration as part of the overall assessment required in order to determine whether the integrating links previously forged with the host Member State have been broken.

Unsurprisingly, when the case returned to the UK courts, the Upper Tribunal in *MG (prison – Article 28(3)(a) of Citizens Directive)* [2014] UKUT 392 (IAC) noted that the case law conflicted in its approach to this question.

Imprisonment will prevent a person maintaining his status as a qualified person:

- A person who is serving a prison sentence cannot claim to be exercising his Treaty rights during the period of incarceration (see *Carvalho* v. *Secretary of State for the Home Department* [2010] EWCA Civ 1406 and *SO (imprisonment breaks continuity of residence) Nigeria* [2011] UKUT 164 (IAC)); therefore residence during imprisonment does not count towards the qualifying period for permanent residence.
- Incarceration in a hospital pursuant to an order of the court under the Mental Health Act 1983 is not to be equated with imprisonment, as the individual has not been convicted of any criminal offence: a 'Hospital Order results from a finding that the individual suffers from a mental disorder and is not therefore criminally responsible for their otherwise culpable behaviour' (*JO (qualified person – hospital order – effect) Slovakia* [2012] UKUT 237 (IAC)).

4.8.3 Imperative grounds of public security

The meaning of the phrase 'imperative grounds of public security' awaits resolution.

Although in *MG and VC (EEA Regulations 2006; 'conductive' deportation) Ireland* [2006] UKAIT 53 the Secretary of State's considered view was said to be that the phrase 'public security' was directed at the risk of 'terrorist offences', by the time of *LG (Italy)* v. *Secretary of State for the Home Department* [2008] EWCA Civ

190 it was noted that 'public security' was not to be equated with 'national security', and that the words might equate to a 'risk to the safety of the public or a section of the public'.

However, in any event there was a need to show an actual risk to public security so compelling that it justifies the exceptional course of removing someone who has become 'integrated' by many years' residence in the host state. That test was not met in *Secretary of State for the Home Department* v. *FV (Italy)* [2012] EWCA Civ 1199 where an appellant was sentenced to eight years' imprisonment for manslaughter.

4.8.4   Relevant factors in considering public interest expulsion

Regardless of which test is to be applied, the following factors must be considered when reaching any decision based on public policy, public security or public health:

- The decision must comply with the principle of proportionality.
- The decision must be based exclusively on the personal conduct of the person concerned.
- The personal conduct of the person concerned must represent a genuine, present and sufficiently serious threat affecting one of the fundamental interests of society.
- Punishment cannot simply be for the purposes of general deterrence and so previous criminal convictions do not in themselves justify the decision.
- In public policy and public security (not public health) cases, account must also be taken of considerations such as the age, state of health, family and economic situation of the person, the person's length of residence in the UK, the person's social and cultural integration into the UK and the extent of the person's links with his country of origin.

In *GW (EEA reg. 21: 'fundamental interests') Netherlands* [2009] UKAIT 50 the Tribunal held that:

- what are the 'fundamental interests' of a society is a question to be determined by reference to the legal rules governing the society in question; and
- it is unlikely that conduct that is not criminalised or otherwise prohibited can be regarded as threatening those interests.

The case concerned the attempt by the Secretary of State to exclude Geert Wilders from visiting the UK on the grounds of his unpleasant views about Islam. Mr Wilders' appeal was upheld.

Any national of a Member State who wishes to seek employment in another Member State may reapply for a residence permit, even after having previously been expelled or refused.

4.9   EEA DEPORTATION APPEALS

It has been government policy since summer 2014 to expel deportees following the refusal of their applications, notwithstanding that their appeals are still pending.

From 28 July 2014, an appeal against a deportation decision made under reg.19(3)(b) of the Immigration (European Economic Area) Regulations 2006 can still be lodged in the UK but it no longer suspends removal proceedings, except where:

- The Secretary of State has not certified that the person would not face a real risk of serious irreversible harm if removed to the country of return before the appeal is finally determined.
- The person has made an application to the courts for an interim order to suspend removal proceedings (e.g. by judicial review: the language of the 2006 Regulations suggests that another remedy might be available, e.g. an appeal, though this has not so far been explored); and that application has not yet been determined, or a court has made an interim order to suspend removal.

Where interim relief is sought, under the 2006 Regulations removal will be suspended pending a hearing on that issue unless:

- the notice of a decision to make a deportation order is based on a previous judicial decision; or
- the person has had previous access to judicial review; or
- the removal decision is based on imperative grounds of public security.

See the Home Office guidance on certification for non-suspensive appeals in EEA deportation cases, *Section 94B of the Nationality, Immigration and Asylum Act 2002* (see **4.4.2.1**).

In addition, a person removed from the UK under this new regime can apply to re-enter the UK under reg.29AA to make submissions at his own appeal hearing. This provision is necessary because Article 31(4) of the Citizens Directive (Directive 2004/38/EC) states that:

> Member States may exclude the individual concerned from their territory pending the redress procedure, but they may not prevent the individual from submitting his/her defence in person, except when his/her appearance may cause serious troubles to public policy or public security or when the appeal or judicial review concerns a denial of entry to the territory.

Regulation 29AA of the Immigration (European Economic Area) Regulations 2006 provides that:

- A person may apply to return once a date for the hearing has been set and if he or she wishes to make submissions in person (reg.29AA(1)(c), (d)).
- The person will be granted temporary admission to do so if his or her application succeeds (reg.29AA(2)).

- The person's application may be refused only if his or her appearance 'may cause serious troubles to public policy or public security': this appears to be a higher test for the Home Office to satisfy than for deportation itself, as the threshold is one of 'serious troubles' (reg.29AA(3)): it is very difficult to see that past convictions alone could represent such a threat.
- The period granted will take account of the date(s) on which the individual will be required to make submissions in person (reg.29AA(4)).
- The person may be removed having made the requisite submissions pending the appeal being finally determined, though may return again if required (reg.29AA(5)).
- The person is liable to detention (reg.29AA(6)–(7)).

The extent of the right to submit a defence in person awaits establishment: it may involve a significant period of residence in this country in order to effectively instruct one's legal team, for example. EU law requires that rights are made practical and effective, and Article 47 of the Charter of Fundamental Rights of the European Union, which operates whenever EU rights are litigated, requires that:

> Everyone whose rights and freedoms guaranteed by the law of the Union are violated has the right to an effective remedy before a tribunal ...
>
> Everyone is entitled to a fair and public hearing within a reasonable time ... Everyone shall have the possibility of being advised, defended and represented.

Legal aid shall be made available to those who lack sufficient resources in so far as such aid is necessary to ensure effective access to justice.

CHAPTER 5

Detention

5.1 STATUTORY FRAMEWORK AND THE POWER TO DETAIN

The original powers of removal are the foundation for the Home Office's power to award temporary admission and conversely to detain. Those core powers are found in IA 1971, although subsequent legislation also addresses bail and affords limited, though important extensions of the detention powers.

Schedules 2 and 3 to IA 1971 (as amended) set out the four main scenarios in which detention of persons may be authorised:

- when they are being examined as to their suitability for entry;
- pending their removal;
- pending deportation;
- as crew members.

NIAA 2002 extended the power to detain so as to include situations where:

- a decision by the Secretary of State on whether or not to make removal directions is being considered (s.62);
- an individual cannot currently be removed, i.e. due to legal impediments arising out of international agreement, or practical difficulties or demands on administrative resources which impede or delay a decision to remove.

5.2 DETENTION PROCESSES

The Home Office *Enforcement Instructions and Guidance* at Chapter 55 (Operational Guidance, Enforcement) explains how detention will operate in practice.

Although the immigration legislation gives broad general powers to detain, there is very little substantive control over how those detention powers will be exercised. The *Enforcement Instructions and Guidance* therefore represents most of the 'law' that immigration lawyers will come across in their dealings with the Home Office. Policies regarding detention should be published and reliance on unpublished guidance to justify detention may result in a migrant being held unlawfully (*Lumba (WL)* v. *Secretary of State for the Home Department* [2011] UKSC 12).

179

Chapter 55 of the *Enforcement Instructions and Guidance* requires that the Secretary of State promptly provide reasons for detention at its outset, using Form IS91R. A failure to do so renders the detention unlawful, although this will not necessarily oblige the detainee's release from detention, if there are nevertheless good reasons for them to be detained (*Saadi* v. *UK* [2008] ECHR 80).

Following the initial detention, regular reviews are necessary by various ranks of officer, the reasons for which must be given on Form IS93. The programme for reviews in a routine case is shown in **Table 5.1**.

Table 5.1   Programme of reviews in a routine case

Timing of review	Responsible officer
24 hours	Immigration Officer
7 days	Immigration Officer
14 days	Inspector
21 days	Immigration Officer
28 days	Inspector
Months 1 and 2	Executive Officer
Months 3 and 4	Senior Executive Officer
Months 5, 6 and 7	Assistant Director
Months 8, 9, 10 and 11	Deputy Director
Month 12 and every three months	Director
Intervening monthly reviews	Deputy Director

A failure to conduct reviews as laid out by the *Enforcement Instructions and Guidance* may render detention unlawful (*SK (Zimbabwe)* v. *Secretary of State for the Home Department* [2011] UKSC 23), although release, and the ability to obtain more than nominal damages, will depend on whether, on the balance of probabilities, detention would have been authorised anyway. So there are two stages in analysing a detention case in relation to *Enforcement Instructions and Guidance*:

1.   Was relevant guidance breached?
2.   If so, would detention have been authorised anyway? Put another way, are the risks of absconding, offending, and danger to the public, sufficiently great for a judge to be confident that detention would have proceeded even if the guidance had been followed? In that case, a judge would only award nominal damages.

Eloise (Kenya)

Eloise is a Kenyan national. She has been detained for five months. On obtaining disclosure under the Data Protection Act 1998, you see that her detention was not reviewed during the first four weeks, and no Form IS96 was issued authorising detention in the first instance.

Eloise's detention in the initial four weeks was therefore unlawful, given the failure to follow the Chapter 55 processes.

Reviewing her file, you note that later detention summaries show that her removal has constantly been pursued, with a real chance of success, and that because of a lack of community ties and a particularly poor immigration history, she presents a high risk of absconding.

Were she to pursue a claim for damages for unlawful detention for the initial period, she would be unlikely to recover any more than nominal damages given that while detention was unlawful by reason of the procedural errors, the Secretary of State on the balance of probabilities is very likely to have authorised detention had the right procedures been followed.

5.3 THE EXERCISE OF THE POWER TO DETAIN

The basic justifications for detention are set out in the *Enforcement Instructions and Guidance*, Chapter 55 and may be described as follows:

1. To effect removal.
2. To establish identity or basis of claim.
3. There is reason to believe the person will fail to comply with conditions.

The burden is on the Secretary of State to justify detention as necessary. She must do so to the ordinary civil standard.

There are limitations on the use of the power which the Secretary of State must contemplate when determining whether to detain:

*   There is a presumption in favour of liberty, so that there must be strong grounds for believing that a person will not comply with conditions of temporary admission or bail for detention to be justified (although for foreign national offenders the presumption may be displaced). See *Enforcement Instructions and Guidance*, para.55.1.2:

    Due to the clear imperative to protect the public from harm from a person whose criminal record is sufficiently serious as to satisfy the deportation criteria, and/or because of the likely consequence of such a criminal record for the assessment of the risk that such a person will abscond, in many cases this is likely to result in the conclusion that the person should be detained, provided detention is, and continues to be, lawful.

*   All reasonable alternatives to detention must be considered before detention is authorised.
*   Each case must be considered on its individual merits.
*   Detention must be reasonable in all the circumstances, particularly having regard to the prospects of removal (the '*Hardial Singh* principle': *R (on the application of Singh)* v. *Governor of Durham Prison* [1984] 1 WLR 704 (QB)).
*   If, before the expiry of the reasonable period, it becomes apparent that the Secretary of State will not be able to effect deportation within that reasonable

period, the power of detention should not be exercised (*R (on the application of I)* v. *Secretary of State for the Home Department* [2003] INLR 196).

• If the purpose of detention is removal, the Secretary of State should act with reasonable diligence and expedition to effect the same (*R (I)*).

5.3.1 Factors influencing decision to detain

Beyond general constraints on the exercise of the power to detain, the relevant factors when considering whether to initiate or persist in detention include (*Enforcement Instructions and Guidance*, para.55.3.1):

• What is the likelihood of the person being removed and, if so, after what timescale?
• Is there any evidence of previous absconding?
• Is there any evidence of a previous failure to comply with conditions of temporary release or bail?
• Has the subject taken part in a determined attempt to breach the immigration laws? (For example, entry in breach of a deportation order, attempted or actual clandestine entry).
• Is there a previous history of complying with the requirements of immigration control? (For example, by applying for a visa or further leave).
• What are the person's ties with the United Kingdom? Are there close relatives (including dependants) here? Does anyone rely on the person for support? If the dependant is a child or vulnerable adult, do they depend heavily on public welfare services for their daily care needs in lieu of support from the detainee? Does the person have a settled address/employment?
• What are the individual's expectations about the outcome of the case? Are there factors such as an outstanding appeal, an application for judicial review or representations which afford incentive to keep in touch? (See also 55.14)
• Is there a risk of offending or harm to the public (this requires consideration of the likelihood of harm *and* the seriousness of the harm if the person does offend)?
• Is the subject under 18?
• Does the subject have a history of torture?
• Does the subject have a history of physical or mental ill health?

5.3.2 Persons considered unsuitable for detention

The *Enforcement Instructions and Guidance* also identifies certain categories of person who are ordinarily regarded as unsuitable for detention save in very exceptional circumstances, including the following (see further paras.55.9.3–55.9.4 and 55.10):

• those in respect of whom there is independent evidence of torture;
• those with a disability which cannot be adequately managed within a detained environment;
• women who are 24 or more weeks pregnant;
• those with a physical or mental medical condition which cannot be adequately treated within a detained environment, or managed for practical reasons (e.g. being infectious or contagious);

- trafficking victims where there is a reasonable grounds decision taken by the competent authority;
- children (whether applicants or dependants), whose claimed date of birth is accepted by the UK Border Agency;
- family cases.

In relation to the latter two categories the *Enforcement Instructions and Guidance* states more particularly that:

(a) Children may be detained for removal in a short-term holding facility for a maximum period of 24 hours, and only for so long as it is reasonably believed that removal will ensue based on directions which are in force, or will be made, within that period.

(b) The Secretary of State must 'aim' to keep the family as a single unit, but:

- a child should be separated from its parents, however, if there is evidence that that is in the child's best interests;
- any such decision must be taken by the local social services department.

Chola (Ecuador)

Chola is an Ecuadorian national. He faces deportation from the UK having been convicted of serious drugs offences.

At the conclusion of his custodial sentence he was detained under immigration powers. His detention has now endured for 13 months as his removal has been complicated by a diplomatic dispute between the UK and Ecuador.

Six months into detention Chola began to present with mental health problems. He was prescribed anti-depressants. The dosage of his medication has been progressively raised as his symptoms have not resolved themselves.

Within the last three weeks Chola has become actively suicidal. He attempted to strangle himself with a ligature and has been refusing food for 12 days. The detention centre has placed him on suicide watch and has relocated him to the hospital wing. It has not been able to persuade Chola to resume eating however.

Chola should not be detained. He falls into a category of person deemed unsuitable for detention by the Secretary of State's own guidance, given his serious mental illness which the detention facility cannot treat effectively.

While Chola does present a risk of harm to the public, offending, and absconding, there is a very strong argument that those factors cannot justify his detention exceptionally given the enduring obstacle to his removal caused by the diplomatic dispute.

5.4 RELEASE AND BAIL

Where an individual is detained under the Immigration Acts consideration must be given to how he or she can be released.

In that regard there are a number of steps that may be pursued. Those steps may be described as follows:

1. Temporary admission.
2. Chief Immigration Officer bail.
3. Tribunal bail.
4. Judicial review.

Each step is considered in more detail below.

5.4.1   Temporary admission and Chief Immigration Officer bail

In the first place verbal communications with the Immigration Service in support of an application for temporary admission may yield some results, though representations should also be put in writing.

If an application for temporary admission proves unsuccessful representations can be made to a Chief Immigration Officer (CIO), for CIO bail.

The details of the local enforcement team responsible for detention should be on any Form IS96 issued to the detainee.

If the detainee is released he will usually be required to comply with conditions which may include:

- residence at a specified address;
- reporting to police station or Immigration Service and electronic tagging;
- sureties.

If he is permitted to work by the terms of his immigration status a bailee can do this so long as there is no restriction imposed by an immigration judge, and the Home Office does not have power to impose work conditions on an immigration judge's grant of bail.

The Secretary of State has the power to provide accommodation to those granted temporary admission. Where this happens, she is empowered to place a condition on their temporary admission/bail requiring them to reside in that accommodation and to impose restrictions on an individual's absence from it.

5.4.2   Tribunal bail

5.4.2.1   The power to grant bail

There is a right to seek bail at every stage in the immigration process. This is contained mainly in IA 1971, Sched.2

There are some firm restrictions imposed by statute on access to bail, however:

- A person cannot be released on bail without the permission of the Secretary of State within 14 days of the date set for any removal (IA 1971, Sched.2).

- Repeat bail applications are prohibited within 28 days of a previous bail refusal by the Tribunal, unless there is a material change of circumstances (Tribunal Procedure (First-tier Tribunal) (Immigration and Asylum Chamber) Rules 2014, rule 39(3)).

5.4.2.2 The process of making a bail application

The 2014 Procedure Rules make specific provision for bail application before the First-tier Tribunal from rule 38 onwards.

They require detailed grounds in support, together with advanced service of a bail address and details of any surety, and similarly envisage service of the Secretary of State's bail summary by 2 pm the day prior to the bail application provided adequate notice was given (rule 40(1)).

An immigration tribunal bail application must be made on a prescribed form, a B1.

An immigration judge may release a person on bail subject to conditions similar to those an Immigration Officer may impose but with the additional power to require recognisance from the detainee and any sureties.

5.4.2.3 Factors relevant to bail

The bail guidance issued by the President of the Immigration and Asylum Chamber of the First-tier Tribunal (*Bail Guidance for Judges Presiding Over Immigration and Asylum Hearings*, July 2011, implemented June 2012 ('Bail Guidance')) is very useful reading for anyone participating in bail hearings.

It reminds judges that bail itself is a restriction on liberty, that there is a presumption in favour of bail and that the burden of proof in justifying detention lies on the Secretary of State, to the standard of a balance of probabilities.

The Bail Guidance states three broad considerations to be taken into account in making a decision on bail:

1. The reason(s) why the person has been detained.
2. The length of the detention to date and its likely future duration.
3. The likelihood of the person complying with conditions of bail.

Although the lawfulness of detention is beyond the jurisdiction of the immigration judge, demonstrating the unlawfulness may still be beneficial on a bail application. The Bail Guidance indicates at para.5 that:

> it will be a good reason [for a judge] to grant bail if for one reason or another continued detention might well be successfully challenged elsewhere.

The Guidance also furnishes some very approximate guidance as to what is considered a long period of detention, stating at para.19 that:

it is generally accepted that detention for three months would be considered a substantial period of time and six months a long period. Imperative considerations of public safety may be necessary to justify detention in excess of six months.

Where a detainee has difficulty providing an address it is possible to arrange accommodation through the Home Office, and a protocol exists between the Home Office and the tribunal and is attached to the tribunal bail guidance.

The guidance also includes a section on bail in principle, whereby bail might be granted in principle but release is dependent on certain information being provided to the immigration judge. This might arise, for example, where an address for release needs to be provided or information provided by a surety.

When recording a decision on bail an immigration judge must also give a reasoned decision in writing, and that decision is open to attack by way of judicial review (as it does not carry a right of appeal to the Upper Tribunal).

5.4.2.4   Sureties and recognisance

There is no requirement in law that sureties or a recognisance be provided, nor that there be any particular sum of money, nor that the money be in especially liquid form.

Where it is proposed to advance sureties, while the standard bail form, Form B1, has spaces for two sureties, there is no requirement that there are two. Nor indeed is an applicant limited to only two.

The details of those sureties whom it is intended to rely upon must be provided to the First-tier Tribunal and Secretary of State in good time (two days) before any application, so that the individuals in question and their addresses can be the subject of investigation via the Police National Computer (PNC).

Those with criminal convictions or insecure immigration status, or whose addresses have in the past been associated with absconding, are unlikely to make good sureties.

The sureties should always attend court. They should have proof of ID, address, occupation, financial status, immigration status (ideally British citizenship or indefinite leave to remain) and evidence of the address that is available to the detainee.

Immigration judges tend to prefer a surety living with or near an applicant who may be able to exercise a measure of control over him. Sureties should explain their relationship to the detainee, and what level of contact they have had with him in the past, and intend to maintain in the future.

For renewals and variations, it may be possible to avoid attendance by the sureties and it may even be possible to avoid a hearing. The current bail guidance allows for no hearing to take place where the Home Office has no objection to the renewal or variation.

If the bailee breaches the bail conditions in any way, the sureties risk forfeiting all or part of their recognisance at a forfeiture hearing at the Tribunal. It is important that the sureties fully understand this risk as they may be liable even though they have done their best to avoid such an event.

Large sums have sometimes been required by immigration judges and adjudicators (or CIOs): sums of several thousands of pounds are not unknown. In order to ensure that sureties understand the seriousness of their obligations, a judge may question them to determine the basis of their confidence in the applicant meeting their bail conditions, and what plans they have to monitor and ensure compliance with bail.

Practice point

Always ask potential sureties about the following:

- any criminal convictions (especially offences of dishonesty or related to immigration);
- their financial situation, including expenses and income – any recent large transactions into their account should be explained;
- liquidity of assets:
    - that they may have to deposit the money in question;
    - whether they have thought through how they might deal with the loss of the money;
    - whether the sum they are offering is credible given their circumstances;
- evidence of support and accommodation arrangements: whether the proposed sources of money raise questions of ethics or immigration offences;
- plans regarding any trips abroad or other engagements which might impact on their effectiveness as surety, or their ability to support subsequent extensions of bail;
- how they know, and how they intend to maintain contact with, or control over, the applicant;
- what they would do in the event that the bailee did breach bail conditions.

Parents and partners are often not powerful sureties because of their close relationship with the applicant. An immigration judge may have had the unpleasant task of conducting forfeiture hearings with such sureties and will consider them not best able to judge a bail applicant's character because of their closeness, or too much under the latter's influence or too willing to do anything to get him or her out of detention, including risking forfeiting large amounts of money.

Close friends or colleagues willing to put up substantial sums and who can explain that they understand the risk may make better sureties.

Generally, Bail Circle volunteers or detention visitors are not considered good sureties by most immigration judges, because they are perceived as having limited knowledge of the detainee and only limited control over their future intentions.

5.4.2.5 Bail conditions

In the event that bail is granted an immigration judge may impose conditions.

Where an immigration appeal is pending, the primary conditions for bail are usually as follows:

- to attend the next and every subsequent hearing of the appeal at such places and times as shall be notified or as otherwise varied in writing by the Tribunal; and
- following final determination of the appeal, unless bail is revoked by the Tribunal or by operation of law, to appear before an immigration officer at such time and place as directed by the Tribunal; and
- the terms of bail may be varied at any time during their currency by application or at the Tribunal's own motion.

An immigration judge is also likely to impose secondary conditions relating to the place of residence and how the person released on bail should maintain contact with the immigration authorities.

Immigration judges will be anxious to avoid a conflict between the grant of bail (or its conditions) and the terms of a licence for release from prison following a criminal sentence. To that end, information from the National Probation Service may well be required. The Criminal Casework Directorate should hold the details of any licence, so this information can usually be provided by the Home Office.

Practice point

Bail summaries provided by the Home Office are known to be less than fully accurate. They may allege that a person was an absconder when in fact he or she had merely changed address, or may fail to record that a person has complied with previous conditions for bail or temporary admission. They may downplay significant periods of a detention history, such as the attempts at removal (or lack of them). It is therefore crucial to take instructions on the accuracy of a bail summary and to ask the Home Office for proof on any contested facts.

It can be very helpful to prepare a witness statement by a bail applicant. Such statements need not be long, but it should be borne in mind that live evidence at a bail hearing, particularly one by video link, is often unhelpful to the applicant. Any applicant for bail can be expected to state that he or she will comply with conditions, for example, and so such assurances therefore carry little weight. Cross-examination of a bail applicant is often a productive exercise for the Home Office, however, particularly with an unprepared witness.

When you take instructions, ensure you recognise any vulnerability of the client, and that any appropriate referral needs (e.g. for mental or physical healthcare) are identified and actioned.

The following are suggestions for instructions to consider taking from clients applying for bail:

- their case in the light of each relevant detention criterion/factor;
- the underlying facts said to give rise to a power to detain, e.g. was the person working in breach of conditions, and/or is the Home Office right to say he has overstayed his leave? Does he seem to have a strong case for leave on human rights or other grounds if an application was made?

5.4.3 Challenges to lawfulness of detention

Detention can be challenged on *Hardial Singh* principles (mentioned previously), relating to whether the length of detention is reasonable. Alternatively, complaint may be advanced on the grounds the detention is not in accordance with Home Office policies.

It would be unusual to challenge lawfulness of detention directly before applying for temporary release and/or bail, as these are the simplest ways to secure a detainee's release from detention, which is likely to be the detainee's main priority.

An understanding of lawfulness of detention can inform such applications, and can be important in securing compensation for a detainee after release.

Applications challenging the lawfulness of detention may be by either:

(a)   writ of Habeas corpus application; or
(b)   judicial review proceedings in the Administrative Court.

The latter alternative has the advantage of enabling the pursuit of damages as part of the proceedings (although the case will be referred to the Queen's Bench Division or a county court for assessment). The former has the advantage of a very quick listing in the Administrative Court, though it is very rarely relied upon these days because judicial review is more straightforward.

Judicial review is available even though one might apply for bail to the First-tier Tribunal, because the two remedies focus on different considerations. See *R (on the application of Konan)* v. *Secretary of State for the Home Department* [2004] EWHC 22 (Admin) at [30]:

> An adjudicator in considering a bail application is not determining (indeed, he has no power to determine) the lawfulness of the detention.

5.5   DETENTION REMEDIES SUMMARY

- **Bail** challenges the wrongful exercise of power, e.g. 'I am not at risk of absconding or to the public because I have good community connections'.
- **Judicial review** challenges the lack of a power, e.g. 'you cannot remove me therefore there is no power to detain'.

Dariush (Iran)

Dariush is from Iran. He has been present in the UK for 12 years but is now facing deportation, having been convicted of a serious assault attracting an 18-month sentence.

His appeal rights were exhausted 21 months ago and he has now been detained for 24 months, having been transferred into immigration detention at the expiration of his custodial term.

The Home Office insists that it is doing everything in its power to remove Dariush, but the Iranian authorities are not co-operating. A face-to-face interview between him and Iranian Embassy officials took place 18 months ago, in detention, in order to obtain an Emergency Travel Document.

The Embassy did not accept Dariush was Iranian, however, and he could not provide alternative written proof of his nationality. A second interview was arranged and took place 15 months ago, but the Iranian authorities maintained their position. It is not clear whether any new information was submitted by the Home Office. A third telephone interview took place three months ago with the same result.

Dariush has applied for bail five times in the last 24 months and has been refused each time because he is a high absconding risk and a high risk of harm. There is strong support for this view, as he has a serious criminal conviction and a poor immigration record.

Nonetheless, Dariush's detention may well be unlawful and probably has been for some time, almost indisputably since the second interview. Since Tribunal bail applications have failed him he can apply for judicial review.

On the claim form he should also specify that he seeks a declaration of unlawful detention and damages. This amount could potentially be tens of thousands of pounds if a substantial part of his detention was deemed unlawful by reason of there demonstrably being no prospect of removal within a reasonable time.

CHAPTER 6

Victims of trafficking

6.1 THE NEEDS OF VICTIMS

Victims of trafficking will often have protection needs and can apply for asylum where necessary, e.g. where they fear retribution from their traffickers or being re-trafficked (see *PO (Nigeria)* v. *Secretary of State for the Home Department* [2011] EWCA Civ 132). Additionally, victims of trafficking may benefit from services, and be granted short periods of discretionary leave under the Council of Europe Convention on Action against Trafficking in Human Beings (CAT).

Trafficking victims may need:

- medical help, both physical and psychological;
- assistance in respect of their current circumstances, and the need for immediate protection;
- assistance with matters of criminal law, with immigration status and detention issues; and
- help with other matters,

all of which may be new to many immigration advisers.

Assisting trafficking victims is a specialist area and advisers who have concerns that their clients may be victims of trafficking should seek specialist advice. An extremely useful resource, for those who are interested in this area, is the *Human Trafficking Handbook: Recognising Trafficking and Modern-Day Slavery in the UK*, edited by Parosha Chandran (LexisNexis, 2011).

6.2 THE CONVENTION ON ACTION AGAINST TRAFFICKING IN HUMAN BEINGS

The government ratified the CAT on 17 December 2008 and implemented it from 1 April 2009. It is accompanied by an Explanatory Report which gives useful supplementary information about many of the terms used.

In order to ensure that trafficking obligations are met, the National Referral Mechanism (NRM) was created, to provide a framework for identifying victims of human trafficking and ensuring they receive the appropriate protection and support.

Two Home Office guidance documents (Operational Guidance under Modernised Guidance, Other Cross-cutting Guidance (Modernised Guidance)) outline the policies and practices of the Home Office in regard to the UK's obligations under the CAT:

- *Victims of Modern Slavery – Frontline Staff Guidance*; and
- *Victims of Modern Slavery – Competent Authority Guidance* ('Competent Authority Guidance').

The website of the Anti-Trafficking Legal Project (ATLeP) (**www.atlep.org.uk**) hosts a great deal of useful information for those representing victims of trafficking.

Normally international Conventions are not directly effective in England and Wales: the CAT does not have an equivalent domestic statutes as is the case with the ECHR and HRA 1998. Nor is it EU law, being a Convention of the Council of Europe rather than flowing from the EU Treaty itself. However, because the government has announced its policy as being to comply with the CAT, it may be relied upon in public law proceedings, as explained in *R (on the application of Minh)* v. *Secretary of State for the Home Department* [2015] EWHC 1725 (Admin) at [53]:

> Since the UK Government has announced that its policy is to give effect to its obligations under the Trafficking Convention, that has consequences in domestic administrative law. Failure to apply the provisions of the Convention may give rise to a successful claim for judicial review: not because the treaty has any direct effect (because it does not), but because the Government has then failed to apply its own published policy ... Thus, the Competent Authority should be taken to have intended to protect the victim's rights, combat trafficking and promote international co-operation (the objectives identified in the Convention) and to promote a human rights based approach.

The scourge of trafficking has long been the subject of international attention. All inter-governmental solutions put forward so far attempt to balance the desire to punish the perpetrators with protecting the victims, without risking the integrity of immigration control: those who have been trafficked are often seen as victims when it comes to punishing their traffickers, but as voluntary migrants when considering their immigration status.

Many of the instruments of the past have concentrated on the criminal justice dimension, only contemplating the victims' status in this country as an adjunct to ensuring the efficient prosecution of their traffickers. However, some protections for victims have emerged (e.g. most recently, the residence permit which may be granted where a person's 'stay is necessary owing to their personal situation' under the CAT).

6.3 ASSESSING THE CLAIM

The Competent Authority Guidance warns that an account should not necessarily be doubted merely because of being incoherent, inconsistent or delayed – the version then extant was cited in *R (on the application of SF)* v. *Secretary of State for the Home Department* [2015] EWHC 2705 (Admin) at [22]:

(a)   'Due to the trauma of trafficking, there may be valid reason why a potential victim's account is inconsistent and lacks sufficient detail'.

(b)   'When you assess the credibility of a claim, there may be mitigating reasons why a potential victim of trafficking is incoherent, inconsistent or delays giving details of material facts. You must take these reasons into account when considering the credibility of a claim. Such factors may include, but are not limited to the following:

   –   trauma (mental, psychological, or emotional)
   –   inability to express themselves clearly
   –   mistrust of authorities
   –   feelings of shame
   –   painful memories (particularly those of a sexual nature)'.

(c)   'Children may be unable to disclose or give a consistent credible account due to such factors as:

   –   their age
   –   their on-going nature of abuse throughout childhood, and/or
   –   fear of traffickers, violence or witchcraft'.

(d)   'Delayed disclosure

   A key symptom of post-traumatic stress is avoidance of trauma triggers, or those that cause frightening memories, flashbacks or other unpleasant physical and psychological experiences. Because of these symptoms a person may be unable to fully explain their experience until they have achieved a minimum level of psychological stability. You must not view a delay in disclosing of facts as necessarily manipulative or untrue. In any cases it is the result of an effective recovery period and the establishment of trust with the person they disclose the information to'.

(e)   'You should assess the material facts of past and present events (material facts being those which are serious and significant in nature) which may indicate that a person is a victim of trafficking'.

The same notions appears in the present version (version 3, 21 March 2016) albeit that it is differently structured.

There is no requirement for corroboration for a trafficking claim to be accepted, and a decision letter which suggests the contrary may well be struck down: see *R (on the application of Mutesi)* v. *Secretary of State for the Home Department* [2015] EWHC 2467 (Admin) at [61] and *R (on the application of SF)* v. *Secretary of State for the Home Department* [2015] EWHC 2705 (Admin) at [191].

As trafficking often raises issues of the assessment of evidence of foreign cultures given by a witness who may have suffered trauma, many of the principles established in asylum claims regarding the assessment of credibility may well be relevant, *MVN* v. *London Borough of Greenwich* [2015] EWHC 1942 (Admin) at [28]:

(1)   Decision makers considering asylum claims should take everything material into

account. Their sources of information will frequently go well beyond the testimony of the applicant and include in-country reports and expert testimony ...

(2)   It is an error of law for a decision maker to seek to assess the credibility of a claim in isolation without considering other relevant evidence such as reports regarding a country that corroborate a person's claims ...

(3)   It is also an error of law to fail to take account of relevant expert evidence when assessing credibility ...

(4)   Further, in assessing credibility in the context of trafficking, this must be done 'in the round' ...

(5)   Allowances should be given to the fact that asylum seekers (and similarly victims of trafficking) may have problems giving coherent accounts of their history: *R (N) v Secretary of State for the Home Department* [2008] EWHC 1952 (Admin) at [25] per Blake J ('most people who have experience of obtaining a narrative from asylum seekers from a different language or different culture recognise that time, confidence in the interviewer and the interview process and some patience and some specific direction to pertinent questions is needed to adduce a comprehensive and adequate account').

Indeed it was said in *R (on the application of Minh)* v. *Secretary of State for the Home Department* [2015] EWHC 1725 (Admin) at [48(m)] that:

> Later disclosure should therefore not be seen as necessarily manipulative or untrue, but in many cases is the result of an effective recovery period and the establishment of trust with the person to whom they are disclosing.

In *Minh* at [90]–[91] such reports assisted as to the plausibility of the route taken to the UK and the kind of labour exploitation. In *AB* v. *Secretary of State for the Home Department* [2015] EWHC 1490 (Admin) a conclusive grounds decision was quashed for failing to engage with the report from the respected support organisation, Ashiana, which had used its expertise in giving its opinion that the applicant was a trafficked person.

Practice point

Always think about obtaining reports that may assist the client. There may be public domain reports that discuss the trafficking situation in a particular country (e.g. the *Global Report on Trafficking in Persons* (United Nations Office on Drugs and Crime (UNODC), 2014) provides country-specific information on reported cases of trafficking in persons, victims, and prosecutions, and the US State Department publishes its Trafficking in Persons Report which includes valuable country narratives on the circumstances prevailing in source, transit and destination countries), and there may be agencies such as Ashiana that will write case-specific reports in relation to victims whom they are supporting.

Victims may of course not identify themselves as such, as accepted in *MVN* v. *London Borough of Greenwich* [2015] EWHC 1942 (Admin) at [72(2)]. Giving false details is also something which may well be understandable, a point made in the Child Exploitation and Online Protection Centre (CEOP) report, *Strategic Threat Assessment: Child Trafficking in the UK* (2010) on page 19 (cited with approval in *MVN*):

> It should be noted, however that coaching victims to provide a vague story is a measure of control as the agent wants to ensure that the victim is not immediately deported. The victim will comply by recounting a fabricated story believing they are in the process of being facilitated, whilst the trafficker hopes to stall authorities long enough to get the victim out of their control and into exploitation.

As noted in *Minh* and *R (on the application of FM)* v. *Secretary of State for the Home Department* [2015] EWHC 844 (Admin), 'due weight' should be given to the reports and views of an organisation supporting the alleged victim and which might have established a degree of trust with them.

As the Competent Authority Guidance puts it (an earlier version of which was summarised in *Minh*):

> Where an assessment of credibility undermines an individual's account to the point that the reasonable grounds standard can no longer be met, the Competent Authority must conclude that the subject is not a victim of trafficking or modern slavery.

Minh at [48(1)] also noted the need for a second caseworker not involved in the asylum decision to review the case.

Sarah

Sarah travelled to the UK under the control of a person who intended to exploit her by forcing her to work as a prostitute. They spent some time in Hungary before she came to the UK because the person controlling her claimed to have business to attend to there. The Home Office as the competent authority has to accept that there are 'reasonable grounds' for thinking her to be a trafficking victim. However, it says that the trafficker would not have acted in the way that she claims, that she would have taken steps to escape from him sooner had her story been true, and that her account is inconsistent because of variations of detail over the interview process. Additionally, it notes she has no corroborative documents confirming the details of her journey here.

Clearly she has a prima facie case of being a victim of trafficking in terms of her story meeting the definition. That does not help her, though, unless the core facts are accepted as established.

The requirement for corroboration is inconsistent with the authorities cited above such as *Mutesi*. No attention has been given to the difficulties of a person who has truly suffered traumatic experiences in giving a coherent account, and the 'mitigating reasons' identified in the guidance have not been explored.

6.4 DEFINITION OF TRAFFICKING

Many victims will not understand themselves to have been trafficked or are unwilling to disclose their true story. The two Home Office policy documents, referred to in **6.2**, provide useful indicators of trafficking and should be consulted where there is concern that a client might be a victim.

The CAT defines trafficking under Article 4. There are three crucial elements in the definition:

- the action of 'recruitment, transportation, transfer, harbouring or receipt of persons';
- by means of 'the threat or use of force or other forms of coercion, of abduction, of fraud, of deception, of the abuse of power or of a position of vulnerability or of the giving or receiving of payments or benefits to achieve the consent of a person having control over another person';
- for the purpose of exploitation which includes 'at a minimum, the exploitation of the prostitution of others or other forms of sexual exploitation, forced labour or services, slavery or practices similar to slavery, servitude or the removal of organs'.

The Explanatory Report at para.83 elaborates on the meaning of vulnerability:

> By abuse of a position of vulnerability is meant abuse of any situation in which the person involved has no real and acceptable alternative to submitting to the abuse. The vulnerability may be of any kind, whether physical, psychological, emotional, family-related, social or economic. The situation might, for example, involve insecurity or illegality of the victim's administrative status, economic dependence or fragile health. In short, the situation can be any state of hardship in which a human being is impelled to accept being exploited.

As already touched upon, children receive specific protections, and CAT, Article 10(3) holds that:

> When the age of the victim is uncertain and there are reasons to believe that the victim is a child, he or she shall be presumed to be a child and shall be accorded special protection measures pending verification of his/her age.

The definition of trafficking does not, it will be seen, itself imply or require any element of cross-border movement – so one might come across a person who entered the UK under her own steam, regularly or irregularly, yet nevertheless qualifies for the protections given against trafficking because of her past experiences, abroad or in this country.

Article 4 emphasises that a person's 'consent' to these practices is irrelevant to his or her status as a victim.

It is evident that a person may be brought to the UK in circumstances that have the flavour of trafficking but without one of the vital three ingredients being present, so it is important to always consider each dimension carefully.

The claimed mistreatment has to reach a certain level of severity: in *R (on the application of Poquiz)* v. *Secretary of State for the Home Department* [2015] EWHC 1759 (Admin) a decision not to recognise a person as a trafficking victim was upheld where she was recruited from an apparently reputable employment agency and had sufficient freedom to seek alternative employment and report her employer at a police station.

6.5 HISTORIC TRAFFICKING

Past trafficking experiences may carry over to the present day in terms of their impact on the victim, as the Home Office Competent Authority Guidance presently puts it (page 103):

> This is because, although they may be far removed from their trafficking situation, they may still have been subjected to exploitation and may therefore be considered a victim of trafficking under the Convention. They may also still be traumatised by their experience.

At one time the Home Office policy took the view that someone who might have been the victim of trafficking was 'no longer in need of the protection and assistance offered by [the CAT] because the individual's circumstances have changed so much since the trafficking occurred'. In *R (on the application of Atamewan)* v. *Secretary of State for the Home Department* [2013] EWHC 2727 (Admin) the court held at [71] that: 'Measures to protect and promote the rights of victims' necessarily addressed the plight of 'anyone who is presently, or who has been the victim of trafficking.'

Not every victim will necessarily need all the benefits for which the CAT provides: *Minh* summarises this guidance at [48]:

n. A gap in time between the trafficking situation and referral should be seen as normal and not itself a reason to conclude that an individual should not be treated as a victim, though there may be circumstances in which it can still be concluded that at the time of the assessment the person no longer meets Convention criteria or needs the protection or assistance they can afford.

o. When trafficking is removed through location (i.e. a migrant who claims to have been exploited overseas but travelled independently of any alleged trafficker to the UK over a period of time passing through a number of other countries), the migrant is very unlikely to benefit from being considered under the Convention, but it is entirely possible that a person who has fled to escape a current trafficking situation will still be traumatised, and subject to Dublin II arrangements (on refoulement of asylum seekers) will need to be afforded the help and protection in the UK that is offered under the Convention. Issues consider include whether the person requires time to recover from the trafficking ordeal.

Veronica (Sri Lanka)

Veronica is a citizen of Sri Lanka who arrived in the UK a year ago and was granted leave to enter as a student. In conference she tells you that she was previously persuaded to leave Sri

197

Lanka by a man who said he loved her and on whom she had become emotionally dependent, but who forced her to work in India for two years in very demanding conditions in his manufacturing business: he confiscated her passport, restricted her movements, and she did not receive her earnings because he said that she needed to contribute towards the household's running costs. She eventually escaped and returned to Sri Lanka.

Veronica may well have a good case to be a trafficking victim even though this did not arise as part of her journey to the UK: she was recruited/transported to travel to India, by abuse of her vulnerability, and then required to undertake forced labour similar to servitude.

6.6   REFERRAL PROCESS

All agencies and organisations that find themselves with grounds for concern that a person may be a victim of human trafficking have a responsibility both for ensuring the safeguarding needs of the child are assessed and addressed and for reporting their trafficking concerns to a first responder.

First responders are the agencies who will refer the child on to the NRM. A first responder may be:

- a local authority;
- UKVI;
- the police;
- the National Crime Agency (NCA);
- Barnardo's;
- the NSPCC's Child Trafficking Advice Centre (CTAC);
- an agency that deals predominantly with adults who have been trafficked (such as Gangmasters Licensing Authority, the Trafficking Awareness Raising Alliance (TARA) in Glasgow, Migrant Help, the Medaille Trust, Kalayaan and the Salvation Army).

Where a first responder finds itself with grounds for concern that a person may be a victim of human trafficking, a formal referral is made to the NRM. The NRM is a victim identification and support process which is designed to make it easier for all the different agencies that could be involved in a trafficking case (e.g. police, Home Office, local authorities and NGOs) to co-operate, share information about potential victims and facilitate their access to advice, accommodation and support.

6.6.1   Competent authorities

Decisions about who is a victim of trafficking are made by one of the two competent authorities – the UK Human Trafficking Centre where the person is a UK or EEA national or where there is an immigration issue but the person is not yet known to Home Office, and the Home Office for situations where trafficking is raised as part of an asylum claim or in the context of another immigration process.

The decision-making process has two stages. Within five days of a referral, the competent authority should apply a 'reasonable grounds' test to consider if the statement, 'I suspect but cannot prove' that the person is a victim of trafficking, holds true. If the answer is positive, the person will be granted a minimum of 45 calendar days for recovery and reflection. No detention or removal action will be taken against the subject during this time.

6.7 DECISION-MAKING PROCESS

6.7.1 The 'reasonable grounds' stage

The test at the 'reasonable grounds' stage was discussed in *Minh* at [68]–[70] which recognises at [75] that holes and inconsistencies in the account are much more likely at this stage, before the victim has established a relationship built on trust with an adviser:

> **68.** This is an objective question: the question is whether the evidence provides grounds upon which a reasonable observer could believe that this person is a trafficking victim, applying the low threshold of suspicion but not proof, and bearing in mind the non-exhaustive list in the [Competent Authority] Guidance of possible reasons for absence of detail or inconsistency.
>
> **69.** The question for the Competent Authority at this stage is not, 'is there evidence which a reasonable observer could consider *proves* that this person is a trafficking victim?'; still less is it, 'on what I know now, do I believe that this person *is* a trafficking victim'?
>
> **70.** It is worth noting that at this preliminary stage of enquiry, there could be both reasonable grounds upon which a reasonable person could believe that a person could be a victim of trafficking *and* reasonable grounds for believe that they might not be. (That may particularly be so in circumstances where there are inconsistencies or gaps in the evidence, but also features of the account which suggest possibly plausible psychological or other reasons to explain those lacunae.) In such circumstances, the question of whether there are 'reasonable grounds' for suspecting that a person is a victim of trafficking must be answered in the affirmative. Provided there are reasonable grounds for belief, then the question of whether there are also reasonable grounds for disbelief is irrelevant. The further question of whether the grounds for disbelief outweigh the grounds for belief is not one for determination at that stage: it is a matter which will fall for determination by a decision-maker making a Conclusive Grounds decision at a later date (after the reflection/recovery period and if necessary after extra enquiries).

Bello (Nigeria)

Following attendance at a hearing of her appeal before the First-tier Tribunal, to pursue her asylum claim based on religious persecution, Bello, a citizen of Nigeria, explains to the judge that after arriving here to join her aunt, she was forced by her aunt and her husband to work as a housekeeper, discouraged from socialising beyond their family, paid minimal wages, and monitored by cameras placed around the house.

The judge raises the possibility that she is a trafficking victim with the Home Office presenting officer. The hearing is adjourned for a reasonable grounds decision to be made.

Thereafter, the competent authority at UKVI accepts that there are reasonable grounds to think her a victim of trafficking. She should now receive a period of 45 days for recovery and reflection during which time her appeal should remain adjourned; any reporting conditions may need to be reconsidered.

6.7.2 'Conclusive grounds' decision

Following a positive reasonable grounds decision, competent authorities are required to make a second identification decision, on 'conclusive grounds', to decide conclusively if the individual is a victim of trafficking. The expectation is that a conclusive grounds decision will be made within 45 calendar days.

This part of the process should include such guidance to the victim as is needed 'to take an informed decision on cooperating with the competent authorities': CAT, Article 13(1). See also *Atamewan* at [78], a decision which also notes that victims should not be found free from protection needs simply because they have not made a complaint to the police, given that Article 27(1) states that investigations and prosecutions should not be dependent on the making of a report.

Once a person is identified as a victim to the reasonable grounds standard, then he or she is owed assistance as identified by Article 12(1) of the CAT:

- appropriate and secure accommodation, psychological and material assistance;
- access to emergency medical treatment;
- translation and interpretation services;
- translated counselling and information as regards the person's legal rights and the services available to him or her;
- assistance to enable their rights and interests to be presented and considered at appropriate stages of criminal proceedings against offenders;
- access to education for children.

As it was put in *Atamewan* at [73]:

if the needs are great, the level of assistance must be greater; but, equally, if they are minimal or they become minimal, it seems to me that the obligation to provide the assistance will be accordingly reduced or exhausted.

A preliminary needs assessment will be held at this stage; thereafter there must be a fuller one following a favourable conclusive grounds decision, *Atamewan* at [78].

6.7.3 Residence permits for those accepted as victims of trafficking

Those found, in a conclusive grounds decision, to be victims of trafficking may be granted a period of 12 months and one day's DL either to assist with police enquiries because of their personal circumstances, unless they are entitled to a more generous form of leave (e.g. as a refugee). The DL can be extended where necessary.

The entitlement to a possible grant of leave of between 12 and 30 months can be found in the asylum policy instruction, *Discretionary Leave* (Operational Guidance, Asylum Policy, Asylum Decision Making Guidance (Asylum Instructions); see also **3.3**). The grant of leave, where granted following the refusal of an asylum claim, allows for an appeal against the refusal of asylum under NIAA 2002 (s.82 of the new-style relevant provisions, s.83 of the old-style saved provisions).

Opportunities for leave to remain are essentially twofold:

- where personal circumstances 'are so compelling' (note that the underlying CAT obligation is for the competent authority to consider whether 'their stay is necessary owing to their personal situation': neither the CAT nor the EU Directive on preventing and combating trafficking (Directive 2011/36/EU – see **6.7.5**) uses the term 'compelling');
- the individual is 'helping police with enquiries and pursuing compensation' as a victim of trafficking.

In *R (on the application of FM)* v. *Secretary of State for the Home Department* [2015] EWHC 844 (Admin) the court noted that once a potential victim of trafficking is identified, Article 12(1) of the CAT required the state to assist in his or her 'physical, psychological and social recovery'. The Home Office guidance made it clear that DL should be granted to allow a victim to finish a course of treatment that would not be readily available abroad.

Veronica (Sri Lanka)

Returning to the case of Veronica, she has plainly had bad experiences in the past that may qualify her as a victim of trafficking. However, even if the facts are accepted in the second stage 'conclusive grounds' decision, this does not of itself mean she will receive a residence permit.

Presuming she is not helping the police presently, she needs to show that her stay is necessary owing to her personal situation. In putting a case to the Home Office, representations need to argue that her situation is 'so compelling' that she should be granted a permit.

You would want to investigate:

- her personal circumstances generally including her vulnerability;
- her mental health needs;
- the prospects for her recovery if she receives assistance here.

6.7.4 Overview of Home Office consideration of trafficking cases

The process in these cases will be that:

- trafficking indicators are identified and acknowledged by the Secretary of State;

- a 'reasonable grounds' decision is made on the lower standard of proof (a 45-day reflection and recovery period will then follow);
- a conclusive decision is made on the balance of probabilities;
- individuals who are identified as victims of trafficking may then be granted leave to remain if their personal circumstances are compelling or they are involved in an ongoing police investigation which requires their presence.

A decision to remove can be challenged in the Tribunal on the basis of a failure by the Home Office to properly consider its duties under the CAT, and on the basis that removal would breach Article 4 of the ECHR (see *EK (Article 4 ECHR: Anti-Trafficking Convention) Tanzania* [2013] UKUT 313 (IAC)).

6.7.5 Extra protection introduced by EU law

The protection available to trafficking victims has now been strengthened with the entry into force of Directive 2011/36/EU on preventing and combating trafficking in human beings and protecting its victims. It focuses on involvement in the criminal process and emphasises that:

- Member States shall take the necessary measures to ensure that a person is provided with assistance and support as soon as the competent authorities have a reasonable-grounds indication for believing that the person might have been subjected to a relevant trafficking offence (whether or not they are cooperating in a criminal investigation) (Article 11(2), (3));
- at Recital 22: 'Assistance and support measures for child victims should focus on their physical and psycho-social recovery and on a durable solution for the person in question. Access to education would help children to be reintegrated into society.'

6.8 IDENTIFICATION OF VICTIMS AND ARTICLE 4 DUTIES

The CAT would be a rather empty Treaty without an effective regime to identify victims: both prosecutors (deprived of witnesses) and the victims (deprived of support) would then lose out. Accordingly, the ECHR steps in to make it clear that there are positive obligations on states to make appropriate enquiries.

In *Rantsev* v. *Cyprus and Russia* (2010) 51 EHRR 1, the Strasbourg Court, having held that trafficking in human beings fell within the scope of Article 4 of the ECHR, observed at [285] that:

> In order to comply with [the positive obligation to prevent trafficking], member States are required to put in place a legislative and administrative framework to prohibit and punish trafficking. The Court observes that the Palermo Protocol and the Anti-Trafficking Convention refer to the need for a comprehensive approach to combat trafficking which includes measures to prevent trafficking and to protect victims, in addition to measures to punish traffickers ... It is clear from the provisions of these two instruments that the Contracting States, including almost all of the member States of the Council of Europe,

have formed the view that only a combination of measures addressing all three aspects can be effective in the fight against trafficking ... Accordingly, the duty to penalise and prosecute trafficking is only one aspect of member States' general undertaking to combat trafficking. The extent of the positive obligations arising under Article 4 must be considered within this broader context.

Thus Article 10 of the CAT provides that states must adopt appropriate legislative and other measures and provide their competent authority with trained, qualified persons. There must also be collaboration between relevant agencies, taking into account the special situation of child and women victims.

Thus in *Atamewan* at [90] the court held that the Home Office:

was under a duty to initiate or trigger an effective investigation by the police into offences that were committed against the claimant in respect of her trafficking to and in the UK.

In *R (on the application of FM)* v. *Secretary of State for the Home Department* [2015] EWHC 844 (Admin) the court found that there was sufficient information in the asylum screening interview for a reasonable decision maker to have initiated further enquiries that might have led to the grant of discretionary leave. In *R (on the application of Haile)* v. *Secretary of State for the Home Department* [2015] EWHC 732 (Admin) we see a case where the judge ruled that it was too late to bring a claim in 2013 relating to asserted oversights in asylum proceedings in 2010 in which the applicant had been represented. Indeed there even a delay of around a year was considered 'prompt and effective' where there was no suggestion that the failure hampered the police, though in *FM* at [60]–[63] a declaration of breach was made because no referral to the police had been made a year after judicial review proceedings had first been brought. In *AB* v. *Secretary of State for the Home Department* [2015] EWHC 1490 (Admin) at [43] the judge, noting evidence of the existence of the Operational Intelligence Unit which had decided a case with a favourable 'reasonable grounds' decision should have been referred onwards to the police, stated:

I was concerned that a body within SSHD seemed to be filtering referrals to the police about potentially trafficked persons at all. We have surely learned by now that we best safeguard the vulnerable by the relevant agencies sharing information as widely as possible so that there can be a 'joining of the dots' rather than each such agency working in relative isolation.

Failure to correctly identify a victim could lead to a damages claim, which should be pleaded under Article 4 of the ECHR and relying on *Rantsev* to show the duty which has been breached. Such a claim must be brought within one year as per HRA 1998, s.7 or 'such longer period as the court or tribunal considers equitable having regard to all the circumstances' (see e.g. *Haile*).

6.9 CHALLENGING TRAFFICKING DECISIONS

The only means of challenging a negative NRM decision is by way of judicial review in the Administrative Court. There is no ground of appeal under the old or new style appeal systems by which decisions of the competent authority on trafficking can be reviewed by an immigration judge.

6.9.1 Approach to NRM decisions on appeal

However, there may be cases where an immigration appeal nevertheless covers the same, or overlapping, territory as that addressed by the NRM decision. The question then arises as to what approach a First-tier Tribunal judge should take to the findings made by the NRM.

In *AS (Afghanistan)* v. *Secretary of State for the Home Department* [2013] EWCA Civ 1469 at [14] the Tribunal accepted that (at least) where such findings were 'perverse' they could not bind the Tribunal, whose overall role is to determine whether decisions are compatible with the Refugee Convention and the ECHR. It is easy to imagine cases in which this principle would be important:

- Under the Refugee Convention a person's subjection to forced labour in the past may be the central basis for their asylum claim, or the effect on them of bad experiences during their journey here may be relevant to their overall credibility.
- In cases where Article 8 of the ECHR is relied upon, trafficking might well have an impact on a person's private life and the public interest in their removal, given the damage to a person's physical and moral integrity that might result and the public interest in ensuring that victims are appropriately treated.

So in those and related circumstances, i.e. where the trafficking story bears significantly on the grounds of appeal to the Tribunal, the judge is able to depart from the findings of fact made by the competent authority where he or she thinks they are unreasonable.

Even this implied limitation on the First-tier Tribunal's usual unfettered fact-finding jurisdiction may seem rather odd; and indeed in *XB* v. *Secretary of State for the Home Department* [2015] EWHC 2557 (Admin) at [32], Collins J goes rather further, saying:

> It seems to me that if a Tribunal is satisfied that the decision of the NRM was wrong, it not only is entitled to but should decide the contrary.

Notably in a case in the criminal Court of Appeal, *R* v. *L and others* [2013] EWCA Crim 991, and again showing that a court will have regard to competent authority decisions though not treat itself as bound by them where there is contradictory evidence available, Lord Judge LCJ stated at [28]:

Whether the concluded decision of the competent authority is favourable or adverse to the individual it will have been made by an authority vested with the responsibility for investigating these issues, and although the court is not bound by the decision, unless there is evidence to contradict it, or significant evidence that was not considered, it is likely that the criminal courts will abide by it.

Tran (Vietnam)

Tran is a citizen of Vietnam. In her own country she was sent by her family to live with neighbours, having been abandoned by her mother at the age of 18. They would shout and beat her if she made a mistake, and she was maltreated and severely abused, and suffered regular beatings. She fetched water, cooked, washed and attended on their personal needs, and they did not pay her. She remained with them for a period between a few months and a year before running away.

Tran claimed asylum following her arrival in the UK, where she has joined her older brother who had also been abandoned and managed to make his way to this country lawfully.

The Home Office refused her asylum claim as it does not accept she would not find state protection against her neighbours and because she could live safely elsewhere in the country. It does not accept she could not integrate back in Vietnam and so refuses her private life claim under Article 8 of the ECHR. Meanwhile a NRM decision rejects her claim to be a trafficking victim based on her past experiences, because her account, when viewed in detail, is thought inconsistent and implausible.

On appeal the First-tier Tribunal is essentially confined to looking at 'asylum' and 'human rights' grounds of appeal: there is no appeal against the NRM decision before it. However, in a case like this one, these grounds may inevitably cover the same territory. Ultimately, it is for the judge of the First-tier Tribunal to decide whether the story is true and its implications for her entitlement to international protection and, probably more relevantly on these facts, for the extent to which she is emotionally dependent on her brother to the extent that interference with her family life with him would be disproportionate.

On appeal, you would be aiming to show that the NRM decision was of very poor quality and failed to have regard to evidence that was before it, or flew in the face of relevant principles such as not demanding corroboration and taking account of explanations for inconsistencies. If additional evidence is available than was before the NRM decision maker, there would be an even better chance of persuading a First-tier Tribunal judge to depart from the NRM approach.

6.9.2 Approach to NRM decisions on judicial review

The courts often issue important rulings as to the intensity with which government decisions should be reviewed in the course of judicial review proceedings. Thus in *R (on the application of SF)* v. *Secretary of State for the Home Department* [2015] EWHC 2705 (Admin) [98]–[103] (and *Minh* and *FM*) it was recognised that given the importance of Article 4 of the ECHR (which enshrined a basic value of democratic states) read with the CAT right to have one's victim status identified meant that:

- There should be a searching review of the primary decision maker's evaluation of the evidence.
- Anxious scrutiny should be applied – i.e. decisions should show by their reasoning that every factor which tells in favour of the applicant has been properly taken into account.

Other recent decisions have emphasised that a high standard of reasoning is required in assessing a person's credibility (*R (on the application of Mutesi)* v. *Secretary of State for the Home Department* [2015] EWHC 2467 (Admin)).

Other rulings of note in trafficking judicial reviews are that:

- It would be wrong to attach 'substantial weight' to a police decision not to pursue a prosecution against the traffickers, given that that would have necessarily taken account of the criminal standard for liability of 'beyond reasonable doubt' rather than the civil standard of 'balance of probabilities' (the relevant one for determining trafficking status). Additionally the police would not have been under the obligation to take particular care before disbelieving a potential victim's account (*R (on the application of SF)* v. *Secretary of State for the Home Department* [2015] EWHC 2705 (Admin)).
- Failure to have regard to Home Office guidance on assessing delayed disclosure of being a trafficking victim and inconsistencies in an account might render a decision unlawful (*R (on the application of FK)* v. *Secretary of State for the Home Department* [2016] EWHC 56 (Admin)).

6.10 SUPPORT BEYOND ASSISTANCE WITH IMMIGRATION STATUS

We are not addressing welfare law issues within this course. However, because a competent adviser needs to be at least aware of matters that are vital to their client's interests, we should just mention these. These provisions of Directive 2011/36/EU among others bear inspection:

Article 11: Assistance and support for victims of trafficking in human beings

1. Member States shall take the necessary measures to ensure that assistance and support are provided to victims before, during and for an appropriate period of time after the conclusion of criminal proceedings ...
5. The assistance and support measures referred to in paragraphs 1 and 2 shall be provided on a consensual and informed basis, and shall include at least standards of living capable of ensuring victims' subsistence through measures such as the provision of appropriate and safe accommodation and material assistance, as well as necessary medical treatment including psychological assistance, counselling and information, and translation and interpretation services where appropriate.

Article 12: Protection of victims of trafficking in human beings in criminal investigation and proceedings

...

2. Member States shall ensure that victims of trafficking in human beings have access without delay to legal counselling, and, in accordance with the role of victims in the relevant justice system, to legal representation, including for the purpose of claiming compensation. Legal counselling and legal representation shall be free of charge where the victim does not have sufficient financial resources.

CHAPTER 7

Victims of domestic violence

7.1 INTRODUCTION

Victims of domestic violence may be granted indefinite leave to remain where the marriage or relationship breaks down permanently during the probationary period as a result of domestic violence (under the Immigration Rules, para.DVILR 1.1 of Appendix FM covering family members; previously under para.289A for spouse and unmarried partner routes – we need not concern ourselves further with these cases now).

7.2 IMMIGRATION RULES: DOMESTIC VIOLENCE ROUTE

The structure of the domestic violence route under Appendix FM requires:

- a valid application to have been made by a person who is in the UK;
- the applicant to be 'suitable' by the standards of the suitability requirements of the indefinite leave to remain route for partners, which contains the usual bars to settlement.

7.2.1 Refusals

Mandatory refusal reasons:

- The applicant is subject to a deportation order.
- The applicant has been sentenced to imprisonment exceeding four years (at any time in the past), or of imprisonment for one to four years (15-year bar), or of imprisonment of up to a year (seven-year bar), or 'been convicted of or admitted an offence for which they received a non-custodial sentence or other out of court disposal that is recorded on their criminal record' (two-year bar).
- The applicant has otherwise offended having caused serious harm or is a persistent offender showing a particular disregard for the law.
- The applicant's character, conduct or associations otherwise make their presence undesirable.

- The applicant has failed to comply, without reasonable excuse, with requirements to attend an interview, provide information or physical data, or undergo a medical examination or provide a medical report.

Discretionary refusal reasons:

- Making false representations or failing to disclose material facts.
- Failing to pay relevant NHS charges.
- Failing to provide a requested maintenance and accommodation undertaking.

7.2.2   Eligibility

In order to be eligible the applicant needs to satisfy certain positive qualifying requirements.

They must show these requirements in respect of their previous grant of leave:

- to have been last granted leave as a partner (though not as a fiancé/proposed civil partner); or
- having been granted such leave, then being granted leave to access public funds pending a domestic violence application (i.e. under the 'destitution – domestic violence' (DDV) concession discussed at **7.6**); or
- having previously been granted only limited leave under the domestic violence route because of an inability to meet the suitability requirements of the settlement route;

and the following requirement as to causation:

- that her relationship with her partner broke down permanently as a result of domestic violence during the last grant of leave as a partner.

Where a person satisfies these requirements, she will be granted indefinite leave to remain. If she fails on the suitability time bar requirements, she will be granted 30-month periods of limited leave.

This provision applies only to those granted limited leave as a spouse, civil partner or unmarried partner of a British citizen or a person settled in the UK. It does not apply where the migrant's partner is a refugee or has humanitarian protection (the Home Office has stated its policy position as being that partners coming here in the latter scenarios would not have any expectation of settlement, as opposed to having to leave the country, at the end of their leave).

7.2.3   Other features of these applications

There is no requirement to have current leave (the guidance explains that where 'late' applications are made, relevant questions will be the timing of the relationship breakdown, the age of supporting evidence and whether this impacts on its verifiability, and how the applicant has since been financially supported). As the relationship must have been caused permanently to break down during the two-year probationary period, there can be a problem where there has not been a clean separation between the couple. Helpfully, *LA (para 289A: causes of breakdown) Pakistan* [2009] UKAIT 19 in the headnote reminds judges that they:

> must be careful to assess the evidence in the round, looking at the totality of the evidence and remembering that a broken marriage may have ended before the parties separate and the marriage may have broken down as a result of domestic violence even if other grounds are given in matrimonial proceedings or raised before the Tribunal.

- No fee is payable where the applicant can show they are destitute.
- As noted, the suitability provisions apply, but not the knowledge of life and language in the UK (KoLL) requirements.

Sameena (Pakistan)

Sameena is a citizen of Pakistan. She came to the UK two years ago, having been granted entry clearance as the partner of her husband Iqbal who is a British citizen: she was granted leave to enter as a partner to expire in around six months from now. She left him having suffered physical violence from him repeatedly. Having fled the family home, she was convicted of theft and sentenced to imprisonment for 13 months.

She will not be able to sustain an application under the Immigration Rules (having been sentenced to imprisonment for between one and four years) for 15 years (see Immigration Rules, Appendix FM, para.S-ILR.1.4). In the meantime, if her application succeeds, she will be granted 30-month extensions of leave.

If Iqbal had refugee status when he sponsored Sameena's application, she would not be able to make an application under the Immigration Rules.

Mirza (Bangladesh)

Mirza is a citizen of Bangladesh. He comes to the UK as the partner of his wife, Maryam. He was granted leave for 30 months on arrival. He explains that some time after his arrival here, his wife and his in-laws became very abusive towards him. He was assaulted by Maryam on two occasions and his relationship with her grew more distant. Around six months later, just before his leave expired, he left the family home. He wants advice on whether he qualifies for the domestic violence route.

The Home Office is likely to argue that, applying Appendix FM, para.E-DVILR.1.3, his application should be refused because the relationship did not break down permanently as a result of the domestic violence, given he only left the family home some time after the last incident of violence.

7.3   DEFINITION OF DOMESTIC VIOLENCE

Domestic violence can be physical, emotional, sexual or financial abuse. It can come from a person other than the partner (e.g. from their family members). Since

31 March 2013, following Home Office circular 003/2013, the new cross-government definition (**www.gov.uk/guidance/domestic-violence-and-abuse**) of domestic violence and abuse is:

> any incident or pattern of incidents of controlling, coercive, threatening behaviour, violence or abuse between those aged 16 or over who are, or have been, intimate partners or family members regardless of gender or sexuality. The abuse can encompass, but is not limited to:
>
> - psychological
> - physical
> - sexual
> - financial
> - emotional
>
> **Controlling behaviour** is a range of acts designed to make a person subordinate and/or dependent by isolating them from sources of support, exploiting their resources and capacities for personal gain, depriving them of the means needed for independence, resistance and escape and regulating their everyday behaviour.
>
> **Coercive behaviour** is an act or a pattern of acts of assault, threats, humiliation and intimidation or other abuse that is used to harm, punish, or frighten their victim.

It will always be necessary to show that the relationship has broken down as a result of the domestic violence. Domestic violence is widely defined and an adviser needs to be sensitive to certain behaviour even if the client does not recognise it to be domestic violence. Signs of domestic violence include (see **www.southallblacksisters.org.uk/domestic-violence**):

- **Forced marriage:** family members, including extended family members, who use physical violence or emotional pressure to make you to marry someone, without your free and full consent;
- **Threats regarding 'honour':** immediate and extended family members, partners and ex-partners justifying a range of abusive and violent behaviour (listed below) in the name of 'honour'. For example, using violence to prevent you from bringing dishonour or shame upon yourself or them.
- **Destructive criticism and verbal abuse:** shouting / mocking / humiliating / accusing / name calling / verbally threatening;
- **Pressure tactics:** sulking; threatening to: withhold money, disconnect the telephone, take the car away, commit suicide, take the children away, report you to welfare agencies unless you comply with his demands regarding bringing up the children; lying to your friends and family about you, telling you that you have no choice in any decisions; demanding more dowry;
- **Disrespect and humiliation:** persistently putting you down in front of other people; not listening or responding when you talk; interrupting your telephone calls; taking money from your purse without asking; refusing to help with child-care or housework;
- **Breaking trust:** lying to you; withholding information from you; being jealous; having other relationships; breaking promises and shared agreements;
- **Isolation:** monitoring or blocking your telephone calls; telling you where you can and cannot go; preventing you from contacting friends and relatives; accompanying you wherever you go.

- **Harassment:** following you; checking up on you; opening your mail; repeatedly checking to see who has telephoned you; embarrassing you in public;
- **Threats:** making angry gestures; using physical size to intimidate; shouting you down; destroying your possessions; breaking things; punching walls; wielding a knife or a gun;
- **Sexual violence:** using force, threats or intimidation to make you perform sexual acts; having sex with you when you don't want to have sex; any degrading treatment based on your sexual orientation;
- **Physical violence:** punching; slapping; hitting; biting; pinching; kicking; pulling hair out; pushing; shoving; burning; strangling; raping;
- **Denial:** saying the abuse doesn't happen; saying you caused the abusive behaviour; being publicly gentle and patient; crying and begging for forgiveness; saying it will never happen again;
- **Suicide:** acting in ways which make you feel suicidal or encouraging you to contemplate or commit suicide.

7.4   EVIDENCING THE CLAIM

The Home Office specifies in its *Victims of Domestic Violence* (Operational Guidance collection under Modernised Guidance, Family of People Settled or Coming to Settle and reproduced at **Appendix E3**), certain types of evidence that it expects to be submitted. This list is less prescriptive than it used to be and does tell caseworkers that other evidence may be considered, but in practice anything that is not considered to be 'impartial and objective' risks rejection. It might be thought that it will be difficult to acquire evidence that is 'impartial and objective' in relation to violence that is by its nature private and experienced only by the victim. On appeal the Tribunal can consider any relevant evidence including personal testimony (see *Ishtiaq* v. *Secretary of State for the Home Department* [2007] EWCA Civ 386).

The Home Office prefers certain kinds of evidence to be put forward:

- an injunction, non-molestation order or other protection order made against the sponsor (other than an *ex parte* or interim order); or
- a relevant court conviction against the sponsor; or
- full details of a relevant police caution issued against the sponsor.

As an alternative, the guidance states that more than one of the following forms of evidence will usually be accepted as proving the case adequately:

- a medical report from a hospital doctor confirming that the applicant has injuries consistent with being a victim of domestic violence; *or* a letter from a GMC registered family practitioner who has examined the applicant and is satisfied that the applicant has injuries consistent with being a victim of domestic violence;
- an undertaking given to a court that the perpetrator of the violence will not approach the applicant who is the victim of the violence;

- a police report confirming attendance at the home of the applicant as a result of a domestic violence incident;
- a letter from a social services department confirming its involvement in connection with domestic violence;
- a letter of support or a report from a domestic violence support organisation.

Where such evidence is not available the more relaxed approach to evidence laid down in *Ishtiaq* is very helpful. Nevertheless, every attempt should be made to obtain evidence as outlined in the Home Office guidance.

Virika (Fiji)

Virika is a citizen of Fiji. She was granted 32 months' leave as a partner of Apenisa, on the basis of a successful entry clearance application. During the time she lived with Apenisa and his mother, the latter shouted and teased her, and sometimes threatened to strike her. She would sometimes say that she would remove their new-born baby to her sister's home because Virika seemed to lack mothering skills.

The Home Office refuses an application for settlement on domestic violence grounds made just before the expiry of Virika's leave, by which time she has moved out of the family home and is living in a woman's refuge; she has not initiated any family law proceedings against Apenisa. She made the application herself and did not have any corroborative evidence beyond her own personal statement. The refusal is because the Home Office does not consider that what she suffered was domestic violence, and because she lacks relevant evidence of the violence she claimed to have suffered.

Clearly, under the published guidance she has an arguable case for having suffered domestic violence via 'destructive criticism/verbal abuse' and 'pressure tactics'.

As to the forms of evidence she put forward, it is true that she lacks any of the examples of the kinds of material preferred by the Home Office. One can imagine that it may be difficult in her position to obtain cautions or family court orders: the most hopeful line of attack may be to get the refuge to provide a letter of support or a report.

She could use these arguments and further evidence either on a further application or if she appeals.

Even if you do not have one of the preferred forms of evidence, think carefully about possible alternatives:

- expert evidence from a psychiatrist or psychologist, particularly one with a track record of expertise in this area;
- a report from a refuge;
- witness statements from neighbours or friends, or figures of authority such as doctors, expressing concerns.

7.4.1 Children

If there are children dependent on the application (or indeed otherwise affected by it) then it will be necessary to take account of the Borders, Citizenship and Immigration Act 2009, s.55 which requires that all immigration decision making safeguards and promotes the welfare of children. This effectively requires that it takes account of the best interests of the child.

7.5 RIGHT OF APPEAL/REVIEW

The Home Office deems certain applications, including most of those made under Appendix FM to the Immigration Rules, as involving human rights claims, so that the remedy on refusal is an appeal. However, Appendix AR (AR3.2(c)) does not include a domestic violence application as one of those that are so treated. So one might think that the remedy would be administrative review.

However, if an application on domestic violence grounds is a latent or patent human rights claim (i.e. if the arguments raised therein amount to a human rights claim, e.g. 'I have no life to return to abroad because I burned my bridges when I came here and now my family have ostracised me, and all my friendships are here'; or if Article 8 of the ECHR was expressly raised), then there may well be a right of appeal, because the refusal of the application involves the refusal of a human rights claim. Ultimately whether it does so is a question for the First-tier Tribunal, so if the Home Office refuses to acknowledge a right of appeal, it may nevertheless be worth lodging notice of appeal to see if the Tribunal will accept jurisdiction.

If the application was refused because documents provided with the application were overlooked, then administrative review, which is well suited to that kind of complaint and is speedy, may well be more appropriate, at least where the Home Office does not recognise a right of appeal.

On appeal, the question for the First-tier Tribunal is not simply whether the domestic violence rules are satisfied, because it has to look at whether the refusal infringes the ECHR. So the primary question will be whether a person's Article 8 rights are infringed, i.e. applying the traditional five-stage test in *R (on the application of Razgar)* v. *Secretary of State for the Home Department* [2004] UKHL 27:

(a)   **Will there be an interference with private and family life?** Has the applicant's personal identity been compromised by their problems? Does he or she have connections in this country beyond the failed relationship?

(b)   **Is the interference sufficiently serious to engage Article 8 of the ECHR?** What would circumstances be abroad compared to those here?

(c)   **Is the interference for a legitimate aim?** Immigration control is accepted by the courts as being a legitimate aim.

(d)   **Is it in accordance with the law?** If the applicant satisfies the requirements of the Immigration Rules, there is a strong argument that the refusal is simply not in accordance with the law: the judge would then allow the appeal and the Home Office would have no option but to implement the rules based on the judge's findings.

(e) **It is proportionate?** If the applicant does not satisfy the requirements of the Immigration Rules, then the question is whether a compelling case has been put for departure from the requirements, in the context of whether a fair balance has been struck between the public interest and the strength of the applicant's Article 8 rights.

It may be that the judge on appeal accepts that the Immigration Rules were satisfied. However, that will not of itself require that the appeal be allowed, because meeting the requirements of the domestic violence rules does not of itself show that the decision was contrary to a person's right to private life. However, if it can be shown that the decision amounted to a serious interference with their private life then meeting the rules may very well constitute a strong argument that the decision was not in accordance with the law (which surely includes the Immigration Rules) or was disproportionate (because there cannot be any significant public interest in removing a person who satisfies the requirements of the rules).

There is a likelihood that a victim of serious domestic violence may face difficulties in giving evidence which may mean that the Joint Presidential Note No.2 on witnesses including vulnerable and sensitive ones should be drawn to the Tribunal's attention.

Where there is no viable appeal because it cannot be argued that a human rights claim was refused, and where administrative review has failed, there is always the possibility of judicial review. As always that remedy will concentrate on the legality of the decision more than its merits, e.g. whether:

- all relevant evidence was taken into account;
- the refusal letter correctly applies the law and understands the Immigration Rules and any relevant guidance; and
- without errors of those kinds, the decision on the substance of the case was simply a conclusion to which no reasonable decision maker could have come.

7.6 'DESTITUTION – DOMESTIC VIOLENCE' (DDV) CONCESSION

This concession allows prospective applicants under the domestic violence rule who can establish themselves as destitute to apply for three months of discretionary leave to allow them to claim benefits and secure temporary accommodation while they make and await a decision on the domestic violence application. The application for settlement must be made within the three month's grant.

Details of the concession and an application form are at: **www.gov.uk/government/publications/application-for-benefits-for-visa-holder-domestic-violence**. There is also a briefing in the House of Commons Library (John Woodhouse and Noel Dempsey, *Domestic Violence in England and Wales*, no.6337,

26 February 2016 at **http://researchbriefings.parliament.uk/researchbriefing/ summary/SN06337**). A person granted DDV leave will not have to pay a fee when applying for ILR under the rules.

7.7   EEA NATIONALS AND THEIR FAMILY MEMBERS

Under the Immigration (European Economic Area) Regulations 2006, the family members of EEA nationals may retain their residence rights in certain circumstances (reg.10(5)). These include the situation where a person satisfies these conditions:

(a)   he ceased to be a family member of a qualified person or of an EEA national with a permanent right of residence on the termination of the marriage or civil partnership of that person;

(b)   he was residing in the United Kingdom in accordance with these Regulations at the date of the termination;

(c)   he satisfies [a requirement of economic self-sufficiency equivalent to the various definitions of qualified person for EEA purposes, i.e. being a worker, self-employed or self-sufficient person]; and

(d)   …

(iv)   the continued right of residence in the United Kingdom of the person is warranted by particularly difficult circumstances, such as he or another family member having been a victim of domestic violence while the marriage or civil partnership was subsisting.

To simplify the regulation, then, the requirements are that:

- the relationship has formally ended by divorce/termination;
- at that time the applicant was the spouse/civil partner of a qualified person;
- the applicant suffered domestic violence during the currency of the formal relationship.

Unsurprisingly it can be difficult to obtain evidence that a former partner was working or otherwise a qualified person at the relevant time following a relationship breakdown. Because of the obvious undesirability of expecting someone to have to approach a person who was violent to them, the Home Office has a policy to investigate the claims of victims of domestic violence (e.g. via enquiries of HM Revenue and Customs) – though only where the same kinds of relatively formal evidence are available as have already been set out above. A judge on appeal to the First-tier Tribunal may make a direction requiring the Home Office to assist an appellant who has been the victim of domestic violence in establishing its case (and it may be that the Tribunal will exercise discretion in broader circumstances than the Home Office policy would suggest.

CHAPTER 8

Public funding

8.1   LEGAL AID, SENTENCING AND PUNISHMENT OF OFFENDERS ACT 2012

The Legal Aid, Sentencing and Punishment of Offenders Act 2012 (LASPO 2012) came into force on 1 May 2012, although the sections dealing with legal aid (Part 1 of the Act) did not come into force until 1 April 2013. The Act completely changed the landscape for legal aid. LASPO 2012 determines the matters that remain in scope for legal aid purposes. Any matters not specified as being in scope under LASPO 2012 do not therefore qualify for legal aid and an application would have to be made for exceptional case funding (ECF) (see **8.4**).

Section 9 of LASPO 2012 is the key provision:

(1)   Civil legal aid services are to be made available to an individual under this Part if –

    (a)   they are civil legal services described in Part 1 of Schedule 1, and

    (b)   the Director has determined that the individual qualifies for the services in accordance with this Part (and has not withdrawn the determination).

(2)   The Lord Chancellor may by order –

    (a)   add services to Part 1 of Schedule 1, or

    (b)   vary or omit services described in that Part,

    (whether by modifying that Part or Part 2, 3 or 4 of the Schedule).

Apart from ECF (which is covered by section 10 of the Act), anything outside Schedule 1 is therefore outside the scope of legal aid.

We shall now turn to Schedule 1 to see what remains in scope.

8.2   WHAT REMAINS IN SCOPE OF LEGAL AID

Part 1 of Schedule 1 to LASPO 2012 contains a somewhat haphazard list of matters that remain in scope for legal aid purposes. The following are the relevant areas for immigration practitioners:

- judicial review (para.19);
- SIAC (para.24);
- detention under immigration powers (paras.25–27);
- victims of domestic violence (paras.28–29);

- asylum claims (para.30);
- asylum support (para.31);
- victims of trafficking in human persons (para.32);
- advocacy (Schedule 1, Part 3).

The following sections will consider the provisions in more detail.

8.2.1 Judicial review

Generally, judicial review remains in scope for immigration cases, although there are specific exclusions, such as where 'the same issue, or substantially the same issue, was the subject of a previous judicial review or an appeal to a court or tribunal', the application was refused and this was less than a year before the current legal aid application (LASPO 2012, Sched.1, Part 1, para.19(5)).

However, fresh claims and other certified cases are still permitted legal aid for judicial review in spite of these restrictions, i.e. where there would not be a right of appeal (see paras.19(7) and (8)).

8.2.2 SIAC cases

All cases before SIAC remain in scope under LASPO 2012. These are usually covered under licensed work, meaning legal aid certificates rather than controlled legal representation.

8.2.3 Detention under immigration powers

These paragraphs include applying for temporary admission or release and applying for CIO's bail or applying for bail to the Tribunal.

8.2.4 Victims of domestic violence

Paragraphs 28 and 29 specify the limited circumstances that remain in scope for victims of domestic violence under LASPO 2012. Paragraph 28 covers the situation where a partner is applying for indefinite leave to remain as the relationship has broken down permanently due to domestic violence. Paragraph 29 covers the following two EEA scenarios: first, an application for a residence card by a victim of domestic violence with a retained right to reside; or, second, with a permanent right to reside where the applicant has ceased to be a family member on the termination of the marriage.

8.2.5 Asylum claims

Paragraph 30 covers applications to enter and remain in the UK under:

- the Refugee Convention;

- Articles 2 or 3 of the ECHR;
- Directive 2001/55/EC (the 'Temporary Protection Directive'); or
- the Qualification Directive.

8.2.6 Asylum support

Paragraph 31 covers the provision of accommodation for National Asylum Support Service (NASS) applications made under s.4 or s.95 of the Immigration and Asylum Act 1999, limited to advice only (not representation in the Tribunal). NASS support falls under the housing category rather than the immigration category.

8.2.7 Victims of trafficking

Paragraph 32 is qualified as the victim of trafficking must have either a 'reasonable grounds' determination (and no conclusive grounds decision) or a 'conclusive grounds' determination to fall under this section.

The drawback with this paragraph is that a victim of trafficking cannot fall under this section if they have not yet had a 'reasonable grounds' decision. However, in most cases the trafficking victim will have an asylum claim and can therefore receive legal aid under that provision.

The advantage for a trafficking victim in falling under this paragraph is that it is widely drafted so covers any type of application for leave to remain in the UK, rather than just being limited to asylum, so Article 8 advice would also be covered by legal aid here.

8.2.8 Advocacy

The basic rule under LASPO 2012 is that if the category of work is in scope, e.g. bail, then advocacy will be permitted (Sched.1, Part 3, para.13).

8.3 WHAT IS 'OUT OF SCOPE' UNDER LASPO 2012

We have looked broadly at what is in scope for legal aid purposes under Part 1 of Schedule 1 to LASPO 2012. Anything not covered is therefore out of scope for legal aid purposes, which includes:

- EU cases;
- post-conviction deportation cases;
- Article 8 of the ECHR;
- applicants with mental health/incapacity issues (other than on ECHR, Article 3 grounds);
- entry clearance applications/appeals, e.g. for family members (including family reunion for the family members of recognised refugees);

- appeals for the excluded cases in this list including to the higher courts, such as the Court of Appeal and Supreme Court.

This has also led to complications with the funding regime under LASPO 2012, where a client is raising more than one ground to remain in the UK, one ground may fall under LASPO 2012 and the other may not. For example, in the case of an appeal against deportation the applicant may be raising asylum/Article 3 claims which are covered under LASPO 2012 and Article 8 claims as they have a British spouse or children, which are not.

So what can you do if the application does not fall within LASPO 2012?

8.4 EXCEPTIONAL CASE FUNDING

Section 10 of LASPO 2012 provides for 'exceptional case determinations' to provide legal aid funding for cases that do not fall within Part 1 of Schedule 1 to LASPO 2012. An application for ECF can be made to the Director of Legal Casework on the ECF application form (**www.gov.uk/government/uploads/system/uploads/attachment_data/file/475820/legal-aid-civ-ecf1.pdf**).

The Legal Aid Agency has made available provider packs for applications (with a separate pack for inquests), giving details of how applications should be made (**www.gov.uk/guidance/legal-aid-apply-for-exceptional-case-funding**).

Section 10(3) of LASPO 2012 sets out the general test for civil legal services:

an exceptional case determination is a determination –

(a)   that it is necessary to make the services available to the individual under this Part because failure to do so would be a breach of –

    (i)   the individual's Convention rights (within the meaning of the Human Rights Act 1998); or

    (ii)   any rights of the individual to the provision of legal services that are enforceable EU rights, or

(b)   that it is appropriate to do so, in the particular circumstances of the case, having regard to any risk that failure to do so would be such a breach.

The Lord Chancellor has also prepared guidance on ECF (**www.gov.uk/government/uploads/system/uploads/attachment_data/file/477317/legal-aid-chancellor-non-inquests.pdf**).

This guidance is intended for Legal Aid Agency caseworkers considering ECF applications and identifies a number of relevant factors as to when ECF should be granted including the consequences to the applicant, whether the claim includes issues relating to life, liberty, health and bodily integrity, child welfare or vulnerable adults, protection from violence or abuse, or physical safety.

The guidance reflects the factors identified in the test case of *R (on the application of Gudanaviciene) v. Director of Legal Aid Casework* [2014] EWCA Civ 1622 including the relevant test being whether withholding legal aid means that someone will be unable to present their case effectively or it will lead to obvious unfairness.

In addition, in another judicial review funding challenge, *IS* v. *Director of Legal Aid Casework and another* [2015] EWHC 1965 (Admin), Collins J cited earlier authority stating that there would be no fair trial where the court 'has no confidence in its ability to grasp the facts and principles of the matter'.

Since the judgment in *Gudanaviciene* there has been a noticeable increase in the number of successful ECF applications granted by the Legal Aid Agency. Certainly for appeals involving deportation, Article 8 of the ECHR and family reunion it is worth applying for ECF provided key factors such as those above are identified and highlighted in the making of an application.

There is a right to request a review from the Legal Aid Agency if an ECF application is refused. If the review is unsuccessful then the only remedy to challenge the review would be by way of judicial review. Legal aid funding is technically available for such a challenge.

8.5   MERITS CRITERIA REGULATIONS

Legal aid can only be granted under an immigration legal aid contract if both the merits of the case and means of the client satisfy the requisite thresholds as set out in Civil Legal Aid (Merits Criteria) Regulations 2013, SI 2013/104 (Merits Criteria Regulations). In this section we will look at the different merits tests that apply to the different levels of legal aid work.

8.5.1   Legal Help

Legal Help covers initial applications to the Home Office, such as asylum. A provider can only grant Legal Help to a client if the matter meets the 'sufficient benefit' test, that is (Merits Criteria Regulations, reg.32(b)):

> there is likely to be sufficient benefit to the individual, having regard to all the circum-
> stances of the case, including the circumstances of the individual, to justify the cost of
> provision of legal help.

This is effectively a cost-benefit analysis, namely would a reasonable privately paying client of moderate means pay for the advice to start or continue the case. It is a continuing test so would need to be borne in mind throughout the lifetime of the case.

There will normally be sufficient benefit to a client in receiving advice on detention and release (Immigration Specification of the Standard Civil Contract 2013, para.8.37).

221

8.5.2 Prospects of success test

For controlled legal representation, investigative representation and full representation there is a 'prospects of success' test laid down in the Merits Criteria Regulations, reg.5 as amended by the Civil Legal Aid (Merits Criteria) (Amendment) (No.2) Regulations 2015, reg.2(2), which sets out a classification system of achieving a successful outcome as follows:

- very good – above 80 per cent;
- good – above 60 per cent but below 80 per cent;
- moderate – above 50 per cent but below 60 per cent;
- borderline – not that the chances are 'unclear' but that it is not possible due to disputed law, fact or expert evidence to decide that a case has a 50 per cent chance of a successful outcome or more or to classify the prospects as poor;
- poor – above 20 per cent but below 50 per cent;
- very poor – below 20 per cent;
- unclear – this means a case cannot be put into one of the categories above as further investigations need to be carried out before the case can be reliably categorised.

We will see in the following sections the importance of these categorisations in considering whether a case has 'merit' for the purposes of legal aid.

8.5.3 Controlled legal representation

Controlled legal representation (CLR) covers appeals to the First-tier and Upper Tribunal.

The merits test for a provider granting CLR is that the reasonable privately playing client test is satisfied (see **8.5.1**), and (Merits Criteria Regulations, reg.60(3) as amended):

The Director must be satisfied that –

(a)   the prospects of success are very good, good or moderate;
(b)   the prospects of success are borderline or poor but it is –

      (i)   necessary for the Director to determine that the criterion in this paragraph is met to prevent a breach of –

          (aa)   the individual's Convention rights; or
          (bb)   any rights of the individual to the provision of legal services that are enforceable EU rights; or

      (ii)   appropriate for the Director to determine that the criterion in this paragraph is met, in the particular circumstances of the case, having regard to any risk that a failure to make such a determination would be such a breach; or

(c)   the prospects of success are unclear, and –

      (i)   the case is of significant wider public interest;
      (ii)   the case is one with overwhelming importance to the individual; or
      (iii)   the substance of the case relates to a breach of Convention rights.

Please note the important amendment that has been introduced by the Civil Legal Aid (Merits Criteria) (Amendment) (No.2) Regulations 2015, reg.2(6) to give effect to the judgment in *IS* v. *Director of Legal Aid Casework and another* [2015] EWHC 1965 (Admin), where a case on the merits might be 'poor' (so above 30 per cent but below 50 per cent) or borderline but it is accepted that a failure to grant legal aid would be a breach of the applicant's ECHR or enforceable EU rights.

An application can be made to the Director of Legal Aid Casework for authority to grant CLR where the prospects of success are poor or borderline. The Legal Aid Agency has confirmed that such applications can be emailed to them, depending on whether they are 'in scope' or ECF cases.

Applications for 'poor' or 'borderline' determinations should be sent to HR&EUInscopeCases@legalaid.gsi.gov.uk for cases covered by legal aid or ECF@legalaid.gsi.gov.uk for exceptional funding cases (**www.gov.uk/ government/news/civil-news-civil-legal-aid-merits-regulations-amended**).

8.5.4 Investigative representation

'Investigative representation' is a type of legal aid certificate, as the name suggests, which providers can obtain to carry out 'substantial' enquiries where the prospects of success are unclear in order to determine the prospects and in addition there are reasonable grounds for believing that once the investigations are complete the case will meet the criteria for a 'full certificate' to be issued (Merits Criteria Regulations, reg.40).

8.5.5 Full representation

Full legal aid certificates are usually issued in the immigration context for judicial review applications in both the Upper Tribunal and Administrative Court and for statutory appeals to the Court of Appeal from the Upper Tribunal, and to the Supreme Court.

The merits test the applicant has to meet is set out in reg.42 of the Merits Criteria Regulations:

Cost benefit criteria for determinations for full representation

(1)   The cost benefit criteria are as follows.

(2)   If the case is primarily a claim for damages or other sum of money and is not of significant wider public interest –

   (a)   if the prospects of success of the case are very good, the Director must be satisfied that the likely damages exceed likely costs;

   (b)   if the prospects of success of the case are good, the Director must be satisfied that the likely damages exceed likely costs by a ratio of two to one; or

   (c)   if the prospects of success of the case are moderate, the Director must be satisfied that the likely damages exceed likely costs by a ratio of four to one.

223

(3)   If the case is –

    (a)   not primarily a claim for damages or other sum of money; and
    (b)   not of significant wider public interest,

the Director must be satisfied that the reasonable private paying individual test is met.

(4)   If the case is of significant wider public interest, the Director must be satisfied that the proportionality test is met.

Please note the amendments made by the Civil Legal Aid (Merits Criteria) (Amendment) (No.2) Regulations 2015, reg.2(3) and (4) again in connection with the chances of success to reflect the *IS* judgment (see **8.5.3**).

It should also be noted that it is now the default position, for legal aid certificates issued on or after 27 March 2015, that if a judicial review application is refused permission to appeal a provider will not be paid for the work (Civil Legal Aid (Remuneration) Regulations 2013, SI 2013/422 as amended by the Civil Legal Aid (Remuneration) (Amendment) Regulations 2015, SI 2015/898). This means that the work is being carried out 'at risk' of not getting paid.

Disbursements (such as court fees) are still recoverable under legal aid (reg.5A(2) of the 2013 Regulations). It should also be noted that work done in respect of interim relief applications can also still be claimed (even where permission to appeal has been refused) (reg.5A(3)(c) of the 2013 Regulations).

A number of other exceptions are covered in the Regulations, e.g. where either permission has been refused following the Home Office withdrawing a decision or where no decision has been made by the court on the permission application and a claim can still be made for profit costs under the certificate (reg.5A(1)(a) to (e) of the 2013 Regulations).

8.5.6   CW4 and provider obligations

Where a provider refuses or withdraws legal aid under controlled legal representation (CLR) for representation before the First-tier Tribunal (Immigration and Asylum) as the provider believes the case does not meet the merits criteria then the provider is under a duty to provide the client with a completed CW4 form, giving the reasons for that decision, within five working days of making the decision. The provider should also send the form to the Legal Aid Agency for the client if this is requested.

This will enable the client to appeal the provider's decision to the Legal Aid Agency within 14 days where the decision will be reviewed. If the provider's decision is overturned by the Agency then the provider will have to provide the client with legal aid under CLR.

This process applies whether the provider is refusing or withdrawing legal aid for a bail application, an appeal covered by LASPO 2012 or an appeal under ECF.

Failure to provide the client with the CW4 form would be a breach of paragraphs 8.41–8.45 of the Immigration Specification of the 2013 Standard Civil Contract.

8.6 IMMIGRATION AND ASYLUM SPECIFICATION OF THE 2013 STANDARD CIVIL CONTRACT

There are a number of important issues to look at under the Immigration and Asylum Specification of the 2013 Standard Civil Contract (Immigration Specification).

8.6.1 Duty to refer unaccompanied asylum-seeking children

Where an unaccompanied asylum-seeking child (UASC) experiences problems with a local authority exercising its duties under the Children Act 1989 then it is very important to ensure the adviser makes the necessary referral to another adviser who can assist the child with legal advice under the family, community care, public or housing contracts. It can either be referred in house or to an external provider (Immigration Specification, paras.8.9–8.10).

It should be noted that this is an additional extra duty on top of the usual referral duties under the Standard Civil Contract.

8.6.2 Immigration and asylum supervisor legal competence standard

There are additional requirements that fee earners have to meet to be supervisors under the immigration specification, namely to have passed either level 2 or 3 of the Immigration and Asylum Accreditation Scheme (IAAS) plus have passed the IAAS supervisor accreditation assessment.

The specification even goes so far to spell out:

> 8.19   The Supervisor must take account of any changes in legislation and case law and maintain access for the duration of the Contract to at least 1 nationally published specialist journal (containing updates on Immigration and Asylum case law and statutes). This may include electronic publications such as subscription case law websites.

No other specification under the Standard Civil Contract goes into so much detail as to what standard a supervisor should meet and this is a legacy of the historically poor standard of advice in this area of legal aid work.

8.6.3 Level of accreditation for contract work

The Immigration Specification at para.8.20 also details the level of responsibility for making decisions on files that fee earners are able to carry out, depending on their level of accreditation:

Type of contract work	Level of accreditation
Conduct of Legal Help matters	Level 1 Accredited caseworker and above
Use of Delegated Functions to make a determination that an individual qualifies for CLR; and conduct of CLR cases	Level 2 Senior caseworker and above
All Contract Work carried out for an UASC	Level 2 Senior caseworker and above

Paragraph 8.21 defines 'conduct' as 'having responsibility for and control of the progression of the case'.

8.6.4 Work restrictions

As well as controlling who will make decisions on the case the Immigration Specification also makes it clear that the level of accreditation determines what work can be carried out on a file:

> 8.15 All caseworkers who carry out Immigration and Asylum Contract Work must:
>
> (a) comply with the terms of the Law Society's Immigration and Asylum Accreditation Scheme and Levels of Accreditation (IAAS);
> (b) comply with our Work Restrictions; and
> (c) if intending to act for a Client who is an UASC have had an enhanced Criminal Records Bureau check in the 24 months prior to instruction.

The 'work restrictions' referred to in para.8.15(b) are set out in a separate document produced by the Legal Aid Agency (*Contract Management – Immigration and Asylum Accreditation Scheme: Work Restrictions*, version 3, April 2013).

For example, only level 2 (and above) accredited fee earners can do work on the files of UASCs and note also the requirement for a criminal records check to be carried out on any fee earner working on files for UASCs in the 24 months prior to instruction at para.8.15(c)).

If fee earners are not accredited to the correct level then they will not be able to make a claim for payment for the work (Immigration Specification, para.8.22).

8.7 FOR THE FUTURE: A RESIDENCE TEST FOR LEGAL AID

In an unprecedented move on 19 April 2016, the Supreme Court stopped an appeal, halfway through, at the end of the first day of a two-day hearing. After minutes of deliberation, the Supreme Court decision was unanimous and a brief announcement was made:

> The issues in this appeal were whether the proposed civil legal aid residence test in the draft Legal Aid, Sentencing and Punishment of Offenders Act (Amendment of Schedule

1) Order 2014 is ultra vires and unjustifiably discriminatory and so in breach of common law and the Human Rights Act 1998. At the end of today's hearing the Supreme Court announced that it was allowing the appeal on ground [of ultra vires] ... The Supreme Court asked the parties whether they wished to address the court on the second issue. The case has been adjourned while this is considered.

The proceedings were brought by Public Law Project, represented by Bindmans and with the Law Society intervening. The written judgment had not yet been handed down when this Handbook went to press.

The Lord Chancellor has been attempting to bring in a 'residence test' to further limit entitlement to legal aid to those lawfully resident in the UK. The Public Law Project brought a judicial review challenge to this. The application was successful in the Administrative Court but was overturned by the Court of Appeal (*Public Law Project* v. *Lord Chancellor* [2015] EWCA Civ 1193).

If the 'residence test' had been introduced this would have further restricted access to justice which, as we have seen above, has already been decimated with the introduction of the LASPO 2012 restrictions in 2013.

Now, if the Ministry of Justice still wants to introduce the residence test, it will have to set out the measures in a bill subject to full debate in Parliament.

APPENDIX A

Statutes

Immigration Act 1971 (extracts)

3   General provisions for regulation and control

(5)   A person who is not a British citizen is liable to deportation from the United Kingdom if –

    (a)   the Secretary of State deems his deportation to be conducive to the public good; or

    (b)   another person to whose family he belongs is or has been ordered to be deported.

(6)   Without prejudice to the operation of subsection (5) above, a person who is not a British citizen shall also be liable to deportation from the United Kingdom if, after he has attained the age of seventeen, he is convicted of an offence for which he is punishable with imprisonment and on his conviction is recommended for deportation by a court empowered by this Act to do so.

3C   Continuation of leave pending variation decision

(1)   This section applies if –

    (a)   a person who has limited leave to enter or remain in the United Kingdom applies to the Secretary of State for variation of the leave,

    (b)   the application for variation is made before the leave expires, and

    (c)   the leave expires without the application for variation having been decided.

(2)   The leave is extended by virtue of this section during any period when –

    (a)   the application for variation is neither decided nor withdrawn,

    (b)   an appeal under section 82(1) of the Nationality, Asylum and Immigration Act 2002 could be brought, while the appellant is in the United Kingdom against the decision on the application for variation (ignoring any possibility of an appeal out of time with permission),

    (c)   an appeal under that section against that decision, brought while the appellant is in the United Kingdom, is pending (within the meaning of section 104 of that Act), or

    (d)   an administrative review of the decision on the application for variation –

        (i)   could be sought, or

        (ii)   is pending.

(3)   Leave extended by virtue of this section shall lapse if the applicant leaves the United Kingdom.

(4)   A person may not make an application for variation of his leave to enter or remain in the United Kingdom while that leave is extended by virtue of this section.

(5)   But subsection (4) does not prevent the variation of the application mentioned in subsection (1)(a).

24   Illegal entry and similar offences

(1)   A person who is not a British citizen shall be guilty of an offence punishable on summary conviction with a fine of not more than level 5 on the standard scale or with imprisonment for not more than six months, or with both, in any of the following cases: –

    (a)   if contrary to this Act he knowingly enters the United Kingdom in breach of a deportation order or without leave;

    (b)   if, having only a limited leave to enter or remain in the United Kingdom, he knowingly either –

        (i)   remains beyond the time limited by the leave; or

        (ii)   fails to observe a condition of the leave;

    (c)   if, having lawfully entered the United Kingdom without leave by virtue of section 8(1) above, he remains without leave beyond the time allowed by section 8(1);

    (d)   if, without reasonable excuse, he fails to comply with any requirement imposed on him under Schedule 2 to this Act to report to a medical officer of health, or to attend, or submit to a test or examination, as required by such an officer;

    (e)   if, without reasonable excuse, he fails to observe any restriction imposed on him under Schedule 2 or 3 to this Act as to residence, as to his employment or occupation or as to reporting to the police, to an immigration officer or to the Secretary of State;

    (f)   if he disembarks in the United Kingdom from a ship or aircraft after being placed on board under Schedule 2 or 3 to this Act with a view to his removal from the United Kingdom;

    (g)   if he embarks in contravention of a restriction imposed by or under an Order in Council under section 3(7) of this Act.

(1A)   A person commits an offence under subsection (1)(b)(i) above on the day when he first knows that the time limited by his leave has expired and continues to commit it throughout any period during which he is in the United Kingdom thereafter; but a person shall not be prosecuted under that provision more than once in respect of the same limited leave.

(2)   [*Repealed*]

(3)   The extended time limit for prosecutions which is provided for by section 28 below shall apply to offences under subsection (1)(a) and (c) above.

(4)   In proceedings for an offence against subsection (1)(a) above of entering the United Kingdom without leave, –

    (a)   any stamp purporting to have been imprinted on a passport or other travel document by an immigration officer on a particular date for the purpose of giving leave shall be presumed to have been duly so imprinted, unless the contrary is proved;

    (b)   proof that a person had leave to enter the United Kingdom shall lie on the defence if, but only if, he is shown to have entered within six months before the date when the proceedings were commenced.

24A Deception

(1)   A person who is not a British citizen is guilty of an offence if, by means which include deception by him –

    (a)   he obtains or seeks to obtain leave to enter or remain in the United Kingdom; or

    (b)   he secures or seeks to secure the avoidance, postponement or revocation of enforcement action against him.

(2)   'Enforcement action', in relation to a person, means –

    (a)   the giving of directions for his removal from the United Kingdom ('directions') under Schedule 2 to this Act or section 10 of the Immigration and Asylum Act 1999;

    (b)   the making of a deportation order against him under section 5 of this Act; or

    (c)   his removal from the United Kingdom in consequence of directions or a deportation order.

(3)   A person guilty of an offence under this section is liable –

    (a)   on summary conviction, to imprisonment for a term not exceeding six months or to a fine not exceeding the statutory maximum, or to both; or

    (b)   on conviction on indictment, to imprisonment for a term not exceeding two years or to a fine, or to both.

(4)   [*Repealed*]

25 Assisting unlawful immigration to member State

(1)   A person commits an offence if he –

    (a)   does an act which facilitates the commission of a breach of immigration law by an individual who is not a citizen of the European Union,

    (b)   knows or has reasonable cause for believing that the act facilitates the commission of a breach of immigration law by the individual, and

    (c)   knows or has reasonable cause for believing that the individual is not a citizen of the European Union.

(2)   In subsection (1) 'immigration law' means a law which has effect in a member State and which controls, in respect of some or all persons who are not nationals of the State, entitlement to –

    (a)   enter the State,

    (b)   transit across the State, or

    (c)   be in the State.

(3)   A document issued by the government of a member State certifying a matter of law in that State –

    (a)   shall be admissible in proceedings for an offence under this section, and

    (b)   shall be conclusive as to the matter certified.

(4)   Subsection (1) applies to things done whether inside or outside the United Kingdom.

(5)   [*Repealed*]

(6)   A person guilty of an offence under this section shall be liable –

    (a)   on conviction on indictment, to imprisonment for a term not exceeding 14 years, to a fine or to both, or

    (b)   on summary conviction, to imprisonment for a term not exceeding six months, to a fine not exceeding the statutory maximum or to both.

(7)   In this section –

   (a)   a reference to a member State includes a reference to a State on a list prescribed for the purposes of this section by order of the Secretary of State (to be known as the 'Section 25 List of Schengen Acquis States'), and

   (b)   a reference to a citizen of the European Union includes a reference to a person who is a national of a State on that list.

(8)   An order under subsection (7)(a) –

   (a)   may be made only if the Secretary of State thinks it necessary for the purpose of complying with the United Kingdom's obligations under the EU Treaties,

   (b)   may include transitional, consequential or incidental provision,

   (c)   shall be made by statutory instrument, and

   (d)   shall be subject to annulment in pursuance of a resolution of either House of Parliament.

25A   Helping asylum-seeker to enter United Kingdom

(1)   A person commits an offence if –

   (a)   he knowingly and for gain facilitates the arrival in, or the entry into, the United Kingdom of an individual, and

   (b)   he knows or has reasonable cause to believe that the individual is an asylum-seeker.

(2)   In this section 'asylum-seeker' means a person who intends to claim that to remove him from or require him to leave the United Kingdom would be contrary to the United Kingdom's obligations under –

   (a)   the Refugee Convention (within the meaning given by section 167(1) of the Immigration and Asylum Act 1999 (c 33) (interpretation)), or

   (b)   the Human Rights Convention (within the meaning given by that section).

(3)   Subsection (1) does not apply to anything done by a person acting on behalf of an organisation which –

   (a)   aims to assist asylum-seekers, and

   (b)   does not charge for its services.

(4)   Subsections (4) and (6) of section 25 apply for the purpose of the offence in subsection (1) of this section as they apply for the purpose of the offence in subsection (1) of that section.

25B   Assisting entry to United Kingdom in breach of deportation or exclusion order

(1)   A person commits an offence if he –

   (a)   does an act which facilitates a breach of a deportation order in force against an individual who is a citizen of the European Union, and

   (b)   knows or has reasonable cause for believing that the act facilitates a breach of the deportation order.

(2)   Subsection (3) applies where the Secretary of State personally directs that the exclusion from the United Kingdom of an individual who is a citizen of the European Union is conducive to the public good.

(3)   A person commits an offence if he –

    (a)   does an act which assists the individual to arrive in, enter or remain in the United Kingdom,

    (b)   knows or has reasonable cause for believing that the act assists the individual to arrive in, enter or remain in the United Kingdom, and

    (c)   knows or has reasonable cause for believing that the Secretary of State has personally directed that the individual's exclusion from the United Kingdom is conducive to the public good.

(4)   Subsections (4) and (6) of section 25 apply for the purpose of an offence under this section as they apply for the purpose of an offence under that section.

26   General offences in connection with administration of Act

(1)   A person shall be guilty of an offence punishable on summary conviction with a fine of not more than level 5 on the standard scale or with imprisonment for not more than six months, or with both, in any of the following cases –

    (a)   if, without reasonable excuse, he refuses or fails to submit to examination under Schedule 2 to this Act;

    (b)   if, without reasonable excuse, he refuses or fails to furnish or produce any information in his possession, or any documents in his possession or control, which he is on an examination under that Schedule required to furnish or produce;

    (c)   if on any such examination or otherwise he makes or causes to be made to an immigration officer or other person lawfully acting in the execution of a relevant enactment a return, statement or representation which he knows to be false or does not believe to be true;

    (d)   if, without lawful authority, he alters any certificate of entitlement, entry clearance, work permit or other document issued or made under or for the purposes of this Act, or uses for the purposes of this Act, or has in his possession for such use, any passport, certificate of entitlement, entry clearance, work permit or other document which he knows or has reasonable cause to believe to be false;

    (e)   if, without reasonable excuse, he fails to complete and produce a landing or embarkation card in accordance with any order under Schedule 2 to this Act;

    (f)   if, without reasonable excuse, he fails to comply with any requirement of regulations under section 4(3) or of an order under section 4(4) above;

    (g)   if, without reasonable excuse, he obstructs an immigration officer or other person lawfully acting in the execution of this Act.

(2)   The extended time limit for prosecutions which is provided for by section 28 below shall apply to offences under subsection (1)(c) and (d) above.

(3)   'Relevant enactment' means –

    (a)   this Act;

    (b)   the Immigration Act 1988;

    (c)   the Asylum and Immigration Appeals Act 1993 (apart from section 4 or 5);

    (d)   the Immigration and Asylum Act 1999 (apart from Part VI); or

    (e)   the Nationality, Immigration and Asylum Act 2002 (apart from Part 5).

Immigration and Asylum Act 1999 (extracts)

10 Removal of persons unlawfully in the United Kingdom

(1)   A person may be removed from the United Kingdom under the authority of the Secretary of State or an immigration officer if the person requires leave to enter or remain in the United Kingdom but does not have it.

(2)   Where a person ('P') is liable to be or has been removed from the United Kingdom under subsection (1), a member of P's family who meets the following three conditions may also be removed from the United Kingdom under the authority of the Secretary of State or an immigration officer, provided that the Secretary of State or immigration officer has given the family member written notice of the intention to remove him or her.

(3)   The first condition is that the family member is –

    (a)   P's partner,
    (b)   P's child, or a child living in the same household as P in circumstances where P has care of the child,
    (c)   in a case where P is a child, P's parent, or
    (d)   an adult dependent relative of P.

(4)   The second condition is that –

    (a)   in a case where the family member has leave to enter or remain in the United Kingdom, that leave was granted on the basis of his or her family life with P;
    (b)   in a case where the family member does not have leave to enter or remain in the United Kingdom, in the opinion of the Secretary of State or immigration officer the family member –

        (i)   would not, on making an application for such leave, be granted leave in his or her own right, but
        (ii)   would be granted leave on the basis of his or her family life with P, if P had leave to enter or remain.

(5)   The third condition is that the family member is neither a British citizen, nor is he or she entitled to enter or remain in the United Kingdom by virtue of an enforceable EU right or of any provision made under section 2(2) of the European Communities Act 1972.

(6)   A notice given to a family member under subsection (2) invalidates any leave to enter or remain in the United Kingdom previously given to the family member.

(7)   For the purposes of removing a person from the United Kingdom under subsection (1) or (2), the Secretary of State or an immigration officer may give any such direction for the removal of the person as may be given under paragraphs 8 to 10 of Schedule 2 to the 1971 Act.

(8)   But subsection (7) does not apply where a deportation order is in force against a

person (and any directions for such a person's removal must be given under Schedule 3 to the 1971 Act).

(9) The following paragraphs of Schedule 2 to the 1971 Act apply in relation to directions under subsection (7) (and the persons subject to those directions) as they apply in relation to directions under paragraphs 8 to 10 of Schedule 2 (and the persons subject to those directions) –

    (a) paragraph 11 (placing of person on board ship or aircraft);

    (b) paragraph 16(2) to (4) (detention of person where reasonable grounds for suspecting removal directions may be given or pending removal in pursuance of directions);

    (c) paragraph 17 (arrest of person liable to be detained and search of premises for person liable to arrest);

    (d) paragraph 18 (supplementary provisions on detention);

    (e) paragraph 18A (search of detained person);

    (f) paragraph 18B (detention of unaccompanied children);

    (g) paragraphs 19 and 20 (payment of expenses of custody etc);

    (h) paragraph 21 (temporary admission to UK of person liable to detention);

    (i) paragraphs 22 to 25 (bail);

    (j) paragraphs 25A to 25E (searches etc).

(10) The Secretary of State may by regulations make further provision about –

    (a) the time period during which a family member may be removed under subsection (2);

    (b) the service of a notice under subsection (2).

(11) In this section 'child' means a person who is under the age of 18.

31 Defences based on Article 31(1) of the Refugee Convention

(1) It is a defence for a refugee charged with an offence to which this section applies to show that, having come to the United Kingdom directly from a country where his life or freedom was threatened (within the meaning of the Refugee Convention), he –

    (a) presented himself to the authorities in the United Kingdom without delay;

    (b) showed good cause for his illegal entry or presence; and

    (c) made a claim for asylum as soon as was reasonably practicable after his arrival in the United Kingdom.

(2) If, in coming from the country where his life or freedom was threatened, the refugee stopped in another country outside the United Kingdom, subsection (1) applies only if he shows that he could not reasonably have expected to be given protection under the Refugee Convention in that other country.

(3) In England and Wales and Northern Ireland the offences to which this section applies are any offence, and any attempt to commit an offence, under –

    (a) Part I of the Forgery and Counterfeiting Act 1981 (forgery and connected offences);

    (aa) section 4 or 6 of the Identity Documents Act 2010;

    (b) section 24A of the 1971 Act (deception); or

    (c) section 26(1)(d) of the 1971 Act (falsification of documents).

(4) In Scotland, the offences to which this section applies are those –

    (a) of fraud,

    (b) of uttering a forged document,

     (ba)   under section 4 or 6 of the Identity Documents Act 2010,

     (c)   under section 24A of the 1971 Act (deception), or

     (d)   under section 26(1)(d) of the 1971 Act (falsification of documents),
       and any attempt to commit any of those offences.

(5)   A refugee who has made a claim for asylum is not entitled to the defence provided by subsection (1) in relation to any offence committed by him after making that claim.

(6)   'Refugee' has the same meaning as it has for the purposes of the Refugee Convention.

(7)   If the Secretary of State has refused to grant a claim for asylum made by a person who claims that he has a defence under subsection (1), that person is to be taken not to be a refugee unless he shows that he is.

PART VI   SUPPORT FOR ASYLUM-SEEKERS

Interpretation

94   Interpretation of Part VI

(1)   In this Part –

    'asylum-seeker' means a person who is not under 18 and has made a claim for asylum which has been recorded by the Secretary of State but which has not been determined;

    'claim for asylum' means a claim that it would be contrary to the United Kingdom's obligations under the Refugee Convention, or under Article 3 of the Human Rights Convention, for the claimant to be removed from, or required to leave, the United Kingdom;

    'the Department' means the Department of Health and Social Services for Northern Ireland;

    'dependant', in relation to an asylum-seeker or a supported person, means a person in the United Kingdom who –

     (a)   is his spouse;

     (b)   is a child of his, or of his spouse, who is under 18 and dependent on him; or

     (c)   falls within such additional category, if any, as may be prescribed;

    'the Executive' means the Northern Ireland Housing Executive;

    'housing accommodation' includes flats, lodging houses and hostels;

    'local authority' means –

     (a)   in England and Wales, a county council, a county borough council, a district council, a London borough council, the Common Council of the City of London or the Council of the Isles of Scilly;

     (b)   in Scotland, a council constituted under section 2 of the Local Government etc (Scotland) Act 1994;

    'Northern Ireland authority' has the meaning given by section 110(9);

    'supported person' means –

     (a)   an asylum-seeker, or

     (b)   a dependant of an asylum-seeker,
      who has applied for support and for whom support is provided under section 95.

(2)   References in this Part to support provided under section 95 include references to support which is provided under arrangements made by the Secretary of State under that section.

(3)   For the purposes of this Part, a claim for asylum is determined at the end of such period beginning –

(a)   on the day on which the Secretary of State notifies the claimant of his decision on the claim, or

(b)   if the claimant has appealed against the Secretary of State's decision, on the day on which the appeal is disposed of,

as may be prescribed.

(4)   An appeal is disposed of when it is no longer pending for the purposes of the Immigration Acts or the Special Immigration Appeals Commission Act 1997.

(5)   If an asylum-seeker's household includes a child who is under 18 and a dependant of his, he is to be treated (for the purposes of this Part) as continuing to be an asylum-seeker while –

(a)   the child is under 18; and

(b)   he and the child remain in the United Kingdom.

(6)   Subsection (5) does not apply if, on or after the determination of his claim for asylum, the asylum-seeker is granted leave to enter or remain in the United Kingdom (whether or not as a result of that claim).

(7)   For the purposes of this Part, the Secretary of State may inquire into, and decide, the age of any person.

(8)   A notice under subsection (3) must be given in writing.

(9)   If such a notice is sent by the Secretary of State by first class post, addressed –

(a)   to the asylum-seeker's representative, or

(b)   to the asylum-seeker's last known address,

it is to be taken to have been received by the asylum-seeker on the second day after the day on which it was posted.

Provision of support

95   Persons for whom support may be provided

(1)   The Secretary of State may provide, or arrange for the provision of, support for –

(a)   asylum-seekers, or

(b)   dependants of asylum-seekers,

who appear to the Secretary of State to be destitute or to be likely to become destitute within such period as may be prescribed.

(2)   In prescribed circumstances, a person who would otherwise fall within subsection (1) is excluded.

(3)   For the purposes of this section, a person is destitute if –

(a)   he does not have adequate accommodation or any means of obtaining it (whether or not his other essential living needs are met); or

(b)   he has adequate accommodation or the means of obtaining it, but cannot meet his other essential living needs.

(4)   If a person has dependants, subsection (3) is to be read as if the references to him were references to him and his dependants taken together.

(5)   In determining, for the purposes of this section, whether a person's accommodation is adequate, the Secretary of State –

    (a)   must have regard to such matters as may be prescribed for the purposes of this paragraph; but

    (b)   may not have regard to such matters as may be prescribed for the purposes of this paragraph or to any of the matters mentioned in subsection (6).

(6)   Those matters are –

    (a)   the fact that the person concerned has no enforceable right to occupy the accommodation;

    (b)   the fact that he shares the accommodation, or any part of the accommodation, with one or more other persons;

    (c)   the fact that the accommodation is temporary;

    (d)   the location of the accommodation.

(7)   In determining, for the purposes of this section, whether a person's other essential living needs are met, the Secretary of State –

    (a)   must have regard to such matters as may be prescribed for the purposes of this paragraph; but

    (b)   may not have regard to such matters as may be prescribed for the purposes of this paragraph.

(8)   The Secretary of State may by regulations provide that items or expenses of such a description as may be prescribed are, or are not, to be treated as being an essential living need of a person for the purposes of this Part.

(9)   Support may be provided subject to conditions.

(9A)   A condition imposed under subsection (9) may, in particular, relate to –

    (a)   any matter relating to the use of the support provided, or

    (b)   compliance with a restriction imposed under paragraph 21 of Schedule 2 to the 1971 Act (temporary admission or release from detention) or paragraph 2 or 5 of Schedule 3 to that Act (restriction pending deportation).

(10)   The conditions must be set out in writing.

(11)   A copy of the conditions must be given to the supported person.

(12)   Schedule 8 gives the Secretary of State power to make regulations supplementing this section.

(13)   Schedule 9 makes temporary provision for support in the period before the coming into force of this section.

Nationality, Immigration and Asylum Act 2002 (extracts)

72 Serious criminal

(1) This section applies for the purpose of the construction and application of Article 33(2) of the Refugee Convention (exclusion from protection).

(2) A person shall be presumed to have been convicted by a final judgment of a particularly serious crime and to constitute a danger to the community of the United Kingdom if he is –

    (a) convicted in the United Kingdom of an offence, and

    (b) sentenced to a period of imprisonment of at least two years.

(3) A person shall be presumed to have been convicted by a final judgment of a particularly serious crime and to constitute a danger to the community of the United Kingdom if –

    (a) he is convicted outside the United Kingdom of an offence,

    (b) he is sentenced to a period of imprisonment of at least two years, and

    (c) he could have been sentenced to a period of imprisonment of at least two years had his conviction been a conviction in the United Kingdom of a similar offence.

(4) A person shall be presumed to have been convicted by a final judgment of a particularly serious crime and to constitute a danger to the community of the United Kingdom if –

    (a) he is convicted of an offence specified by order of the Secretary of State, or

    (b) he is convicted outside the United Kingdom of an offence and the Secretary of State certifies that in his opinion the offence is similar to an offence specified by order under paragraph (a).

(5) An order under subsection (4) –

    (a) must be made by statutory instrument, and

    (b) shall be subject to annulment in pursuance of a resolution of either House of Parliament.

(6) A presumption under subsection (2), (3) or (4) that a person constitutes a danger to the community is rebuttable by that person.

(7) A presumption under subsection (2), (3) or (4) does not apply while an appeal against conviction or sentence –

    (a) is pending, or

    (b) could be brought (disregarding the possibility of appeal out of time with leave).

(8) Section 34(1) of the Anti-terrorism, Crime and Security Act 2001 (c 24) (no need to

consider gravity of fear or threat of persecution) applies for the purpose of considering whether a presumption mentioned in subsection (6) has been rebutted as it applies for the purpose of considering whether Article 33(2) of the Refugee Convention applies.

(9)   Subsection (10) applies where –

(a)   a person appeals under section 82 of this Act or under section 2 of the Special Immigration Appeals Commission Act 1997 (c 68) wholly or partly on the ground mentioned in section 84(1)(a) or (3)(a) of this Act (breach of the United Kingdom's obligations under the Refugee Convention), and

(b)   the Secretary of State issues a certificate that presumptions under subsection (2), (3) or (4) apply to the person (subject to rebuttal).

(10)   The Tribunal or Commission hearing the appeal –

(a)   must begin substantive deliberation on the appeal by considering the certificate, and

(b)   if in agreement that presumptions under subsection (2), (3) or (4) apply (having given the appellant an opportunity for rebuttal) must dismiss the appeal in so far as it relies on the ground specified in subsection (9)(a).

(10A)   Subsection (10) also applies in relation to the Upper Tribunal when it acts under section 12(2)(b)(ii) of the Tribunals, Courts and Enforcement Act 2007.

(11)   For the purposes of this section –

(a)   'the Refugee Convention' means the Convention relating to the Status of Refugees done at Geneva on 28th July 1951 and its Protocol, and

(b)   a reference to a person who is sentenced to a period of imprisonment of at least two years –

(i)   does not include a reference to a person who receives a suspended sentence (unless a court subsequently orders that the sentence or any part of it is to take effect),

(ia)   does not include a reference to a person who is sentenced to a period of imprisonment of at least two years only by virtue of being sentenced to consecutive sentences which amount in aggregate to more than two years,

(ii)   includes a reference to a person who is sentenced to detention, or ordered or directed to be detained, in an institution other than a prison (including, in particular, a hospital or an institution for young offenders), and

(iii)   includes a reference to a person who is sentenced to imprisonment or detention, or ordered or directed to be detained, for an indeterminate period (provided that it may last for two years).

76   Revocation of leave to enter or remain

(1)   The Secretary of State may revoke a person's indefinite leave to enter or remain in the United Kingdom if the person –

(a)   is liable to deportation, but
(b)   cannot be deported for legal reasons.

(2)   The Secretary of State may revoke a person's indefinite leave to enter or remain in the United Kingdom if –

(a)   the leave was obtained by deception.

(3)   The Secretary of State may revoke a person's indefinite leave to enter or remain in the United Kingdom if the person, or someone of whom he is a dependant, ceases to be a refugee as a result of –

(a)   voluntarily availing himself of the protection of his country of nationality,
(b)   voluntarily re-acquiring a lost nationality,
(c)   acquiring the nationality of a country other than the United Kingdom and availing himself of its protection, or
(d)   voluntarily establishing himself in a country in respect of which he was a refugee.

(4)   In this section –

'indefinite leave' has the meaning given by section 33(1) of the Immigration Act 1971 (c 77) (interpretation),
'liable to deportation' has the meaning given by section 3(5) and (6) of that Act (deportation),
'refugee' has the meaning given by the Convention relating to the Status of Refugees done at Geneva on 28th July 1951 and its Protocol.

(5)   A power under subsection (1) or (2) to revoke leave may be exercised –

(a)   in respect of leave granted before this section comes into force;
(b)   in reliance on anything done before this section comes into force.

(6)   A power under subsection (3) to revoke leave may be exercised –

(a)   in respect of leave granted before this section comes into force, but
(b)   only in reliance on action taken after this section comes into force.

(7)   [*Repealed*]

78   No removal while appeal pending

(1)   While a person's appeal under section 82(1) is pending he may not be –

(a)   removed from the United Kingdom in accordance with a provision of the Immigration Acts, or
(b)   required to leave the United Kingdom in accordance with a provision of the Immigration Acts.

(2)   In this section 'pending' has the meaning given by section 104.
(3)   Nothing in this section shall prevent any of the following while an appeal is pending –

(a)   the giving of a direction for the appellant's removal from the United Kingdom,
(b)   the making of a deportation order in respect of the appellant (subject to section 79), or
(c)   the taking of any other interim or preparatory action.

(4)   This section applies only to an appeal brought while the appellant is in the United Kingdom in accordance with section 92.

78A   Restriction on removal of children and their parents etc

(1)   This section applies in a case where –

(a)   a child is to be removed from or required to leave the United Kingdom, and
(b)   an individual who –

(i)   is a parent of the child or has care of the child, and

(ii)   is living in a household in the United Kingdom with the child,

is also to be removed from or required to leave the United Kingdom (a 'relevant parent or carer').

(2)   During the period of 28 days beginning with the day on which the relevant appeal rights are exhausted –

(a)   the child may not be removed from or required to leave the United Kingdom; and

(b)   a relevant parent or carer may not be removed from or required to leave the United Kingdom if, as a result, no relevant parent or carer would remain in the United Kingdom.

(3)   The relevant appeal rights are exhausted at the time when –

(a)   neither the child, nor any relevant parent or carer, could bring an appeal under section 82 (ignoring any possibility of an appeal out of time with permission), and

(b)   no appeal brought by the child, or by any relevant parent or carer, is pending within the meaning of section 104.

(4)   Nothing in this section prevents any of the following during the period of 28 days mentioned in subsection (2) –

(a)   the giving of a direction for the removal of a person from the United Kingdom,

(b)   the making of a deportation order in respect of a person, or

(c)   the taking of any other interim or preparatory action.

(5)   In this section –

'child' means a person who is aged under 18;

references to a person being removed from or required to leave the United Kingdom are to the person being removed or required to leave in accordance with a provision of the Immigration Acts

PART 5

Appeals in respect of protection and human rights claims

82   Right of appeal to the Tribunal

(1)   A person ('P') may appeal to the Tribunal where –

(a)   the Secretary of State has decided to refuse a protection claim made by P,

(b)   the Secretary of State has decided to refuse a human rights claim made by P, or

(c)   the Secretary of State has decided to revoke P's protection status.

(2)   For the purposes of this Part –

(a)   a 'protection claim' is a claim made by a person ('P') that removal of P from the United Kingdom –

(i)   would breach the United Kingdom's obligations under the Refugee Convention, or

(ii)   would breach the United Kingdom's obligations in relation to persons eligible for a grant of humanitarian protection;

(b)   P's protection claim is refused if the Secretary of State makes one or more of the following decisions –

(i)   that removal of P from the United Kingdom would not breach the United Kingdom's obligations under the Refugee Convention;

(ii)   that removal of P from the United Kingdom would not breach the United Kingdom's obligations in relation to persons eligible for a grant of humanitarian protection;

(c)   a person has 'protection status' if the person has been granted leave to enter or remain in the United Kingdom as a refugee or as a person eligible for a grant of humanitarian protection;

(d)   'humanitarian protection' is to be construed in accordance with the immigration rules;

(e)   'refugee' has the same meaning as in the Refugee Convention.

(3)   The right of appeal under subsection (1) is subject to the exceptions and limitations specified in this Part.

83   [Repealed]

[Repealed]

83A   [Repealed]

[Repealed]

84   Grounds of Appeal

(1)   An appeal under section 82(1)(a) (refusal of protection claim) must be brought on one or more of the following grounds –

(a)   that removal of the appellant from the United Kingdom would breach the United Kingdom's obligations under the Refugee Convention;

(b)   that removal of the appellant from the United Kingdom would breach the United Kingdom's obligations in relation to persons eligible for a grant of humanitarian protection;

(c)   that removal of the appellant from the United Kingdom would be unlawful under section 6 of the Human Rights Act 1998 (public authority not to act contrary to Human Rights Convention).

(2)   An appeal under section 82(1)(b) (refusal of human rights claim) must be brought on the ground that the decision is unlawful under section 6 of the Human Rights Act 1998.

(3)   An appeal under section 82(1)(c) (revocation of protection status) must be brought on one or more of the following grounds –

(a)   that the decision to revoke the appellant's protection status breaches the United Kingdom's obligations under the Refugee Convention;

(b)   that the decision to revoke the appellant's protection status breaches the United Kingdom's obligations in relation to persons eligible for a grant of humanitarian protection.

85 Matters to be considered

(1) An appeal under section 82(1) against a decision shall be treated by the Tribunal as including an appeal against any decision in respect of which the appellant has a right of appeal under section 82(1).

(2) If an appellant under section 82(1) makes a statement under section 120, the Tribunal shall consider any matter raised in the statement which constitutes a ground of appeal of a kind listed in section 84 against the decision appealed against.

(3) Subsection (2) applies to a statement made under section 120 whether the statement was made before or after the appeal was commenced.

(4) On an appeal under section 82(1) against a decision the Tribunal may consider any matter which it thinks relevant to the substance of the decision, including a matter arising after the date of the decision.

(5) But the Tribunal must not consider a new matter unless the Secretary of State has given the Tribunal consent to do so.

(6) A matter is a 'new matter' if –

  (a) it constitutes a ground of appeal of a kind listed in section 84, and
  (b) the Secretary of State has not previously considered the matter in the context of –

    (i) the decision mentioned in section 82(1), or
    (ii) a statement made by the appellant under section 120.

86 Determination of appeal

(1) This section applies on an appeal under section 82(1).
(2) The Tribunal must determine –

  (a) any matter raised as a ground of appeal, and
  (b) any matter which section 85 requires it to consider.

92 Place from which an appeal may be brought or continued

(1) This section applies to determine the place from which an appeal under section 82(1) may be brought or continued.

(2) In the case of an appeal under section 82(1)(a) (protection claim appeal), the appeal must be brought from outside the United Kingdom if –

  (a) the claim to which the appeal relates has been certified under section 94(1) or (7) (claim clearly unfounded or removal to safe third country), or
  (b) paragraph 5(3)(a), 10(3), 15(3) or 19(b) of Schedule 3 to the Asylum and Immigration (Treatment of Claimants, etc) Act 2004 (removal of asylum seeker to safe third country) applies.

Otherwise, the appeal must be brought from within the United Kingdom.

(3) In the case of an appeal under section 82(1)(b) (human rights claim appeal) where the claim to which the appeal relates was made while the appellant was in the United Kingdom, the appeal must be brought from outside the United Kingdom if –

  (a) the claim to which the appeal relates has been certified under section 94(1) or (7) (claim clearly unfounded or removal to safe third country) or section 94B (certification of human rights claims made by persons liable to deportation), or
  (b) paragraph 5(3)(b) or (4), 10(4), 15(4) or 19(c) of Schedule 3 to the Asylum and Immigration (Treatment of Claimants, etc) Act 2004 (removal of asylum seeker to safe third country) applies.

Otherwise, the appeal must be brought from within the United Kingdom.

(4) In the case of an appeal under section 82(1)(b) (human rights claim appeal) where the claim to which the appeal relates was made while the appellant was outside the United Kingdom, the appeal must be brought from outside the United Kingdom.

(5) In the case of an appeal under section 82(1)(c) (revocation of protection status) –

(a) the appeal must be brought from within the United Kingdom if the decision to which the appeal relates was made while the appellant was in the United Kingdom;

(b) the appeal must be brought from outside the United Kingdom if the decision to which the appeal relates was made while the appellant was outside the United Kingdom.

(6) If, after an appeal under section 82(1)(a) or (b) has been brought from within the United Kingdom, the Secretary of State certifies the claim to which the appeal relates under section 94(1) or (7) or section 94B, the appeal must be continued from outside the United Kingdom.

(7) Where a person brings or continues an appeal under section 82(1)(a) (refusal of protection claim) from outside the United Kingdom, for the purposes of considering whether the grounds of appeal are satisfied, the appeal is to be treated as if the person were not outside the United Kingdom.

(8) Where an appellant brings an appeal from within the United Kingdom but leaves the United Kingdom before the appeal is finally determined, the appeal is to be treated as abandoned unless the claim to which the appeal relates has been certified under section 94(1) or (7) or section 94B.

94 Appeal from within United Kingdom: unfounded human rights or protection claim

(1) The Secretary of State may certify a protection claim or human rights claim as clearly unfounded.

(2) [*Repealed*]

(3) If the Secretary of State is satisfied that a claimant is entitled to reside in a State listed in subsection (4) he shall certify the claim under subsection (1) unless satisfied that it is not clearly unfounded.

(4) Those States are –

...

(k) the Republic of Albania,

...

(n) Jamaica,

(o) Macedonia,

(p) the Republic of Moldova,

...

(s) Bolivia,

(t) Brazil,

(u) Ecuador,

(v) ...

(w) South Africa, and

(x) Ukraine,

(y) India,

(z) Mongolia,

(aa) Ghana (in respect of men),

(bb) Nigeria (in respect of men),

(cc) Bosnia-Herzegovina,
(dd) Gambia (in respect of men),
(ee) Kenya (in respect of men),
(ff) Liberia (in respect of men),
(gg) Malawi (in respect of men),
(hh) Mali (in respect of men),
(ii) Mauritius,
(jj) Montenegro,
(kk) Peru,
(ll) Serbia,
(mm) Sierra Leone (in respect of men),
(nn) Kosovo,
(oo) South Korea.

(5) The Secretary of State may by order add a State, or part of a State, to the list in subsection (4) if satisfied that –

(a) there is in general in that State or part no serious risk of persecution of persons entitled to reside in that State or part, and
(b) removal to that State or part of persons entitled to reside there will not in general contravene the United Kingdom's obligations under the Human Rights Convention.

(5A) If the Secretary of State is satisfied that the statements in subsection (5) (a) and (b) are true of a State or part of a State in relation to a description of person, an order under subsection (5) may add the State or part to the list in subsection (4) in respect of that description of person.

...

(5D) In deciding whether the statements in subsection (5) (a) and (b) are true of a State or part of a State, the Secretary of State –

(a) shall have regard to all the circumstances of the State or part (including its laws and how they are applied), and
(b) shall have regard to information from any appropriate source (including other member States and international organisations).

...

(7) The Secretary of State may certify a protection claim or human rights claim made by a person if –

(a) it is proposed to remove the person to a country of which he is not a national or citizen, and
(b) there is no reason to believe that the person's rights under the Human Rights Convention will be breached in that country.

(8) In determining whether a person in relation to whom a certificate has been issued under subsection (7) may be removed from the United Kingdom, the country specified in the certificate is to be regarded as –

(a) a place where a person's life and liberty is not threatened by reason of his race, religion, nationality, membership of a particular social group, or political opinion, and
(b) a place from which a person will not be sent to another country otherwise than in accordance with the Refugee Convention or with the United Kingdom's obligations in relation to persons eligible for a grant of humanitarian protection.

94A   European Common List of Safe Countries of Origin

(1)   The Secretary of State shall by order prescribe a list of States to be known as the 'European Common List of Safe Countries of Origin'.

(2)   Subsections (3) and (4) apply where a person makes a protection claim or a human rights claim (or both) and that person is –

    (a)   a national of a State which is listed in the European Common List of Safe Countries of Origin, or

    (b)   a Stateless person who was formerly habitually resident in such a State.

(3)   The Secretary of State shall consider the claim or claims mentioned in subsection (2) to be unfounded unless satisfied that there are serious grounds for considering that the State in question is not safe in the particular circumstances of the person mentioned in that subsection.

(4)   The Secretary of State shall also certify the claim or claims mentioned in subsection (2) under section 94(1) unless satisfied that the claim or claims is or are not clearly unfounded.

(5)   An order under subsection (1) –

    (a)   may be made only if the Secretary of State thinks it necessary for the purpose of complying with the United Kingdom's obligations under EU law,

    (b)   may include transitional, consequential or incidental provision,

    (c)   shall be made by statutory instrument, and

    (d)   shall be subject to annulment in pursuance of a resolution of either House of Parliament.

94B   Appeal from within the United Kingdom: certification of human rights claims made by persons liable to deportation

(1)   This section applies where a human rights claim has been made by a person ('P') who is liable to deportation under –

    (a)   section 3(5)(a) of the Immigration Act 1971 (Secretary of State deeming deportation conducive to public good), or

    (b)   section 3(6) of that Act (court recommending deportation following conviction).

(2)   The Secretary of State may certify the claim if the Secretary of State considers that, despite the appeals process not having been begun or not having been exhausted, removal of P to the country or territory to which P is proposed to be removed, pending the outcome of an appeal in relation to P's claim, would not be unlawful under section 6 of the Human Rights Act 1998 (public authority not to act contrary to Human Rights Convention).

(3)   The grounds upon which the Secretary of State may certify a claim under subsection (2) include (in particular) that P would not, before the appeals process is exhausted, face a real risk of serious irreversible harm if removed to the country or territory to which P is proposed to be removed.

96   Earlier right of appeal

(1)   A person may not bring an appeal under section 82 against a decision ('the new decision') if the Secretary of State or an immigration officer certifies –

    (a)   that the person was notified of a right of appeal under that section against another decision ('the old decision') (whether or not an appeal was brought and whether or not any appeal brought has been determined),

(b)   that the claim or application to which the new decision relates relies on a ground that could have been raised in an appeal against the old decision, and

(c)   that, in the opinion of the Secretary of State or the immigration officer, there is no satisfactory reason for that ground not having been raised in an appeal against the old decision.

(2)   A person may not bring an appeal under section 82 if the Secretary of State or an immigration officer certifies –

(a)   that the person has received a notice under section 120(2),

(b)   that the appeal relies on a ground that should have been, but has not been, raised in a statement made under section 120(2) or (5), and

(c)   that, in the opinion of the Secretary of State or the immigration officer, there is no satisfactory reason for that ground not having been raised in a statement under section 120(2) or (5).

(3)   [*Repealed*]

(4)   In subsection (1) 'notified' means notified in accordance with regulations under section 105.

(5)   Subsections (1) and (2) apply to prevent a person's right of appeal whether or not he has been outside the United Kingdom since an earlier right of appeal arose or since a requirement under section 120 was imposed.

(6)   In this section a reference to an appeal under section 82(1) includes a reference to an appeal under section 2 of the Special Immigration Appeals Commission Act 1997 (c 68) which is or could be brought by reference to an appeal under section 82(1).

(7)   A certificate under subsection (1) or (2) shall have no effect in relation to an appeal instituted before the certificate is issued.

97   National security, &c

(1)   An appeal under section 82(1) against a decision in respect of a person may not be brought or continued if the Secretary of State certifies that the decision is or was taken –

(a)   by the Secretary of State wholly or partly on a ground listed in subsection (2), or

(b)   in accordance with a direction of the Secretary of State which identifies the person to whom the decision relates and which is given wholly or partly on a ground listed in subsection (2).

(2)   The grounds mentioned in subsection (1) are that the person's exclusion or removal from the United Kingdom is –

(a)   in the interests of national security, or

(b)   in the interests of the relationship between the United Kingdom and another country.

(3)   An appeal under section 82(1) against a decision may not be brought or continued if the Secretary of State certifies that the decision is or was taken wholly or partly in reliance on information which in his opinion should not be made public –

(a)   in the interests of national security,

(b)   in the interests of the relationship between the United Kingdom and another country, or

(c)   otherwise in the public interest.

(4)   In subsections (1)(a) and (b) and (3) a reference to the Secretary of State is to the Secretary of State acting in person.

104   Pending appeal

(1)   An appeal under section 82(1) is pending during the period –

    (a)   beginning when it is instituted, and

    (b)   ending when it is finally determined, withdrawn or abandoned (or when it lapses under section 99).

(2)   An appeal under section 82(1) is not finally determined for the purpose of subsection (1)(b) while –

    (a)   an application for permission to appeal under section 11 or 13 of the Tribunals, Courts and Enforcement Act 2007 could be made or is awaiting determination,

    (b)   permission to appeal under either of those sections has been granted and the appeal is awaiting determination, or

    (c)   an appeal has been remitted under section 12 or 14 of that Act and is awaiting determination.; and

(3)   [Repealed]

(4)   [Repealed]

(4A)   An appeal under section 82(1) brought by a person while he is in the United Kingdom shall be treated as abandoned if the appellant is granted leave to enter or remain in the United Kingdom (subject to subsection (4B).

(4B)   Subsection (4A) shall not apply to an appeal in so far as it is brought on a ground specified in section 84(1)(a) or (b) or 84(3) (asylum or humanitarian protection) where the appellant –

    (a)   [Repealed]

    (b)   gives notice, in accordance with Tribunal Procedure Rules, that he wishes to pursue the appeal in so far as it is brought on that ground.

(4C)   [Repealed]

(5)   [Repealed]

113   Interpretation

(1)   In this Part, unless a contrary intention appears –

'asylum claim' means a claim made by a person to the Secretary of State at a place designated by the Secretary of State that to remove the person from or require him to leave the United Kingdom would breach the United Kingdom's obligations under the Refugee Convention,

'humanitarian protection' has the meaning given in section 82 (2);

'human rights claim' means a claim made by a person to the Secretary of State at a place designated by the Secretary of State that to remove the person from or require him to leave the United Kingdom or to refuse him entry into the United Kingdom would be unlawful under section 6 of the Human Rights Act 1998 (c 42) (public authority not to act contrary to Convention).

'the Human Rights Convention' has the same meaning as 'the Convention' in the Human Rights Act 1998 and 'Convention rights' shall be construed in accordance with section 1 of that Act,

'immigration rules' means rules under section 1(4) of the Immigration Act 1971 (general immigration rules), 'protection claim' has the meaning given in section 82 (2);

'protection status' has the meaning given in section 82 (2);

'the Refugee Convention' means the Convention relating to the Status of Refugees done at Geneva on 28th July 1951 and its Protocol,

PART 5A

Article 8 of the ECHR: public interest considerations

117A Application of this Part

(1)   This Part applies where a court or tribunal is required to determine whether a decision made under the Immigration Acts –

    (a)   breaches a person's right to respect for private and family life under Article 8, and

    (b)   as a result would be unlawful under section 6 of the Human Rights Act 1998.

(2)   In considering the public interest question, the court or tribunal must (in particular) have regard –

    (a)   in all cases, to the considerations listed in section 117B, and

    (b)   in cases concerning the deportation of foreign criminals, to the considerations listed in section 117C.

(3)   In subsection (2), 'the public interest question' means the question of whether an interference with a person's right to respect for private and family life is justified under Article 8(2).

117B Article 8: public interest considerations applicable in all cases

(1)   The maintenance of effective immigration controls is in the public interest.

(2)   It is in the public interest, and in particular in the interests of the economic well-being of the United Kingdom, that persons who seek to enter or remain in the United Kingdom are able to speak English, because persons who can speak English –

    (a)   are less of a burden on taxpayers, and

    (b)   are better able to integrate into society.

(3)   It is in the public interest, and in particular in the interests of the economic well-being of the United Kingdom, that persons who seek to enter or remain in the United Kingdom are financially independent, because such persons –

    (a)   are not a burden on taxpayers, and

    (b)   are better able to integrate into society.

(4)   Little weight should be given to –

    (a)   a private life, or

    (b)   a relationship formed with a qualifying partner,

that is established by a person at a time when the person is in the United Kingdom unlawfully.

(5)   Little weight should be given to a private life established by a person at a time when the person's immigration status is precarious.

(6)   In the case of a person who is not liable to deportation, the public interest does not require the person's removal where –

    (a)   the person has a genuine and subsisting parental relationship with a qualifying child, and

    (b)   it would not be reasonable to expect the child to leave the United Kingdom.

117C   Article 8: additional considerations in cases involving foreign criminals

(1)   The deportation of foreign criminals is in the public interest.

(2)   The more serious the offence committed by a foreign criminal, the greater is the public interest in deportation of the criminal.

(3)   In the case of a foreign criminal ('C') who has not been sentenced to a period of imprisonment of four years or more, the public interest requires C's deportation unless Exception 1 or Exception 2 applies.

(4)   Exception 1 applies where –

    (a)   C has been lawfully resident in the United Kingdom for most of C's life,

    (b)   C is socially and culturally integrated in the United Kingdom, and

    (c)   there would be very significant obstacles to C's integration into the country to which C is proposed to be deported.

(5)   Exception 2 applies where C has a genuine and subsisting relationship with a qualifying partner, or a genuine and subsisting parental relationship with a qualifying child, and the effect of C's deportation on the partner or child would be unduly harsh.

(6)   In the case of a foreign criminal who has been sentenced to a period of imprisonment of at least four years, the public interest requires deportation unless there are very compelling circumstances, over and above those described in Exceptions 1 and 2.

(7)   The considerations in subsections (1) to (6) are to be taken into account where a court or tribunal is considering a decision to deport a foreign criminal only to the extent that the reason for the decision was the offence or offences for which the criminal has been convicted.

117D   Interpretation of this Part

(1)   In this Part –

'Article 8' means Article 8 of the European Convention on Human Rights;
'qualifying child' means a person who is under the age of 18 and who –

    (a)   is a British citizen, or

    (b)   has lived in the United Kingdom for a continuous period of seven years or more;

'qualifying partner' means a partner who –

    (a)   is a British citizen, or

    (b)   who is settled in the United Kingdom (within the meaning of the Immigration Act 1971 – see section 33(2A) of that Act).

(2)   In this Part, 'foreign criminal' means a person –

    (a)   who is not a British citizen,

    (b)   who has been convicted in the United Kingdom of an offence, and

    (c)   who –

        (i)   has been sentenced to a period of imprisonment of at least 12 months,

253

     (ii)   has been convicted of an offence that has caused serious harm, or

     (iii)   is a persistent offender.

(3)   For the purposes of subsection (2)(b), a person subject to an order under –

     (a)   section 5 of the Criminal Procedure (Insanity) Act 1964 (insanity etc),

     (b)   section 57 of the Criminal Procedure (Scotland) Act 1995 (insanity etc), or

     (c)   Article 50A of the Mental Health (Northern Ireland) Order 1986 (insanity etc),

has not been convicted of an offence.

(4)   In this Part, references to a person who has been sentenced to a period of imprisonment of a certain length of time –

     (a)   do not include a person who has received a suspended sentence (unless a court subsequently orders that the sentence or any part of it (of whatever length) is to take effect);

     (b)   do not include a person who has been sentenced to a period of imprisonment of that length of time only by virtue of being sentenced to consecutive sentences amounting in aggregate to that length of time;

     (c)   include a person who is sentenced to detention, or ordered or directed to be detained, in an institution other than a prison (including, in particular, a hospital or an institution for young offenders) for that length of time; and

     (d)   include a person who is sentenced to imprisonment or detention, or ordered or directed to be detained, for an indeterminate period, provided that it may last for at least that length of time.

(5)   If any question arises for the purposes of this Part as to whether a person is a British citizen, it is for the person asserting that fact to prove it.

…

120   Requirement to state additional grounds for application etc

(1)   Subsection (2) applies to a person ('P') if –

     (a)   P has made a protection claim or a human rights claim,

     (b)   P has made an application to enter or remain in the United Kingdom, or

     (c)   a decision to deport or remove P has been or may be taken.

(2)   The Secretary of State or an immigration officer may serve a notice on P requiring P to provide a statement setting out –

     (a)   P's reasons for wishing to enter or remain in the United Kingdom,

     (b)   any grounds on which P should be permitted to enter or remain in the United Kingdom, and

     (c)   any grounds on which P should not be removed from or required to leave the United Kingdom.

(3)   A statement under subsection (2) need not repeat reasons or grounds set out in –

     (a)   P's protection or human rights claim,

     (b)   the application mentioned in subsection (1)(b), or

     (c)   an application to which the decision mentioned in subsection (1)(c) relates.

(4)   Subsection (5) applies to a person ('P') if P has previously been served with a notice under subsection (2) and –

     (a)   P requires leave to enter or remain in the United Kingdom but does not have it, or

(b)   P has leave to enter or remain in the United Kingdom only by virtue of section 3C or 3D of the Immigration Act 1971 (continuation of leave pending decision or appeal).

(5)   Where P's circumstances have changed since the Secretary of State or an immigration officer was last made aware of them (whether in the application or claim mentioned in subsection (1) or in a statement under subsection (2) or this subsection) so that P has –

(a)   additional reasons for wishing to enter or remain in the United Kingdom,

(b)   additional grounds on which P should be permitted to enter or remain in the United Kingdom, or

(c)   additional grounds on which P should not be removed from or required to leave the United Kingdom, P must, as soon as reasonably practicable, provide a supplementary statement to the Secretary of State or an immigration officer setting out the new circumstances and the additional reasons or grounds.

(6)   In this section –

'human rights claim' and 'protection claim' have the same meanings as in Part 5;

references to 'grounds' are to grounds on which an appeal under Part 5 may be brought (see section 84).

Asylum and Immigration (Treatment of Claimants, etc.) Act 2004 (extracts)

Offences

1   Assisting unlawful immigration

(1)   At the end of section 25 of the Immigration Act 1971 (c 77) (offence of assisting unlawful immigration to member State) add –

    '(7) In this section –

        (a)   a reference to a member State includes a reference to a State on a list prescribed for the purposes of this section by order of the Secretary of State (to be known as the 'Section 25 List of Schengen Acquis States'), and

        (b)   a reference to a citizen of the European Union includes a reference to a person who is a national of a State on that list.

    (8) An order under subsection (7)(a) –

        (a)   may be made only if the Secretary of State thinks it necessary for the purpose of complying with the United Kingdom's obligations under the Community Treaties,

        (b)   may include transitional, consequential or incidental provision,

        (c)   shall be made by statutory instrument, and

        (d)   shall be subject to annulment in pursuance of a resolution of either House of Parliament.'

(2)   In section 25C(9)(a) of that Act (forfeiture of vehicle, ship or aircraft) for '(within the meaning of section 25)' substitute '(for which purpose 'member State' and 'immigration law' have the meanings given by section 25(2) and (7))'.

2   Entering United Kingdom without passport, &c

(1)   A person commits an offence if at a leave or asylum interview he does not have with him an immigration document which –

        (a)   is in force, and

        (b)   satisfactorily establishes his identity and nationality or citizenship.

(2)   A person commits an offence if at a leave or asylum interview he does not have with him, in respect of any dependent child with whom he claims to be travelling or living, an immigration document which –

        (a)   is in force, and

        (b)   satisfactorily establishes the child's identity and nationality or citizenship.

(3)   But a person does not commit an offence under subsection (1) or (2) if –

    (a)   the interview referred to in that subsection takes place after the person has entered the United Kingdom, and

    (b)   within the period of three days beginning with the date of the interview the person provides to an immigration officer or to the Secretary of State a document of the kind referred to in that subsection.

(4)   It is a defence for a person charged with an offence under subsection (1) –

    (a)   to prove that he is an EEA national,

    (b)   to prove that he is a member of the family of an EEA national and that he is exercising a right under the EU Treaties in respect of entry to or residence in the United Kingdom,

    (c)   to prove that he has a reasonable excuse for not being in possession of a document of the kind specified in subsection (1),

    (d)   to produce a false immigration document and to prove that he used that document as an immigration document for all purposes in connection with his journey to the United Kingdom, or

    (e)   to prove that he travelled to the United Kingdom without, at any stage since he set out on the journey, having possession of an immigration document.

(5)   It is a defence for a person charged with an offence under subsection (2) in respect of a child –

    (a)   to prove that the child is an EEA national,

    (b)   to prove that the child is a member of the family of an EEA national and that the child is exercising a right under the EU Treaties in respect of entry to or residence in the United Kingdom,

    (c)   to prove that the person has a reasonable excuse for not being in possession of a document of the kind specified in subsection (2),

    (d)   to produce a false immigration document and to prove that it was used as an immigration document for all purposes in connection with the child's journey to the United Kingdom, or

    (e)   to prove that he travelled to the United Kingdom with the child without, at any stage since he set out on the journey, having possession of an immigration document in respect of the child.

(6)   Where the charge for an offence under subsection (1) or (2) relates to an interview which takes place after the defendant has entered the United Kingdom –

    (a)   subsections (4)(c) and (5)(c) shall not apply, but

    (b)   it is a defence for the defendant to prove that he has a reasonable excuse for not providing a document in accordance with subsection (3).

(7)   For the purposes of subsections (4) to (6) –

    (a)   the fact that a document was deliberately destroyed or disposed of is not a reasonable excuse for not being in possession of it or for not providing it in accordance with subsection (3), unless it is shown that the destruction or disposal was –

        (i)   for a reasonable cause, or

        (ii)   beyond the control of the person charged with the offence, and

    (b)   in paragraph (a)(i) 'reasonable cause' does not include the purpose of –

        (i)   delaying the handling or resolution of a claim or application or the taking of a decision,

        (ii)   increasing the chances of success of a claim or application, or

        (iii)   complying with instructions or advice given by a person who offers advice about, or facilitates, immigration into the United Kingdom, unless in the circumstances of the case it is unreasonable to expect non-compliance with the instructions or advice.

(8)   A person shall be presumed for the purposes of this section not to have a document with him if he fails to produce it to an immigration officer or official of the Secretary of State on request.

(9)   A person guilty of an offence under this section shall be liable –

    (a)   on conviction on indictment, to imprisonment for a term not exceeding two years, to a fine or to both, or

    (b)   on summary conviction, to imprisonment for a term not exceeding twelve months, to a fine not exceeding the statutory maximum or to both.

(10)   If an immigration officer reasonably suspects that a person has committed an offence under this section he may arrest the person without warrant.

(11)   An offence under this section shall be treated as –

    (a)   a relevant offence for the purposes of sections 28B and 28D of the Immigration Act 1971 (c 77) (search, entry and arrest), and

    (b)   an offence under Part III of that Act (criminal proceedings) for the purposes of sections 28(4), 28E, 28G and 28H (search after arrest, &c) of that Act.

(12)   In this section –

'EEA national' means a national of a State which is a contracting party to the Agreement on the European Economic Area signed at Oporto on 2nd May 1992 (as it has effect from time to time),

'immigration document' means –

    (a)   a passport, and

    (b)   a document which relates to a national of a State other than the United Kingdom and which is designed to serve the same purpose as a passport, and

'leave or asylum interview' means an interview with an immigration officer or an official of the Secretary of State at which a person –

    (a)   seeks leave to enter or remain in the United Kingdom, or

    (b)   claims that to remove him from or require him to leave the United Kingdom would breach the United Kingdom's obligations under the Refugee Convention or would be unlawful under section 6 of the Human Rights Act 1998 (c 42) as being incompatible with his Convention rights.

(13)   For the purposes of this section –

    (a)   a document which purports to be, or is designed to look like, an immigration document, is a false immigration document, and

    (b)   an immigration document is a false immigration document if and in so far as it is used –

        (i)   outside the period for which it is expressed to be valid,

        (ii)   contrary to provision for its use made by the person issuing it, or

        (iii) by or in respect of a person other than the person to or for whom it was issued.

(14)   Section 11 of the Immigration Act 1971 (c 77) shall have effect for the purpose of the construction of a reference in this section to entering the United Kingdom.

(15)   In so far as this section extends to England and Wales, subsection (9)(b) shall, until the commencement of section 154 of the Criminal Justice Act 2003 (c 44) (increased limit on magistrates' power of imprisonment), have effect as if the reference to twelve months were a reference to six months.

(16)   In so far as this section extends to Scotland, subsection (9)(b) shall have effect as if the reference to twelve months were a reference to six months.

(17)   In so far as this section extends to Northern Ireland, subsection (9)(b) shall have effect as if the reference to twelve months were a reference to six months.

4 Trafficking people for exploitation [*repealed except in Scotland*]

(1)   A person commits an offence if he arranges or facilitates the arrival in, or the entry into, the United Kingdom of an individual (the 'passenger') and –

(a)   he intends to exploit the passenger in the United Kingdom or elsewhere, or

(b)   he believes that another person is likely to exploit the passenger in the United Kingdom or elsewhere.

(2)   A person commits an offence if he arranges or facilitates travel within the United Kingdom by an individual (the 'passenger') in respect of whom he believes that an offence under subsection (1) may have been committed and –

(a)   he intends to exploit the passenger in the United Kingdom or elsewhere, or

(b)   he believes that another person is likely to exploit the passenger in the United Kingdom or elsewhere.

(3)   A person commits an offence if he arranges or facilitates the departure from the United Kingdom of an individual (the 'passenger') and –

(a)   he intends to exploit the passenger outside the United Kingdom, or

(b)   he believes that another person is likely to exploit the passenger outside the United Kingdom.

(3A)   A person to whom section 5(2) applies commits an offence if –

(a)   in relation to an individual (the 'passenger'), he arranges or facilitates –

    (i)   the arrival in or the entry into a country other than the United Kingdom of the passenger,

    (ii)   travel by the passenger within a country other than the United Kingdom,

    (iii)   the departure of the passenger from a country other than the United Kingdom, and

(b)   he –

    (i)   intends to exploit the passenger, or

    (ii)   believes that another person is likely to exploit the passenger,

(wherever the exploitation is to occur).

(4)   For the purposes of this section a person is exploited if (and only if) –

(a)   he is the victim of behaviour that contravenes Article 4 of the Human Rights Convention (slavery and forced labour),

(b)   he is encouraged, required or expected to do anything

    (i)   as a result of which he or another person would commit an offence under Part 1 of the Human Tissue (Scotland) Act 2006 (asp 4) or under section 32 or 33 of the Human Tissue Act 2004, or

       (ii)   which, were it done in England and Wales, would constitute an offence within sub-paragraph (i),

  (ba) he is encouraged, required or expected to do anything in connection with the removal of any part of a human body –

       (i)   as a result of which he or another person would commit an offence under the law of Scotland (other than an offence mentioned in paragraph (b)(i)), or

       (ii)   which, were it done in Scotland, would constitute such an offence,

  (c) he is subjected to force, threats or deception designed to induce him –

       (i)   to provide services of any kind,

       (ii)   to provide another person with benefits of any kind, or

       (iii)   to enable another person to acquire benefits of any kind, or

  (d) a person uses or attempts to use him for any purpose within sub-paragraph (i), (ii) or (iii) of paragraph (c), having chosen him for that purpose on the grounds that –

       (i)   he is mentally or physically ill or disabled, he is young or he has a family relationship with a person, and

       (ii)   a person without the illness, disability, youth or family relationship would be likely to refuse to be used for that purpose.

(4A)   A person who is a UK national commits an offence under this section regardless of –

  (a) where the arranging or facilitating takes place, or

  (b) which country is the country of arrival, entry, travel or (as the case may be) departure.

(4B)   A person who is not a UK national commits an offence under this section if –

  (a) any part of the arranging or facilitating takes place in the United Kingdom, or

  (b) the United Kingdom is the country of arrival, entry, travel or (as the case may be) departure.

(5)   A person guilty of an offence under this section shall be liable –

  (a) on conviction on indictment, to imprisonment for a term not exceeding 14 years, to a fine or to both, or

  (b) on summary conviction, to imprisonment for a term not exceeding twelve months, to a fine not exceeding the statutory maximum or to both.

Treatment of claimants

8 Claimant's credibility

(1)   In determining whether to believe a statement made by or on behalf of a person who makes an asylum claim or a human rights claim, a deciding authority shall take account, as damaging the claimant's credibility, of any behaviour to which this section applies.

(2)   This section applies to any behaviour by the claimant that the deciding authority thinks –

  (a) is designed or likely to conceal information,

  (b) is designed or likely to mislead, or

(c)   is designed or likely to obstruct or delay the handling or resolution of the claim or the taking of a decision in relation to the claimant.

(3)   Without prejudice to the generality of subsection (2) the following kinds of behaviour shall be treated as designed or likely to conceal information or to mislead –

(a)   failure without reasonable explanation to produce a passport on request to an immigration officer or to the Secretary of State,

(b)   the production of a document which is not a valid passport as if it were,

(c)   the destruction, alteration or disposal, in each case without reasonable explanation, of a passport,

(d)   the destruction, alteration or disposal, in each case without reasonable explanation, of a ticket or other document connected with travel, and

(e)   failure without reasonable explanation to answer a question asked by a deciding authority.

(4)   This section also applies to failure by the claimant to take advantage of a reasonable opportunity to make an asylum claim or human rights claim while in a safe country.

(5)   This section also applies to failure by the claimant to make an asylum claim or human rights claim before being notified of an immigration decision, unless the claim relies wholly on matters arising after the notification.

(6)   This section also applies to failure by the claimant to make an asylum claim or human rights claim before being arrested under an immigration provision, unless –

(a)   he had no reasonable opportunity to make the claim before the arrest, or

(b)   the claim relies wholly on matters arising after the arrest.

(7)   In this section –

'asylum claim' has the meaning given by section 113(1) of the Nationality, Immigration and Asylum Act 2002 (c 41) (subject to subsection (9) below),
'deciding authority' means –

(a)   an immigration officer,

(b)   the Secretary of State,

(c)   the First-tier Tribunal, or

(d)   the Special Immigration Appeals Commission,

'human rights claim' has the meaning given by section 113(1) of the Nationality, Immigration and Asylum Act 2002 (subject to subsection (9) below),
'immigration decision' means –

(a)   refusal of leave to enter the United Kingdom,

(b)   refusal to vary a person's leave to enter or remain in the United Kingdom,

(c)   grant of leave to enter or remain in the United Kingdom,

(d)   a decision that a person is to be removed from the United Kingdom by way of directions under section 10 of the Immigration and Asylum Act 1999 (c 33)(removal of persons unlawfully in United Kingdom),

(e)   a decision that a person is to be removed from the United Kingdom by way of directions under paragraphs 8 to 12 of Schedule 2 to the Immigration Act 1971 (c 77) (control of entry: removal),

(f)   a decision to make a deportation order under section 5(1) of that Act, and

(g)   a decision to take action in relation to a person in connection with extradition from the United Kingdom,

'immigration provision' means –

(a)   sections 28A, 28AA, 28B, 28C and 28CA of the Immigration Act 1971 (immigration offences: enforcement),

(b)   paragraph 17 of Schedule 2 to that Act (control of entry),

(c)   section 14 of this Act, and

(d)   a provision of the Extradition Act 1989 (c 33) or 2003 (c 41),

'notified' means notified in such manner as may be specified by regulations made by the Secretary of State,

'passport' includes a document which relates to a national of a country other than the United Kingdom and which is designed to serve the same purpose as a passport, and

'safe country' means a country to which Part 2 of Schedule 3 applies.

(8)   A passport produced by or on behalf of a person is valid for the purposes of subsection (3)(b) if it –

(a)   relates to the person by whom or on whose behalf it is produced,

(b)   has not been altered otherwise than by or with the permission of the authority who issued it, and

(c)   was not obtained by deception.

...

SCHEDULE 3

Part 2   First List of Safe Countries (Refugee Convention and Human Rights (1)
2.   This Part applies to –

(a)   Austria,

(b)   Belgium,

(ba)   Bulgaria,

(c)   Republic of Cyprus,

(d)   Czech Republic,

(e)   Denmark,

(f)   Estonia,

(g)   Finland,

(h)   France,

(i)   Germany,

(j)   Greece,

(k)   Hungary,

(l)   Iceland,

(m)   Ireland,

(n)   Italy,

(o)   Latvia,

(p)   Lithuania,

(q)   Luxembourg,

(r)   Malta,

(s)   Netherlands,

(t)   Norway,

(u)   Poland,

(v)   Portugal,

(va)   Romania,

(w)   Slovak Republic,

(x)   Slovenia,

    (y)   Spain,

    (z)   Sweden,

    (z1) Switzerland.

3.   (1)   This paragraph applies for the purposes of the determination by any person, tribunal or court whether a person who has made an asylum claim or a human rights claim may be removed –

        (a)   from the United Kingdom, and

        (b)   to a State of which he is not a national or citizen.

    (2)   A State to which this Part applies shall be treated, in so far as relevant to the question mentioned in sub-paragraph (1), as a place –

        (a)   where a person's life and liberty are not threatened by reason of his race, religion, nationality, membership of a particular social group or political opinion,

        (b)   from which a person will not be sent to another State in contravention of his Convention rights, and

        (c)   from which a person will not be sent to another State otherwise than in accordance with the Refugee Convention.

4.   Section 77 of the Nationality, Immigration and Asylum Act 2002 (c 41) (no removal while claim for asylum pending) shall not prevent a person who has made a claim for asylum from being removed –

    (a)   from the United Kingdom, and

    (b)   to a State to which this Part applies;

provided that the Secretary of State certifies that in his opinion the person is not a national or citizen of the State.

5.   (1)   This paragraph applies where the Secretary of State certifies that –

        (a)   it is proposed to remove a person to a State to which this Part applies, and

        (b)   in the Secretary of State's opinion the person is not a national or citizen of the State.

    (2)   [Repealed]

    (3)   The person may not bring an immigration appeal from within the United Kingdom in reliance on –

        (a)   an asylum claim which asserts that to remove the person to a specified State to which this Part applies would breach the United Kingdom's obligations under the Refugee Convention, or

        (b)   a human rights claim in so far as it asserts that to remove the person to a specified State to which this Part applies would be unlawful under section 6 of the Human Rights Act 1998 because of the possibility of removal from that State to another State.

    (4)   The person may not bring an immigration appeal from within the United Kingdom in reliance on a human rights claim to which this sub-paragraph applies if the Secretary of State certifies that the claim is clearly unfounded; and the Secretary of State shall certify a human rights claim to which this sub-paragraph applies unless satisfied that the claim is not clearly unfounded.

    (5)   Sub-paragraph (4) applies to a human rights claim if, or in so far as, it asserts a matter other than that specified in sub-paragraph (3)(b).

6.   A person who is outside the United Kingdom may not bring an immigration appeal on any ground that is inconsistent with treating a State to which this Part applies as a place –

(a)   where a person's life and liberty are not threatened by reason of his race, religion, nationality, membership of a particular social group or political opinion,

(b)   from which a person will not be sent to another State in contravention of his Convention rights, and

(c)   from which a person will not be sent to another State otherwise than in accordance with the Refugee Convention.

UK Borders Act 2007 (extracts)

Deportation of criminals

32   Automatic deportation

(1)   In this section 'foreign criminal' means a person –

   (a)   who is not a British citizen,
   (b)   who is convicted in the United Kingdom of an offence, and
   (c)   to whom Condition 1 or 2 applies.

(2)   Condition 1 is that the person is sentenced to a period of imprisonment of at least 12 months.

(3)   Condition 2 is that –

   (a)   the offence is specified by order of the Secretary of State under section 72(4)(a) of the Nationality, Immigration and Asylum Act 2002 (c 41) (serious criminal), and
   (b)   the person is sentenced to a period of imprisonment.

(4)   For the purpose of section 3(5)(a) of the Immigration Act 1971 (c 77), the deportation of a foreign criminal is conducive to the public good.

(5)   The Secretary of State must make a deportation order in respect of a foreign criminal (subject to section 33).

(6)   The Secretary of State may not revoke a deportation order made in accordance with subsection (5) unless –

   (a)   he thinks that an exception under section 33 applies,
   (b)   the application for revocation is made while the foreign criminal is outside the United Kingdom, or
   (c)   section 34(4) applies.

(7)   Subsection (5) does not create a private right of action in respect of consequences of non-compliance by the Secretary of State.

33   Exceptions

(1)   Section 32(4) and (5) –

   (a)   do not apply where an exception in this section applies (subject to subsection (7) below), and
   (b)   are subject to sections 7 and 8 of the Immigration Act 1971 (Commonwealth citizens, Irish citizens, crew and other exemptions).

(2)   Exception 1 is where removal of the foreign criminal in pursuance of the deportation order would breach –

    (a)   a person's Convention rights, or

    (b)   the United Kingdom's obligations under the Refugee Convention.

(3)   Exception 2 is where the Secretary of State thinks that the foreign criminal was under the age of 18 on the date of conviction.

(4)   Exception 3 is where the removal of the foreign criminal from the United Kingdom in pursuance of a deportation order would breach rights of the foreign criminal under the EU treaties.

(5)   Exception 4 is where the foreign criminal –

    (a)   is the subject of a certificate under section 2 or 70 of the Extradition Act 2003 (c 41),

    (b)   is in custody pursuant to arrest under section 5 of that Act,

    (c)   is the subject of a provisional warrant under section 73 of that Act,

    (d)   is the subject of an authority to proceed under section 7 of the Extradition Act 1989 (c 33) or an order under paragraph 4(2) of Schedule 1 to that Act, or

    (e)   is the subject of a provisional warrant under section 8 of that Act or of a warrant under paragraph 5(1)(b) of Schedule 1 to that Act.

(6)   Exception 5 is where any of the following has effect in respect of the foreign criminal –

    (a)   a hospital order or guardianship order under section 37 of the Mental Health Act 1983 (c 20),

    (b)   a hospital direction under section 45A of that Act,

    (c)   a transfer direction under section 47 of that Act,

    (d)   a compulsion order under section 57A of the Criminal Procedure (Scotland) Act 1995 (c 46),

    (e)   a guardianship order under section 58 of that Act,

    (f)   a hospital direction under section 59A of that Act,

    (g)   a transfer for treatment direction under section 136 of the Mental Health (Care and Treatment) (Scotland) Act 2003 (asp 13), or

    (h)   an order or direction under a provision which corresponds to a provision specified in paragraphs (a) to (g) and which has effect in relation to Northern Ireland.

(6A)   Exception 6 is where the Secretary of State thinks that the application of section 32(4) and (5) would contravene the United Kingdom's obligations under the Council of Europe Convention on Action against Trafficking in Human Beings (done at Warsaw on 16th May 2005).

(7)   The application of an exception –

    (a)   does not prevent the making of a deportation order;

    (b)   results in it being assumed neither that deportation of the person concerned is conducive to the public good nor that it is not conducive to the public good;

but section 32(4) applies despite the application of Exception 1 or 4.

34   Timing

(1)   Section 32(5) requires a deportation order to be made at a time chosen by the Secretary of State.

(2)   A deportation order may not be made under section 32(5) while an appeal or further appeal against the conviction or sentence by reference to which the order is to be made –

    (a)   has been instituted and neither withdrawn nor determined, or

    (b)   could be brought.

(3)   For the purpose of subsection (2)(b) –

    (a)   the possibility of an appeal out of time with permission shall be disregarded, and

    (b)   a person who has informed the Secretary of State in writing that the person does not intend to appeal shall be treated as being no longer able to appeal.

(4)   The Secretary of State may withdraw a decision that section 32(5) applies, or revoke a deportation order made in accordance with section 32(5), for the purpose of –

    (a)   taking action under the Immigration Acts or rules made under section 3 of the Immigration Act 1971 (c 77) (immigration rules), and

    (b)   subsequently taking a new decision that section 32(5) applies and making a deportation order in accordance with section 32(5).

35   Appeal

(1)   The Nationality, Immigration and Asylum Act 2002 (c 41) is amended as follows.

(2)   At the end of section 79 (no deportation order pending appeal) add –

  '(3)   This section does not apply to a deportation order which states that it is made in accordance with section 32(5) of the UK Borders Act 2007.

    (4)   But a deportation order made in reliance on subsection (3) does not invalidate leave to enter or remain, in accordance with section 5(1) of the Immigration Act 1971, if and for so long as section 78 above applies.'

(3)   [*Repealed*]

36   Detention

(1)   A person who has served a period of imprisonment may be detained under the authority of the Secretary of State –

    (a)   while the Secretary of State considers whether section 32(5) applies, and

    (b)   where the Secretary of State thinks that section 32(5) applies, pending the making of the deportation order.

(2)   Where a deportation order is made in accordance with section 32(5) the Secretary of State shall exercise the power of detention under paragraph 2(3) of Schedule 3 to the Immigration Act 1971 (c 77) (detention pending removal) unless in the circumstances the Secretary of State thinks it inappropriate.

(3)   A court determining an appeal against conviction or sentence may direct release from detention under subsection (1) or (2).

(4)   Provisions of the Immigration Act 1971 which apply to detention under paragraph 2(3) of Schedule 3 to that Act shall apply to detention under subsection (1) (including provisions about bail).

(5)   Paragraph 2(5) of Schedule 3 to that Act (residence, occupation and reporting restrictions) applies to a person who is liable to be detained under subsection (1).

37 Family

(1)   Where a deportation order against a foreign criminal states that it is made in accordance with section 32(5) ('the automatic deportation order') this section shall have effect in place of the words from 'A deportation order' to 'after the making of the deportation order against him' in section 5(3) of the Immigration Act 1971 (period during which family members may also be deported).

(2)   A deportation order may not be made against a person as belonging to the family of the foreign criminal after the end of the relevant period of 8 weeks.

(3)   In the case of a foreign criminal who has not appealed in respect of the automatic deportation order, the relevant period begins when an appeal can no longer be brought (ignoring any possibility of an appeal out of time with permission).

(4)   In the case of a foreign criminal who has appealed in respect of the automatic deportation order, the relevant period begins when the appeal is no longer pending (within the meaning of section 104 of the Nationality, Immigration and Asylum Act 2002 (c 41)).

38 Interpretation

(1)   In section 32(2) the reference to a person who is sentenced to a period of imprisonment of at least 12 months –

   (a)   does not include a reference to a person who receives a suspended sentence (unless a court subsequently orders that the sentence or any part of it (of whatever length) is to take effect),

   (b)   does not include a reference to a person who is sentenced to a period of imprisonment of at least 12 months only by virtue of being sentenced to consecutive sentences amounting in aggregate to more than 12 months,

   (c)   includes a reference to a person who is sentenced to detention, or ordered or directed to be detained, in an institution other than a prison (including, in particular, a hospital or an institution for young offenders) for at least 12 months, and

   (d)   includes a reference to a person who is sentenced to imprisonment or detention, or ordered or directed to be detained, for an indeterminate period (provided that it may last for 12 months).

(2)   In section 32(3)(b) the reference to a person who is sentenced to a period of imprisonment –

   (a)   does not include a reference to a person who receives a suspended sentence (unless a court subsequently orders that the sentence or any part of it is to take effect), and

   (b)   includes a reference to a person who is sentenced to detention, or ordered or directed to be detained, in an institution other than a prison (including, in particular, a hospital or an institution for young offenders).

(3)   For the purposes of section 32 a person subject to an order under section 5 of the Criminal Procedure (Insanity) Act 1964 (c 84) (insanity, &c.) has not been convicted of an offence.

(4)   In sections 32 and 33 –

   (a)   'British citizen' has the same meaning as in section 3(5) of the Immigration Act 1971 (c 77) (and section 3(8) (burden of proof) shall apply),

   (b)   'Convention rights' has the same meaning as in the Human Rights Act 1998 (c 42),

(c)   'deportation order' means an order under section 5, and by virtue of section 3(5), of the Immigration Act 1971, and

(d)   'the Refugee Convention' means the Convention relating to the Status of Refugees done at Geneva on 28th July 1951 and its Protocol.

Borders, Citizenship and Immigration Act 2009 (extract)

Children

55 Duty regarding the welfare of children

(1) The Secretary of State must make arrangements for ensuring that –

    (a) the functions mentioned in subsection (2) are discharged having regard to the need to safeguard and promote the welfare of children who are in the United Kingdom, and

    (b) any services provided by another person pursuant to arrangements which are made by the Secretary of State and relate to the discharge of a function mentioned in subsection (2) are provided having regard to that need.

(2) The functions referred to in subsection (1) are –

    (a) any function of the Secretary of State in relation to immigration, asylum or nationality;

    (b) any function conferred by or by virtue of the Immigration Acts on an immigration officer;

    (c) any general customs function of the Secretary of State;

    (d) any customs function conferred on a designated customs official.

(3) A person exercising any of those functions must, in exercising the function, have regard to any guidance given to the person by the Secretary of State for the purpose of subsection (1).

(4) The Director of Border Revenue must make arrangements for ensuring that –

    (a) the Director's functions are discharged having regard to the need to safeguard and promote the welfare of children who are in the United Kingdom, and

    (b) any services provided by another person pursuant to arrangements made by the Director in the discharge of such a function are provided having regard to that need.

(5) A person exercising a function of the Director of Border Revenue must, in exercising the function, have regard to any guidance given to the person by the Secretary of State for the purpose of subsection (4).

(6) In this section –

'children' means persons who are under the age of 18;

'customs function', 'designated customs official' and 'general customs function' have the meanings given by Part 1.

(7)   A reference in an enactment (other than this Act) to the Immigration Acts includes a reference to this section.

(8)   Section 21 of the UK Borders Act 2007 (c 30) (children) ceases to have effect.

Identity Documents Act 2010 (extracts)

4 Possession of false identity documents etc with improper intention

(1)   It is an offence for a person ('P') with an improper intention to have in P's possession or under P's control –

    (a)   an identity document that is false and that P knows or believes to be false,

    (b)   an identity document that was improperly obtained and that P knows or believes to have been improperly obtained, or

    (c)   an identity document that relates to someone else.

(2)   Each of the following is an improper intention –

    (a)   the intention of using the document for establishing personal information about P;

    (b)   the intention of allowing or inducing another to use it for establishing, ascertaining or verifying personal information about P or anyone else.

(3)   In subsection (2)(b) the reference to P or anyone else does not include, in the case of a document within subsection (1)(c), the individual to whom it relates.

(4)   A person guilty of an offence under this section is liable, on conviction on indictment, to imprisonment for a term not exceeding 10 years or a fine (or both).

...

7 Meaning of 'identity document'

(1)   For the purposes of sections 4 to 6 'identity document' means any document that is or purports to be –

    (a)   an immigration document,

    (b)   a United Kingdom passport (within the meaning of the Immigration Act 1971),

    (c)   a passport issued by or on behalf of the authorities of a country or territory outside the United Kingdom or by or on behalf of an international organisation,

    (d)   a document that can be used (in some or all circumstances) instead of a passport,

    (e)   a licence to drive a motor vehicle granted under Part 3 of the Road Traffic 1988 or under Part 2 of the Road Traffic (Northern Ireland) Order 1981, or

    (f)   a driving licence issued by or on behalf of the authorities of a country or territory outside the United Kingdom.

(2)   In subsection (1)(a) 'immigration document' means –

    (a)   a document used for confirming the right of a person under the EU Treaties in respect of entry or residence in the United Kingdom,

      (b)   a document that is given in exercise of immigration functions and records information about leave granted to a person to enter or to remain in the United Kingdom, or

      (c)   a registration card (within the meaning of section 26A of the Immigration Act 1971).

(3)   In subsection (2)(b) 'immigration functions' means functions under the Immigration Acts (within the meaning of the Asylum and Immigration (Treatment of Claimants, etc.) Act 2004).

(4)   References in subsection (1) to the issue of a document include its renewal, replacement or re-issue (with or without modifications).

(5)   In this section 'document' includes a stamp or label.

(6)   The Secretary of State may by order amend the definition of 'identity document'.

APPENDIX B

Court procedure rules

Tribunal Procedure (First-tier Tribunal) (Immigration and Asylum Chamber) Rules 2014

PART 1

Introduction

Citation, commencement, application and interpretation

1. (1) These Rules may be cited as the Tribunal Procedure (First-tier Tribunal) (Immigration and Asylum Chamber) Rules 2014 and come into force on 20th October 2014.

    (2) They apply to proceedings before the Immigration and Asylum Chamber of the First-tier Tribunal.

    (3) The Schedule of Fast Track Rules has effect in the circumstances and in the manner specified in that Schedule.

    (4) In these Rules –

    'the 1999 Act' means the Immigration and Asylum Act 1999;

    'the 2002 Act' means the Nationality, Immigration and Asylum Act 2002;

    'the 2004 Act' means the Asylum and Immigration (Treatment of Claimants, etc.) Act 2004;

    'the 2006 Regulations' means the Immigration (European Economic Area) Regulations 2006;

    'the 2007 Act' means the Tribunals, Courts and Enforcement Act 2007;

    'appealable decision' means a decision from which there is a right of appeal to the Immigration and Asylum Chamber of the First-tier Tribunal;

    'appellant' means a person who has provided a notice of appeal to the Tribunal against an appealable decision in accordance with these Rules;

    'asylum claim' has the meaning given in section 113(1) of the 2002 Act;

    'certificate of fee satisfaction' means a certificate of fee satisfaction issued by the Lord Chancellor under article 8 of the Fees Order;

    'decision maker' means the maker of a decision against which an appeal is brought;

    'dispose of proceedings' includes, unless indicated otherwise, disposing of a part of the proceedings;

    'document' means anything in which information is recorded in any form, and an obligation under these Rules to provide or allow access to a document or

277

a copy of a document for any purpose means, unless the Tribunal directs otherwise, an obligation to provide or allow access to such document or copy in a legible form or in a form which can be readily made into a legible form;

'Fast Track Rules' means the rules contained in the Schedule to this statutory instrument;

'the Fees Order' means the First-tier Tribunal (Immigration and Asylum Chamber) Fees Order 2011;

'hearing' means an oral hearing and includes a hearing conducted in whole or in part by video link, telephone or other means of instantaneous two-way electronic communication;

'the Immigration Acts' means the Acts referred to in section 61 of the UK Borders Act 2007;

'party' means –

(a)   an appellant or respondent to proceedings;

(b)   a party to a bail application as provided for in rule 37(3) and 37(4); and

(c)   the UNHCR where notice has been given to the Tribunal in accordance with rule 8(3);

'practice direction' means a direction given under section 23 of the 2007 Act;

'qualified representative' means a person who is a qualified person in accordance with section 84(2) of the 1999 Act;

'respondent' means –

(a)   the decision maker specified in the notice of decision against which a notice of appeal has been provided; and

(b)   a person substituted or added as a respondent in accordance with rule 8.

'Tribunal' means the First-tier Tribunal;

'the UNHCR' means the United Kingdom Representative of the United Nations High Commissioner for Refugees; and

'working day' means any day except –

(a)   a Saturday or Sunday, Christmas Day, Good Friday or a bank holiday under section 1 of the Banking and Financial Dealings Act 1971; and

(b)   27th to 31st December inclusive.

(5)   A rule or Part referred to by number alone, means a rule in, or Part of, these Rules.

Overriding objective and parties' obligation to co-operate with the Tribunal

2.   (1)   The overriding objective of these Rules is to enable the Tribunal to deal with cases fairly and justly.

(2)   Dealing with a case fairly and justly includes –

(a)   dealing with the case in ways which are proportionate to the importance of the case, the complexity of the issues, the anticipated costs and the resources of the parties and of the Tribunal;

(b)   avoiding unnecessary formality and seeking flexibility in the proceedings;

(c)   ensuring, so far as practicable, that the parties are able to participate fully in the proceedings;

(d)   using any special expertise of the Tribunal effectively; and

(e)   avoiding delay, so far as compatible with proper consideration of the issues.

(3)   The Tribunal must seek to give effect to the overriding objective when it –

        (a)   exercises any power under these Rules; or

        (b)   interprets any rule or practice direction.

  (4)   Parties must –

        (a)   help the Tribunal to further the overriding objective; and

        (b)   co-operate with the Tribunal generally.

PART 2

General Powers and Provisions

Delegation to staff

3.   (1)   Anything of a formal or administrative nature which is required or permitted to be done by the Tribunal under these Rules may be done by a member of the Tribunal's staff.

      (2)   Staff appointed by the Lord Chancellor may, with the approval of the Senior President of Tribunals, carry out functions of a judicial nature permitted or required to be done by the Tribunal.

      (3)   The approval referred to at paragraph (2) may apply generally to the carrying out of specified functions by members of staff of a specified description in specified circumstances.

      (4)   Within 14 days after the date on which the Tribunal sends notice of a decision made by a member of staff under paragraph (2) to a party, that party may apply in writing to the Tribunal for that decision to be considered afresh by a judge.

Case management powers

4.   (1)   Subject to the provisions of the 2007 Act and any other enactment, the Tribunal may regulate its own procedure.

      (2)   The Tribunal may give a direction in relation to the conduct or disposal of proceedings at any time, including a direction amending, suspending or setting aside an earlier direction.

      (3)   In particular, and without restricting the general powers in paragraphs (1) and (2), the Tribunal may –

        (a)   extend or shorten the time for complying with any rule, practice direction or direction;

        (b)   consolidate or hear together two or more sets of proceedings or parts of proceedings raising common issues;

        (c)   permit or require a party to amend a document;

        (d)   permit or require a party or another person to provide documents, information, evidence or submissions to the Tribunal or a party;

        (e)   provide for a particular matter to be dealt with as a preliminary issue;

        (f)   hold a hearing to consider any matter, including a case management issue;

        (g)   decide the form of any hearing;

        (h)   adjourn or postpone a hearing;

        (i)   require a party to produce a bundle for a hearing;

        (j)   stay (or, in Scotland, sist) proceedings;

(k) transfer proceedings to another court or tribunal if that other court or tribunal has jurisdiction in relation to the proceedings and –

(i) because of a change of circumstances since the proceedings were started, the Tribunal no longer has jurisdiction in relation to the proceedings; or

(ii) the Tribunal considers that the other court or tribunal is a more appropriate forum for the determination of the case; or

(l) suspend the effect of its own decision pending the determination by the Tribunal or the Upper Tribunal of an application for permission to appeal against, and any appeal or review of, that decision.

Procedure for applying for and giving directions

5. (1) The Tribunal may give a direction on the application of one or more of the parties or on its own initiative.

(2) An application for a direction may be made –

(a) by sending or delivering a written application to the Tribunal; or

(b) orally during the course of a hearing.

(3) An application for a direction must include the reason for making that application.

(4) Unless the Tribunal considers that there is good reason not to do so, the Tribunal must send written notice of any direction to every party and to any other person affected by the direction.

(5) If a party or any other person sent notice of the direction under paragraph (4) wishes to challenge the direction which the Tribunal has given, they may do so by applying for another direction which amends, suspends or sets aside the first direction.

Failure to comply with rules etc

6. (1) An irregularity resulting from a failure to comply with any requirement in these Rules, a practice direction or a direction does not of itself render void the proceedings or any step taken in the proceedings.

(2) If a party has failed to comply with a requirement in these Rules, a practice direction or a direction, the Tribunal may take such action as it considers just, which may include –

(a) waiving the requirement;

(b) requiring the failure to be remedied; or

(c) exercising its power under paragraph (3).

(3) The Tribunal may refer to the Upper Tribunal, and ask the Upper Tribunal to exercise its power under section 25 (supplementary powers of Upper Tribunal) of the 2007 Act in relation to, any failure by a person to comply with a requirement imposed by the Tribunal –

(a) to attend at any place for the purpose of giving evidence;

(b) otherwise to make themselves available to give evidence;

(c) to swear an oath in connection with the giving of evidence;

(d) to give evidence as a witness;

(e) to produce a document; or

(f)   to facilitate the inspection of a document or any other thing (including any premises).

Striking out of an appeal for non-payment of fee and reinstatement

7.   (1)   Where the Tribunal is notified by the Lord Chancellor that a certificate of fee satisfaction has been revoked, the appeal shall automatically be struck out without order of the Tribunal and the Tribunal must notify each party that the appeal has been struck out.

        (2)   Where an appeal has been struck out in accordance with paragraph (1), the appeal may be reinstated if –

            (a)   the appellant applies to have the appeal reinstated; and
            (b)   the Lord Chancellor has issued a new certificate of fee satisfaction.

        (3)   An application made under paragraph (2)(a) must be made in writing and received by the Tribunal within 14 days, or if the appellant is outside the United Kingdom within 28 days, of the date on which the Tribunal sent notification of the striking out to the appellant.

Substitution and addition of parties

8.   (1)   The Tribunal may give a direction substituting a respondent if –

            (a)   the wrong person has been named as a respondent; or
            (b)   the substitution has become necessary because of a change in circumstances since the start of proceedings.

        (2)   The Tribunal may give a direction adding a person to the proceedings as a respondent.

        (3)   The UNHCR may give notice to the Tribunal that they wish to participate in any proceedings where the appellant has made an asylum claim and on giving such notice becomes a party to the proceedings.

        (4)   If –

            (a)   the Tribunal gives a direction under paragraph (1) or (2); or
            (b)   the UNHCR gives notice to the Tribunal under paragraph (3),

the Tribunal may give such consequential directions as it considers appropriate.

Orders for payment of costs and interest on costs (or, in Scotland, expenses)

9.   (1)   If the Tribunal allows an appeal, it may order a respondent to pay by way of costs to the appellant an amount no greater than –

            (a)   any fee paid under the Fees Order that has not been refunded; and
            (b)   any fee which the appellant is or may be liable to pay under that Order.

        (2)   The Tribunal may otherwise make an order in respect of costs only –

            (a)   under section 29(4) of the 2007 Act (wasted costs) and costs incurred in applying for such costs; or
            (b)   if a person has acted unreasonably in bringing, defending or conducting proceedings.

        (3)   The Tribunal may make an order under this rule on an application or on its own initiative.

(4)   A person making an application for an order for costs –

    (a)   must, unless the application is made orally at a hearing, send or deliver an application to the Tribunal and to the person against whom the order is sought to be made; and

    (b)   may send or deliver together with the application a schedule of the costs claimed in sufficient detail to allow summary assessment of such costs by the Tribunal.

(5)   An application for an order for costs may be made at any time during the proceedings but must be made within 28 days after the date on which the Tribunal sends –

    (a)   a notice of decision recording the decision which disposes of the proceedings; or

    (b)   notice that a withdrawal has taken effect under rule 17 (withdrawal).

(6)   The Tribunal may not make an order for costs against a person (in this rule called the 'paying person') without first giving that person an opportunity to make representations.

(7)   The amount of costs to be paid under an order under this rule may be determined by –

    (a)   summary assessment by the Tribunal;

    (b)   agreement of a specified sum by the paying person and the person entitled to receive the costs (in this rule called the 'receiving person');

    (c)   detailed assessment of the whole or a specified part of the costs (including the costs of the assessment) incurred by the receiving person, if not agreed.

(8)   Except in relation to paragraph (9), in the application of this rule in relation to Scotland, any reference to costs is to be read as a reference to expenses.

(9)   Following an order for detailed assessment made by the Tribunal under paragraph (7)(c) the paying person or the receiving person may apply –

    (a)   in England and Wales, to the county court for a detailed assessment of the costs on the standard basis or, if specified in the order, on the indemnity basis; and the Civil Procedure Rules 1998, section 74 (interest on judgment debts, etc) of the County Courts Act 1984 and the County Court (Interest on Judgment Debts) Order 1991 shall apply, with necessary modifications, to that application and assessment as if the proceedings in the Tribunal had been proceedings in a court to which the Civil Procedure Rules 1998 apply;

    (b)   in Scotland, to the Auditor of the Sheriff Court or the Court of Session (as specified in the order) for the taxation of the expenses according to the fees payable in that court; or

    (c)   in Northern Ireland, to the Taxing Office of the High Court of Northern Ireland for taxation on the standard basis or, if specified in the order, on the indemnity basis.

Representatives

10.   (1)   A party may be represented by any person not prohibited from representing by section 84 of the 1999 Act.

    (2)   Where a party is or has been represented by a person prohibited from

representing by section 84 of the 1999 Act, that does not of itself render void the proceedings or any step taken in the proceedings.

(3) If a party appoints a representative, that party (or the representative if the representative is a qualified representative) must send or deliver to the Tribunal written notice of the representative's name and address, which may be done at a hearing.

(4) Anything permitted or required to be done by a party under these Rules, a practice direction or a direction may be done by the representative of that party, except signing a witness statement.

(5) A person who receives notice of the appointment of a representative –

    (a) must provide to the representative any document which is required to be provided to the represented party, and need not provide that document to the represented party; and

    (b) may assume that the representative is and remains authorised as such until they receive written notification that this is not so from the representative or the represented party.

(6) As from the date on which a person has notified the Tribunal that they are acting as the representative of an appellant and has given an address for service, if any document is provided to the appellant a copy must also at the same time be provided to the appellant's representative.

Calculating time

11. (1) An act required or permitted to be done on or by a particular day by these Rules, a practice direction or a direction must, unless otherwise directed, be done by midnight on that day.

    (2) Subject to the Tribunal directing that this paragraph does not apply, if the time specified by these Rules, a practice direction or a direction for doing any act ends on a day other than a working day, the act is done in time if it is done on the next working day.

Sending, delivery and language of documents

12. (1) Any document to be provided to the Tribunal or any person under these Rules, a practice direction or a direction must be –

    (a) delivered, or sent by post, to an address;

    (b) sent via a document exchange to a document exchange number or address;

    (c) sent by fax to a fax number;

    (d) sent by e-mail to an e-mail address; or

    (e) sent or delivered by any other method,

identified for that purpose by the Tribunal or person to whom the document is directed.

    (2) A document to be provided to an individual may be provided by leaving it with that individual.

    (3) If the respondent believes that the address specified under paragraph (1) for the provision of documents to the appellant is not appropriate for that purpose, the respondent must notify the Tribunal in writing of that fact and, if aware of it, an address which would be appropriate.

    (4) If any document is provided to a person who has notified the Tribunal that they

are acting as the representative of a party, it shall be deemed to have been provided to that party.

(5)   Subject to paragraph (6) –

    (a)   any notice of appeal or application notice provided to the Tribunal must be completed in English; and
    (b)   if a document provided to the Tribunal is not written in English, it must be accompanied by an English translation.

(6)   In proceedings that are in Wales or have a connection with Wales, a document or translation may be provided to the Tribunal in Welsh.

Use of documents and information

13.   (1)   The Tribunal may make an order prohibiting the disclosure or publication of –

    (a)   specified documents or information relating to the proceedings; or
    (b)   any matter likely to lead members of the public to identify any person whom the Tribunal considers should not be identified.

(2)   The Tribunal may give a direction prohibiting the disclosure of a document or information to a person if –

    (a)   the Tribunal is satisfied that such disclosure would be likely to cause that person or some other person serious harm; and
    (b)   the Tribunal is satisfied, having regard to the interests of justice, that it is proportionate to give such a direction.

(3)   If a party ('the first party') considers that the Tribunal should give a direction under paragraph (2) prohibiting the disclosure of a document or information to another party ('the second party'), the first party must –

    (a)   exclude the relevant document or information from any documents to be provided to the second party; and
    (b)   provide to the Tribunal the excluded document or information, and the reason for its exclusion, so that the Tribunal may decide whether the document or information should be disclosed to the second party or should be the subject of a direction under paragraph (2).

(4)   The Tribunal must conduct proceedings as appropriate in order to give effect to a direction given under paragraph (2).

(5)   If the Tribunal gives a direction under paragraph (2) which prevents disclosure to a party who has appointed a representative, the Tribunal may give a direction that the documents or information be disclosed to that representative if the Tribunal is satisfied that –

    (a)   disclosure to the representative would be in the interests of the party; and
    (b)   the representative will act in accordance with paragraph (6).

(6)   Documents or information disclosed to a representative in accordance with a direction under paragraph (5) must not be disclosed either directly or indirectly to any other person without the Tribunal's consent.

(7)   The Tribunal may, on the application of a party or on its own initiative, give a direction that certain documents or information must or may be disclosed to the Tribunal on the basis that the Tribunal will not disclose such documents or information to other persons, or specified other persons.

(8)   A party making an application for a direction under paragraph (7) may

withhold the relevant documents or information from other parties until the Tribunal has granted or refused the application.

(9)   In a case involving matters relating to national security, the Tribunal must ensure that information is not disclosed contrary to the interests of national security.

(10)   The Tribunal must conduct proceedings and record its decision and reasons appropriately so as not to undermine the effect of an order made under paragraph (1), a direction given under paragraph (2), (5) or (7) or the duty imposed by paragraph (9).

Evidence and submissions

14.   (1)   Without restriction on the general powers in rule 4 (case management powers), the Tribunal may give directions as to –

        (a)   issues on which it requires evidence or submissions;

        (b)   the nature of the evidence or submissions it requires;

        (c)   whether the parties are permitted or required to provide expert evidence;

        (d)   any limit on the number of witnesses whose evidence a party may put forward, whether in relation to a particular issue or generally;

        (e)   the manner in which any evidence or submissions are to be provided, which may include a direction for them to be given –

            (i)   orally at a hearing; or

            (ii)   by witness statement or written submissions; and

        (f)   the time at which any evidence or submissions are to be provided.

      (2)   The Tribunal may admit evidence whether or not –

        (a)   the evidence would be admissible in a civil trial in the United Kingdom; or

        (b)   subject to section 85A(4) of the 2002 Act, the evidence was available to the decision maker.

      (3)   The Tribunal may consent to a witness giving, or require any witness to give, evidence on oath or affirmation, and may administer an oath or affirmation for that purpose.

Summoning or citation of witnesses and orders to answer questions or produce documents

15.   (1)   On the application of a party or on its own initiative, the Tribunal may –

        (a)   by summons (or, in Scotland, citation) require any person to attend as a witness at a hearing at the time and place specified in the summons or citation; or

        (b)   order any person to answer any questions or produce any documents in that person's possession or control which relate to any issue in the proceedings.

      (2)   A summons or citation under paragraph (1)(a) must –

        (a)   give the person required to attend 14 days' notice of the hearing or such shorter period as the Tribunal may direct; and

        (b)   where the person is not a party, make provision for the person's necessary expenses of attendance to be paid, and state who is to pay them.

(3)   No person may be compelled to give any evidence or produce any document that the person could not be compelled to give or produce on a trial of an action in a court of law in the part of the United Kingdom where the proceedings are to be determined.

(4)   A summons, citation or order under this rule must –

(a)   state that the person on whom the requirement is imposed may apply to the Tribunal to vary or set aside the summons, citation or order, if they have not had an opportunity to object to it; and

(b)   state the consequences of failure to comply with the summons, citation or order.

Appeal treated as abandoned or finally determined

16.   (1)   A party must notify the Tribunal if they are aware that –

(a)   the appellant has left the United Kingdom;

(b)   the appellant has been granted leave to enter or remain in the United Kingdom;

(c)   a deportation order has been made against the appellant; or

(d)   a document listed in paragraph 4(2) of Schedule 2 to the 2006 Regulations has been issued to the appellant.

(2)   Where an appeal is treated as abandoned pursuant to section 104(4A) of the 2002 Act or paragraph 4(2) of Schedule 2 to 2006 Regulations, the Tribunal must send the parties a notice informing them that the appeal is being treated as abandoned or finally determined, as the case may be.

(3)   Where an appeal would otherwise fall to be treated as abandoned pursuant to section 104(4A) of the 2002 Act, but the appellant wishes to pursue their appeal, the appellant must provide a notice, which must comply with any relevant practice direction, to the Tribunal and each other party so that it is received within 28 days of the date on which the appellant was sent notice of the grant of leave to enter or remain in the United Kingdom or was sent the document listed in paragraph 4(2) of Schedule 2 to the 2006 Regulations, as the case may be.

Withdrawal

17.   (1)   A party may give notice of the withdrawal of their appeal –

(a)   by providing to the Tribunal a written notice of withdrawal of the appeal; or

(b)   orally at a hearing,

and in either case must specify the reasons for that withdrawal.

(2)   The Tribunal must (save for good reason) treat an appeal as withdrawn if the respondent notifies the Tribunal and each other party that the decision (or, where the appeal relates to more than one decision, all of the decisions) to which the appeal relates has been withdrawn and specifies the reasons for the withdrawal of the decision.

(3)   The Tribunal must notify each party in writing that a withdrawal has taken effect under this rule and that the proceedings are no longer regarded by the Tribunal as pending.

Certification of pending appeal

18.   (1)   The Secretary of State must, upon issuing a certificate under section 97 or 98 of the 2002 Act which relates to a pending appeal, provide notice of the certification to the Tribunal.

        (2)   Where a notice of certification is provided under paragraph (1), the Tribunal must –

            (a)   notify the parties; and

            (b)   take no further action in relation to the appeal.

PART 3

Proceedings Before the Tribunal

CHAPTER 1   Before the Hearing

Notice of appeal

19.   (1)   An appellant must start proceedings by providing a notice of appeal to the Tribunal.

        (2)   If the person is in the United Kingdom, the notice of appeal must be received not later than 14 days after they are sent the notice of the decision against which the appeal is brought.

        (3)   If the person is outside the United Kingdom, the notice of appeal must be received –

            (a)   not later than 28 days after their departure from the United Kingdom if the person –

                (i)   was in the United Kingdom when the decision against which they are appealing was made, and

                (ii)   may not appeal while they are in the United Kingdom by reason of a provision of the 2002 Act; or

            (b)   in any other case, not later than 28 days after they receive the notice of the decision.

        (4)   The notice of appeal must –

            (a)   set out the grounds of appeal;

            (b)   be signed and dated by the appellant or their representative;

            (c)   if the notice of appeal is signed by the appellant's representative, the representative must certify in the notice of appeal that it has been completed in accordance with the appellant's instructions;

            (d)   state whether the appellant requires an interpreter at any hearing and if so for which language and dialect;

            (e)   state whether the appellant intends to attend at any hearing; and

            (f)   state whether the appellant will be represented at any hearing.

        (5)   The appellant must provide with the notice of appeal –

(a)   the notice of decision against which the appellant is appealing or if it is not practicable to include the notice of decision, the reasons why it is not practicable;

(b)   any statement of reasons for that decision;

(c)   any documents in support of the appellant's case which have not been supplied to the respondent;

(d)   an application for the Lord Chancellor to issue a certificate of fee satisfaction;

(e)   any further information or documents required by an applicable practice direction.

(6)   The Tribunal must send a copy of the notice of appeal and the accompanying documents or information provided by the appellant to the respondent.

(7)   An appellant may, with the permission of the Tribunal, vary the grounds on which they rely in the notice of appeal.

Late notice of appeal

20.   (1)   Where a notice of appeal is provided outside the time limit in rule 19, including any extension of time directed under rule 4(3)(a) (power to extend time), the notice of appeal must include an application for such an extension of time and the reason why the notice of appeal was not provided in time.

(2)   If, upon receipt of a notice of appeal, the notice appears to the Tribunal to have been provided outside the time limit but does not include an application for an extension of time, the Tribunal must (unless it extends time of its own initiative) notify the person in writing that it proposes to treat the notice of appeal as being out of time.

(3)   Where the Tribunal gives notification under paragraph (2), the person may by written notice to the Tribunal contend that –

(a)   the notice of appeal was given in time; or

(b)   time for providing the notice of appeal should be extended,

and, if so, that person may provide the Tribunal with written evidence in support of that contention.

(4)   The Tribunal must decide any issue under this rule as to whether a notice of appeal was given in time, or whether to extend the time for appealing, as a preliminary issue, and may do so without a hearing.

(5)   Where the Tribunal makes a decision under this rule it must provide to the parties written notice of its decision, including its reasons.

Special provision for imminent removal cases (late notice of appeal)

21.   (1)   This rule applies in any case to which rule 20 applies, where the respondent notifies the Tribunal that directions have been given for the removal of that person from the United Kingdom on a date within 5 days of the date on which the notice of appeal was received.

(2)   The Tribunal must, if reasonably practicable, make any decision under rule 20 before the date and time proposed for the removal.

(3)   Rule 20 shall apply, subject to the modifications that the Tribunal may –

(a)   give notification under rule 20(2) orally, which may include giving it by telephone,

(b)   direct a time for providing evidence under rule 20(3), and

(c)   direct that evidence in support of a contention under rule 20(3) is to be given orally, which may include requiring the evidence to be given by telephone, and hold a hearing for the purpose of receiving such evidence.

Circumstances in which the Tribunal may not accept a notice of appeal

22.　(1)　Where a person has provided a notice of appeal to the Tribunal and any of the circumstances in paragraph (2) apply, the Tribunal may not accept the notice of appeal.

　　(2)　The circumstances referred to in paragraph (1) are that –

　　　(a)　there is no appealable decision; or
　　　(b)　the Lord Chancellor has refused to issue a certificate of fee satisfaction.

　　(3)　Where the Tribunal does not accept a notice of appeal, it must –

　　　(a)　notify the person providing the notice of appeal and the respondent; and
　　　(b)　take no further action on that notice of appeal.

Response: entry clearance cases

23.　(1)　This rule applies to an appeal against a refusal of entry clearance or a refusal of an EEA family permit (which has the meaning given in regulation 2(1) of the 2006 Regulations).

　　(2)　When a respondent is provided with a copy of a notice of appeal from a refusal of entry clearance or a refusal of an EEA family permit, the respondent must provide the Tribunal with –

　　　(a)　the notice of the decision to which the notice of appeal relates and any other document the respondent provided to the appellant giving reasons for that decision;
　　　(b)　a statement of whether the respondent opposes the appellant's case and, if so, the grounds for such opposition;
　　　(c)　any statement of evidence or application form completed by the appellant;
　　　(d)　any record of an interview with the appellant in relation to the decision being appealed;
　　　(e)　any other unpublished document which is referred to in a document mentioned in subparagraph (a) or relied upon by the respondent; and
　　　(f)　the notice of any other appealable decision made in relation to the appellant.

　　(3)　The respondent must send to the Tribunal and the other parties the documents listed in paragraph (2) within 28 days of the date on which the respondent received from the Tribunal a copy of the notice of appeal and any accompanying documents or information provided under rule 19(6).

Response: other cases

24.　(1)　Except in appeals to which rule 23 applies, when a respondent is provided with a copy of a notice of appeal, the respondent must provide the Tribunal with –

　　　(a)　the notice of the decision to which the notice of appeal relates and any other document the respondent provided to the appellant giving reasons for that decision;

(b)   any statement of evidence or application form completed by the appellant;

(c)   any record of an interview with the appellant in relation to the decision being appealed;

(d)   any other unpublished document which is referred to in a document mentioned in subparagraph (a) or relied upon by the respondent; and

(e)   the notice of any other appealable decision made in relation to the appellant.

(2)   The respondent must, if the respondent intends to change or add to the grounds or reasons relied upon in the notice or the other documents referred to in paragraph (1)(a), provide the Tribunal and the other parties with a statement of whether the respondent opposes the appellant's case and the grounds for such opposition.

(3)   The documents listed in paragraph (1) and any statement required under paragraph (2) must be provided in writing within 28 days of the date on which the Tribunal sent to the respondent a copy of the notice of appeal and any accompanying documents or information provided under rule 19(6).

CHAPTER 2   Hearings

Consideration of decision with or without a hearing

25.   (1)   The Tribunal must hold a hearing before making a decision which disposes of proceedings except where –

(a)   each party has consented to, or has not objected to, the matter being decided without a hearing;

(b)   the appellant has not consented to the appeal being determined without a hearing but the Lord Chancellor has refused to issue a certificate of fee satisfaction for the fee payable for a hearing;

(c)   the appellant is outside the United Kingdom and does not have a representative who has an address for service in the United Kingdom;

(d)   it is impracticable to give the appellant notice of the hearing;

(e)   a party has failed to comply with a provision of these Rules, a practice direction or a direction and the Tribunal is satisfied that in all the circumstances, including the extent of the failure and any reasons for it, it is appropriate to determine the appeal without a hearing;

(f)   the appeal is one to which rule 16(2) or 18(2) applies; or

(g)   subject to paragraph (2), the Tribunal considers that it can justly determine the matter without a hearing.

(2)   Where paragraph (1)(g) applies, the Tribunal must not make the decision without a hearing without first giving the parties notice of its intention to do so, and an opportunity to make written representations as to whether there should be a hearing.

(3)   This rule does not apply to decisions under Part 4 or Part 5.

Notice of hearings

26.   The Tribunal must give each party entitled to attend a hearing reasonable notice of the time and place of the hearing (including any adjourned or postponed hearing) and any changes to the time and place of the hearing.

Public and private hearings

27.   (1)   Subject to the following paragraphs and to section 108 of the 2002 Act, all hearings must be held in public.

        (2)   The Tribunal may give a direction that a hearing, or part of it, is to be held in private.

        (3)   Where a hearing, or part of it, is to be held in private, the Tribunal may determine who is permitted to attend the hearing or part of it.

        (4)   The Tribunal may give a direction excluding from any hearing, or part of it –

            (a)   any person whose conduct the Tribunal considers is disrupting or is likely to disrupt the hearing;

            (b)   any person whose presence the Tribunal considers is likely to prevent another person from giving evidence or making submissions freely;

            (c)   any person who the Tribunal considers should be excluded in order to give effect to a direction under rule 13(2) (withholding a document or information likely to cause serious harm); or

            (d)   any person where the purpose of the hearing would be defeated by the attendance of that person.

        (5)   The Tribunal may give a direction excluding a witness from a hearing until that witness gives evidence.

Hearing in a party's absence

28.   If a party fails to attend a hearing the Tribunal may proceed with the hearing if the Tribunal –

        (a)   is satisfied that the party has been notified of the hearing or that reasonable steps have been taken to notify the party of the hearing; and

        (b)   considers that it is in the interests of justice to proceed with the hearing.

CHAPTER 3   Decisions

Decisions and notice of decisions

29.   (1)   The Tribunal may give a decision orally at a hearing.

        (2)   Subject to rule 13(2) (withholding information likely to cause serious harm), the Tribunal must provide to each party as soon as reasonably practicable after making a decision (other than a decision under Part 4) which disposes of the proceedings –

            (a)   a notice of decision stating the Tribunal's decision; and

            (b)   notification of any right of appeal against the decision and the time within which, and the manner in which, such right of appeal may be exercised.

        (3)   Where the decision of the Tribunal relates to –

            (a)   an asylum claim or a humanitarian protection claim, the Tribunal must provide, with the notice of decision in paragraph (2)(a), written reasons for its decision;

            (b)   any other matter, the Tribunal may provide written reasons for its decision but, if it does not do so, must notify the parties of the right to apply for a written statement of reasons.

(4) Unless the Tribunal has already provided a written statement of reasons, a party may make a written application to the Tribunal for such statement following a decision which disposes of the proceedings.

(5) An application under paragraph (4) must be received within 28 days of the date on which the Tribunal sent or otherwise provided to the party a notice of decision relating to the decision which disposes of the proceedings.

(6) If a party makes an application in accordance with paragraphs (4) and (5) the Tribunal must, subject to rule 13(2) (withholding a document or information likely to cause serious harm), send a written statement of reasons to each party as soon as reasonably practicable.

PART 4

Correcting, Setting Aside, Reviewing and Appealing Tribunal Decisions

Interpretation

30. In this Part –

'appeal' means the exercise of a right of appeal on a point of law under section 11 of the 2007 Act;

'review' means the review of a decision by the Tribunal under section 9 of the 2007 Act.

Clerical mistakes and accidental slips or omissions

31. The Tribunal may at any time correct any clerical mistake or other accidental slip or omission in a decision, direction or any document produced by it, by –

(a) providing notification of the amended decision or direction, or a copy of the amended document, to all parties; and

(b) making any necessary amendment to any information published in relation to the decision, direction or document.

Setting aside a decision which disposes of proceedings

32. (1) The Tribunal may set aside a decision which disposes of proceedings, or part of such a decision, and re-make the decision, or the relevant part of it, if –

(a) the Tribunal considers that it is in the interests of justice to do so; and

(b) one or more of the conditions in paragraph (2) are satisfied.

(2) The conditions are –

(a) a document relating to the proceedings was not provided to, or was not received at an appropriate time by, a party or a party's representative;

(b) a document relating to the proceedings was not provided to the Tribunal at an appropriate time;

(c) a party, or a party's representative, was not present at a hearing related to the proceedings; or

(d) there has been some other procedural irregularity in the proceedings.

(3) An application for a decision, or part of a decision, to be set aside under paragraph (1) must be made –

(a)   if the appellant is outside the United Kingdom, within 28 days; or

(b)   in any other case, within 14 days,

of the date on which the party was sent the notice of decision.

Application for permission to appeal to the Upper Tribunal

33.   (1)   A party seeking permission to appeal to the Upper Tribunal must make a written application to the Tribunal for permission to appeal.

    (2)   Subject to paragraph (3), an application under paragraph (1) must be provided to the Tribunal so that it is received no later than 14 days after the date on which the party making the application was provided with written reasons for the decision.

    (3)   Where an appellant is outside the United Kingdom, an application to the Tribunal under paragraph (1) must be provided to the Tribunal so that it is received no later than 28 days after the date on which the party making the application was provided with written reasons for the decision.

    (4)   The time within which a party may apply for permission to appeal against an amended notice of decision runs from the date on which the party is sent the amended notice of decision.

    (5)   An application under paragraph (1) must –

        (a)   identify the decision of the Tribunal to which it relates;

        (b)   identify the alleged error or errors of law in the decision; and

        (c)   state the result the party making the application is seeking and include any application for an extension of time and the reasons why such an extension should be given.

    (6)   If a person makes an application under paragraph (1) when the Tribunal has not given a written statement of reasons for its decision –

        (a)   the Tribunal must, if no application for a written statement of reasons has been made, treat the application for permission as such an application; and

        (b)   may –

            (i)   direct under rule 36 that the application is not to be treated as an application for permission to appeal; or

           (ii)   determine the application for permission to appeal.

    (7)   If an application for a written statement of reasons has been, or is, refused because the application was received out of time, the Tribunal must only admit the application for permission if the Tribunal considers that it is in the interests of justice to do so.

Tribunal's consideration of an application for permission to appeal to the Upper Tribunal

34.   (1)   On receiving an application for permission to appeal the Tribunal must first consider whether to review the decision in accordance with rule 35.

    (2)   If the Tribunal decides not to review the decision, or reviews the decision and decides to take no action in relation to the decision, or part of it, the Tribunal must consider whether to give permission to appeal in relation to the decision or that part of it.

    (3)   The Tribunal must send a record of its decision to the parties as soon as practicable.

(4)   If the Tribunal refuses permission to appeal it must send with the record of its decision –

    (a)   a statement of its reasons for such refusal; and

    (b)   notification of the right to make an application to the Upper Tribunal for permission to appeal and the time within which, and the manner in which, such application must be made.

(5)   The Tribunal may give permission to appeal on limited grounds, but must comply with paragraph (4) in relation to any grounds on which it has refused permission.

Review of a decision

35.   (1)   The Tribunal may only undertake a review of a decision –

    (a)   pursuant to rule 34 (review on an application for permission to appeal); and

    (b)   if it is satisfied that there was an error of law in the decision.

(2)   The Tribunal must notify the parties in writing of the outcome of any review, and of any right of appeal in relation to the outcome.

(3)   If the Tribunal takes any action in relation to a decision following a review without first giving every party an opportunity to make representations –

    (a)   the notice under paragraph (2) must state that any party that did not have an opportunity to make representations may apply for such action to be set aside; and

    (b)   the Tribunal may regard the review as incomplete and act accordingly.

Power to treat an application as a different type of application

36.   The Tribunal may treat an application for a decision to be corrected, set aside or reviewed, or for permission to appeal against a decision, as an application for any other one of those things.

PART 5

Bail

Scope of this Part and interpretation

37.   (1)   This Part applies to bail proceedings, meaning bail applications and any matter relating to bail which the Tribunal is considering on its own initiative.

(2)   In this Part, 'bail party' means a person released on bail or applying to the Tribunal to be released on bail.

(3)   Except where paragraph (4) applies, the parties to bail proceedings are the bail party and the Secretary of State.

(4)   Where the proceedings concern forfeiture of a recognizance, the parties are the Secretary of State and any person who entered into the recognizance in question, whether as principal or surety.

Bail applications

38.   (1)   A bail application must be made by sending or delivering to the Tribunal an application notice containing the information specified below.

        (2)   A bail application must specify whether it is for –

        (a)   the bail party to be released on bail;
        (b)   variation of bail conditions;
        (c)   continuation of bail; or
        (d)   forfeiture of a recognizance.

        (3)   Subject to paragraph (4), a bail application must contain the following details –

        (a)   the bail party's –

        (i)   full name;
        (ii)   date of birth; and
        (iii)   date of their most recent arrival in the United Kingdom;

        (b)   the address of any place where the bail party is detained;
        (c)   the address where the bail party will reside if the bail application is granted, or, if unable to give such an address, the reason why an address is not given;
        (d)   the amount of any recognizance in which the bail party is, or is proposed to be, bound;
        (e)   whether the bail party has a pending appeal to the Tribunal or any pending application for further appeal relating to such an appeal;
        (f)   the full name, address, date of birth and any occupation of any person who is acting or is proposed to act as a surety for the recognizance and the amount in which the surety is, or is proposed to be, bound;
        (g)   where the bail party is aged 18 or over, whether the bail party will, if required, agree as a condition of bail to co-operate with electronic monitoring under section 36 of the 2004 Act;
        (h)   the grounds on which the application is made and, where a previous application has been refused, when it was refused and details of any material change in circumstances since the refusal; and
        (i)   whether an interpreter will be required at the hearing, and in respect of what language and dialect.

        (4)   Where the application is for forfeiture of a recognizance, paragraph (3) applies except for subparagraphs (a)(iii), (b), (c), (e) and (g) of that paragraph.

        (5)   An application made by the bail party must be signed by the bail party or their representative.

        (6)   On receipt of a bail application, the Tribunal must record the date on which it was received and provide a copy of the application to the Secretary of State as soon as reasonably practicable.

Bail hearings

39.   (1)   Subject to paragraph (3), where a bail application is for the bail party to be released on bail, the Tribunal must, as soon as reasonably practicable, hold a hearing of the application.

        (2)   In all other bail proceedings, the Tribunal may determine the matter without a hearing if it considers it can justly do so.

        (3)   Where an application for release on bail is received by the Tribunal within 28

days after a Tribunal decision made at a hearing under paragraph (1) not to release the bail party on bail, the Tribunal –

    (a)   must determine whether the bail party has demonstrated that there has been a material change in circumstances since the decision;

    (b)   if the Tribunal so determines, must apply paragraph (1);

    (c)   otherwise, must dismiss the application without a hearing.

(4)   Paragraph (3) has no effect until the date on which section 7(3)(c) of the Immigration Act 2014 (inserting paragraph 25(2) of Schedule 2 to the Immigration Act 1971) comes into force.

Response to a bail application

40.   (1)   If the Secretary of State opposes a bail application, the Secretary of State must provide the Tribunal and the bail party with a written statement of the reasons for doing so –

    (a)   not later than 2.00 pm on the working day before the hearing; or

    (b)   if the Secretary of State was provided with notice of the hearing less than 24 hours before that time, as soon as reasonably practicable.

(2)   Where the Secretary of State's reasons for opposition include that directions are in force for the removal of the bail party from the United Kingdom, the Secretary of State must provide a copy of the notice of those directions.

Decision in bail proceedings

41.   (1)   The Tribunal must provide written notice of its decision to –

    (a)   the parties; and

    (b)   if the bail application is for the bail party to be released on bail, the person having custody of the bail party.

(2)   Where bail is granted, varied or continued, the notice must state any bail conditions, including any amounts in which the bail party and any sureties are to be bound.

(3)   Where bail is refused or where the Tribunal orders forfeiture of the recognizance, the notice must include reasons for the decision.

(4)   Where, instead of granting or refusing bail, the Tribunal fixes the amount and conditions of the bail with a view to the recognizance being taken subsequently by a person specified by the Tribunal, the notice must include the matters stated in paragraph (2) and the name or office of the person so specified.

(5)   Paragraph (6) applies where the Tribunal determines that directions for the removal of the bail party from the United Kingdom are for the time being in force and the directions require the bail party to be removed from the United Kingdom within 14 days of the date of the decision to release the bail party on bail or under paragraph (4).

(6)   The notice provided under paragraph (1) must state –

    (a)   the determination of the Tribunal under paragraph (5);

    (b)   whether the Secretary of State has consented to the release of the bail party;

    (c)   where the Secretary of State has not consented to that release, that the bail party must therefore not be released on bail.

Recognizances

42. (1) Any recognizance must be in writing and must state –

    (a) the bail conditions, including the amount of the recognizance and any amount in which any surety agrees to be bound; and

    (b) that the bail party and any surety understand the bail conditions and that, if the bail party fails to comply with those conditions, they may be ordered to pay all or part of the amount in which they are bound.

    (2) The recognizance must be signed by the bail party and any surety and provided to the Tribunal, and a copy provided to –

    (a) the parties,

    (b) any person having custody of the bail party, and

    (c) any surety.

Release of bail party

43. The person having custody of the bail party must release the bail party upon –

    (a) being provided with a notice of decision to grant bail; or

    (b) being –

        (i) provided with a notice of decision fixing the amount and conditions of the bail, and

        (ii) satisfied that the recognizance required by that decision has been entered into.

Application of this Part to Scotland

44. This Part applies to Scotland with the following modifications –

    (a) in rule 37, for paragraph (4) substitute –

    '(4) Where the proceedings concern forfeiture of bail, the parties are the Secretary of State and any person who entered into the bail bond in question, whether that is the bail party or cautioner.'

    (b) in rule 38 –

        (i) for paragraph (2)(d) substitute –

        '(d) forfeiture of bail.';

        (ii) for paragraph (3)(d) substitute –

        '(d) the amount, if any, deposited or to be deposited if bail is granted;';

        (iii) for paragraph (3)(f) substitute –

        '(f) the full name, address, date of birth and any occupation of any person acting or offering to act as a cautioner if the application for bail is granted, and the amount, if any, deposited or to be deposited;'; and

        (iv) for paragraph (4) substitute –

        '(4) Where the application is for forfeiture of bail, paragraph (3) applies with the exception of sub-paragraphs (a)(iii) and (b), (c), (e) and (g) of that paragraph';

    (c) in rule 41, for paragraphs (2), (3) and (4) substitute –

    '(2) Where bail is granted, varied or continued, the notice must state any bail conditions, including the amounts (if any) to be deposited by the bail party and any cautioners.

(3)   Where bail is refused or where the Tribunal orders forfeiture of bail, the notice must include reasons for the decision.

(4)   Where, instead of granting or refusing bail, the Tribunal fixes the amount and conditions of bail with a view to a bail bond being entered into subsequently before a person specified by the Tribunal, the notice must include the matters stated in paragraph (2) and the name or office of the person so specified.';

(d)   for rule 42 substitute –

'42.   Bail bond

(1)   Any bail bond of a bail party or cautioner must be in writing and, where the deposit of money is required as a condition of bail, must state –

        (a)   the amount to be deposited; and

        (b)   that the bail party and any cautioner understand that, if the bail party fails to answer to bail, all or part of the amount deposited may be forfeited.

(2)   The bail bond must be signed by the bail party and any cautioner and provided to the Tribunal, and a copy provided to –

        (a)   the parties,

        (b)   any person having custody of the bail party, and

        (c)   any cautioner.'

(e)   in rule 43, for sub-paragraph (b) substitute –

'(b)   being –

        (i)   provided with the notice of decision fixing the amount and conditions of the bail, and

        (ii)   satisfied that the amount, if any, to be deposited in accordance with those conditions has been deposited.'.

Tribunal Procedure (Upper Tribunal) Rules 2008 (extracts)

2. Overriding objective and parties' obligation to co-operate with the Upper Tribunal

(1)   The overriding objective of these Rules is to enable the Upper Tribunal to deal with cases fairly and justly.

(2)   Dealing with a case fairly and justly includes –

    (a)   dealing with the case in ways which are proportionate to the importance of the case, the complexity of the issues, the anticipated costs and the resources of the parties;

    (b)   avoiding unnecessary formality and seeking flexibility in the proceedings;

    (c)   ensuring, so far as practicable, that the parties are able to participate fully in the proceedings;

    (d)   using any special expertise of the Upper Tribunal effectively; and

    (e)   avoiding delay, so far as compatible with proper consideration of the issues.

(3)   The Upper Tribunal must seek to give effect to the overriding objective when it –

    (a)   exercises any power under these Rules; or

    (b)   interprets any rule or practice direction.

(4)   Parties must –

    (a)   help the Upper Tribunal to further the overriding objective; and

    (b)   co-operate with the Upper Tribunal generally.

5. Case management powers

(1)   Subject to the provisions of the 2007 Act and any other enactment, the Upper Tribunal may regulate its own procedure.

(2)   The Upper Tribunal may give a direction in relation to the conduct or disposal of proceedings at any time, including a direction amending, suspending or setting aside an earlier direction.

(3)   In particular, and without restricting the general powers in paragraphs (1) and (2), the Upper Tribunal may –

    (a)   extend or shorten the time for complying with any rule, practice direction or direction;

    (b)   consolidate or hear together two or more sets of proceedings or parts of proceedings raising common issues, or treat a case as a lead case;

    (c)   permit or require a party to amend a document;

    (d)   permit or require a party or another person to provide documents, information, evidence or submissions to the Upper Tribunal or a party;

    (e)   deal with an issue in the proceedings as a preliminary issue;

(f)   hold a hearing to consider any matter, including a case management issue;

(g)   decide the form of any hearing;

(h)   adjourn or postpone a hearing;

(i)   require a party to produce a bundle for a hearing;

(j)   stay (or, in Scotland, sist) proceedings;

(k)   transfer proceedings to another court or tribunal if that other court or tribunal has jurisdiction in relation to the proceedings and –

    (i)   because of a change of circumstances since the proceedings were started, the Upper Tribunal no longer has jurisdiction in relation to the proceedings; or

    (ii)   the Upper Tribunal considers that the other court or tribunal is a more appropriate forum for the determination of the case;

(l)   suspend the effect of its own decision pending an appeal or review of that decision;

(m)   in an appeal, or an application for permission to appeal, against the decision of another tribunal, suspend the effect of that decision pending the determination of the application for permission to appeal, and any appeal;

(n)   require any person, body or other tribunal whose decision is the subject of proceedings before the Upper Tribunal to provide reasons for the decision, or other information or documents in relation to the decision or any proceedings before that person, body or tribunal.

(4)   The Upper Tribunal may direct that a fast-track case cease to be treated as a fast-track case if –

(a)   all the parties consent; or

(b)   the Upper Tribunal is satisfied that the appeal or application could not be justly determined if it were treated as a fast-track case;

…

6. Procedure for applying for and giving directions

(1)   The Upper Tribunal may give a direction on the application of one or more of the parties or on its own initiative.

(2)   An application for a direction may be made –

(a)   by sending or delivering a written application to the Upper Tribunal; or

(b)   orally during the course of a hearing.

(3)   An application for a direction must include the reason for making that application.

(4)   Unless the Upper Tribunal considers that there is good reason not to do so, the Upper Tribunal must send written notice of any direction to every party and to any other person affected by the direction.

(5)   If a party or any other person sent notice of the direction under paragraph (4) wishes to challenge a direction which the Upper Tribunal has given, they may do so by applying for another direction which amends, suspends or sets aside the first direction.

12. Calculating time

(1)   An act required by these Rules, a practice direction or a direction to be done on or by a particular day must be done by 5pm on that day.

(2)   If the time specified by these Rules, a practice direction or a direction for doing any act ends on a day other than a working day, the act is done in time if it is done on the next working day.

(3)   In a special educational needs case or a disability discrimination in schools case, the following days must not be counted when calculating the time by which an act must be done –

    (a)   25th December to 1st January inclusive; and

    (b)   any day in August.

(3A)   In an asylum case or an immigration case, when calculating the time by which an act must be done, in addition to the days specified in the definition of 'working days' in rule 1(interpretation), the following days must also not be counted as working days –

    (a)   27th to 31st December inclusive;

(4)   Paragraph (3) or (3A) does not apply where the Upper Tribunal directs that an act must be done by or on a specified date.

...

13. Sending and delivery of documents

(1)   Any document to be provided to the Upper Tribunal under these Rules, a practice direction or a direction must be –

    (a)   sent by pre-paid post or by document exchange, or delivered by hand,[1] to the address specified for the proceedings;

    (b)   sent by fax to the number specified for the proceedings; or

    (c)   sent or delivered by such other method as the Upper Tribunal may permit or direct.

(2)   Subject to paragraph (3), if a party provides a fax number, email address or other details for the electronic transmission of documents to them, that party must accept delivery of documents by that method.

(3)   If a party informs the Upper Tribunal and all other parties that a particular form of communication, other than pre-paid post or delivery by hand, should not be used to provide documents to that party, that form of communication must not be so used.

(4)   If the Upper Tribunal or a party sends a document to a party or the Upper Tribunal by email or any other electronic means of communication, the recipient may request that the sender provide a hard copy of the document to the recipient. The recipient must make such a request as soon as reasonably practicable after receiving the document electronically.

(5)   The Upper Tribunal and each party may assume that the address provided by a party or its representative is and remains the address to which documents should be sent or delivered until receiving written notification to the contrary.

(6)   Subject to paragraph (7), if a document submitted to the Upper Tribunal is not written in English, it must be accompanied by an English translation.

(7)   In proceedings that are in Wales or have a connection with Wales, a document or translation may be submitted to the Upper Tribunal in Welsh.

15. Evidence and submissions

(1)   Without restriction on the general powers in rule 5(1) and (2) (case management powers), the Upper Tribunal may give directions as to –

    (a)   issues on which it requires evidence or submissions;

(b)   the nature of the evidence or submissions it requires;

(c)   whether the parties are permitted or required to provide expert evidence, and if so whether the parties must jointly appoint a single expert to provide such evidence;

(d)   any limit on the number of witnesses whose evidence a party may put forward, whether in relation to a particular issue or generally;

(e)   the manner in which any evidence or submissions are to be provided, which may include a direction for them to be given –

    (i)   orally at a hearing; or

    (ii)   by written submissions or witness statement; and

(f)   the time at which any evidence or submissions are to be provided.

(2)   The Upper Tribunal may –

(a)   admit evidence whether or not –

    (i)   the evidence would be admissible in a civil trial in the United Kingdom; or

    (ii)   the evidence was available to a previous decision maker; or

(b)   exclude evidence that would otherwise be admissible where –

    (i)   the evidence was not provided within the time allowed by a direction or a practice direction;

    (ii)   the evidence was otherwise provided in a manner that did not comply with a direction or a practice direction; or

    (iii)   it would otherwise be unfair to admit the evidence.

(2A)   In an asylum case or an immigration case –

(a)   if a party wishes the Upper Tribunal to consider evidence that was not before the First-tier Tribunal, that party must send or deliver a notice to the Upper Tribunal and any other party –

    (i)   indicating the nature of the evidence; and

    (ii)   explaining why it was not submitted to the First-tier Tribunal; and

(b)   when considering whether to admit evidence that was not before the First-tier Tribunal, the Upper Tribunal must have regard to whether there has been unreasonable delay in producing that evidence.

(3)   The Upper Tribunal may consent to a witness giving, or require any witness to give, evidence on oath, and may administer an oath for that purpose.

17. Withdrawal

(1)   Subject to paragraph (2), a party may give notice of the withdrawal of its case, or any part of it –

(a)   . . . by sending or delivering to the Upper Tribunal a written notice of withdrawal; or

(b)   orally at a hearing.

(2)   Notice of withdrawal will not take effect unless the Upper Tribunal consents to the withdrawal except in relation to an application for permission to appeal.

(3)   A party which has withdrawn its case may apply to the Upper Tribunal for the case to be reinstated.

(4)   An application under paragraph (3) must be made in writing and be received by the Upper Tribunal within 1 month after –

    (a)   the date on which the Upper Tribunal received the notice under paragraph (1)(a); or

    (b)   the date of the hearing at which the case was withdrawn orally under paragraph (1)(b).

(5)   The Upper Tribunal must notify each party in writing that a withdrawal has taken effect under this rule.

(6)   Paragraph (3) does not apply to a financial services case other than a reference against a penalty.

17A.   Appeal treated as abandoned or finally determined in an asylum case or an immigration case

(1)   A party to an asylum case or an immigration case before the Upper Tribunal must notify the Upper Tribunal if they are aware that –

    (a)   the appellant has left the United Kingdom;

    (b)   the appellant has been granted leave to enter or remain in the United Kingdom;

    (c)   a deportation order has been made against the appellant; or

    (d)   a document listed in paragraph 4(2) of Schedule 2 to the Immigration (European Economic Area) Regulations 2006 has been issued to the appellant.

(2)   Where an appeal is treated as abandoned pursuant to section 104(4) or (4A) of the Nationality, Immigration and Asylum Act 2002 or paragraph 4(2) of Schedule 2 to the Immigration (European Economic Area) Regulations 2006, or as finally determined pursuant to section 104(5) of the Nationality, Immigration and Asylum Act 2002, the Upper Tribunal must send the parties a notice informing them that the appeal is being treated as abandoned or finally determined.

(3)   Where an appeal would otherwise fall to be treated as abandoned pursuant to section 104(4A) of the Nationality, Immigration and Asylum Act 2002, but the appellant wishes to pursue their appeal, the appellant must send or deliver a notice, which must comply with any relevant practice directions, to the Upper Tribunal and the respondent so that it is received within thirty days of the date on which the notice of the grant of leave to enter or remain in the United Kingdom was sent to the appellant.

(4)   Where a notice of grant of leave to enter or remain is sent electronically or delivered personally, the time limit in paragraph (3) is twenty eight days.

(5)   Notwithstanding rule 5(3)(a) (case management powers) and rule 7(2) (failure to comply with rules etc.), the Upper Tribunal must not extend the time limits in paragraph (3) and (4).

21.   Application to the Upper Tribunal for permission to appeal

(1)   [*Repealed*]

(2)   A person may apply to the Upper Tribunal for permission to appeal to the Upper Tribunal against a decision of another tribunal only if –

    (a)   they have made an application for permission to appeal to the tribunal which made the decision challenged; and

    (b)   that application has been refused or has not been admitted or has been granted only on limited grounds.

(3)   An application for permission to appeal must be made in writing and received by the Upper Tribunal no later than –

(a) in the case of an application under section 4 of the Safeguarding Vulnerable Groups Act 2006, 3 months after the date on which written notice of the decision being challenged was sent to the appellant;

(aa) in an asylum case or an immigration case where the appellant is in the United Kingdom at the time that the application is made –

    (i) 14 days after the date on which notice of the First-tier Tribunal's refusal of permission was sent to the appellant; or

    (ii) if the case is a fast-track case, four working days after the date on which notice of the First-tier Tribunal's refusal of permission was sent to the appellant;

(b) otherwise, a month after the date on which the tribunal that made the decision under challenge sent notice of its refusal of permission to appeal, or refusal to admit the application for permission to appeal, to the appellant.

(4) The application must state –

(a) the name and address of the appellant;
(b) the name and address of the representative (if any) of the appellant;
(c) an address where documents for the appellant may be sent or delivered;
(d) details (including the full reference) of the decision challenged;
(e) the grounds on which the appellant relies; and
(f) whether the appellant wants the application to be dealt with at a hearing.

(5) The appellant must provide with the application a copy of –

(a) any written record of the decision being challenged;
(b) any separate written statement of reasons for that decision; and
(c) if the application is for permission to appeal against a decision of another tribunal, the notice of refusal of permission to appeal, or notice of refusal to admit the application for permission to appeal, from that other tribunal.

(6) If the appellant provides the application to the Upper Tribunal later than the time required by paragraph (3) or by an extension of time allowed under rule 5(3)(a) (power to extend time) –

(a) the application must include a request for an extension of time and the reason why the application was not provided in time; and
(b) unless the Upper Tribunal extends time for the application under rule 5(3)(a) (power to extend time) the Upper Tribunal must not admit the application.

(7) If the appellant makes an application to the Upper Tribunal for permission to appeal against the decision of another tribunal, and that other tribunal refused to admit the appellant's application for permission to appeal because the application for permission or for a written statement of reasons was not made in time –

(a) the application to the Upper Tribunal for permission to appeal must include the reason why the application to the other tribunal for permission to appeal or for a written statement of reasons, as the case may be, was not made in time; and
(b) the Upper Tribunal must only admit the application if the Upper Tribunal considers that it is in the interests of justice for it to do so.

(8) In this rule, a reference to notice of a refusal of permission to appeal is to be taken to include a reference to notice of a grant of permission to appeal on limited grounds.

22A.   Special procedure for providing notice of a refusal of permission to appeal in an asylum case

(1)   This rule applies to a decision in an asylum case to refuse permission to appeal or to refuse to admit a late application for permission to appeal, where –

    (a)   the appellant is not the Secretary of State;

    (b)   at the time the application is made the appellant is in the United Kingdom; and

    (c)   the decision is not made in a fast-track case.

(2)   The Upper Tribunal must provide written notice of the refusal and of the reasons for the refusal ('the notice') to the Secretary of State as soon as reasonably practicable.

(3)   The Secretary of State must –

    (a)   send the notice to the appellant not later than 30 days after the Upper Tribunal provided it to the Secretary of State; and

    (b)   as soon as practicable after doing so, inform the Upper Tribunal of the date on which, and the means by which, it was sent.

(4)   If the Secretary of State does not give the Upper Tribunal the information required by paragraph (3)(b) within 31 days after the notice was provided to the Secretary of State, the Upper Tribunal must send the notice to the appellant as soon as reasonably practicable.

24.   Response to the notice of appeal

(1)   This rule and rule 25 do not apply to a road transport case, in respect of which Schedule 1 makes alternative provision.

(1A)   Subject to any direction given by the Upper Tribunal, a respondent may provide a response to a notice of appeal.

(2)   Any response provided under paragraph (1A) must be in writing and must be sent or delivered to the Upper Tribunal so that it is received –

    (a)   if an application for permission to appeal stands as the notice of appeal, no later than one month after the date on which the respondent was sent notice that permission to appeal had been granted;

    (aa)   in a fast-track case, two days before the hearing of the appeal;

    (ab)   in a quality contracts scheme case, no later than 1 month after the date on which a copy of the notice of appeal is sent to the respondent; or

    (b)   in any other case, no later than 1 month after the date on which the Upper Tribunal sent a copy of the notice of appeal to the respondent.

(3)   The response must state –

    (a)   the name and address of the respondent;

    (b)   the name and address of the representative (if any) of the respondent;

    (c)   an address where documents for the respondent may be sent or delivered;

    (d)   whether the respondent opposes the appeal;

    (e)   the grounds on which the respondent relies, including (in the case of an appeal against the decision of another tribunal) any grounds on which the respondent was unsuccessful in the proceedings which are the subject of the appeal, but intends to rely in the appeal; and

    (f)   whether the respondent wants the case to be dealt with at a hearing.

(4)   If the respondent provides the response to the Upper Tribunal later than the time required by paragraph (2) or by an extension of time allowed under rule 5(3)(a)

(power to extend time), the response must include a request for an extension of time and the reason why the response was not provided in time.

(5)   When the Upper Tribunal receives the response it must send a copy of the response and any accompanying documents to the appellant and each other party.

25. Appellant's reply

(1)   Subject to any direction given by the Upper Tribunal, the appellant may provide a reply to any response provided under rule 24 (response to the notice of appeal).

(2)   Subject to paragraph (2A), any reply provided under paragraph (1) must be in writing and must be sent or delivered to the Upper Tribunal so that it is received within one month after the date on which the Upper Tribunal sent a copy of the response to the appellant.

(2A)   In an asylum case or an immigration case, the time limit in paragraph (2) is –

    (a)   one month after the date on which the Upper Tribunal sent a copy of the response to the appellant, or five days before the hearing of the appeal, whichever is the earlier; and

    (b)   in a fast-track case, the day of the hearing.

...

(3)   When the Upper Tribunal receives the reply it must send a copy of the reply and any accompanying documents to each respondent.

...

36A. Special time limits for hearing an appeal in a fast-track case

(1)   Subject to rule 36(2)(aa) (notice of hearings) and paragraph (2) of this rule, where permission to appeal to the Upper Tribunal has been given in a fast-track case, the Upper Tribunal must start the hearing of the appeal not later than –

    (a)   five working days after the date on which the First-tier Tribunal or the Upper Tribunal sent notice of its grant of permission to appeal to the appellant; or

    (b)   where the notice of its grant of permission to appeal is sent electronically or delivered personally, two working days after the date on which the First-tier Tribunal or the Upper Tribunal sent notice of its grant of permission to appeal to the appellant.

(2)   If the Upper Tribunal is unable to arrange for the hearing to start within the time specified in paragraph (1), it must set a date for the hearing as soon as is reasonably practicable.

44. Application for permission to appeal

(1)   Subject to paragraphs (4A) and (4B), a person seeking permission to appeal must make a written application to the Upper Tribunal for permission to appeal.

...

(3A)   An application under paragraph (1) in respect of a decision in an asylum case or an immigration case must be sent or delivered to the Upper Tribunal so that it is received within the appropriate period after the Upper Tribunal or, as the case may be in an asylum case, the Secretary of State for the Home Department, sent any of the documents in paragraph (3) to the party making the application.

(3B)   The appropriate period referred to in paragraph (3A) is as follows –

       (a)   where the person who appealed to the First-tier Tribunal is in the United Kingdom at the time that the application is made –

           (i)   twelve working days; or
           (ii)   if the party making the application is in detention under the Immigration Acts, seven working days; and

       (b)   where the person who appealed to the First-tier Tribunal is outside the United Kingdom at the time that the application is made, thirty eight days.

(3C)   Where a notice of decision is sent electronically or delivered personally, the time limits in paragraph (3B) are –

       (a)   in sub-paragraph (a)(i), ten working days;
       (b)   in sub-paragraph (a)(ii), five working days; and
       (c)   in sub-paragraph (b), ten working days.

…

(4A)   Where a decision that disposes of immigration judicial review proceedings is given at a hearing, a party may apply at that hearing for permission to appeal, and the Upper Tribunal must consider at the hearing whether to give or refuse permission to appeal.

(4B)   Where a decision that disposes of immigration judicial review proceedings is given at a hearing and no application for permission to appeal is made at that hearing –

       (a)   the Upper Tribunal must nonetheless consider at the hearing whether to give or refuse permission to appeal; and
       (b)   if permission to appeal is given to a party, it shall be deemed for the purposes of section 13(4) of the 2007 Act to be given on application by that party.

(4C)   Where a decision that disposes of immigration judicial review proceedings is given pursuant to rule 30 and the Upper Tribunal records under rule 30(4A) that the application is totally without merit, an application under paragraph (1) must be sent or delivered to the Upper Tribunal so that it is received within 7 days after the later of the dates on which the Upper Tribunal sent to the applicant –

       (a)   written reasons for the decision; or
       (b)   notification of amended reasons for, or correction of, the decision following a review.

(5)   The date in paragraph (3)(c) or (4)(c) applies only if the application for the decision to be set aside was made within the time stipulated in rule 43 (setting aside a decision which disposes of proceedings) or any extension of that time granted by the Upper Tribunal.

(6)   If the person seeking permission to appeal provides the application to the Upper Tribunal later than the time required by paragraph (3), (3A), (3D) or (4), or by any extension of time under rule 5(3)(a) (power to extend time) –

       (a)   the application must include a request for an extension of time and the reason why the application notice was not provided in time; and
       (b)   unless the Upper Tribunal extends time for the application under rule 5(3)(a) (power to extend time) the Upper Tribunal must refuse the application.

(7)   An application under paragraph (1) or (4A)(a) must –

       (a)   identify the decision of the Tribunal to which it relates;
       (b)   identify the alleged error or errors of law in the decision; and
       (c)   state the result the party making the application is seeking.

45. Upper Tribunal's consideration of application for permission to appeal

(1)   On receiving an application for permission to appeal the Upper Tribunal may review the decision in accordance with rule 46 (review of a decision), but may only do so if –

  (a)   when making the decision the Upper Tribunal overlooked a legislative provision or binding authority which could have had a material effect on the decision; or

  (b)   since the Upper Tribunal's decision, a court has made a decision which is binding on the Upper Tribunal and which, had it been made before the Upper Tribunal's decision, could have had a material effect on the decision.

(2)   If the Upper Tribunal decides not to review the decision, or reviews the decision and decides to take no action in relation to the decision or part of it, the Upper Tribunal must consider whether to give permission to appeal in relation to the decision or that part of it.

(3)   The Upper Tribunal must send a record of its decision to the parties as soon as practicable.

(4)   If the Upper Tribunal refuses permission to appeal it must send with the record of its decision –

  (a)   a statement of its reasons for such refusal; and

  (b)   notification of the right to make an application to the relevant appellate court for permission to appeal and the time within which, and the method by which, such application must be made.

(5)   The Upper Tribunal may give permission to appeal on limited grounds, but must comply with paragraph (4) in relation to any grounds on which it has refused permission.

46. Review of a decision

(1)   The Upper Tribunal may only undertake a review of a decision pursuant to rule 45(1) (review on an application for permission to appeal).

(2)   The Upper Tribunal must notify the parties in writing of the outcome of any review and of any rights of review or appeal in relation to the outcome.

(3)   If the Upper Tribunal decides to take any action in relation to a decision following a review without first giving every party an opportunity to make representations, the notice under paragraph (2) must state that any party that did not have an opportunity to make representations may apply for such action to be set aside and for the decision to be reviewed again.

Practice Directions: Immigration and Asylum Chambers of the First-tier Tribunal and the Upper Tribunal (extracts)

PART 3
PRACTICE DIRECTIONS FOR THE IMMIGRATION AND ASYLUM CHAMBER OF THE UPPER TRIBUNAL

3 Procedure on appeal

3.1   Where permission to appeal to the Upper Tribunal has been granted, then, unless and to the extent that they are directed otherwise, for the purposes of preparing for a hearing in the Upper Tribunal the parties should assume that:–

(a)   the Upper Tribunal will decide whether the making of the decision of the First-tier Tribunal involved the making of an error on a point of law, such that the decision should be set aside under section 12(2)(a) of the 2007 Act;

(b)   except as specified in Practice Statement 7.2 (disposal of appeals by Upper Tribunal), the Upper Tribunal will proceed to re-make the decision under section 12(2)(b)(ii), if satisfied that the original decision should be set aside; and

(c)   in that event, the Upper Tribunal will consider whether to remake the decision by reference to the First-tier Tribunal's findings of fact and any new documentary evidence submitted under UT rule 15(2A) which it is reasonably practicable to adduce for consideration at that hearing.

3.2   The parties should be aware that, in the circumstances described in paragraph 3.1(c), the Upper Tribunal will generally expect to proceed, without any further hearing, to re-make the decision, where this can be undertaken without having to hear oral evidence. In certain circumstances, the Upper Tribunal may give directions for the giving of oral evidence at the relevant hearing, where it appears appropriate to do so. Such directions may be given before or at that hearing.

3.3   In a case where no oral evidence is likely to be required in order for the Upper Tribunal to re-make the decision, the Upper Tribunal will therefore expect any documentary evidence relevant to the re-making of the decision to be adduced in accordance with Practice Direction 4 so that it may be considered at the relevant hearing; and, accordingly, the party seeking to rely on such documentary evidence will be expected to show good reason why it is not reasonably practicable to adduce the same in order for it to be considered at that hearing.

3.4   If the Upper Tribunal nevertheless decides that it cannot proceed as described in paragraph 3.1(c) because findings of fact are needed which it is not in a position to make, the Upper Tribunal will make arrangements for the adjournment of the hearing, so that the proceedings may be completed before the same constitution of the Tribunal; or, if that is not reasonably practicable, for their transfer to a different constitution, in either case so as to enable evidence to be adduced for that purpose.

3.5 Where proceedings are transferred in the circumstances described in paragraph 3.4, any documents sent to or given by the Tribunal from which the proceedings are transferred shall be deemed to have been sent to or given by the Tribunal to which those proceedings are transferred.

3.6 Where such proceedings are transferred, the Upper Tribunal shall prepare written reasons for finding that the First-tier Tribunal made an error of law, such that its decision fell to be set aside, and those written reasons shall be sent to the parties before the next hearing.

3.7 The written reasons shall be incorporated in full in, and form part of, the determination of the Upper Tribunal that re-makes the decision. Only in very exceptional cases can the decision contained in those written reasons be departed from or varied by the Upper Tribunal which re-makes the decision under section 12(2)(b)(ii) of the 2007 Act.

3.8 Unless directed otherwise, the parties to any fast track appeal which is before the Upper Tribunal will be expected to attend with all necessary witnesses and evidence that may be required if the Upper Tribunal should decide that it is necessary to set aside the decision of the First-tier Tribunal and re-make the decision. It will be unusual for the Upper Tribunal to adjourn or transfer, but, if it does so, paragraph 3.6 and 3.7 will, so far as appropriate, apply. 3.9 In this Practice Direction and Practice Direction 4, 'the relevant hearing' means a hearing fixed by the Upper Tribunal at which it will consider if the First-tier Tribunal made an error of law.

3.10 Without prejudice to the generality of paragraph 1.5, where, by virtue of any transitional provisions in Schedule 4 to the Transfer of Functions Order, the Upper Tribunal is undertaking the reconsideration of a decision of the AIT, references in this Practice Direction and Practice Direction 4 to the First-tier Tribunal shall be construed as references to the AIT.

4   Evidence

4.1 UT rule 15(2A) imposes important procedural requirements where the Upper Tribunal is asked to consider evidence that was not before the First-tier Tribunal. UT rule 15(2A) must be complied with in every case where permission to appeal is granted and a party wishes the Upper Tribunal to consider such evidence. Notice under rule 15(2A)(a), indicating the nature of the evidence and explaining why it was not submitted to the First-tier Tribunal, must be filed with the Upper Tribunal and served on the other party within the time stated in any specific directions given by the Upper Tribunal; or, if no such direction has been given, as soon as practicable after permission to appeal has been granted.

4.2 A party who wishes the Upper Tribunal to consider any evidence that was not before the First-tier Tribunal must indicate in the notice whether the evidence is sought to be adduced:–

   (a)   in connection with the issue of whether the First-tier Tribunal made an error of law, requiring its decision to be set aside; or

   (b)   in connection with the re-making of the decision by the Upper Tribunal, in the event of the First-tier Tribunal being found to have made such an error.

4.3 The notice must clearly indicate whether the party concerned wishes the evidence to be considered at the relevant hearing and state whether the evidence is in oral or documentary form.

4.4 Where a party wishes, in the circumstances described in paragraph 4.2(b), to adduce only documentary evidence, Practice Direction 3.3 will apply.

4.5   Where a party wishes, in the circumstances described in paragraph 4.2(b), to adduce oral evidence at the relevant hearing, the notice must explain why it is considered desirable to proceed in such a manner and give details of the oral evidence and a time estimate.

4.6   Where the Upper Tribunal acts under Practice Direction 3 to adjourn or transfer the hearing, it shall consider any notice given under UT rule 15(2A) and give any directions arising therefrom, if and to the extent that this has not already been done.

4.7   This Practice Direction does not apply in the case of a fast track appeal (as to which, see Practice Direction 3.8).

PART 4
PRACTICE DIRECTIONS FOR THE IMMIGRATION AND ASYLUM CHAMBER OF THE FIRST-TIER TRIBUNAL AND THE UPPER TRIBUNAL

7   Case management review hearings and directions

7.1   Where the Tribunal so directs, a CMR hearing will be held in the case of an appeal where the party who is or was the appellant before the First-tier Tribunal:–

(a)   is present in the United Kingdom; and
(b)   has a right of appeal whilst in the United Kingdom.

7.2   It is important that the parties and their representatives understand that a CMR hearing is a hearing in the appeal and that the appeal may be determined under the relevant Procedure Rules if a party does not appear and is not represented at that hearing.

7.3   In addition to any information required by First-tier rule 19 (notice of appeal), the appellant before the First-tier Tribunal must provide that Tribunal and the respondent at the CMR hearing with:–

(a)   particulars of any application for permission to vary the grounds of appeal;
(b)   particulars of any amendments to the reasons in support of the grounds of appeal;
(c)   particulars of any witnesses to be called or whose written statement or report is proposed to be relied upon at the full hearing; and
(d)   the draft of any directions that the appellant is requesting the Tribunal to make at the CMR hearing.

7.4   In addition to any documents required by relevant Procedure Rules, the party who is or was the respondent before the First-tier Tribunal must provide the Tribunal and the other party at the CMR hearing with:–

(a)   any amendment that has been made or is proposed to be made to the notice of decision to which the appeal relates or to any other document served on the person concerned giving reasons for that decision; and
(b)   a draft of any directions that the Tribunal is requested to make at the CMR hearing.

7.5   In most cases, including those appeals where a CMR hearing is to be held, the Tribunal will normally have given to the parties the following directions with the notice of hearing:-

(a)   not later than 5 working days before the full hearing (or 10 days in the case of an out-of-country appeal) the appellant shall serve on the Tribunal and the respondent:

      (i)   witness statements of the evidence to be called at the hearing, such statements to stand as evidence in chief at the hearing;

      (ii)   a paginated and indexed bundle of all the documents to be relied on at the hearing with a schedule identifying the essential passages;

      (iii) a skeleton argument, identifying all relevant issues including human rights claims and citing all the authorities relied upon; and

      (iv) a chronology of events;

   (b)   not later than 5 working days before the full hearing, the respondent shall serve on the Tribunal and the appellant a paginated and indexed bundle of all the documents to be relied upon at the hearing, with a schedule identifying the relevant passages, and a list of any authorities relied upon.

7.6   At the end of the CMR hearing, the Tribunal will give the parties any further written directions relating to the conduct of the appeal.

7.7   Although in normal circumstances a witness statement should stand as evidence-in-chief, there may be cases where it will be appropriate for appellants or witnesses to have the opportunity of adding to or supplementing their witness statements.

7.8   In addition to the directions referred to above, at the end of the CMR hearing the Tribunal will also give to the parties written confirmation of:–

   (a)   any issues that have been agreed at the CMR hearing as being relevant to the determination of the appeal; and

   (b)   any concessions made at the CMR hearing by a party.

9   Adjournments

9.1   Applications for the adjournment of appeals (other than fast track appeals) listed for hearing before the Tribunal must be made not later than 5.00p.m. one clear working day before the date of the hearing.

9.2   For the avoidance of doubt, where a case is listed for hearing on, for example, a Friday, the application must be received by 5.00p.m. on the Wednesday.

9.3   The application for an adjournment must be supported by full reasons and must be made in accordance with relevant Procedure Rules.

9.4   Any application made later than the end of the period mentioned in paragraph 9.1 must be made to the Tribunal at the hearing and will require the attendance of the party or the representative of the party seeking the adjournment.

9.5   It will be only in the most exceptional circumstances that a late application for an adjournment will be considered without the attendance of a party or representative.

9.6   Parties must not assume that an application, even if made in accordance with paragraph 9.1, will be successful and they must always check with the Tribunal as to the outcome of the application.

9.7   Any application for the adjournment of a fast track appeal must be made to the Tribunal at the hearing and will be considered by the Tribunal in accordance with relevant Procedure Rules.

9.8   If an adjournment is not granted and the party fails to attend the hearing, the Tribunal may in certain circumstances proceed with the hearing in that party's absence.

10   Expert evidence

10.1   A party who instructs an expert must provide clear and precise instructions to the expert, together with all relevant information concerning the nature of the appellant's case, including the appellant's immigration history, the reasons why the appellant's claim or application has been refused by the respondent and copies of any relevant previous reports prepared in respect of the appellant.

10.2   It is the duty of an expert to help the Tribunal on matters within the expert's own expertise. This duty is paramount and overrides any obligation to the person from whom the expert has received instructions or by whom the expert is paid.

10.3   Expert evidence should be the independent product of the expert uninfluenced by the pressures of litigation.

10.4   An expert should assist the Tribunal by providing objective, unbiased opinion on matters within his or her expertise, and should not assume the role of an advocate.

10.5   An expert should consider all material facts, including those which might detract from his or her opinion.

10.6   An expert should make it clear:–

(a)   when a question or issue falls outside his or her expertise; and

(b)   when the expert is not able to reach a definite opinion, for example because of insufficient information.

10.7   If, after producing a report, an expert changes his or her view on any material matter, that change of view should be communicated to the parties without delay, and when appropriate to the Tribunal.

10.8   An expert's report should be addressed to the Tribunal and not to the party from whom the expert has received instructions.

10.9   An expert's report must:–

(a)   give details of the expert's qualifications;

(b)   give details of any literature or other material which the expert has relied on in making the report;

(c)   contain a statement setting out the substance of all facts and instructions given to the expert which are material to the opinions expressed in the report or upon which those opinions are based;

(d)   make clear which of the facts stated in the report are within the expert's own knowledge;

(e)   say who carried out any examination, measurement or other procedure which the expert has used for the report, give the qualifications of that person, and say whether or not the procedure has been carried out under the expert's supervision;

(f)   where there is a range of opinion on the matters dealt with in the report:

(i)   summarise the range of opinion, so far as reasonably practicable, and

(ii)   give reasons for the expert's own opinion;

(g)   contain a summary of the conclusions reached;

(h)   if the expert is not able to give an opinion without qualification, state the qualification; and

(j)   contain a statement that the expert understands his or her duty to the Tribunal, and has complied and will continue to comply with that duty.

10.10   An expert's report must be verified by a Statement of Truth as well as containing the statements required in paragraph 10.9(h) and (j).

10.11   The form of the Statement of Truth is as follows:-

'I confirm that insofar as the facts stated in my report are within my own knowledge I have made clear which they are and I believe them to be true, and that the opinions I have expressed represent my true and complete professional opinion'.

10.12   The instructions referred to in paragraph 10.9(c) are not protected by privilege but cross-examination of the expert on the contents of the instructions will not be allowed unless the Tribunal permits it (or unless the party who gave the instructions consents to it). Before it gives permission the Tribunal must be satisfied that there are reasonable grounds to consider that the statement in the report or the substance of the instructions is inaccurate or incomplete. If the Tribunal is so satisfied, it will allow the cross-examination where it appears to be in the interests of justice to do so.

10.13 In this Practice Direction:–

'appellant' means the party who is or was the appellant before the First-tier Tribunal; and

'respondent' means the party who is or was the respondent before the First-tier Tribunal.

11 Citation of unreported determinations

11.1 A determination of the Tribunal which has not been reported may not be cited in proceedings before the Tribunal unless:–

(a) the person who is or was the appellant before the First-tier Tribunal, or a member of that person's family, was a party to the proceedings in which the previous determination was issued; or

(b) the Tribunal gives permission.

11.2 An application for permission to cite a determination which has not been reported must:–

(a) include a full transcript of the determination;

(b) identify the proposition for which the determination is to be cited; and

(c) certify that the proposition is not to be found in any reported determination of the Tribunal, the IAT or the AIT and had not been superseded by the decision of a higher authority.

11.3 Permission under paragraph 11.1 will be given only where the Tribunal considers that it would be materially assisted by citation of the determination, as distinct from the adoption in argument of the reasoning to be found in the determination. Such instances are likely to be rare; in particular, in the case of determinations which were unreportable (see Practice Statement 11 (reporting of determinations)). It should be emphasised that the Tribunal will not exclude good arguments from consideration but it will be rare for such an argument to be capable of being made only by reference to an unreported determination.

11.4 The provisions of paragraph 11.1 to 11.3 apply to unreported and unreportable determinations of the AIT, the IAT and adjudicators, as those provisions apply respectively to unreported and unreportable determinations of the Tribunal.

11.5 A party citing a determination of the IAT bearing a neutral citation number prior to 2003 (including all series of 'bracket numbers') must be in a position to certify that the matter or proposition for which the determination is cited has not been the subject of more recent, reported, determinations of the IAT, the AIT or the Tribunal.

11.6 In this Practice Direction and Practice Direction 12, 'determination' includes any decision of the AIT or the Tribunal.

12 Starred and Country Guidance determinations

12.1 Reported determinations of the Tribunal, the AIT and the IAT which are 'starred' shall be treated by the Tribunal as authoritative in respect of the matter to which the 'starring' relates, unless inconsistent with other authority that is binding on the Tribunal.

12.2 A reported determination of the Tribunal, the AIT or the IAT bearing the letters 'CG' shall be treated as an authoritative finding on the country guidance issue identified in the determination, based upon the evidence before the members of the Tribunal, the AIT or the IAT that determine the appeal. As a result, unless it has been expressly superseded or replaced by any later 'CG' determination, or is inconsistent with other authority that is binding on the Tribunal, such a country guidance case is authoritative in any subsequent appeal, so far as that appeal:–

(a)   relates to the country guidance issue in question; and
(b)   depends upon the same or similar evidence.

12.3 A list of current CG cases will be maintained on the Tribunal's website. Any representative of a party to an appeal concerning a particular country will be expected to be conversant with the current 'CG' determinations relating to that country.

12.4 Because of the principle that like cases should be treated in like manner, any failure to follow a clear, apparently applicable country guidance case or to show why it does not apply to the case in question is likely to be regarded as grounds for appeal on a point of law.

13   Bail applications

13.1 Subject to First-tier Rule 39(3), an application for bail must if practicable be listed for hearing within three working days of receipt by the Tribunal of the notice of application.

13.2 Any such notice which is received by the Tribunal after 3.30p.m. on a particular day will be treated for the purposes of this paragraph as if it were received on the next business day.

13.3 An Upper Tribunal judge may exercise bail jurisdiction under the Immigration Act 1971 by reason of being also a First-tier judge.

13.4 Notwithstanding paragraph 13.3, it will usually be appropriate for a bail application to be made to an Upper Tribunal judge only where the appeal in question is being heard by the Upper Tribunal, or where a hearing before the Upper Tribunal is imminent. In case of doubt, a potential applicant should consult the bails section of the First-tier Tribunal.

14   This Practice Direction is made by the Senior President of Tribunals with the agreement of the Lord Chancellor. It is made in the exercise of powers conferred by the Tribunals, Courts and Enforcement Act 2007.

B4

Practice Statements: Immigration and Asylum Chambers of the First-tier Tribunal and the Upper Tribunal (extracts)

3 Where the Tribunal may not accept a notice of appeal

3.1 First-tier rule 22 (where the Tribunal may not accept a notice of appeal) imposes a duty on the Tribunal not to accept an invalid notice of appeal (in the circumstances described in rule 22(2)) and to serve notice to this effect on the person who gave the notice of appeal and on the respondent.

3.2 The Tribunal will scrutinise a notice of appeal as soon as practicable after it has been given. First-tier rule 22 makes no provision for the issue of validity to be determined by means of a hearing or by reference to any representations of the parties.

3.3 Once the Tribunal has served the notice described in paragraph 3.1, First tier rule 9 provides that the Tribunal must take no further action in relation to the notice of appeal. The decision under First-tier rule 22 is, accordingly, a procedural or preliminary decision.

3.4 The fact that a hearing date may have been given to the parties does not mean that the appeal must be treated as valid. Accordingly, if at a hearing (including a CMR hearing) it transpires that the notice of appeal does not relate to a decision against which there is, in the circumstances, an exercisable right of appeal, the Tribunal must so find; but it will do so in the form of a determination, rather than by means of a notice under First tier rule 9.

5 Record of proceedings

5.1 The Tribunal shall keep a record of proceedings of any hearing and attach that record to the Tribunal's case file.

7 Disposal of appeals in Upper Tribunal

7.1 Where under section 12(1) of the 2007 Act (proceedings on appeal to the Upper Tribunal) the Upper Tribunal finds that the making of the decision concerned involved the making of an error on a point of law, the Upper Tribunal may set aside the decision and, if it does so, must either remit the case to the First-tier Tribunal under section 12(2)(b)(i) or proceed (in accordance with relevant Practice Directions) to re-make the decision under section 12(2)(b)(ii).

7.2 The Upper Tribunal is likely on each such occasion to proceed to re-make the decision, instead of remitting the case to the First-tier Tribunal, unless the Upper Tribunal is satisfied that:–

(a) the effect of the error has been to deprive a party before the First-tier Tribunal of a fair hearing or other opportunity for that party's case to be put to and considered by the First-tier Tribunal; or

(b)   the nature or extent of any judicial fact finding which is necessary in order for the decision in the appeal to be re-made is such that, having regard to the overriding objective in rule 2, it is appropriate to remit the case to the First-tier Tribunal.

7.3   Remaking rather than remitting will nevertheless constitute the normal approach to determining appeals where an error of law is found, even if some further fact finding is necessary.

International conventions and EU-derived statutory instruments

Immigration (European Economic Area) Regulations 2006 (extracts)

'Family member who has retained the right of residence'

10.   (1)   In these Regulations, 'family member who has retained the right of residence' means, subject to paragraph (8), a person who satisfies the conditions in paragraph (2), (3), (4) or (5).

     …

     (5)   A person satisfies the conditions in this paragraph if –

        (a)   he ceased to be a family member of a qualified person or of an EEA national with a permanent right of residence on the termination of the marriage or civil partnership of that person;

        (b)   he was residing in the United Kingdom in accordance with these Regulations at the date of the termination;

        (c)   he satisfies the condition in paragraph (6); and

        (d)   either –

            (i)   prior to the initiation of the proceedings for the termination of the marriage or the civil partnership the marriage or civil partnership had lasted for at least three years and the parties to the marriage or civil partnership had resided in the United Kingdom for at least one year during its duration;

            (ii)   the former spouse or civil partner of the qualified person has custody of a child of the qualified person or the EEA national with a permanent right of residence;

            (iii)   the former spouse or civil partner of the qualified person or the EEA national with a permanent right of residence has the right of access to a child of the qualified person or the EEA national with a permanent right of residence, where the child is under the age of 18 and where a court has ordered that such access must take place in the United Kingdom; or

            (iv)   the continued right of residence in the United Kingdom of the person is warranted by particularly difficult circumstances, such as he or another family member having been a victim of domestic violence while the marriage or civil partnership was subsisting.

     (6)   The condition in this paragraph is that the person –

        (a)   is not an EEA national but would, if he were an EEA national, be a worker, a self-employed person or a self-sufficient person under regulation 6; or

        (b)   is the family member of a person who falls within paragraph (a). (7) In this regulation, 'educational course' means a course within the scope of

Article 12 of Council Regulation (EEC) No. 1612/68 on freedom of movement for workers.

...

PART 4   REFUSAL OF ADMISSION AND REMOVAL ETC

Exclusion and removal from the United Kingdom

19.   (1)   A person is not entitled to be admitted to the United Kingdom by virtue of regulation 11 if his exclusion is justified on grounds of public policy, public security or public health in accordance with regulation 21.

(1A) A person is not entitled to be admitted to the United Kingdom by virtue of regulation 11 if that person is subject to a deportation or exclusion order, except where the person is temporarily admitted pursuant to regulation 29AA.

(1AB)A person is not entitled to be admitted to the United Kingdom by virtue of regulation 11 if the Secretary of State considers there to be reasonable grounds to suspect that his admission would lead to the abuse of a right to reside in accordance with regulation 21B(1).

(1B) If the Secretary of State considers that the exclusion of an EEA national or the family member of an EEA national is justified on the grounds of public policy, public security or public health in accordance with regulation 21 the Secretary of State may make an order for the purpose of these Regulations prohibiting that person from entering the United Kingdom.

(2)   A person is not entitled to be admitted to the United Kingdom as the family member of an EEA national under regulation 11(2) unless, at the time of his arrival –

(a)   he is accompanying the EEA national or joining him in the United Kingdom; and

(b)   the EEA national has a right to reside in the United Kingdom under these Regulations.

(3)   Subject to paragraphs (4) and (5), an EEA national who has entered the United Kingdom or the family member of such a national who has entered the United Kingdom may be removed if –

(a)   that person does not have or ceases to have a right to reside under these Regulations;

(b)   the Secretary of State has decided that the person's removal is justified on grounds of public policy, public security or public health in accordance with regulation 21; or

(c)   the Secretary of State has decided that the person's removal is justified on grounds of abuse of rights in accordance with regulation 21B(2).

(4)   A person must not be removed under paragraph (3) as the automatic consequence of having recourse to the social assistance system of the United Kingdom.

(5)   A person must not be removed under paragraph (3) if he has a right to remain in the United Kingdom by virtue of leave granted under the 1971 Act unless his removal is justified on the grounds of public policy, public security or public health in accordance with regulation 21.

Refusal to issue or renew and revocation of residence documentation

20.   (1)   The Secretary of State may refuse to issue, revoke or refuse to renew a registration certificate, a residence card, a document certifying permanent residence or a permanent residence card if the refusal or revocation is justified on grounds of public policy, public security or public health or on grounds of abuse of rights in accordance with regulation 21B(2).

    (1A) A decision under regulation 19(3) or 24(4) to remove a person from the United Kingdom, or a decision under regulation 23A to revoke a person's admission to the United Kingdom, will (save during any period in which a right of residence is deemed to continue as a result of regulation 15B(2)) invalidate a registration certificate, residence card, document certifying permanent residence or permanent residence card held by that person or an application made by that person for such a certificate, card or document.

    (2)   The Secretary of State may revoke a registration certificate or a residence card or refuse to renew a residence card if the holder of the certificate or card has ceased to have, or never had a right to reside under these Regulations.

    (3)   The Secretary of State may revoke a document certifying permanent residence or a permanent residence card or refuse to renew a permanent residence card if the holder of the certificate or card has ceased to have, or never had, a right of permanent residence under regulation 15.

    (4)   An immigration officer may, at the time of a person's arrival in the United Kingdom –

        (a)   revoke that person's residence card if he is not at that time the family member of a qualified person or of an EEA national who has a right of permanent residence under regulation 15, a family member who has retained the right of residence or a person with a right of permanent residence under regulation 15;

        (b)   revoke that person's permanent residence card if he is not at that time a person with a right of permanent residence under regulation 15.

    (5)   An entry clearance officer or immigration officer may at any time revoke a person's EEA family permit if –

        (a)   the revocation is justified on grounds of public policy, public security or public health; or

        (b)   the person is not at that time the family member of an EEA national with the right to reside in the United Kingdom under these Regulations or is not accompanying that national or joining him in the United Kingdom.

    (6)   Any action taken under this regulation on grounds of public policy, public security or public health shall be in accordance with regulation 21.

Cancellation of a right of residence

20A.   (1)   Where the conditions in paragraph (2) are met the Secretary of State may cancel a person's right to reside in the United Kingdom pursuant to these Regulations.

    (2)   The conditions in this paragraph are met where –

        (a)   a person has a right to reside in the United Kingdom as a result of these Regulations;

        (b)   the Secretary of State has decided that the cancellation of that person's right to reside in the United Kingdom is justified on grounds of public policy, public security or public health in accordance with regulation 21 or on grounds of abuse of rights in accordance with regulation 21B(2);

(c)   the circumstances are such that the Secretary of State cannot make a decision under regulation 20(1); and

(d)   it is not possible for the Secretary of State to remove the person from the United Kingdom pursuant to regulation 19(3)(b) or (c).

Verification of a right of residence

20B.   (1)   This regulation applies when the Secretary of State –

(a)   has reasonable doubt as to whether a person ('A') has a right to reside under regulation 14(1) or (2); or

(b)   wants to verify the eligibility of a person ('A') to apply for documentation issued under Part 3.

(2)   The Secretary of State may invite A to –

(a)   provide evidence to support the existence of a right to reside, or to support an application for documentation under Part 3; or

(b)   attend an interview with the Secretary of State.

(3)   If A purports to be entitled to a right to reside on the basis of a relationship with another person ('B'), the Secretary of State may invite B to –

(a)   provide information about their relationship with A; or

(b)   attend an interview with the Secretary of State.

(4)   If, without good reason, A or B fail to provide the additional information requested or, on at least two occasions, fail to attend an interview if so invited, the Secretary of State may draw any factual inferences about A's entitlement to a right to reside as appear appropriate in the circumstances.

(5)   The Secretary of State may decide following an inference under paragraph (4) that A does not have or ceases to have a right to reside.

(6)   But the Secretary of State must not decide that A does not have or ceases to have a right to reside on the sole basis that A failed to comply with this regulation.

(7)   This regulation may not be invoked systematically.

(8)   In this regulation, 'a right to reside' means a right to reside under these Regulations.

Decisions taken on public policy, public security and public health grounds

21.   (1)   In this regulation a 'relevant decision' means an EEA decision taken on the grounds of public policy, public security or public health.

(2)   A relevant decision may not be taken to serve economic ends.

(3)   A relevant decision may not be taken in respect of a person with a permanent right of residence under regulation 15 except on serious grounds of public policy or public security.

(4)   A relevant decision may not be taken except on imperative grounds of public security in respect of an EEA national who –

(a)   has resided in the United Kingdom for a continuous period of at least ten years prior to the relevant decision; or

(b)   is under the age of 18, unless the relevant decision is necessary in his best interests, as provided for in the Convention on the Rights of the Child adopted by the General Assembly of the United Nations on 20th November 1989.

(5) Where a relevant decision is taken on grounds of public policy or public security it shall, in addition to complying with the preceding paragraphs of this regulation, be taken in accordance with the following principles –

(a) the decision must comply with the principle of proportionality;

(b) the decision must be based exclusively on the personal conduct of the person concerned;

(c) the personal conduct of the person concerned must represent a genuine, present and sufficiently serious threat affecting one of the fundamental interests of society;

(d) matters isolated from the particulars of the case or which relate to considerations of general prevention do not justify the decision;

(e) a person's previous criminal convictions do not in themselves justify the decision.

(6) Before taking a relevant decision on the grounds of public policy or public security in relation to a person who is resident in the United Kingdom the decision maker must take account of considerations such as the age, state of health, family and economic situation of the person, the person's length of residence in the United Kingdom, the person's social and cultural integration into the United Kingdom and the extent of the person's links with his country of origin.

(7) In the case of a relevant decision taken on grounds of public health –

(a) a disease that does not have epidemic potential as defined by the relevant instruments of the World Health Organisation or is not a disease listed in Schedule 1 to the Health Protection (Notification) Regulations 2010 shall not constitute grounds for the decision; and

(b) if the person concerned is in the United Kingdom, diseases occurring after the three month period beginning on the date on which he arrived in the United Kingdom shall not constitute grounds for the decision.

Application of Part 4 to persons with a derivative right of residence

21A. (1) Where this regulation applies Part 4 of these Regulations applies subject to the modifications listed in paragraph (3).

(2) This regulation applies where a person –

(a) would, notwithstanding Part 4 of these Regulations, have a right to be admitted to, or reside in, the United Kingdom by virtue of a derivative right of residence arising under regulation 15A(2), (4), (4A) or (5);

(b) holds a derivative residence card; or

(c) has applied for a derivative residence card.

(3) Where this regulation applies Part 4 applies in relation to the matters listed in paragraph (2) as if –

(a) references to a matter being justified on grounds of public policy, public security or public health in accordance with regulation 21 referred instead to a matter being 'conducive to the public good';

(b) the reference in regulation 20(5)(a) to a matter being 'justified on grounds of public policy, public security or public health' referred instead to a matter being 'conducive to the public good';

(c) references to 'the family member of an EEA national' referred instead to 'a person with a derivative right of residence';

(d) references to 'a registration certificate, a residence card, a document certifying permanent residence or a permanent residence card' referred instead to 'a derivative residence card';

(e) the reference in regulation 19(1A) to a deportation or exclusion order referred also to a deportation or exclusion order made under any provision of the immigration Acts.

(f) regulation 20(4) instead conferred on an immigration officer the power to revoke a derivative residence card where the holder is not at that time a person with a derivative right of residence; and

(g) regulations 20(3), 20(6) and 21 were omitted.

Abuse of rights or fraud

21B.   (1)   The abuse of a right to reside includes –

(a) engaging in conduct which appears to be intended to circumvent the requirement to be a qualified person;

(b) attempting to enter the United Kingdom within 12 months of being removed pursuant to regulation 19(3)(a), where the person attempting to do so is unable to provide evidence that, upon re-entry to the United Kingdom, the conditions for any right to reside, other than the initial right of residence under regulation 13, will be met;

(c) entering, attempting to enter or assisting another person to enter or attempt to enter, a marriage or civil partnership of convenience; or

(d) fraudulently obtaining or attempting to obtain, or assisting another to obtain or attempt to obtain, a right to reside.

(2)   The Secretary of State may take an EEA decision on the grounds of abuse of rights where there are reasonable grounds to suspect the abuse of a right to reside and it is proportionate to do so.

(3)   Where these Regulations provide that an EEA decision taken on the grounds of abuse in the preceding twelve months affects a person's right to reside, the person who is the subject of that decision may apply to the Secretary of State to have the effect of that decision set aside on grounds that there has been a material change in the circumstances which justified that decision.

(4)   An application under paragraph (3) may only be made whilst the applicant is outside the United Kingdom.

(5)   This regulation may not be invoked systematically.

(6)   In this regulation, 'a right to reside' means a right to reside under these Regulations.

…

PART 6   APPEALS UNDER THESE REGULATIONS

Interpretation of Part 6

25.   (1)   In this Part –

'Commission' has the same meaning as in the Special Immigration Appeals Commission Act 1997;

(2) For the purposes of this Part, and subject to paragraphs (3) and (4), an appeal is to be treated as pending during the period when notice of appeal is given and ending when the appeal is finally determined, withdrawn or abandoned.

(3) An appeal is not to be treated as finally determined while a further appeal may be brought; and, if such a further appeal is brought, the original appeal is not to be treated as finally determined until the further appeal is determined, withdrawn or abandoned.

(4) A pending appeal is not to be treated as abandoned solely because the appellant leaves the United Kingdom.

Appeal rights

26. (1) Subject to the following paragraphs of this regulation, a person may appeal under these Regulations against an EEA decision.

(2) If a person claims to be an EEA national, he may not appeal under these Regulations unless he produces a valid national identity card or passport issued by an EEA State.

(2A) If a person claims to be in a durable relationship with an EEA national he may not appeal under these Regulations unless he produces –

(a) a passport; and
(b) either –

(i) an EEA family permit; or
(ii) sufficient evidence to satisfy the Secretary of State that he is in a relationship with that EEA national.

(3) If a person to whom paragraph (2) does not apply claims to be a family member who has retained the right of residence or the family member or relative of an EEA national he may not appeal under these Regulations unless he produces –

(a) a passport; and
(b) either –

(i) an EEA family permit;
(ia) a qualifying EEA State residence card;
(ii) proof that he is the family member or relative of an EEA national; or
(iii) in the case of a person claiming to be a family member who has retained the right of residence, proof that he was a family member of the relevant person.

(3A) If a person claims to be a person with a derivative right of entry or residence he may not appeal under these Regulations unless he produces a valid national identity card issued by an EEA State or a passport, and either –

(a) an EEA family permit; or
(b) proof that –

(i) where the person claims to have a derivative right of entry or residence as a result of regulation 15A(2), he is a direct relative or guardian of an EEA national who is under the age of 18;

(ii)   where the person claims to have a derivative right of entry or residence as a result of regulation 15A(3), he is the child of an EEA national;

(iii)   where the person claims to have a derivative right of entry or residence as a result of regulation 15A(4), he is a direct relative or guardian of the child of an EEA national;

(iv)   where the person claims to have a derivative right of entry or residence as a result of regulation 15A(5), he is under the age of 18 and is a dependant of a person satisfying the criteria in (i) or (iii);

(v)   where the person claims to have a derivative right of entry or residence as a result of regulation 15A(4A), he is a direct relative or guardian of a British citizen.

(4)   A person may not bring an appeal under these Regulations on a ground certified under paragraph (5) or rely on such a ground in an appeal brought under these Regulations.

(5)   The Secretary of State or an immigration officer may certify a ground for the purposes of paragraph (4) if it has been considered in a previous appeal brought under these Regulations or under section 82(1) of the 2002 Act.

(6)   Except where an appeal lies to the Commission, an appeal under these Regulations lies to the First-tier Tribunal.

(7)   The provisions of or made under the 2002 Act referred to in Schedule 1 shall have effect for the purposes of an appeal under these Regulations to the First-tier Tribunal in accordance with that Schedule.

(8)   For the avoidance of doubt, nothing in this Part prevents a person who enjoys a right of appeal under this regulation from appealing to the First-tier Tribunal under section 82(1) of the 2002 Act (right of appeal to the Tribunal), or, where relevant, to the Commission pursuant to section 2 of the Special Immigration Appeals Act 1997 (jurisdiction of the Commission: appeals), provided the criteria for bringing such an appeal under those Acts are met.

Out of country appeals

27.   (1)   Subject to paragraphs (2) and (3), a person may not appeal under regulation 26 whilst he is in the United Kingdom against an EEA decision –

(a)   to refuse to admit him to the United Kingdom;

(zaa)   to revoke his admission to the United Kingdom;

(aa)   to make an exclusion order against him;

(b)   to refuse to revoke a deportation or exclusion order made against him;

(c)   to refuse to issue him with an EEA family permit; . . .

(ca)   to revoke, or to refuse to issue or renew any document under these Regulations where that decision is taken at a time when the relevant person is outside the United Kingdom; or

(d)   to remove him from the United Kingdom after he has entered the United Kingdom in breach of a deportation or exclusion order, or in circumstances where that person was not entitled to be admitted pursuant to regulation 19(1) or (1AB).

(2)   Paragraphs (1)(a) to (aa) do not apply where the person is in the United Kingdom and –

(a)   the person held a valid EEA family permit, registration certificate,

residence card, derivative residence card, document certifying permanent residence or permanent residence card or qualifying EEA State
residence card on his arrival in the United Kingdom or can otherwise
prove that he is resident in the United Kingdom; or

(b)   the person is deemed not to have been admitted to the United Kingdom
under regulation 22(3) but at the date on which notice of the decision to
refuse to admit him is given he has been in the United Kingdom for at
least 3 months.

(c)   [*Repealed*]

(3)   [*Repealed*]

...

Temporary admission in order to submit case in person

29AA. (1)   This regulation applies where –

(a)   a person ('P') was removed from the United Kingdom pursuant to
regulation 19(3)(b);

(b)   P has appealed against the decision referred to in sub-paragraph (a);

(c)   a date for P's appeal has been set by the First Tier Tribunal or Upper
Tribunal; and

(d)   P wants to make submissions before the First Tier Tribunal or Upper
Tribunal in person.

(2)   P may apply to the Secretary of State for permission to be temporarily
admitted (within the meaning of paragraphs 21 to 24 of Schedule 2 to the 1971
Act, as applied by this regulation) to the United Kingdom in order to make
submissions in person.

(3)   The Secretary of State must grant P permission, except when P's appearance
may cause serious troubles to public policy or public security.

(4)   When determining when P is entitled to be given permission, and the duration
of P's temporary admission should permission be granted, the Secretary of
State must have regard to the dates upon which P will be required to make
submissions in person.

(5)   Where –

(a)   P is temporarily admitted to the United Kingdom pursuant to this
regulation;

(b)   a hearing of P's appeal has taken place; and

(c)   the appeal is not finally determined,

P may be removed from the United Kingdom pending the remaining stages of
the redress procedure (but P may apply to return to the United Kingdom to
make submissions in person during the remaining stages of the redress
procedure in accordance with this regulation).

(6)   Where the Secretary of State grants P permission to be temporarily admitted to
the United Kingdom under this regulation, upon such admission P is to be
treated as if P were a person refused leave to enter under the 1971 Act for the
purposes of paragraphs 8, 10, 10A, 11, 16 to 18 and 21 to 24 of Schedule 2 to
the 1971 Act.

(7)   Where Schedule 2 to the 1971 Act so applies, it has effect as if –

(a)   the reference in paragraph 8(1) to leave to enter were a reference to
admission to the United Kingdom under these Regulations; and

(b)   the reference in paragraph 16(1) to detention pending a decision regarding leave to enter or remain in the United Kingdom were to detention pending submission of P's case in person in accordance with this regulation.

(8)   P will be deemed not to have been admitted to the United Kingdom during any time during which P is temporarily admitted pursuant to this regulation.

PART 7   GENERAL

Alternative evidence of identity and nationality

29A.   (1)   Subject to paragraph (2), where a provision of these Regulations requires a person to hold or produce a valid identity card issued by an EEA State or a valid passport the Secretary of State may accept alternative evidence of identity and nationality where the person is unable to obtain or produce the required document due to circumstances beyond his or her control.

       (2)   This regulation does not apply to regulation 11.

Refugee or Person in Need of International Protection (Qualification) Regulations 2006

1. Citation and commencement

(1)   These Regulations may be cited as The Refugee or Person in Need of International Protection (Qualification) Regulations 2006 and shall come into force on 9th October 2006.

(2)   These Regulations apply to any application for asylum which has not been decided and any immigration appeal brought under the Immigration Acts (as defined in section 64(2) of the Immigration, Asylum and Nationality Act 2006) which has not been finally determined.

2. Interpretation

In these Regulations –

'application for asylum' means the request of a person to be recognised as a refugee under the Geneva Convention;

'Geneva Convention' means the Convention Relating to the Status of Refugees done at Geneva on 28 July 1951 and the New York Protocol of 31 January 1967;

'immigration rules' means rules made under section 3(2) of the Immigration Act 1971;

'persecution' means an act of persecution within the meaning of Article 1(A) of the Geneva Convention;

'person eligible for humanitarian protection' means a person who is eligible for a grant of humanitarian protection under the immigration rules;

'refugee' means a person who falls within Article 1(A) of the Geneva Convention and to whom regulation 7 does not apply;

'residence permit' means a document confirming that a person has leave to enter or remain in the United Kingdom whether limited or indefinite;

'serious harm' means serious harm as defined in the immigration rules;

'person' means any person who is not a British citizen.

3. Actors of persecution or serious harm

In deciding whether a person is a refugee or a person eligible for humanitarian protection, persecution or serious harm can be committed by:

(a)   the State;

(b)   any party or organisation controlling the State or a substantial part of the territory of the State;

(c)   any non-State actor if it can be demonstrated that the actors mentioned in paragraphs

331

(a) and (b), including any international organisation, are unable or unwilling to provide protection against persecution or serious harm.

4. Actors of protection

(1)   In deciding whether a person is a refugee or a person eligible for humanitarian protection, protection from persecution or serious harm can be provided by:

    (a)   the State; or

    (b)   any party or organisation, including any international organisation, controlling the State or a substantial part of the territory of the State.

(2)   Protection shall be regarded as generally provided when the actors mentioned in paragraph (1)(a) and (b) take reasonable steps to prevent the persecution or suffering of serious harm by operating an effective legal system for the detection, prosecution and punishment of acts constituting persecution or serious harm, and the person mentioned in paragraph (1) has access to such protection.

(3)   In deciding whether a person is a refugee or a person eligible for humanitarian protection the Secretary of State may assess whether an international organisation controls a State or a substantial part of its territory and provides protection as described in paragraph (2).

5. Act of persecution

(1)   In deciding whether a person is a refugee an act of persecution must be:

    (a)   sufficiently serious by its nature or repetition as to constitute a severe violation of a basic human right, in particular a right from which derogation cannot be made under Article 15 of the Convention for the Protection of Human Rights and Fundamental Freedoms; or

    (b)   an accumulation of various measures, including a violation of a human right which is sufficiently severe as to affect an individual in a similar manner as specified in (a).

(2)   An act of persecution may, for example, take the form of:

    (a)   an act of physical or mental violence, including an act of sexual violence;

    (b)   a legal, administrative, police, or judicial measure which in itself is discriminatory or which is implemented in a discriminatory manner;

    (c)   prosecution or punishment, which is disproportionate or discriminatory;

    (d)   denial of judicial redress resulting in a disproportionate or discriminatory punishment;

    (e)   prosecution or punishment for refusal to perform military service in a conflict, where performing military service would include crimes or acts falling under regulation 7.

(3)   An act of persecution must be committed for at least one of the reasons in Article 1(A) of the Geneva Convention.

6. Reasons for persecution

(1)   In deciding whether a person is a refugee:

    (a)   the concept of race shall include consideration of, for example, colour, descent, or membership of a particular ethnic group;

    (b)   the concept of religion shall include, for example, the holding of theistic, non-theistic and atheistic beliefs, the participation in, or abstention from, formal worship in private or in public, either alone or in community with others, other religious acts or expressions of view, or forms of personal or communal conduct based on or mandated by any religious belief;

(c) the concept of nationality shall not be confined to citizenship or lack thereof but shall include, for example, membership of a group determined by its cultural, ethnic, or linguistic identity, common geographical or political origins or its relationship with the population of another State;

(d) a group shall be considered to form a particular social group where, for example:

 (i) members of that group share an innate characteristic, or a common background that cannot be changed, or share a characteristic or belief that is so fundamental to identity or conscience that a person should not be forced to renounce it, and

 (ii) that group has a distinct identity in the relevant country, because it is perceived as being different by the surrounding society;

(e) a particular social group might include a group based on a common characteristic of sexual orientation but sexual orientation cannot be understood to include acts considered to be criminal in accordance with national law of the United Kingdom;

(f) the concept of political opinion shall include the holding of an opinion, thought or belief on a matter related to the potential actors of persecution mentioned in regulation 3and to their policies or methods, whether or not that opinion, thought or belief has been acted upon by the person.

(2) In deciding whether a person has a well-founded fear of being persecuted, it is immaterial whether he actually possesses the racial, religious, national, social or political characteristic which attracts the persecution, provided that such a characteristic is attributed to him by the actor of persecution.

7. Exclusion

(1) A person is not a refugee, if he falls within the scope of Article 1D, 1E or 1F of the Geneva Convention.

(2) In the construction and application of Article 1F(b) of the Geneva Convention:

(a) the reference to serious non-political crime includes a particularly cruel action, even if it is committed with an allegedly political objective;

(b) the reference to the crime being committed outside the country of refuge prior to his admission as a refugee shall be taken to mean the time up to and including the day on which a residence permit is issued.

(3) Article 1F(a) and (b) of the Geneva Convention shall apply to a person who instigates or otherwise participates in the commission of the crimes or acts specified in those provisions.

C3

European Convention on Human Rights (extracts)

Article 1

Obligation to respect Human Rights

The High Contracting Parties shall secure to everyone within their jurisdiction the rights and freedoms defined in Section I of this Convention.

SECTION I
RIGHTS AND FREEDOMS

Article 2

Right to life

1.　　Everyone's right to life shall be protected by law. No one shall be deprived of his life intentionally save in the execution of a sentence of a court following his conviction of a crime for which this penalty is provided by law.
2.　　Deprivation of life shall not be regarded as inflicted in contravention of this Article when it results from the use of force which is no more than absolutely necessary:

　　(a)　　in defence of any person from unlawful violence;
　　(b)　　in order to effect a lawful arrest or to prevent the escape of a person lawfully detained;
　　(c)　　in action lawfully taken for the purpose of quelling a riot or insurrection.

Article 3

Prohibition of torture

No one shall be subjected to torture or to inhuman or degrading treatment or punishment.

Article 4

Prohibition of slavery and forced labour

1.　　No one shall be held in slavery or servitude.
2.　　No one shall be required to perform forced or compulsory labour.

3. For the purpose of this Article the term forced or compulsory labour' shall not include:

    (a) any work required to be done in the ordinary course of detention imposed according to the provisions of Article 5 of this Convention or during conditional release from such detention;
    (b) any service of a military character or, in case of conscientious objectors in countries where they are recognised, service exacted instead of compulsory military service;
    (c) any service exacted in case of an emergency or calamity threatening the life or well-being of the community;
    (d) any work or service which forms part of normal civic obligations.

Article 5

Right to liberty and security

1. Everyone has the right to liberty and security of person.

    No one shall be deprived of his liberty save in the following cases and in accordance with a procedure prescribed by law:

    (a) the lawful detention of a person after conviction by a competent court;
    (b) the lawful arrest or detention of a person for non-compliance with the lawful order of a court or in order to secure the fulfilment of any obligation prescribed by law;
    (c) the lawful arrest or detention of a person effected for the purpose of bringing him before the competent legal authority on reasonable suspicion of having committed an offence or when it is reasonably considered necessary to prevent his committing an offence or fleeing after having done so;
    (d) the detention of a minor by lawful order for the purpose of educational supervision or his lawful detention for the purpose of bringing him before the competent legal authority;
    (e) the lawful detention of persons for the prevention of the spreading of infectious diseases, of persons of unsound mind, alcoholics or drug addicts, or vagrants;
    (f) the lawful arrest or detention of a person to prevent his effecting an unauthorised entry into the country or of a person against whom action is being taken with a view to deportation or extradition.

2. Everyone who is arrested shall be informed promptly, in a language which he understands, of the reasons for his arrest and of any charge against him.

3. Everyone arrested or detained in accordance with the provisions of paragraph 1(c) of this Article shall be brought promptly before a judge or other officer authorised by law to exercise judicial power and shall be entitled to trial within a reasonable time or to release pending trial. Release may be conditioned by guarantees to appear for trial.

4. Everyone who is deprived of his liberty by arrest or detention shall be entitled to take proceedings by which the lawfulness of his detention shall be decided speedily by a court and his release ordered if the detention is not lawful.

5. Everyone who has been the victim of arrest or detention in contravention of the provisions of this Article shall have an enforceable right to compensation.

Article 6

Right to a fair trial

1.   In the determination of his civil rights and obligations or of any criminal charge against him, everyone is entitled to a fair and public hearing within a reasonable time by an independent and impartial tribunal established by law. Judgment shall be pronounced publicly but the press and public may be excluded from all or part of the trial in the interests of morals, public order or national security in a democratic society, where the interests of juveniles or the protection of the private life of the parties so require, or to the extent strictly necessary in the opinion of the court in special circumstances where publicity would prejudice the interests of justice.

2.   Everyone charged with a criminal offence shall be presumed innocent until proved guilty according to law.

3.   Everyone charged with a criminal offence has the following minimum rights:

   (a)   to be informed promptly, in a language which he understands and in detail, of the nature and cause of the accusation against him;

   (b)   to have adequate time and facilities for the preparation of his defence;

   (c)   to defend himself in person or through legal assistance of his own choosing or, if he has not sufficient means to pay for legal assistance, to be given it free when the interests of justice so require;

   (d)   to examine or have examined witnesses against him and to obtain the attendance and examination of witnesses on his behalf under the same conditions as witnesses against him;

   (e)   to have the free assistance of an interpreter if he cannot understand or speak the language used in court.

Article 7

No punishment without law

1.   No one shall be held guilty of any criminal offence on account of any act or omission which did not constitute a criminal offence under national or international law at the time when it was committed. Nor shall a heavier penalty be imposed than the one that was applicable at the time the criminal offence was committed.

2.   This Article shall not prejudice the trial and punishment of any person for any act or omission which, at the time when it was committed, was criminal according to the general principles of law recognised by civilised nations.

Article 8

Right to respect for private and family life

1.   Everyone has the right to respect for his private and family life, his home and his correspondence.

2.   There shall be no interference by a public authority with the exercise of this right except such as is in accordance with the law and is necessary in a democratic society in the interests of national security, public safety or the economic well-being of the country, for the prevention of disorder or crime, for the protection of health or morals, or for the protection of the rights and freedoms of others.

Article 9

Freedom of thought, conscience and religion

1. Everyone has the right to freedom of thought, conscience and religion; this right includes freedom to change his religion or belief, and freedom, either alone or in community with others and in public or private, to manifest his religion or belief, in worship, teaching, practice and observance.
2. Freedom to manifest one's religion or beliefs shall be subject only to such limitations as are prescribed by law and are necessary in a democratic society in the interests of public safety, for the protection of public order, health or morals, or for the protection of the rights and freedoms of others.

Article 10

Freedom of expression

1. Everyone has the right to freedom of expression. This right shall include freedom to hold opinions and to receive and impart information and ideas without interference by public authority and regardless of frontiers. This Article shall not prevent States from requiring the licensing of broadcasting, television or cinema enterprises.
2. The exercise of these freedoms, since it carries with it duties and responsibilities, may be subject to such formalities, conditions, restrictions or penalties as are prescribed by law and are necessary in a democratic society, in the interests of national security, territorial integrity or public safety, for the prevention of disorder or crime, for the protection of health or morals, for the protection of the reputation or rights of others, for preventing the disclosure of information received in confidence, or for maintaining the authority and impartiality of the judiciary.

Article 11

Freedom of assembly and association

1. Everyone has the right to freedom of peaceful assembly and to freedom of association with others, including the right to form and to join trade unions for the protection of his interests.
2. No restrictions shall be placed on the exercise of these rights other than such as are prescribed by law and are necessary in a democratic society in the interests of national security or public safety, for the prevention of disorder or crime, for the protection of health or morals or for the protection of the rights and freedoms of others. This Article shall not prevent the imposition of lawful restrictions on the exercise of these rights by members of the armed forces, of the police or of the administration of the State.

Article 12

Right to marry

Men and women of marriageable age have the right to marry and to found a family, according to the national laws governing the exercise of this right.

337

Article 13

Right to an effective remedy

Everyone whose rights and freedoms as set forth in this Convention are violated shall have an effective remedy before a national authority notwithstanding that the violation has been committed by persons acting in an official capacity.

Article 14

Prohibition of discrimination

The enjoyment of the rights and freedoms set forth in this Convention shall be secured without discrimination on any ground such as sex, race, colour, language, religion, political or other opinion, national or social origin, association with a national minority, property, birth or other status.

Article 15

Derogation in time of emergency

1.   In time of war or other public emergency threatening the life of the nation any High Contracting Party may take measures derogating from its obligations under this Convention to the extent strictly required by the exigencies of the situation, provided that such measures are not inconsistent with its other obligations under international law.
2.   No derogation from Article 2, except in respect of deaths resulting from lawful acts of war, or from Articles 3, 4 (paragraph 1) and 7 shall be made under this provision.
3.   Any High Contracting Party availing itself of this right of derogation shall keep the Secretary-General of the Council of Europe fully informed of the measures which it has taken and the reasons therefor. It shall also inform the Secretary-General of the Council of Europe when such measures have ceased to operate and the provisions of the Convention are again being fully executed.

UNHCR 1951 Refugee Convention (extracts)

Article 1 – Definition of the term 'refugee'

A.   For the purposes of the present Convention, the term 'refugee' shall apply to any person who:

    ...

(2)   ... owing to wellfounded fear of being persecuted for reasons of race, religion, nationality, membership of a particular social group or political opinion, is outside the country of his nationality and is unable or, owing to such fear, is unwilling to avail himself of the protection of that country; or who, not having a nationality and being outside the country of his former habitual residence as a result of such events, is unable or, owing to such fear, is unwilling to return to it.

In the case of a person who has more than one nationality, the term 'the country of his nationality' shall mean each of the countries of which he is a national, and a person shall not be deemed to be lacking the protection of the country of his nationality if, without any valid reason based on well-founded fear, he has not availed himself of the protection of one of the countries of which he is a national.

...

C.   This Convention shall cease to apply to any person falling under the terms of section A if:

(1)   He has voluntarily re-availed himself of the protection of the country of his nationality; or

(2)   Having lost his nationality, he has voluntarily re-acquired it; or

(3)   He has acquired a new nationality, and enjoys the protection of the country of his new nationality; or

(4)   He has voluntarily re-established himself in the country which he left or outside which he remained owing to fear of persecution; or

(5)   He can no longer, because the circumstances in connexion with which he has been recognized as a refugee have ceased to exist, continue to refuse to avail himself of the protection of the country of his nationality;

Provided that this paragraph shall not apply to a refugee falling under section A (1) of this article who is able to invoke compelling reasons arising out of previous persecution for refusing to avail himself of the protection of the country of nationality;

(6)   Being a person who has no nationality he is, because of the circumstances in connexion with which he has been recognized as a refugee have ceased to exist, able to return to the country of his former habitual residence;

Provided that this paragraph shall not apply to a refugee falling under section A (1) of this article who is able to invoke compelling reasons arising out of previous persecution for refusing to return to the country of his former habitual residence.

D.   This Convention shall not apply to persons who are at present receiving from organs or agencies of the United Nations other than the United Nations High Commissioner for Refugees protection or assistance. When such protection or assistance has ceased for any reason, without the position of such persons being definitively settled in accordance with the relevant resolutions adopted by the General Assembly of the United Nations, these persons shall ipso facto be entitled to the benefits of this Convention.

E.   This Convention shall not apply to a person who is recognized by the competent authorities of the country in which he has taken residence as having the rights and obligations which are attached to the possession of the nationality of that country.

F.   The provisions of this Convention shall not apply to any person with respect to whom there are serious reasons for considering that:

(a)   he has committed a crime against peace, a war crime, or a crime against humanity, as defined in the international instruments drawn up to make provision in respect of such crimes;

(b)   he has committed a serious non-political crime outside the country of refuge prior to his admission to that country as a refugee;

(c)   he has been guilty of acts contrary to the purposes and principles of the United Nations.

Article 31 – Refugees unlawfully in the country of refugee

1.   The Contracting States shall not impose penalties, on account of their illegal entry or presence, on refugees who, coming directly from a territory where their life or freedom was threatened in the sense of article 1, enter or are present in their territory without authorization, provided they present themselves without delay to the authorities and show good cause for their illegal entry or presence.

2.   The Contracting States shall not apply to the movements of such refugees restrictions other than those which are necessary and such restrictions shall only be applied until their status in the country is regularized or they obtain admission into another country. The Contracting States shall allow such refugees a reasonable period and all the necessary facilities to obtain admission into another country.

Article 32 – Expulsion

1.   The Contracting States shall not expel a refugee lawfully in their territory save on grounds of national security or public order.

2.   The expulsion of such a refugee shall be only in pursuance of a decision reached in accordance with due process of law. Except where compelling reasons of national security otherwise require, the refugee shall be allowed to submit evidence to clear himself, and to appeal to and be represented for the purpose before competent authority or a person or persons specially designated by the competent authority.

3.   The Contracting States shall allow such a refugee a reasonable period 30 convention and protocol within which to seek legal admission into another country. The Contracting States reserve the right to apply during that period such internal measures as they may deem necessary.

Article 33 – Prohibition of expulsion or return ('refoulement')

1.   No Contracting State shall expel or return ('refouler') a refugee in any manner whatsoever to the frontiers of territories where his life or freedom would be threatened on account of his race, religion, nationality, membership of a particular social group or political opinion.

2.   The benefit of the present provision may not, however, be claimed by a refugee whom there are reasonable grounds for regarding as a danger to the security of the country in which he is, or who, having been convicted by a final judgment of a particularly serious crime, constitutes a danger to the community of that country.

C5

Council of Europe Convention on Action against Trafficking in Human Beings (extracts)

Article 1 – Purposes of the Convention

1   The purposes of this Convention are:

     a.   to prevent and combat trafficking in human beings, while guaranteeing gender equality;

     b.   to protect the human rights of the victims of trafficking, design a comprehensive framework for the protection and assistance of victims and witnesses, while guaranteeing gender equality, as well as to ensure effective investigation and prosecution;

     c.   to promote international cooperation on action against trafficking in human beings.

2   In order to ensure effective implementation of its provisions by the Parties, this Convention sets up a specific monitoring mechanism.

Article 2 – Scope

This Convention shall apply to all forms of trafficking in human beings, whether national or transnational, whether or not connected with organised crime.

Article 3 – Non-discrimination principle

The implementation of the provisions of this Convention by Parties, in particular the enjoyment of measures to protect and promote the rights of victims, shall be secured without discrimination on any ground such as sex, race, colour, language, religion, political or other opinion, national or social origin, association with a national minority, property, birth or other status.

Article 4 – Definitions

For the purposes of this Convention:

     a.   'Trafficking in human beings' shall mean the recruitment, transportation, transfer, harbouring or receipt of persons, by means of the threat or use of force or other forms of coercion, of abduction, of fraud, of deception, of the abuse of power or of a position of vulnerability or of the giving or receiving of payments or benefits to achieve the consent of a person having control over another person, for the purpose of exploitation. Exploitation shall include, at a minimum, the exploitation of the prostitution of others or other forms of sexual exploitation, forced labour or services, slavery or practices similar to slavery, servitude or the removal of organs;

b.   The consent of a victim of 'trafficking in human beings' to the intended exploitation set forth in subparagraph (a) of this article shall be irrelevant where any of the means set forth in subparagraph (a) have been used;

c.   The recruitment, transportation, transfer, harbouring or receipt of a child for the purpose of exploitation shall be considered 'trafficking in human beings' even if this does not involve any of the means set forth in subparagraph (a) of this article;

d.   'Child' shall mean any person under eighteen years of age;

e.   'Victim' shall mean any natural person who is subject to trafficking in human beings as defined in this article.

Article 10 – Identification of the victims

1   Each Party shall provide its competent authorities with persons who are trained and qualified in preventing and combating trafficking in human beings, in identifying and helping victims, including children, and shall ensure that the different authorities collaborate with each other as well as with relevant support organisations, so that victims can be identified in a procedure duly taking into account the special situation of women and child victims and, in appropriate cases, issued with residence permits under the conditions provided for in Article 14 of the present Convention.

2   Each Party shall adopt such legislative or other measures as may be necessary to identify victims as appropriate in collaboration with other Parties and relevant support organisations. Each Party shall ensure that, if the competent authorities have reasonable grounds to believe that a person has been victim of trafficking in human beings, that person shall not be removed from its territory until the identification process as victim of an offence provided for in Article 18 of this Convention has been completed by the competent authorities and shall likewise ensure that that person receives the assistance provided for in Article 12, paragraphs 1 and 2.

3   When the age of the victim is uncertain and there are reasons to believe that the victim is a child, he or she shall be presumed to be a child and shall be accorded special protection measures pending verification of his/her age.

4   As soon as an unaccompanied child is identified as a victim, each Party shall:

a.   provide for representation of the child by a legal guardian, organisation or authority which shall act in the best interests of that child;

b.   take the necessary steps to establish his/her identity and nationality;

c.   make every effort to locate his/her family when this is in the best interests of the child.

Article 12 – Assistance to victims

1   Each Party shall adopt such legislative or other measures as may be necessary to assist victims in their physical, psychological and social recovery. Such assistance shall include at least:

a.   standards of living capable of ensuring their subsistence, through such measures as: appropriate and secure accommodation, psychological and material assistance;

b.   access to emergency medical treatment;

c.   translation and interpretation services, when appropriate;

d.   counselling and information, in particular as regards their legal rights and the services available to them, in a language that they can understand;

e.   assistance to enable their rights and interests to be presented and considered at appropriate stages of criminal proceedings against offenders;

f.   access to education for children.

2   Each Party shall take due account of the victim's safety and protection needs.

3   In addition, each Party shall provide necessary medical or other assistance to victims lawfully resident within its territory who do not have adequate resources and need such help.

4   Each Party shall adopt the rules under which victims lawfully resident within its territory shall be authorised to have access to the labour market, to vocational training and education.

5   Each Party shall take measures, where appropriate and under the conditions provided for by its internal law, to co-operate with non-governmental organisations, other relevant organisations or other elements of civil society engaged in assistance to victims.

6   Each Party shall adopt such legislative or other measures as may be necessary to ensure that assistance to a victim is not made conditional on his or her willingness to act as a witness.

7   For the implementation of the provisions set out in this article, each Party shall ensure that services are provided on a consensual and informed basis, taking due account of the special needs of persons in a vulnerable position and the rights of children in terms of accommodation, education and appropriate health care.

Article 13 – Recovery and reflection period

1   Each Party shall provide in its internal law a recovery and reflection period of at least 30 days, when there are reasonable grounds to believe that the person concerned is a victim. Such a period shall be sufficient for the person concerned to recover and escape the influence of traffickers and/or to take an informed decision on cooperating with the competent authorities. During this period it shall not be possible to enforce any expulsion order against him or her. This provision is without prejudice to the activities carried out by the competent authorities in all phases of the relevant national proceedings, and in particular when investigating and prosecuting the offences concerned. During this period, the Parties shall authorise the persons concerned to stay in their territory.

2   During this period, the persons referred to in paragraph 1 of this Article shall be entitled to the measures contained in Article 12, paragraphs 1 and 2.

3   The Parties are not bound to observe this period if grounds of public order prevent it or if it is found that victim status is being claimed improperly.

Article 14 – Residence permit

1   Each Party shall issue a renewable residence permit to victims, in one or other of the two following situations or in both:

a.   the competent authority considers that their stay is necessary owing to their personal situation;

b.   the competent authority considers that their stay is necessary for the purpose of their co-operation with the competent authorities in investigation or criminal proceedings.

2   The residence permit for child victims, when legally necessary, shall be issued in accordance with the best interests of the child and, where appropriate, renewed under the same conditions.

3   The non-renewal or withdrawal of a residence permit is subject to the conditions
         provided for by the internal law of the Party.

4   If a victim submits an application for another kind of residence permit, the Party
         concerned shall take into account that he or she holds, or has held, a residence permit
         in conformity with paragraph 1.

5   Having regard to the obligations of Parties to which Article 40 of this Convention
         refers, each Party shall ensure that granting of a permit according to this provision
         shall be without prejudice to the right to seek and enjoy asylum.

APPENDIX D

Immigration Rules

Immigration Rules, Part 11 – Asylum (paragraphs 326A to 352H)

Procedure

326A. The procedures set out in these Rules shall apply to the consideration of admissible applications for asylum and humanitarian protection.

326B. Where the Secretary of State is considering a claim for asylum or humanitarian protection under this Part, she will consider any Article 8 elements of that claim in line with the provisions of Appendix FM (family life) and in line with paragraphs 276ADE to 276DH (private life) of these Rules which are relevant to those elements unless the person is someone to whom Part 13 of these Rules applies.

Definition of EU asylum applicant

326C. Under this Part an EU asylum applicant is a national of a Member State of the European Union who either;

(a) makes a request to be recognised a refugee under the Geneva Convention on the basis that it would be contrary to the United Kingdom's obligations under the Geneva Convention for him to be removed from or required to leave the United Kingdom, or

(b) otherwise makes a request for international protection. 'EU asylum application' shall be construed accordingly.

326D. 'Member State' has the same meaning as in Schedule 1 to the European Communities Act 1972'.

Inadmissibility of EU asylum applications

326E. An EU asylum application will be declared inadmissible and will not be considered unless the requirement in paragraph 326F is met.

326F. An EU asylum application will only be admissible if the applicant satisfies the Secretary of State that there are exceptional circumstances which require the application to be admitted for full consideration. Exceptional circumstances may include in particular:

(a) the Member State of which the applicant is a national has derogated from the European Convention on Human Rights in accordance with Article 15 of that Convention;

(b) the procedure detailed in Article 7(1) of the Treaty on European Union has been initiated, and the Council or, where appropriate, the European Council, has yet to make a decision as required in respect of the Member State of which the applicant is a national; or

(c) the Council has adopted a decision in accordance with Article 7(1) of the Treaty on European Union in respect of the Member State of which the applicant is a national, or the European Council has adopted a decision in accordance with Article 7(2) of that Treaty in respect of the Member State of which the applicant is a national.

Definition of asylum applicant

327. Under the Rules an asylum applicant is a person who either;

(a) makes a request to be recognised as a refugee under the Geneva Convention on the basis that it would be contrary to the United Kingdom's obligations under the Geneva Convention for him to be removed from or required to leave the United Kingdom, or

(b) otherwise makes a request for international protection. 'Application for asylum' shall be construed accordingly.

327A. Every person has the right to make an application for asylum on his own behalf.

Applications for asylum

328. All asylum applications will be determined by the Secretary of State in accordance with the Geneva Convention. Every asylum application made by a person at a port or airport in the United Kingdom will be referred by the Immigration Officer for determination by the Secretary of State in accordance with these Rules.

328A. The Secretary of State shall ensure that authorities which are likely to be addressed by someone who wishes to make an application for asylum are able to advise that person how and where such an application may be made.

329. Until an asylum application has been determined by the Secretary of State or the Secretary of State has issued a certificate under Part 2, 3, 4 or 5 of Schedule 3 to the Asylum and Immigration (Treatment of Claimants, etc.) Act 2004 no action will be taken to require the departure of the asylum applicant or his dependants from the United Kingdom.

330. If the Secretary of State decides to grant refugee status and the person has not yet been given leave to enter, the Immigration Officer will grant limited leave to enter.

331. If a person seeking leave to enter is refused asylum or their application for asylum is withdrawn or treated as withdrawn under paragraph 333C of these Rules, the Immigration Officer will consider whether or not he is in a position to decide to give or refuse leave to enter without interviewing the person further. If the Immigration Officer decides that a further interview is not required he may serve the notice giving or refusing leave to enter by post. If the Immigration Officer decides that a further interview is required, he will then resume his examination to determine whether or not to grant the person leave to enter under any other provision of these Rules. If the person fails at any time to comply with a requirement to report to an Immigration Officer for examination, the Immigration Officer may direct that the person's examination shall be treated as concluded at that time. The Immigration Officer will then consider any outstanding applications for entry on the basis of any evidence before him.

332. If a person who has been refused leave to enter makes an application for asylum and that application is refused or withdrawn or treated as withdrawn under paragraph 333C of these Rules, leave to enter will again be refused unless the applicant qualifies for admission under any other provision of these Rules.

333. Written notice of decisions on applications for asylum shall be given in reasonable time. Where the applicant is legally represented, notice may instead be given to the representative. Where the applicant has no legal representative and free legal assistance is not available, he shall be informed of the decision on the application for asylum and, if the application is rejected, how to challenge the decision, in a language that he may reasonably be supposed to understand.

333A. The Secretary of State shall ensure that a decision is taken by him on each application for asylum as soon as possible, without prejudice to an adequate and complete examination.

Where a decision on an application for asylum cannot be taken within six months of the date it was recorded, the Secretary of State shall either:

(a)   inform the applicant of the delay; or
(b)   if the applicant has made a specific written request for it, provide information on the timeframe within which the decision on his application is to be expected. The provision of such information shall not oblige the Secretary of State to take a decision within the stipulated time-frame.

333B. Applicants for asylum shall be allowed an effective opportunity to consult, at their own expense or at public expense in accordance with provision made for this by the Legal Services Commission or otherwise, a person who is authorised under Part V of the Immigration and Asylum Act 1999 to give immigration advice. This paragraph shall also apply where the Secretary of State is considering revoking a person's refugee status in accordance with these Rules.

Withdrawal of applications

333C. If an application for asylum is withdrawn either explicitly or implicitly, consideration of it may be discontinued. An application will be treated as explicitly withdrawn if the applicant signs the relevant form provided by the Secretary of State. An application may be treated as impliedly withdrawn if an applicant leaves the United Kingdom without authorisation at any time prior to the conclusion of his or her asylum claim, or fails to complete an asylum questionnaire as requested by the Secretary of State, or fails to attend the personal interview as provided in paragraph 339NA of these Rules unless the applicant demonstrates within a reasonable time that that failure was due to circumstances beyond his or her control. The Secretary of State will indicate on the applicant's asylum file that the application for asylum has been withdrawn and consideration of it has been discontinued.

Grant of refugee status

334. An asylum applicant will be granted refugee status in the United Kingdom if the Secretary of State is satisfied that:

(i)   he is in the United Kingdom or has arrived at a port of entry in the United Kingdom;
(ii)   he is a refugee, as defined in regulation 2 of The Refugee or Person in Need of International Protection (Qualification) Regulations 2006;
(iii) there are no reasonable grounds for regarding him as a danger to the security of the United Kingdom;
(iv)   having been convicted by a final judgment of a particularly serious crime, he does not constitute danger to the community of the United Kingdom; and
(v)   refusing his application would result in him being required to go (whether immediately or after the time limited by any existing leave to enter or remain) in breach of the Geneva Convention, to a country in which his life or freedom would

351

threatened on account of his race, religion, nationality, political opinion or membership of a particular social group.

335. If the Secretary of State decides to grant refugee status to a person who has previously been given leave to enter (whether or not the leave has expired) or to a person who has entered without leave, the Secretary of State will vary the existing leave or grant limited leave to remain.

Refusal of asylum

336. An application which does not meet the criteria set out in paragraph 334 will be refused. Where an application for asylum is refused, the reasons in fact and law shall be stated in the decision and information provided in writing on how to challenge the decision.

337. [*deleted*]

338. When a person in the United Kingdom is notified that asylum has been refused he may, if he is liable to removal as an illegal entrant, removal under section 10 of the Immigration and Asylum Act 1999 or to deportation, at the same time be notified of removal directions, served with a notice of intention to make a deportation order, or served with a deportation order, as appropriate.

339. [*deleted*]

Revocation or refusal to renew a grant of refugee status

338A. A person's grant of refugee status under paragraph 334 shall be revoked or not renewed if any of paragraphs 339A to 339AB apply. A person's grant of refugee status under paragraph 334 may be revoked or not renewed if paragraph 339AC applies.

Refugee Convention ceases to apply (cessation)

339A. This paragraph applies when the Secretary of State is satisfied that one or more of the following applies:

(i) he has voluntarily re-availed himself of the protection of the country of nationality;

(ii) having lost his nationality, he has voluntarily re-acquired it;

(iii) he has acquired a new nationality, and enjoys the protection of the country of his new nationality;

(iv) he has voluntarily re-established himself in the country which he left or outside which he remained owing to a fear of persecution;

(v) he can no longer, because the circumstances in connection with which he has been recognised as a refugee have ceased to exist, continue to refuse to avail himself of the protection of the country of nationality; or

(vi) being a stateless person with no nationality, he is able, because the circumstances in connection with which he has been recognised a refugee have ceased to exist, to return to the country of former habitual residence.

In considering (v) and (vi), the Secretary of State shall have regard to whether the change of circumstances is of such a significant and non-temporary nature that the refugee's fear of persecution can no longer be regarded as well-founded.

Exclusion from the Refugee Convention

339AA. This paragraph applies where the Secretary of State is satisfied that the person should have been or is excluded from being a refugee in accordance with regulation 7 of The Refugee or Person in Need of International Protection (Qualification) Regulations 2006.

As regards the application of Article 1F of the Refugee Convention, this paragraph also applies where the Secretary of State is satisfied that the person has instigated or otherwise participated in the crimes or acts mentioned therein.

Misrepresentation

339AB. This paragraph applies where the Secretary of State is satisfied that the person's misrepresentation or omission of facts, including the use of false documents, were decisive for the grant of refugee status.

Danger to the United Kingdom

339AC. This paragraph applies where the Secretary of State is satisfied that:

(i)   there are reasonable grounds for regarding the person as a danger to the security of the United Kingdom; or

(ii) having been convicted by a final judgment of a particularly serious crime, the person constitutes a danger to the community of the United Kingdom.

339B. When a person's refugee status is revoked or not renewed any limited or indefinite leave which they have may be curtailed or cancelled.

339BA. Where the Secretary of State is considering revoking refugee status in accordance with these Rules, the following procedure will apply. The person concerned shall be informed in writing that the Secretary of State is reconsidering his qualification for refugee status and the reasons for the reconsideration. That person shall be given the opportunity to submit, in a personal interview or in a written statement, reasons as to why his refugee status should not be revoked. If there is a personal interview, it shall be subject to the safeguards set out in these Rules.

339BB. The procedure in paragraph 339BA is subject to the following exceptions:

(i)   where a person acquires British citizenship status, his refugee status is automatically revoked in accordance with paragraph 339A (iii) upon acquisition of that status without the need to follow the procedure.

(ii) where refugee status is revoked under paragraph 339A, or if the person has unequivocally renounced his recognition as a refugee, his refugee status may be considered to have lapsed by law without the need to follow the procedure.

339BC. If the person leaves the UK, the procedure set out in paragraph 339BA may be initiated, and completed, while the person is outside the UK.

Grant of humanitarian protection

339C. A person will be granted humanitarian protection in the United Kingdom if the Secretary of State is satisfied that:

(i)   he is in the United Kingdom or has arrived at a port of entry in the United Kingdom;

(ii) he does not qualify as a refugee as defined in regulation 2 of The Refugee or Person in Need of International Protection (Qualification) Regulations 2006;

353

    (iii) substantial grounds have been shown for believing that the person concerned, if he returned to the country of return, would face a real risk of suffering serious harm and is unable, or, owing to such risk, unwilling to avail himself of the protection of that country; and

    (iv) he is not excluded from a grant of humanitarian protection.

Serious harm consists of:

    (i) the death penalty or execution;

    (ii) unlawful killing;

    (iii) torture or inhuman or degrading treatment or punishment of a person in the country of return; or

    (iv) serious and individual threat to a civilian's life or person by reason of indiscriminate violence in situations of international or internal armed conflict.

Exclusion from humanitarian protection

339D. A person is excluded from a grant of humanitarian protection under paragraph 339C (iv) where the Secretary of State is satisfied that:

    (i) there are serious reasons for considering that he has committed a crime against peace, a war crime, a crime against humanity, or any other serious crime or instigated or otherwise participated in such crimes;

    (ii) there are serious reasons for considering that he is guilty of acts contrary to the purposes and principles of the United Nations or has committed, prepared or instigated such acts or encouraged or induced others to commit, prepare or instigate instigated such acts;

    (iii) there are serious reasons for considering that he constitutes a danger to the community or to the security of the United Kingdom; or

    (iv) prior to his admission to the United Kingdom the person committed a crime outside the scope of (i) and (ii) that would be punishable by imprisonment were it committed in the United Kingdom and the person left his country of origin solely in order to avoid sanctions resulting from the crime.

339E. If the Secretary of State decides to grant humanitarian protection and the person has not yet been given leave to enter, the Secretary of State or an Immigration Officer will grant limited leave to enter. If the Secretary of State decides to grant humanitarian protection to a person who has been given limited leave to enter (whether or not that leave has expired) or a person who has entered without leave, the Secretary of State will vary the existing leave or grant limited leave to remain.

Refusal of humanitarian protection

339F. Where the criteria set out in paragraph 339C is not met humanitarian protection will be refused.

Revocation of humanitarian protection

339G. A person's humanitarian protection granted under paragraph 339C will be revoked or not renewed if any of paragraphs 339GA to 339GC apply. A person's humanitarian protection granted under paragraph 339C may be revoked or not renewed if paragraph 339GD applies.

Cessation

339GA. This paragraph applies where the Secretary of State is satisfied that the circumstances which led to the grant of humanitarian protection have ceased to exist or have changed to such a degree that such protection is no longer required.

In applying this paragraph the Secretary of State shall have regard to whether the change of circumstances is of such a significant and non-temporary nature that the person no longer faces a real risk of serious harm.

Exclusion

339GB. This paragraph applies where the Secretary of State is satisfied that:

    (i)   the person granted humanitarian protection should have been or is excluded from humanitarian protection because there are serious reasons for considering that he has committed a crime against peace, a war crime, a crime against humanity, or any other serious crime or instigated or otherwise participated in such crimes;

    (ii)   the person granted humanitarian protection should have been or is excluded from humanitarian protection because there are serious reasons for considering that he is guilty of acts contrary to the purposes and principles of the United Nations or has committed, prepared or instigated such acts or encouraged or induced others to commit, prepare or instigate such acts;

    (iii)   the person granted humanitarian protection should have been or is excluded from humanitarian protection because there are serious reasons for considering that he constitutes a danger to the community or to the security of the United Kingdom;

339GC. This paragraph applies where the Secretary of State is satisfied that the person granted humanitarian protection should have been or is excluded from humanitarian protection because prior to his admission to the United Kingdom the person committed a crime outside the scope of paragraph 339GB (i) and (ii) that would be punishable by imprisonment had it been committed in the United Kingdom and the person left his country of origin solely in order to avoid sanctions resulting from the crime.

Misrepresentation

339GD. This paragraph applies where the Secretary of State is satisfied that the person granted humanitarian protection misrepresented or omitted facts, including the use of false documents, which were decisive to the grant of humanitarian protection.

339H. When a person's humanitarian protection is revoked or not renewed any limited or indefinite leave which they have may be curtailed or cancelled.

Consideration of applications

339HA. The Secretary of State shall ensure that the personnel examining applications for asylum and taking decisions on his behalf have the knowledge with respect to relevant standards applicable in the field of asylum and refugee law.

339I. When the Secretary of State considers a person's asylum claim, eligibility for a grant of humanitarian protection or human rights claim it is the duty of the person to submit to the Secretary of State as soon as possible all material factors needed to substantiate the asylum claim or establish that he is a person eligible for humanitarian protection or substantiate the human rights claim, which the Secretary of State shall assess in cooperation with the person.

The material factors include:

(i)   the person's statement on the reasons for making an asylum claim or on eligibility for a grant of humanitarian protection or for making a human rights claim;

(ii)   all documentation at the person's disposal regarding the person's age, background (including background details of relevant relatives), identity, nationality(ies), country(ies) and place(s) of previous residence, previous asylum applications, travel routes; and

(iii)   identity and travel documents.

339IA. For the purposes of examining individual applications for asylum

(i)   information provided in support of an application and the fact that an application has been made shall not be disclosed to the alleged actor(s) of persecution of the applicant, and

(ii)   information shall not be obtained from the alleged actor(s) of persecution that would result in their being directly informed that an application for asylum has been made by the applicant in question and would jeopardise the physical integrity of the applicant and his dependants, or the liberty and security of his family members still living in the country of origin.

This paragraph shall also apply where the Secretary of State is considering revoking a person's refugee status in accordance with these Rules.

339J. The assessment by the Secretary of State of an asylum claim, eligibility for a grant of humanitarian protection or a human rights claim will be carried out on an individual, objective and impartial basis. This will include taking into account in particular:

(i)   all relevant facts as they relate to the country of origin or country of return at the time of taking a decision on the grant; including laws and regulations of the country of origin or country of return and the manner in which they are applied;

(ii)   relevant statements and documentation presented by the person including information on whether the person has been or may be subject to persecution or serious harm;

(iii)   the individual position and personal circumstances of the person, including factors such as background, gender and age, so as to assess whether, on the basis of the person's personal circumstances, the acts to which the person has been or could be exposed would amount to persecution or serious harm;

(iv)   whether the person's activities since leaving the country of origin or country of return were engaged in for the sole or main purpose of creating the necessary conditions for making an asylum claim or establishing that he is a person eligible for humanitarian protection or a human rights claim, so as to assess whether these activities will expose the person to persecution or serious harm if he returned to that country; and

(v)   whether the person could reasonably be expected to avail himself of the protection of another country where he could assert citizenship.

339JA. Reliable and up-to-date information shall be obtained from various sources as to the general situation prevailing in the countries of origin of applicants for asylum and, where necessary, in countries through which they have transited. Such information shall be made available to the personnel responsible for examining applications and taking decisions and may be provided to them in the form of a consolidated country information report.

This paragraph shall also apply where the Secretary of State is considering revoking a person's refugee status in accordance with these Rules.

339K. The fact that a person has already been subject to persecution or serious harm, or to direct threats of such persecution or such harm, will be regarded as a serious indication of the person's well-founded fear of persecution or real risk of suffering serious harm, unless there are good reasons to consider that such persecution or serious harm will not be repeated.

339L. It is the duty of the person to substantiate the asylum claim or establish that he is a person eligible humanitarian protection or substantiate his human rights claim. Where aspects of the person's statements are not supported by documentary or other evidence, those aspects will not need confirmation when all of the following conditions are met:

(i) the person has made a genuine effort to substantiate his asylum claim or establish that he is a person eligible humanitarian protection or substantiate his human rights claim;

(ii) all material factors at the person's disposal have been submitted, and a satisfactory explanation regarding any lack of other relevant material has been given;

(iii) the person's statements are found to be coherent and plausible and do not run counter to available specific and general information relevant to the person's case;

(iv) the person has made an asylum claim or sought to establish that he is a person eligible for humanitarian protection or made a human rights claim at the earliest possible time, unless the person can demonstrate good reason for not having done so; and

(v) the general credibility of the person has been established.

339M. The Secretary of State may consider that a person has not substantiated his asylum claim or established that he is a person eligible for humanitarian protection or substantiated his human rights claim, and thereby reject his application for asylum, determine that he is not eligible for humanitarian protection or reject his human rights claim, if he fails, without reasonable explanation, to make a prompt and full disclosure of material facts, either orally or in writing, or otherwise to assist the Secretary of State in establishing the facts of the case; this includes, for example, failure to report to a designated place to be fingerprinted, failure to complete an asylum questionnaire or failure to comply with a requirement to report to an immigration officer for examination.

339MA. Applications for asylum shall be neither rejected nor excluded from examination on the sole ground that they have not been made as soon as possible.

339N. In determining whether the general credibility of the person has been established the Secretary of State will apply the provisions in s.8 of the Asylum and Immigration (Treatment of Claimants, etc.) Act 2004.

Personal interview

339NA. Before a decision is taken on the application for asylum, the applicant shall be given the opportunity of a personal interview on his application for asylum with a representative of the Secretary of State who is legally competent to conduct such an interview.

The personal interview may be omitted where:

(i) the Secretary of State is able to take a positive decision on the basis of evidence available;

(ii) the Secretary of State has already had a meeting with the applicant for the purpose of assisting him with completing his application and submitting the essential information regarding the application;

(iii) the applicant, in submitting his application and presenting the facts, has only raised issues that are not relevant or of minimal relevance to the examination of whether he is a refugee, as defined in regulation 2 of the Refugee or Person in Need of International Protection (Qualification) Regulations 2006;

(iv) the applicant has made inconsistent, contradictory, improbable or insufficient representations which make his claim clearly unconvincing in relation to his having been the object of persecution;

(v) the applicant has submitted a subsequent application which does not raise any relevant new elements with respect to his particular circumstances or to the situation in his country of origin;

(vi) the applicant is making an application merely in order to delay or frustrate the enforcement of an earlier or imminent decision which would result in his removal;

(vii) it is not reasonably practicable, in particular where the Secretary of State is of the opinion that the applicant is unfit or unable to be interviewed owing to enduring circumstances beyond his control; or

(viii) the applicant is an EU national whose claim the Secretary of State has nevertheless decided to consider substantively in accordance with paragraph 326F above.

The omission of a personal interview shall not prevent the Secretary of State from taking a decision on the application.

Where the personal interview is omitted, the applicant and dependants shall be given a reasonable opportunity to submit further information.

339NB.

(i) The personal interview mentioned in paragraph 339NA above shall normally take place without the presence of the applicant's family members unless the Secretary of State considers it necessary for an appropriate examination to have other family members present.

(ii) The personal interview shall take place under conditions which ensure appropriate confidentiality.

339NC.

(i) A written report shall be made of every personal interview containing at least the essential information regarding the asylum application as presented by the applicant in accordance with paragraph 339I of these Rules.

(ii) The Secretary of State shall ensure that the applicant has timely access to the report of the personal interview and that access is possible as soon as necessary for allowing an appeal to be prepared and lodged in due time.

339ND. The Secretary of State shall provide at public expense an interpreter for the purpose of allowing the applicant to submit his case, wherever necessary. The Secretary of State shall select an interpreter who can ensure appropriate communication between the applicant and the representative of the Secretary of State who conducts the interview.

Internal relocation

339O.

(i) The Secretary of State will not make:

(a) a grant of refugee status if in part of the country of origin a person would not have a well founded fear of being persecuted, and the person can reasonably be expected to stay in that part of the country; or

(b) a grant of humanitarian protection if in part of the country of return a person would not face a real risk of suffering serious harm, and the person can reasonably be expected to stay in that part of the country.

(ii) In examining whether a part of the country of origin or country of return meets the requirements in (i) the Secretary of State, when making his decision on whether to grant asylum or humanitarian protection, will have regard to the general circumstances prevailing in that part of the country and to the personal circumstances of the person.

(iii) (i) applies notwithstanding technical obstacles to return to the country of origin or country of return

Sur place claims

339P. A person may have a well-founded fear of being persecuted or a real risk of suffering serious harm based on events which have taken place since the person left the country of origin or country of return and/or activates which have been engaged in by a person since he left the country of origin or country of return, in particular where it is established that the activities relied upon constitute the expression and continuation of convictions or orientations held in the country of origin or country of return.

Residence Permits

339Q.

(i) The Secretary of State will issue to a person granted refugee status in the United Kingdom a United Kingdom Residence Permit (UKRP) as soon as possible after the grant of refugee status. The UKRP may be valid for five years and renewable, unless compelling reasons of national security or public order otherwise require or where there are reasonable grounds for considering that the applicant is a danger to the security of the UK or having been convicted by a final judgment of a particularly serious crime, the applicant constitutes a danger to the community of the UK or the person's character, conduct or associations otherwise require.

(ii) The Secretary of State will issue to a person granted humanitarian protection in the United Kingdom a UKRP as soon as possible after the grant of humanitarian protection. The UKRP may be valid for five years and renewable, unless compelling reasons of national security or public order otherwise require or where there are reasonable grounds for considering that the person granted humanitarian protection is a danger to the security of the UK or having been convicted by a final judgment of a serious crime, this person constitutes a danger to the community of the UK or the person's character, conduct or associations otherwise require.

(iii) The Secretary of State will issue a UKRP to a family member of a person granted refugee status or humanitarian protection where the family member does not qualify for such status. A UKRP may be granted for a period of five years. The UKRP is renewable on the terms set out in (i) and (ii) respectively. 'Family member' for the purposes of this sub-paragraph refers only to those who are treated as dependants for the purposes of paragraph 349.

(iv) The Secretary of State may revoke or refuse to renew a person's UKRP where their grant of refugee status or humanitarian protection is revoked under the provisions in the immigration rules.

Requirements for indefinite leave to remain for persons granted refugee status or humanitarian protection

339R. The requirements for indefinite leave to remain for a person granted refugee status or humanitarian protection, or their dependants granted asylum or humanitarian protection in line with the main applicant or any dependant granted in accordance with the requirements of paragraphs 352A to 352FJ of these Rules (Family Reunion), are that:

(i) the applicant has held a UK Residence Permit (UKRP) issued under paragraph 339Q for a continuous period of five years in the UK; and

(ii) the applicant's UKRP has not been revoked or not renewed under paragraphs 339A or 339G of the immigration rules; and

(iii) the applicant has not:

    a. been convicted of an offence for which they have been sentenced to imprisonment for at least 4 years; or

    b. been convicted of an offence for which they have been sentenced to imprisonment for at least 12 months but less than 4 years, unless a period of 15 years has passed since the end of the sentence; or

    c. been convicted of an offence for which they have been sentenced to imprisonment for less than 12 months, unless a period of 7 years has passed since the end of the sentence; or

    d. within the 24 months prior to the date on which the application has been decided, been convicted of or admitted an offence for which they have received a non-custodial sentence or other out of court disposal that is recorded on their criminal record; or

    e. in the view of the Secretary of State caused serious harm by their offending or persistently offended and shown a particular disregard for the law; or

    f. in the view of the Secretary of State, at the date on which the application has been decided, demonstrated the undesirability of granting settlement in the United Kingdom in light of his or her conduct (including convictions which do not fall within paragraphs 339R(iii)(a-e)), character or associations or the fact that he or she represents a threat to national security.

Indefinite leave to remain for a person granted refugee status or humanitarian protection

339S. Indefinite leave to remain for a person granted refugee status or humanitarian protection will be granted where each of the requirements in paragraph 339R is met.

Refusal of indefinite leave to remain for a person granted refugee status or humanitarian protection

339T.

(i) Indefinite leave to remain for a person granted refugee status or humanitarian protection is to be refused if any of the requirements of paragraph 339R is not met.

(ii) An applicant refused indefinite leave to remain under paragraph 339T(i) may apply to have their UK Residence Permit extended in accordance with paragraph 339Q.

Consideration of asylum applications and human rights claims

340. [*deleted*]

341. [*deleted*]

342. The actions of anyone acting as an agent of the asylum applicant or human rights claimant may also be taken into account in regard to the matters set out in paragraphs 340 and 341.

343. [*deleted*]

344. [*deleted*]

Travel documents

344A.

- (i) After having received a complete application for a travel document, the Secretary of State will issue to a person granted refugee status in the United Kingdom and their family members travel documents, in the form set out in the Schedule to the Geneva Convention, for the purpose of travel outside the United Kingdom, unless compelling reasons of national security or public order otherwise require.
- (ii) After having received a complete application for a travel document, the Secretary of State will issue to a person granted humanitarian protection in the United Kingdom and their family members a travel document where that person is unable to obtain a national passport or other identity documents which enable him to travel, unless compelling reasons of national security or public order otherwise require.
- (iii) Where the person referred to in (ii) can obtain a national passport or identity documents but has not done so, the Secretary of State will issue that person with a travel document where he can show that he has made reasonable attempts to obtain a national passport or identity document and there are serious humanitarian reasons for travel.
- (iv) For the purposes of paragraph 344A, a 'family member' refers only to a person who has been treated as a dependant under paragraph 349 of these Rules or a person who has been granted leave to enter or remain in accordance with paragraphs 352A-352FJ of these Rules.

Access to Employment

344B. The Secretary of State will not impose conditions restricting the employment or occupation in the United Kingdom of a person granted refugee status or humanitarian protection.

Information

344C. A person who is granted refugee status or humanitarian protection will be provided with access to information in a language that they may reasonably be supposed to understand which sets out the rights and obligations relating to that status. The Secretary of State will provide the information as soon as possible after the grant of refugee status or humanitarian protection.

Third country cases

345.

- (1) In a case where the Secretary of State is satisfied that the conditions set out in Paragraphs 4 and 5(1), 9 and 10(1), 14 and 15(1) or 17 of Schedule 3 to the Asylum and Immigration (Treatment of Claimants, etc.) Act 2004 are fulfilled, he will normally decline to examine the asylum application substantively and issue a certificate under Part 2, 3, 4 or 5 of Schedule 3 to the Asylum and Immigration (Treatment of Claimants, etc.) Act 2004 as appropriate.
- (2) The Secretary of State shall not issue a certificate under Part 2, 3, 4 or 5 of Schedule 3 to the Asylum and Immigration (Treatment of Claimants, etc.) Act 2004 unless:

(i)   the asylum applicant has not arrived in the United Kingdom directly from the country in which he claims to fear persecution and has had an opportunity at the border or within the third country or territory to make contact with the authorities of that third country or territory in order to seek their protection; or

(ii)   there is other clear evidence of his admissibility to a third country or territory.

Provided that he is satisfied that a case meets these criteria, the Secretary of State is under no obligation to consult the authorities of the third country or territory before the removal of an asylum applicant to that country or territory.

(2A)   Where a certificate is issued under Part 2, 3, 4 or 5 of Schedule 3 to the Asylum and Immigration (Treatment of Claimants, etc.) Act 2004 the asylum applicant shall:

(i)   be informed in a language that he may reasonably be expected to understand regarding his removal to a safe third country;

(ii)   be provided with a document informing the authorities of the safe third country, in the language of that country, that the asylum application has not been examined in substance by the authorities in the United Kingdom;

(iii)   sub-paragraph 345(2A)(ii) shall not apply if removal takes place with reference to the arrangements set out in Regulation (EC) No. 343/2003 (the Dublin Regulation) or Regulation (EC) No. 604/2013; and

(iv)   if an asylum applicant removed under this paragraph is not admitted to the safe third country (not being a country to which the Dublin Regulation applies as specified in paragraph 345(2A)(iii)), subject to determining and resolving the reasons for his non-admission, the asylum applicant shall be admitted to the asylum procedure in the United Kingdom.

(3)   Where a certificate is issued under Part 2, 3, 4 or 5 of Schedule 3 to the Asylum and Immigration (Treatment of Claimants, etc.) Act 2004 in relation to the asylum claim and the person is seeking leave to enter the Immigration Officer will consider whether or not he is in a position to decide to give or refuse leave to enter without interviewing the person further. If the Immigration Officer decides that a further interview is not required he may serve the notice giving or refusing leave to enter by post. If the Immigration Officer decides that a further interview is required, he will then resume his examination to determine whether or not to grant the person leave to enter under any other provision of these Rules. If the person fails at any time to comply with a requirement to report to an Immigration Officer for examination, the Immigration Officer may direct that the person's examination shall be treated as concluded at that time. The Immigration Officer will then consider any outstanding applications for entry on the basis of any evidence before him.

(4)   Where a certificate is issued under Part 2, 3, 4 or 5 of Schedule 3 to the Asylum and Immigration (Treatment of Claimants, etc.) Act 2004 the person may, if liable to removal as an illegal entrant, or removal under section 10 of the Immigration and Asylum Act 1999 or to deportation, at the same time be notified of removal directions, served with a notice of intention to make a deportation order, or served with a deportation order, as appropriate.

Previously rejected applications

346. [*deleted*]

347. [*deleted*]

Rights of appeal

348. [*deleted*]

Dependants

349. A spouse, civil partner, unmarried or same-sex partner, or minor child accompanying a principal applicant may be included in his application for asylum as his dependant, provided, in the case of an adult dependant with legal capacity, the dependant consents to being treated as such at the time the application is lodged. A spouse, civil partner, unmarried or same-sex partner or minor child may also claim asylum in his own right. If the principal applicant is granted refugee status or humanitarian protection and leave to enter or remain any spouse, civil partner, unmarried or same-sex partner or minor child will be granted leave to enter or remain for the same duration. The case of any dependant who claims asylum in his own right will be also considered individually in accordance with paragraph 334 above. An applicant under this paragraph, including an accompanied child, may be interviewed where he makes a claim as a dependant or in his own right.

If the spouse, civil partner, unmarried or same-sex partner, or minor child in question has a claim in his own right, that claim should be made at the earliest opportunity. Any failure to do so will be taken into account and may damage credibility if no reasonable explanation for it is given. Where an asylum or humanitarian protection application is unsuccessful, at the same time that asylum or humanitarian protection is refused the applicant may be notified of removal directions or served with a notice of the Secretary of State's intention to deport him, as appropriate. In this paragraph and paragraphs 350-352 a child means a person who is under 18 years of age or who, in the absence of documentary evidence establishing age, appears to be under that age. An unmarried or same sex partner for the purposes of this paragraph, is a person who has been living together with the principal applicant in a subsisting relationship akin to marriage or a civil partnership for two years or more.

Unaccompanied children

350. Unaccompanied children may also apply for asylum and, in view of their potential vulnerability, particular priority and care is to be given to the handling of their cases.

351. A person of any age may qualify for refugee status under the Convention and the criteria in paragraph 334 apply to all cases. However, account should be taken of the applicant's maturity and in assessing the claim of a child more weight should be given to objective indications of risk than to the child's state of mind and understanding of his situation. An asylum application made on behalf of a child should not be refused solely because the child is too young to understand his situation or to have formed a well founded fear of persecution. Close attention should be given to the welfare of the child at all times.

352. Any child over the age of 12 who has claimed asylum in his own right shall be interviewed about the substance of his claim unless the child is unfit or unable to be interviewed. When an interview takes place it shall be conducted in the presence of a parent, guardian, representative or another adult independent of the Secretary of State who has responsibility for the child. The interviewer shall have specialist training in the interviewing of children and have particular regard to the possibility that a child will feel inhibited or alarmed. The child shall be allowed to express himself in his own way and at his own speed. If he appears tired or distressed, the interview will be suspended. The interviewer should then consider whether it would be appropriate for the interview to be resumed the same day or on another day.

352ZA. The Secretary of State shall as soon as possible after an unaccompanied child makes an application for asylum take measures to ensure that a representative represents and/or assists the unaccompanied child with respect to the examination of the application and ensure that the representative is given the opportunity to inform the unaccompanied child about the meaning and possible consequences of the interview and, where appropriate, how to prepare himself for the interview. The representative shall have the right to be present at the interview and ask questions and make comments in the interview, within the framework set by the interviewer.

352ZB. The decision on the application for asylum shall be taken by a person who is trained to deal with asylum claims from children.

Requirements for limited leave to remain as an unaccompanied asylum seeking child.

352ZC. The requirements to be met in order for a grant of limited leave to remain to be made in relation to an unaccompanied asylum seeking child under paragraph 352ZE are:

(a)   the applicant is an unaccompanied asylum seeking child under the age of 17 ½ years throughout the duration of leave to be granted in this capacity;

(b)   the applicant must have applied for asylum and been granted neither refugee status nor Humanitarian Protection;

(c)   there are no adequate reception arrangements in the country to which they would be returned if leave to remain was not granted;

(d)   the applicant must not be excluded from being a refugee under Regulation 7 of the Refugee or Person in Need of International Protection (Qualification) Regulations 2006 or excluded from a grant of Humanitarian Protection under paragraph 339D or both;

(e)   there are no reasonable grounds for regarding the applicant as a danger to the security of the United Kingdom;

(f)   the applicant has not been convicted by a final judgment of a particularly serious crime, and the applicant does not constitute a danger to the community of the United Kingdom; and

(g)   the applicant is not, at the date of their application, the subject of a deportation order or a decision to make a deportation order.

352ZD. An unaccompanied asylum seeking child is a person who:

(a)   is under 18 years of age when the asylum application is submitted.

(b)   is applying for asylum in their own right; and

(c)   is separated from both parents and is not being cared for by an adult who in law or by custom has responsibility to do so.

352ZE. Limited leave to remain should be granted for a period of 30 months or until the child is 17 ½ years of age whichever is shorter, provided that the Secretary of State is satisfied that the requirements in paragraph 352ZC are met.

352ZF. Limited leave granted under this provision will cease if

(a)   any one or more of the requirements listed in paragraph 352ZC cease to be met, or

(b)   a misrepresentation or omission of facts, including the use of false documents, were decisive for the grant of leave under 352ZE.

Refugee family reunion

352A. The requirements to be met by a person seeking leave to enter or remain in the United Kingdom as the spouse civil partner of a person granted refugee status are that:

(i)   the applicant is married to or the civil partner of a person who has been granted refugee status; and

(ii)   the marriage or civil partnership did not take place after the person granted refugee status left the country of his former habitual residence in order to seek asylum; an

(iii)   the applicant would not be excluded from protection by virtue of article 1F of the United Nations Convention and Protocol relating to the Status of Refugees if he were to seek asylum in his own right; and

(iv)   each of the parties intends to live permanently with the other as his or her spouse civil partner and the marriage is subsisting; and

(v)   if seeking leave to enter, the applicant holds a valid United Kingdom entry clearance for entry in this capacity.

352AA. The requirements to be met by a person seeking leave to enter or remain in the United Kingdom as the unmarried or the same-sex partner of a person granted refugee status are that:

(i)   the applicant is the unmarried or same-sex partner of a person who has been granted refugee status in the United Kingdom on or after 9th October 2006; and

(ii)   the parties have been living together in a relationship akin to either a marriage or a civil partnership which has subsisted for two years or more; and

(iii)   the relationship existed before the person granted refugee status left the country of his former habitual residence in order to seek asylum; and

(iv)   the applicant would not be excluded from protection by virtue of paragraph 334(iii) or (iv) of these Rules or Article 1F of the Geneva Convention if he were to seek of these Rules or article 1F of the Geneva Convention if he were to seek asylum in his own right; and

(v)   each of the parties intends to live permanently with the other as his or her unmarried or same-sex partner and the relationship is subsisting; and

(vi)   the parties are not involved in a consanguineous relationship with one another; and

(viii) if seeking leave to enter, the applicant holds a valid United Kingdom entry clearance for entry in this capacity.

352B. Limited leave to enter the United Kingdom as the spouse civil partner of a person who has been granted refugee status may be granted provided a valid United Kingdom entry clearance for entry in this capacity is produced to the Immigration Officer on arrival. Limited leave to remain in the United Kingdom as the spouse of a person who has been granted refugee status may be granted provided the Secretary of State is satisfied that each of the requirements of paragraph 352A (i)–(v) are met.

352BA. Limited leave to enter the United Kingdom as the unmarried or same-sex partner of a person who has been granted refugee status may be granted provided a valid United Kingdom entry clearance for entry in this capacity is produced to the Immigration Officer on arrival. Limited leave to remain in the United Kingdom as the unmarried or same sex partner of a refugee may be granted provided the Secretary of State is satisfied that each of the requirements of paragraph 352AA (i) – (vii) are met.

352C. Limited leave to enter the United Kingdom as the spouse civil partner of a person who has been granted refugee status is to be refused if a valid United Kingdom entry clearance for entry in this capacity is not produced to the Immigration Officer on arrival. Limited leave to remain as the spouse civil partner of a refugee is to be refused if the Secretary of State is not satisfied that each of the requirements of paragraph 352A (i) – (v) are met.

352CA. Limited leave to enter the United Kingdom as the unmarried or same-sex partner of a person who has been granted refugee status is to be refused if a valid United Kingdom entry clearance for entry in this capacity is not produced to the Immigration Officer on arrival. Limited leave to remain as the unmarried or same sex partner of a refugee is to be refused if the Secretary of State is not satisfied that each of the requirements of paragraph 352AA (i) – (vi) are met.

352D. The requirements to be met by a person seeking leave to enter or remain in the United Kingdom in order to join or remain with the parent who has been granted refugee status are that the applicant:

(i)   is the child of a parent who is currently a refugee granted status as such under the immigration rules in the United Kingdom; and

(ii)   is under the age of 18, and

(iii) is not leading an independent life, is unmarried and is not a civil partner, and has not formed an independent family unit; and

(iv) was part of the family unit of the person granted asylum at the time that the person granted asylum left the country of his habitual residence in order to seek asylum; and

(v)   would not be excluded from protection by virtue of article 1F of the United Nations Convention and Protocol relating to the Status of Refugees if he were to seek asylum in his own right; and

(vi) if seeking leave to enter, holds a valid United Kingdom entry clearance for entry in this capacity.

352E. Limited leave to enter the United Kingdom as the child of a person who has been granted refugee status may be granted provided a valid United Kingdom entry clearance for entry in this capacity is produced to the Immigration Officer on arrival. Limited leave to remain in the United Kingdom as the child of a refugee may be granted provided the Secretary of State is satisfied that each of the requirements of paragraph 352D (i)–(v) are met.

352F. Limited leave to enter the United Kingdom as the child of a person who has been granted refugee status is to be refused if a valid United Kingdom entry clearance for entry in this capacity is not produced to the Immigration Officer on arrival. Limited leave to remain as the child of a refugee is to be refused if the Secretary of State is not satisfied that each of the requirements of paragraph 352D (i)–(v) are met.

352FA. The requirements to be met by a person seeking leave to enter or remain in the United Kingdom as the spouse or civil partner of a person who has been granted humanitarian protection and was granted that status on or after 30 August 2005 are that:

(i)   the applicant is married to or the civil partner of a person who has been granted humanitarian protection and was granted that status on or after 30 August 2005; and

(ii)   the marriage or civil partnership did not take place after the person granted humanitarian protection left the country of his former habitual residence in order to seek asylum in the UK; and

(iii) the applicant would not be excluded from a grant of humanitarian protection for any of the reasons in paragraph 339D; and

(iv)   each of the parties intend to live permanently with the other as his or her spouse or civil partner and the marriage or civil partnership is subsisting; and

(v)   if seeking leave to enter, the applicant holds a valid United Kingdom entry clearance for entry in this capacity.

352FB. Limited leave to enter the United Kingdom as the spouse or civil partner of a person granted humanitarian protection may be granted provided a valid United Kingdom entry clearance for entry in this capacity is produced to the Immigration Officer on arrival. Limited leave to remain in the United Kingdom as the spouse or civil partner of a person granted humanitarian protection may be granted provided the Secretary of State is satisfied that each of the requirements in sub paragraphs 352FA(i)–(iv) are met.

352FC. Limited leave to enter the United Kingdom as the spouse or civil partner of a person granted humanitarian protection is to be refused if a valid United Kingdom entry clearance for entry in this capacity is not produced to the Immigration Officer on arrival. Limited leave to remain as the spouse or civil partner of a person granted humanitarian protection is to be refused if the Secretary of State is not satisfied that each of the requirements in sub paragraphs 352FA (i)–(iv) are met.

352FD. The requirements to be met by a person seeking leave to enter or remain in the United Kingdom as the unmarried or same-sex partner of a person who has been granted humanitarian protection are that:

(i)   the applicant is the unmarried or same-sex partner of a person who has been granted humanitarian protection and has been granted that status on or after 9th October 2006; and

(ii)   the parties have been living together in a relationship akin to either a marriage or a civil partnership which has subsisted for two years or more; and

(iii) the relationship existed before the person granted humanitarian protection left the country of his former habitual residence in order to seek asylum; and

(iv)   the applicant would not be excluded from a grant of humanitarian protection for any of the reasons in paragraph 339D; and

(v)   each of the parties intends to live permanently with the other as his or her unmarried or same-sex partner and the relationship is subsisting; and

(vi)   the parties are not involved in a consanguineous relationship with one another; and

(vii) if seeking leave to enter, the applicant holds a valid United Kingdom entry clearance for entry in this capacity.

352FE. Limited leave to enter the United Kingdom as the unmarried or same-sex partner of a person granted humanitarian protection may be granted provided a valid United Kingdom entry clearance for entry in this capacity is produced to the Immigration Officer on arrival. Limited leave to remain in the United Kingdom as the unmarried or same sex partner of a person granted humanitarian protection may be granted provided the Secretary of State is satisfied that each of the requirements in subparagraphs 352FD (i)–(vi) are met.

352FF. Limited leave to enter the United Kingdom as the unmarried or same-sex partner of a person granted humanitarian protection is to be refused if a valid United Kingdom entry clearance for entry in this capacity is not produced to the Immigration Officer on arrival. Limited leave to remain as the unmarried or same sex partner of a person granted humanitarian protection is to be refused if the Secretary of State is not satisfied that each of the requirements in sub paragraphs 352FD(i)–(vi) are met.

D1

352FG. The requirements to be met by a person seeking leave to enter or remain in the United Kingdom in order to join or remain with their parent who has been granted humanitarian protection and was granted that status on or after 30 August 2005 are that the applicant:

(i)   is the child of a parent who has been granted humanitarian protection and was granted that status on or after 30 August 2005; and

(ii)   is under the age of 18, and

(iii)   is not leading an independent life, is unmarried or is not in a civil partnership, and has not formed an independent family unit; and

(iv)   was part of the family unit of the person granted humanitarian protection at the time that the person granted humanitarian protection left the country of his habitual residence in order to seek asylum in the UK; and

(v)   would not be excluded from a grant of humanitarian protection for any of the reasons in paragraph 339D; and

(vi)   if seeking leave to enter, holds a valid United Kingdom entry clearance for entry in this capacity.

352FH. Limited leave to enter the United Kingdom as the child of a person granted humanitarian protection may be granted provided a valid United Kingdom entry clearance for entry in this capacity is produced to the Immigration Officer on arrival. Limited leave to remain in the United Kingdom as the child of a person granted humanitarian protection may be granted provided the Secretary of State is satisfied that each of the requirements in sub paragraphs 352FG (i)–(v) are met.

352FI. Limited leave to enter the United Kingdom as the child of a person granted humanitarian protection is to be refused if a valid United Kingdom entry clearance for entry in this capacity is not produced to the Immigration Officer on arrival. Limited leave to remain as the child of a person granted humanitarian protection is to be refused if the Secretary of State is not satisfied that each of the requirements in sub paragraphs 352FG (i)–(v) are met.

352FJ. Nothing in paragraphs 352A–352FI shall allow a person to be granted leave to enter or remain in the United Kingdom as the spouse or civil partner, unmarried or same sex partner or child of a person who has been granted refugee status, or of a person granted humanitarian protection under the immigration rules in the United Kingdom on or after 30 August 2005, if the person granted refugee status or, as the case may be, person granted humanitarian protection, is a British Citizen.

Interpretation

352G. For the purposes of this Part:

(a)   'Geneva Convention' means the United Nations Convention and Protocol relating to the Status of Refugees;

(b)   'Country of return' means a country or territory listed in paragraph 8(c) of Schedule 2 of the Immigration Act 1971;

(c)   'Country of origin' means the country or countries of nationality or, for a stateless person, or former habitual residence.

Restriction on study

352H. Where a person is granted leave in accordance with the provisions set out in Part 11 of the Immigration Rules that leave will, in addition to any other conditions which may apply, be granted subject to the condition in Part 15 of these Rules.

Immigration Rules, Part 11B – Asylum (paragraphs 357 to 361)

Reception Conditions for non-EU asylum applicants

357. Part 11B only applies to asylum applicants (within the meaning of these Rules) who are not nationals of a member State.

Information to be provided to asylum applicants

357A. The Secretary of State shall inform asylum applicants in a language they may reasonably be supposed to understand and within a reasonable time after their claim for asylum has been recorded of the procedure to be followed, their rights and obligations during the procedure, and the possible consequences of non-compliance and non-co-operation. They shall be informed of the likely timeframe for consideration of the application and the means at their disposal for submitting all relevant information.

358. The Secretary of State shall inform asylum applicants within a reasonable time not exceeding fifteen days after their claim for asylum has been recorded of the benefits and services that they may be eligible to receive and of the rules and procedures with which they must comply relating to them. The Secretary of State shall also provide information on non-governmental organisations and persons that provide legal assistance to asylum applicants and which may be able to help asylum applicants or provide information on available benefits and services.

358A. The Secretary of State shall ensure that the information referred to in paragraph 358 is available in writing and, to the extent possible, will provide the information in a language that asylum applicants may reasonably be supposed to understand. Where appropriate, the Secretary of State may also arrange for this information to be supplied orally.

Information to be provided by asylum applicants

358B. An asylum applicant must notify the Secretary of State of his current address and of any change to his address or residential status. If not notified beforehand, any change must be notified to the Secretary of State without delay after it occurs.

The United Nations High Commissioner for Refugees

358C. A representative of the United Nations High Commissioner for Refugees (UNHCR) or an organisation working in the United Kingdom on behalf of the UNHCR pursuant to an agreement with the government shall:

    (a)   have access to applicants for asylum, including those in detention;

    (b)   have access to information on individual applications for asylum, on the course of the procedure and on the decisions taken on applications for asylum, provided that the applicant for asylum agrees thereto;

(c) be entitled to present his views, in the exercise of his supervisory responsibilities under Article 35 of the Geneva Convention, to the Secretary of State regarding individual applications for asylum at any stage of the procedure.

This paragraph shall also apply where the Secretary of State is considering revoking a person's refugee status in accordance with these Rules.

Documentation

359. The Secretary of State shall ensure that, within three working days of recording an asylum application, a document is made available to that asylum applicant, issued in his own name, certifying his status as an asylum applicant or testifying that he is allowed to remain in the United Kingdom while his asylum application is pending. For the avoidance of doubt, in cases where the Secretary of State declines to examine an application it will no longer be pending for the purposes of this rule.

359A. The obligation in paragraph 359 above shall not apply where the asylum applicant is detained under the Immigration Acts, the Immigration and Asylum Act 1999 or the Nationality, Immigration and Asylum Act 2002.

359B. A document issued to an asylum applicant under paragraph 359 does not constitute evidence of the asylum applicant's identity.

359C. In specific cases the Secretary of State or an Immigration Officer may provide an asylum applicant with evidence equivalent to that provided under rule 359. This might be, for example, in circumstances in which it is only possible or desirable to issue a time-limited document.

Right to request permission to take up employment

360. An asylum applicant may apply to the Secretary of State for permission to take up employment if a decision at first instance has not been taken on the applicant's asylum application within one year of the date on which it was recorded. The Secretary of State shall only consider such an application if, in the Secretary of State's opinion, any delay in reaching a decision at first instance cannot be attributed to the applicant.

360A. If permission to take up employment is granted under paragraph that permission will be subject to the following restrictions:

(i) employment may only be taken up in a post which is, at the time an offer of employment is accepted, included on the list of shortage occupations published by the United Kingdom Border Agency (as that list is amended from time to time);

(ii) no work in a self-employed capacity; and

(iii) no engagement in setting up a business.

360B. If an asylum applicant is granted permission to take up employment under paragraph 360 this shall only be until such time as his asylum application has been finally determined.

360C. Where an individual makes further submissions which raise asylum grounds and which fall to be considered under paragraph 353 of these Rules, that individual may apply to the Secretary of State for permission to take up employment if a decision pursuant to paragraph 353 of these Rules has not been taken on the further submissions within one year of the date on which they were recorded. The Secretary of State shall only consider such an application if, in the Secretary of State's opinion, any delay in reaching a decision pursuant to paragraph 353 of these Rules cannot be attributed to the individual.

360D. If permission to take up employment is granted under paragraph 360C, that permission will be subject to the following restrictions:

   (i)   employment may only be taken up in a post which is, at the time an offer of employment is accepted, included on the list of shortage occupations published by the United Kingdom Border Agency (as that list is amended from time to time);

   (ii)   no work in a self-employed capacity; and

   (iii) no engagement in setting up a business.

360E. Where permission to take up employment is granted pursuant to paragraph 360C, this shall only be until such time as:

   (i)   a decision has been taken pursuant to paragraph 353 that the further submissions do not amount to a fresh claim; or

   (ii)   where the further submissions are considered to amount to a fresh claim for asylum pursuant to paragraph 353, all rights of appeal from the immigration decision made in consequence of the rejection of the further submissions have been exhausted.

Interpretation

361. For the purposes of this Part -

   (a)   'working day' means any day other than a Saturday or Sunday, a bank holiday, Christmas day or Good Friday;

   (b)   'member State' has the same meaning as in Schedule 1 to the European Communities Act 1972.

Immigration Rules, Part 12 – Procedure and rights of appeal (paragraphs 353 to 353B)

Fresh Claims

353. When a human rights or asylum claim has been refused or withdrawn or treated as withdrawn under paragraph 333C of these Rules and any appeal relating to that claim is no longer pending, the decision maker will consider any further submissions and, if rejected, will then determine whether they amount to a fresh claim. The submissions will amount to a fresh claim if they are significantly different from the material that has previously been considered. The submissions will only be significantly different if the content:

(i)   had not already been considered; and
(ii) taken together with the previously considered material, created a realistic prospect of success, notwithstanding its rejection.

This paragraph does not apply to claims made overseas.

353A. Consideration of further submissions shall be subject to the procedures set out in these Rules. An applicant who has made further submissions shall not be removed before the Secretary of State has considered the submissions under paragraph 353 or otherwise.

Exceptional Circumstances

353B. Where further submissions have been made and the decision maker has established whether or not they amount to a fresh claim under paragraph 353 of these Rules, or in cases with no outstanding further submissions whose appeal rights have been exhausted and which are subject to a review, the decision maker will also have regard to the migrant's:

(i)   character, conduct and associations including any criminal record and the nature of any offence of which the migrant concerned has been convicted;
(ii) compliance with any conditions attached to any previous grant of leave to enter or remain and compliance with any conditions of temporary admission or immigration bail where applicable;
(iii) length of time spent in the United Kingdom spent for reasons beyond the migrant's control after the human rights or asylum claim has been submitted or refused; in deciding whether there are exceptional circumstances which mean that removal from the United Kingdom is no longer appropriate.

This paragraph does not apply to submissions made overseas.

This paragraph does not apply where the person is liable to deportation.

Immigration Rules, Part 13 – Deportation (paragraphs A362 to 400)

A deportation order

A362. Where Article 8 is raised in the context of deportation under Part 13 of these Rules, the claim under Article 8 will only succeed where the requirements of these rules as at 28 July 2014 are met, regardless of when the notice of intention to deport or the deportation order, as appropriate, was served.

362. A deportation order requires the subject to leave the United Kingdom and authorises his detention until he is removed. It also prohibits him from re-entering the country for as long as it is in force and invalidates any leave to enter or remain in the United Kingdom given him before the Order is made or while it is in force.

363. The circumstances in which a person is liable to deportation include:

(i)   where the Secretary of State deems the person's deportation to be conducive to the public good;
(ii) where the person is the spouse or civil partner or child under 18 of a person ordered to be deported; and
(iii) where a court recommends deportation in the case of a person over the age of 17 who has been convicted of an offence punishable with imprisonment.

363A.   Prior to 2 October 2000, a person would have been liable to deportation in certain circumstances in which he is now liable to administrative removal. However, such a person remains liable to deportation, rather than administrative removal where:

(i)   a decision to make a deportation order against him was taken before 2 October 2000; or
(ii) the person has made a valid application under the Immigration (Regularisation Period for Overstayers) Regulations 2000.

Deportation of family members

364. [*deleted*]

364A. [*deleted*]

365. The Secretary of State will not normally decide to deport the spouse or civil partner of a deportee under section 5 of the Immigration Act 1971 where:

(i)   he has qualified for settlement in his own right; or
(ii) he has been living apart from the deportee.

366. The Secretary of State will not normally decide to deport the child of a deportee under section 5 of the Immigration Act 1971 where:
    (i)   he and his mother or father are living apart from the deportee; or
    (ii) he has left home and established himself on an independent basis; or
    (iii) he married or formed a civil partnership before deportation came into prospect.

367. [*deleted*]

368. [*deleted*]

Right of appeal against destination

369. [*deleted*]

Restricted right of appeal against deportation in cases of breach of limited leave

370. [*deleted*]

Exemption to the restricted right of appeal

371. [*deleted*]

372. [*deleted*]

A deportation order made on the recommendation of a Court

373. [*deleted*]

Where deportation is deemed to be conducive to the public good

374. [*deleted*]

375. [*deleted*]

Hearing of appeals

376. [*deleted*]

377. [*deleted*]

378. [*deleted*]

Persons who have claimed asylum

379. [*deleted*]

379A. [*deleted*]

380. [*deleted*]

Procedure

381. When a decision to make a deportation order has been taken (otherwise than on the recommendation of a court) a notice will be given to the person concerned informing him of the decision.

382. Following the issue of such a notice the Secretary of State may authorise detention or make an order restricting a person as to residence, employment or occupation and requiring him to report to the police, pending the making of a deportation order.

383. [*deleted*]

384. [*deleted*]

Arrangements for removal

385. A person against whom a deportation order has been made will normally be removed from the United Kingdom. The power is to be exercised so as to secure the person's return to the country of which he is a national, or which has most recently provided him with a travel document, unless he can show that another country will receive him. In considering any departure from the normal arrangements, regard will be had to the public interest generally, and to any additional expense that may fall on public funds.

386. [*deleted*]

Supervised departure

387. [*deleted*]

Returned deportees

388. Where a person returns to the UK when a deportation order is in force against him, he may be deported under the original order. The Secretary of State will consider every such case in the light of all the relevant circumstances before deciding whether to enforce the order.

Returned family members

389. Persons deported in the circumstances set out in paragraphs 365-368 above (deportation of family members) may be able to seek re-admission to the United Kingdom under the Immigration Rules where:

    (i)   a child reaches 18 (when he ceases to be subject to the deportation order); or

    (ii)   in the case of a spouse or civil partner, the marriage or civil partnership comes to an end.

Revocation of deportation order

390. An application for revocation of a deportation order will be considered in the light of all the circumstances including the following:

    (i)   the grounds on which the order was made;

    (ii)   any representations made in support of revocation;

(iii) the interests of the community, including the maintenance of an effective immigration control;

(iv) the interests of the applicant, including any compassionate circumstances.

390A. Where paragraph 398 applies the Secretary of State will consider whether paragraph 399 or 399A applies and, if it does not, it will only be in exceptional circumstances that the public interest in maintaining the deportation order will be outweighed by other factors.

391. In the case of a person who has been deported following conviction for a criminal offence, the continuation of a deportation order against that person will be the proper course:

(a) in the case of a conviction for an offence for which the person was sentenced to a period of imprisonment of less than 4 years, unless 10 years have elapsed since the making of the deportation order, when, if an application for revocation is received, consideration will be given on a case by case basis to whether the deportation order should be maintained, or

(b) in the case of a conviction for an offence for which the person was sentenced to a period of imprisonment of at least 4 years, at any time,

Unless, in either case, the continuation would be contrary to the Human Rights Convention or the Convention and Protocol Relating to the Status of Refugees, or there are other exceptional circumstances that mean the continuation is outweighed by compelling factors.

391A. In other cases, revocation of the order will not normally be authorised unless the situation has been materially altered, either by a change of circumstances since the order was made, or by fresh information coming to light which was not before the appellate authorities or the Secretary of State. The passage of time since the person was deported may also in itself amount to such a change of circumstances as to warrant revocation of the order.

392. Revocation of a deportation order does not entitle the person concerned to re-enter the United Kingdom; it renders him eligible to apply for admission under the Immigration Rules. Application for revocation of the order may be made to the Entry Clearance Officer or direct to the Home Office.

Rights of appeal in relation to a decision not to revoke a deportation order

393. [*deleted*]

394. [*deleted*]

395. [*deleted*]

396. Where a person is liable to deportation the presumption shall be that the public interest requires deportation. It is in the public interest to deport where the Secretary of State must make a deportation order in accordance with section 32 of the UK Borders Act 2007.

397. A deportation order will not be made if the person's removal pursuant to the order would be contrary to the UK's obligations under the Refugee Convention or the Human Rights Convention. Where deportation would not be contrary to these obligations, it will only be in exceptional circumstances that the public interest in deportation is outweighed.

Deportation and Article 8

A398. These rules apply where:

(a)   a foreign criminal liable to deportation claims that his deportation would be contrary to the United Kingdom's obligations under Article 8 of the Human Rights Convention;

(b)   a foreign criminal applies for a deportation order made against him to be revoked

398. Where a person claims that their deportation would be contrary to the UK's obligations under Article 8 of the Human Rights Convention, and

(a)   the deportation of the person from the UK is conducive to the public good and in the public interest because they have been convicted of an offence for which they have been sentenced to a period of imprisonment of at least 4 years;

(b)   the deportation of the person from the UK is conducive to the public good and in the public interest because they have been convicted of an offence for which they have been sentenced to a period of imprisonment of less than 4 years but at least 12 months; or

(c)   the deportation of the person from the UK is conducive to the public good and in the public interest because, in the view of the Secretary of State, their offending has caused serious harm or they are a persistent offender who shows a particular disregard for the law,

the Secretary of State in assessing that claim will consider whether paragraph 399 or 399A applies and, if it does not, the public interest in deportation will only be outweighed by other factors where there are very compelling circumstances over and above those described in paragraphs 399 and 399A.

399. This paragraph applies where paragraph 398 (b) or (c) applies if –

(a)   the person has a genuine and subsisting parental relationship with a child under the age of 18 years who is in the UK, and

    (i)   the child is a British Citizen; or

    (ii) the child has lived in the UK continuously for at least the 7 years immediately preceding the date of the immigration decision; and in either case

        (a)   it would be unduly harsh for the child to live in the country to which the person is to be deported; and

        (b)   it would be unduly harsh for the child to remain in the UK without the person who is to be deported; or

(b)   the person has a genuine and subsisting relationship with a partner who is in the UK and is a British Citizen or settled in the UK, and

    (i)   the relationship was formed at a time when the person (deportee) was in the UK lawfully and their immigration status was not precarious; and

    (ii) it would be unduly harsh for that partner to live in the country to which the person is to be deported, because of compelling circumstances over and above those described in paragraph EX.2. of Appendix FM; and

    (iii) it would be unduly harsh for that partner to remain in the UK without the person who is to be deported.

399A. This paragraph applies where paragraph 398(b) or (c) applies if –

(a)   the person has been lawfully resident in the UK for most of his life; and

(b)   he is socially and culturally integrated in the UK; and

(c)   there would be very significant obstacles to his integration into the country to which it is proposed he is deported.

399B. Where an Article 8 claim from a foreign criminal is successful:

(a) in the case of a person who is in the UK unlawfully or whose leave to enter or remain has been cancelled by a deportation order, limited leave may be granted for periods not exceeding 30 months and subject to such conditions as the Secretary of State considers appropriate;

(b) in the case of a person who has not been served with a deportation order, any limited leave to enter or remain may be curtailed to a period not exceeding 30 months and conditions may be varied to such conditions as the Secretary of State considers appropriate;

(c) indefinite leave to enter or remain may be revoked under section 76 of the 2002 Act and limited leave to enter or remain granted for a period not exceeding 30 months subject to such conditions as the Secretary of State considers appropriate;

(d) revocation of a deportation order does not confer entry clearance or leave to enter or remain or re-instate any previous leave.

399C. Where a foreign criminal who has previously been granted a period of limited leave under this Part applies for further limited leave or indefinite leave to remain his deportation remains conducive to the public good and in the public interest notwithstanding the previous grant of leave.

399D. Where a foreign criminal has been deported and enters the United Kingdom in breach of a deportation order enforcement of the deportation order is in the public interest and will be implemented unless there are very exceptional circumstances.

400. Where a person claims that their removal under paragraphs 8 to 10 of Schedule 2 to the Immigration Act 1971, section 10 of the Immigration and Asylum Act 1999 or section 47 of the Immigration, Asylum and Nationality Act 2006 would be contrary to the UK's obligations under Article 8 of the Human Rights Convention, the Secretary of State may require an application under paragraph 276ADE(1) (private life) or under paragraphs R-LTRP.1.1.(a), (b) and (d), R-LTRPT.1.1.(a), (b) and (d) and EX.1. of Appendix FM (family life as a partner or parent) of these rules. Where an application is not required, in assessing that claim the Secretary of State or an immigration officer will, subject to paragraph 353, consider that claim against the requirements to be met (except the requirement to make a valid application) under paragraph 276ADE(1) (private life) or paragraphs R-LTRP.1.1.(a), (b) and (d), R-LTRPT.1.1.(a), (b) and (d) and EX.1. of Appendix FM (family life as a partner or parent) of these rules as appropriate and if appropriate the removal decision will be cancelled.

Immigration Rules, Appendix FM – Family members (extracts)

Section DVILR: Indefinite leave to remain (settlement) as a victim of domestic violence

DVILR.1.1. The requirements to be met for indefinite leave to remain in the UK as a victim of domestic violence are that-

(a) the applicant must be in the UK;

(b) the applicant must have made a valid application for indefinite leave to remain as a victim of domestic violence;

(c) the applicant must not fall for refusal under any of the grounds in Section S-ILR: Suitability-indefinite leave to remain; and

(d) the applicant must meet all of the requirements of Section E-DVILR: Eligibility for indefinite leave to remain as a victim of domestic violence.

Section E-DVILR: Eligibility for indefinite leave to remain as a victim of domestic violence

E-DVILR.1.1. To meet the eligibility requirements for indefinite leave to remain as a victim of domestic violence all of the requirements of paragraphs E-DVILR.1.2. and 1.3. must be met.

E-DVILR.1.2. The applicant's first grant of limited leave under this Appendix must have been as a partner (other than a fiancé(e) or proposed civil partner) of a British Citizen or a person settled in the UK under paragraph D-ECP.1.1., D-LTRP.1.1. or D-LTRP.1.2. of this Appendix and any subsequent grant of limited leave must have been:

(a) granted as a partner (other than a fiancé(e) or proposed civil partner) of a British Citizen or a person settled in the UK under paragraph D-ECP.1.1., D-LTRP.1.1. or D-LTRP.1.2. of this Appendix; or

(b) granted to enable access to public funds pending an application under DVILR and the preceding grant of leave was granted as a partner (other than a fiancé(e) or proposed civil partner) of a British Citizen or a person settled in the UK under paragraph D-ECP.1.1., D-LTRP.1.1. or D-LTRP.1.2. of this Appendix; or

(c) granted under paragraph D-DVILR.1.2. E-DVILR.1.3. The applicant must provide evidence that during the last period of limited leave as a partner of a British Citizen or a person settled in the UK under paragraph D-ECP.1.1., D-LTRP.1.1 or D-LTRP.1.2 of this Appendix the applicant's relationship with their partner broke down permanently as a result of domestic violence.

Section D-DVILR: Decision on application for indefinite leave to remain as a victim of domestic violence

D-DVILR.1.1. If the applicant meets all of the requirements for indefinite leave to remain as a victim of domestic violence the applicant will be granted indefinite leave to remain.

D-DVILR.1.2. If the applicant does not meet the requirements for indefinite leave to remain as a victim of domestic violence only because paragraph S-ILR.1.5. or S-ILR.1.6. applies, the applicant will be granted further limited leave to remain for a period not exceeding 30 months.

D-DVILR.1.3. If the applicant does not meet the requirements for indefinite leave to remain as a victim of domestic violence, or further limited leave to remain under paragraph D-DVILR.1.2. the application will be refused.

APPENDIX E

Home Office guidance and policy

Asylum Policy Instruction: Discretionary Leave (extracts)[1]

3.5   Modern Slavery cases (including trafficking)

Victims of slavery, servitude and forced and compulsory labour who are conclusively recognised as such by the National Referral Mechanism (NRM) may be eligible for DL based on the same criteria of personal circumstances, helping police with enquires and pursuing compensation as victims of human trafficking, and this provision applies across the UK.

A person will not normally qualify for DL solely because they have been identified as a victim of modern slavery or trafficking – there must be compelling reasons based on their individual circumstances to justify a grant of DL where they do not qualify for other leave such as asylum or humanitarian protection.

As part of the positive reasonable grounds decision letter issued by the Competent Authority of the NRM the potential victim of human trafficking in the UK, and modern slavery in England and Wales, will be asked if they would like to be considered for DL in the event of a positive conclusive grounds decision from the NRM. Where they indicate they would like to be considered for DL this will be considered under the criteria relating to personal circumstances, helping police with enquires and pursuing compensation detailed in the Competent Authority guidance once a positive conclusive grounds decision is issued. The person will not need to fill in an application form or pay a fee for an initial consideration of DL on this basis. A person who has claimed asylum will receive automatic consideration for DL on this basis if they are not granted asylum or humanitarian protection.

5.4   Modern Slavery cases (including trafficking)

Where a person qualifies for DL under the criteria relating to personal circumstances, helping police with enquires or pursuing compensation the period of leave to be granted will depend on the individual facts of the case and should normally be sufficient to cover the amount of time it is anticipated they will need to remain in the UK. However, leave should normally be granted for a minimum of 12 months, and normally not more than 30 months (2.5 years). A further period of leave may be granted if required and appropriate.

---

[1]   Version 7, 18 August 2015.

E2

Victims of Modern Slavery – Competent Authority Guidance (extracts)[1]

THE 2 STAGE NATIONAL REFERRAL MECHANISM CONSIDERATION PROCESS

This section explains the 2 stage National Referral Mechanism (NRM) process for identifying victims of trafficking, stipulated by the Council of Europe Convention on Action against Trafficking in Human Beings.

Part 1

The first part is the Reasonable Grounds test, which acts as an initial filter to identify potential victims.

Part 2

The second is a substantive Conclusive Grounds decision as to whether the person is in fact a victim. This 2 stage test covers all human trafficking cases in any part of the UK (and slavery, servitude, or forced or compulsory labour in England or Wales).

Making a Reasonable Grounds decision

Timescales

The expectation is that the Competent Authority will make a reasonable grounds decision within 5 working days of the NRM referral being received at the UK Human Trafficking Centre (UKHTC) where possible.

Reasonable grounds decisions for cases in immigration detention will be considered as soon as possible.

If the potential victim is the subject of criminal proceedings, it is important that the reasonable grounds decision is made before the court hearing to prevent confusion with remand processes. Staff in the Competent Authority must find out the date of any court hearing.

In some cases dealt with by criminal casework, a person may already have been convicted and sentenced when criminal casework receives the referral.

---

[1]   Version 3, 21 March 2016.

Standard of proof for Reasonable Grounds decision

The Reasonable Grounds test

This is designed to determine whether someone is a potential victim. When the Competent Authority receives a referral, they must decide whether on the information available it is reasonable to believe that a person is a victim of the crime of human trafficking (in Scotland and Northern Ireland) or modern slavery (in England and Wales).

The test the Competent Authority must apply is: whether the statement 'I suspect but cannot prove' (the person is a victim of human trafficking in Scotland and Northern Ireland, or the person is a victim of modern slavery which includes human trafficking or slavery, servitude, or forced or compulsory labour in England or Wales):

- is true
- whether a reasonable person having regard to the information in the mind of the decision maker, would think there are reasonable grounds to believe the individual had been a victim of human trafficking or modern slavery

For England and Wales cases: indicators of all forms of modern slavery are likely to be similar – it may not be initially clear to the Competent Authority whether a potential victim has been subject to human trafficking or slavery, servitude, or forced or compulsory labour. So to reach a positive reasonable grounds decision the Competent Authority just needs to determine that, on the information available, it is reasonable to believe that a person is a victim of the crime of modern slavery; the Competent Authority does not need to distinguish at the reasonable grounds stage which form of modern slavery they have experienced.

Reasonable suspicion would not normally be met on the basis of an unsubstantiated claim alone, without reliable, credible, precise and up to date:

- intelligence or information
- evidence of some specific behaviour by the person concerned

Where reliable, credible, precise and up to date intelligence, information or evidence is present, it must be considered in reaching a reasonable grounds decision.

...

ACTIONS FOR HOME OFFICE AND UKHTC IF THE REASONABLE GROUNDS DECISION IS POSITIVE

Action 1: provide the potential victim with support if they want it for a minimum of 45 days during a recovery and reflection period

If the Competent Authority makes a positive reasonable grounds decision, the individual must be given support if they want it during a 45 day recovery and reflection period. This temporary period provides the conditions for a full evaluation to conclusively decide if the person was a victim of human trafficking or modern slavery at the date of the reasonable grounds decision. This is a not an immigration decision.

The recovery and reflection period is a legal concept that triggers certain rights and measures under the Council of Europe Convention on Action against Trafficking in Human Beings and in no circumstances should the Competent Authority deny an identified victim these rights where the victim indicates they want them. This recovery and reflection period is being extended to cover positive Reasonable Grounds decisions in all modern slavery cases in England and Wales.

...

MAKING A CONCLUSIVE GROUNDS DECISION

When a Competent Authority makes a positive reasonable grounds decision, at the end of the recovery and reflection period they then have to conclusively decide whether the individual is a victim of human trafficking (Scotland and Northern Ireland) or modern slavery (England and Wales).

The Competent Authority is responsible for making a conclusive decision on whether, 'on the balance of probabilities', there are sufficient grounds to decide that the individual being considered is a victim of human trafficking or modern slavery. We refer to this as the Conclusive Grounds decision.

...

England and Wales

The Competent Authority's consideration of the case in England and Wales is in 2 parts:

1. Are there sufficient grounds to decide that the individual is a victim of trafficking?
2. If not, are sufficient grounds to decide that the individual is a victim of slavery servitude, or forced or compulsory labour?

There are therefore 3 potential outcomes for each case:

- the individual is recognised as a victim of modern slavery (human trafficking)
- the individual is recognised as a victim of modern slavery (slavery, servitude or forced and compulsory labour)
- there is insufficient evidence to recognise the individual as a victim of modern slavery, including trafficking

Timescale for Conclusive Grounds decision

The expectation is that a Conclusive Grounds decision will be made as soon as possible following day 45 of the recovery and reflection period. There is no target to make a conclusive grounds decision within 45 days. The timescale for making a conclusive grounds decision will be based on all the circumstances of the case.

Standard of proof for conclusive grounds decision

At the conclusive grounds decision stage, the Competent Authority must consider whether, 'on the balance of probabilities', there is sufficient information to decide if the individual is a victim of human trafficking or modern slavery.

The balance of probabilities

The 'balance of probabilities' essentially means that, based on the evidence available, human trafficking or modern slavery is more likely than not to have happened. This standard of proof does not require the Competent Authority to be certain that the event occurred.

In reaching their decision the Competent Authority must weigh the balance of probabilities by considering the whole human trafficking or modern slavery process and the different and interrelated actions that need to have taken place. To make their decision, they must weigh the strength of the indicators or evidence presented, including the credibility of the claim, and use common sense and logic based on the particular circumstances of each case. See Assessment of modern slavery by the Competent Authority.

Evidence gathering

Competent Authority staff may need to gather more information to make a conclusive grounds decision.

The Competent Authority must make every effort to secure all available information that could prove useful in establishing if there are conclusive grounds.

If they cannot make a conclusive grounds decision based on the evidence available, they must gather evidence or make further enquiries during the 45 day recovery and reflection period.

The Competent Authority must gather this information, where appropriate, from:

- the first responder
- support provider
- police
- Local Authority (in the case of children)

Some of the indicators on the referral form may not be apparent on the initial encounter but will become clear during subsequent interviews with an interpreter and/or at a safe location (for example in a police station). The Competent Authority must be mindful of any ongoing process which may be able to provide additional information.

Police and intelligence reports relating to the alleged crime can provide objective evidence to strengthen a claim. The Competent Authority must also give due weight to the reports and views of:

- Local Authority children's services (for child victims)
- the organisation supporting the individual

The Competent Authority must also take into account any medical reports submitted, particularly those from qualified health practitioners. See View of experts during the NRM process.

NEXT STEPS FOR THE COMPETENT AUTHORITY IF THE CONCLUSIVE GROUNDS DECISION IS POSITIVE

...

When is discretionary leave to remain relevant?

Someone will not normally qualify for a grant of leave solely because they have been identified as a victim of human trafficking or slavery, servitude and forced or compulsory labour ¡V there must be compelling reasons based on their individual circumstances to justify a grant of discretionary leave, where they do not qualify for other leave on any other basis such as asylum or humanitarian protection.

The Home Office will consider whether a grant of discretionary leave is appropriate following a positive conclusive grounds decision. This consideration will happen automatically where the individual has received a positive conclusive grounds decision from the Home Office under the criteria relating to personal circumstances, helping police with enquires, and pursuing compensation detailed below once a positive conclusive grounds decision is issued. The police need to make a formal request to the Home Office competent authority where the police are asking for discretionary leave be granted to the individual under the helping police with their enquiries criteria.

Only the Home Office Competent Authority has an immigration function and other Competent Authorities like UKHTC cannot determine eligibility for or issue discretionary leave. This means that an automatic consideration of discretionary leave does not take place where UKHTC has taken a positive conclusive grounds decision, but those cases can still be granted discretionary leave under this policy where they or the police request discretionary leave on their behalf from the Home Office directly.

Where an individual receives a positive conclusive grounds decision from another competent authority, for example the UKHTC then that individual will need to apply to the Home Office if they are seeking discretionary leave under this policy and relying on the criteria relating to personal circumstances, or pursuing compensation.

Where an individual receives a positive conclusive grounds decision from another competent authority, for example the UKHTC, then the police rather than the individual will need to make a formal request to the Home Office competent authority where the police are asking for discretionary leave be granted to the individual under the criteria of helping the police with their enquiries.

Applications for further discretionary leave can be made by the individual under this policy under the criteria relating to personal circumstances, and pursuing compensation detailed below. Extensions are not considered automatically but must be applied for regardless of which Competent Authority took the positive conclusive grounds decision.

The police rather than the individual will need to make a formal request to the Home Office competent authority under this policy where the police are asking for further discretionary leave to be granted to the individual under the criteria of helping the police with their enquiries. This might be sought if a criminal prosecution takes longer than expected and the police request that the individual be granted further discretionary leave in order to remain in the UK as a witness in the investigation.

For further advice on cases relating to Scotland and Northern Ireland see Section below on Victims of modern slavery in Scotland and Northern Ireland ¡V Discretionary Leave.

Criteria for granting Discretionary Leave to Remain

A grant of discretionary leave will be considered where the Competent Authority has conclusively identified (with a positive conclusive grounds decision) that an individual is a victim of trafficking (within the meaning of Article 4 of the Council of Europe Convention on Action against Trafficking in Human Beings) and either:

- they have particularly compelling personal circumstances which justify a grant of discretionary leave to allow them to remain in the UK for a temporary period of time
- they need to stay in the UK in order to pursue a claim for compensation against their traffickers (the fact that someone is seeking compensation will be relevant to the consideration but does not in itself merit a grant of leave – leave must only be granted where it would be unreasonable for them to pursue that claim from outside the UK)
- the victim needs to stay in the UK to assist with police enquiries (the victim needs to have agreed to cooperate with the enquiry, and the police must make a formal request for them to be granted leave on this basis)

Each case must be considered on its individual merits and in full compliance with the UK¡¦s obligations under EU Directive 2011/36 on preventing and combating trafficking and the Council of Europe Convention on Action against Trafficking in Human Beings.

As a matter of policy a grant of discretionary leave will be also considered where the Competent Authority has conclusively identified an individual as a victim of slavery, servitude and forced or compulsory labour but where they have not been trafficked. This means that anyone with a positive conclusive grounds decision on the basis of modern slavery can be considered for discretionary leave.

The modern slavery victims who were not trafficked have to meet the same criteria to be granted discretionary leave due to personal circumstances, pursuing compensation (but against their modern slavery facilitators rather than traffickers) or assisting police with their enquiries. Where leave is being requested on the basis of assisting the police with their enquiries, the police must make the request that leave be granted on this basis.

Personal circumstances

When a victim receives a positive conclusive grounds decision, it may be appropriate to grant a victim of modern slavery a period of discretionary leave to remain in the UK if their personal circumstances are compelling, in line with Article 14 of the Council of Europe Convention on Action against Trafficking in Human Beings. This must be considered in line with the discretionary leave policy.

Personal circumstances might mean for example, to allow them to finish a course of medical treatment that would not be readily available if they were to return home. Such leave would normally be granted for the duration of the course of treatment or up to 30 months, whichever is shorter.

Victims who pursue compensation

When a victim receives a positive conclusive grounds decision, it may be appropriate to grant a victim of modern slavery a period of discretionary leave to remain in the UK to pursue compensation in line with Article 15 of the Council of Europe Convention on Action against Trafficking in Human Beings which deals with the right of victims to compensation from traffickers.

It may be appropriate to grant a confirmed victim of modern slavery who has been trafficked discretionary leave where it is clear that they need to stay in the UK on the grounds that they are pursuing a claim for compensation against their traffickers.

The same approach will apply as a matter of policy to a confirmed victim of modern slavery who has not been trafficked. It may be appropriate to grant a confirmed victim of modern slavery who has not been trafficked a period of discretionary leave where it is clear that they need to stay in the UK on the grounds that they are pursuing a claim for compensation against their facilitators.

The fact that someone is seeking compensation through the civil courts does not in itself merit victim status or a residence permit. When determining whether to grant a residence permit the Home Office must consider:

- the type of compensation being sought
- the grounds of the claim
- how credible the claim is for example does the compensation claim relate to the claim of trafficking/slavery accepted or rejected by the a competent authority, is the victim claiming compensation for an injury (eg and seeking the cost of medical treatment) when the competent authority is aware that the victim incurred such costs or did not incur such costs, or the competent authority is has seen or not seen evidence that the victim suffered an injury – other issues might also be relevant to credibility
- the likely length of the claim
- whether the person needs to be physically in the UK for the duration of their claim – in some instances it may be more appropriate to facilitate return to the UK nearer to the hearing date or to arrange video conferencing facilities

Victims who are helping police with their enquiries

When a victim receives a positive conclusive grounds decision, it may be appropriate to grant a victim of modern slavery a period of discretionary leave to remain in the UK in line with the Council of Europe Convention on Action against Trafficking in Human Beings (the Convention), where a victim has agreed to cooperate with police enquiries.

In every case where a person is conclusively found to be a victim of human trafficking or slavery, servitude and forced or compulsory labour and has agreed to assist with police enquiries from the UK, the police must make a formal request for them to be granted leave to remain on this basis. Further periods of discretionary leave may be granted where necessary, for example, where a criminal prosecution takes longer than expected and the police have confirmed this and requested an extension.

Requests for discretionary leave, or further periods of discretionary leave on this basis, should be made by the investigating police force, rather than the victim or their representatives. Legal representatives should not make an application for leave to remain on the basis that their client is a witness in an ongoing investigation.

There is no set format in which the police need to make such a request. The police should not complete an application form. They can for example send an email to the Home Office Competent Authority. Requests from the police should be sent to:

- For non EEA cases the request from the police should go to the NRM team in UK Visas and Immigration or Immigration Enforcement who made the positive conclusive grounds decision.
- For EEA cases the request from the police should be sent to the following mailbox for cases in England, Scotland and Northern Ireland. Mailbox for police requests for DL for cases in England, Scotland and Northern Ireland
- For EEA cases the request from the police should be sent to the following mailbox for cases in Wales. Mailbox for police requests for DL for cases in Wales.

If the police make a request before a conclusive grounds decision is taken, they should be notified that no decision on whether to grant discretionary leave will be taken before a conclusive grounds decision is taken.

After the police make a request, the Competent Authority may seek further information from the confirmed victim such as asking them to complete an application form (the FLR(O) or FLR(DL) as appropriate) and return it to the Competent Authority.

...

Assessing credibility – detail and consistency

Level of detail

The level of detail with which a potential victim presents their claim is a factor when the Competent Authority assesses credibility. It is reasonable to assume that a victim giving an account of their human trafficking or modern slavery experience will be more expressive and more likely to include sensory details (for example what they saw, heard, felt or thought about an event) than someone who has not had this experience.

Where there is insufficient evidence to support a claim that the individual is a victim of human trafficking or modern slavery the Competent Authority is entitled to question whether the reasonable grounds or conclusive grounds threshold is met. However, they must also consider whether they need more information.

Consistency

It is also reasonable to assume that a potential victim who has experienced an event will be able to recount the central elements in a broadly consistent manner. A potential victim's inability to remain consistent throughout their written and oral accounts of past and current events may lead the Competent Authority to disbelieve their claim. However, before the Competent Authority come to a negative conclusion, they must first refer back to the first responder or other expert witnesses to clarify any inconsistencies in the claim.

Due to the trauma of human trafficking or modern slavery, there may be valid reasons why a potential victim's account is inconsistent or lacks sufficient detail.

Assessing credibility – considering gender and culture

Competent Authority staff need to know how to consider gender and cultural issues in considering credibility.

When making reasonable grounds and conclusive grounds decisions the Competent Authority must take into account the individual position and personal circumstances of the person and consider culture and gender issues.

Men and women from the same country of origin may have different experience due to their cultural, ethnic, gender and sexual identity. Women may be unable to disclose relevant details due to cultural and social norms.

Assessing credibility – mitigating circumstances

Competent Authority staff need to know about the mitigating circumstances which can affect whether a potential victim's account of human trafficking or modern slavery is credible.

When the Competent Authority assesses the credibility of a claim, there may be mitigating reasons why a potential victim of human trafficking or modern slavery is incoherent, inconsistent or delays giving details of material facts. The Competent Authority must take these reasons into account when considering the credibility of a claim. Such factors may include, but are not limited to, the following:

- trauma (mental, psychological, or emotional)
- inability to express themselves clearly
- mistrust of authorities
- feelings of shame
- painful memories (including those of a sexual nature)

Children may be unable to disclose or give a consistent credible account due to additional factors such as:

- their age
- the on-going nature of abuse throughout childhood
- fear of traffickers or modern slavery facilitators, violence, or witchcraft

Delayed disclosure

A key symptom of post-traumatic stress is avoidance of trauma triggers, or of those things that cause frightening memories, flashbacks or other unpleasant physical and psychological experiences. Because of these symptoms a person may be unable to fully explain their experience until they have achieved a minimum level of psychological stability. The Competent Authority must not view a delay in disclosing of facts as necessarily manipulative or untrue. It may be the result of an effective recovery and reflection period and the establishment of trust with the person to whom they disclose the information.

Difficulty recalling facts

As a result of trauma, victims in some cases might not be able to recall concrete dates and facts and in some cases their initial account might contradict their later statement. This may be connected to their traumatic experience. However, the need to be sensitive does not remove the need to assess all information critically and objectively when the Competent Authority considers the credibility of a case.

Assessing credibility – potential prosecution of traffickers or facilitators of modern slavery

Competent Authority staff need to know about how prosecution of traffickers or facilitators of modern slavery impacts reasonable grounds and conclusive grounds decisions.

When the Competent Authority is deciding whether there are reasonable or conclusive grounds that a person is a victim of trafficking or modern slavery, their decision may be influenced by whether the alleged trafficker or facilitator or modern slavery is being prosecuted. However, their decision must not be dependent on:

- there being a criminal investigation
- whether the victim cooperates in any criminal proceedings

The victim identification process is independent of any criminal proceedings against those responsible for the human trafficking or modern slavery. The criminal standard of proof, that is 'beyond all reasonable doubt', is higher than that of the reasonable or conclusive grounds test.

...

E3

Victims of Domestic Violence (extracts)[1]

DEFINITION OF DOMESTIC VIOLENCE

The government introduced a new definition of domestic violence from 31 March 2013. The definition of domestic violence and abuse is:

> any incident or pattern of incidents controlling, coercive or threatening behaviour, violence or abuse between those aged 16 or over who are or have been intimate partners or family members regardless of gender or sexuality – this can include, but is not limited to, the following types of abuse:

- psychological
- physical
- sexual
- financial
- emotional

controlling behaviour is a range of acts designed to make a person subordinate and/or dependent by:

- isolating them from sources of support o exploiting their resources and capacities for personal gain
- depriving them of the means needed for independence resistance and escape or
- regulating their everyday behaviour

coercive behaviour is:

- an act or a pattern of acts of assault, threats, humiliation and intimidation
- other abuse that is used to harm, punish, or frighten their victim

There is no difference between psychological (mental) abuse and physical abuse when it comes to assessing if a person has been the victim of domestic violence.

…

A person must be 18 years or over to qualify for leave as a partner. This means no-one under the age of 18 can apply under the domestic violence rule as the main applicant.

In the domestic violence context, family members, whether directly related, in-laws or stepfamily, are defined as:

- mother
- father
- son
- daughter
- brother
- sister
- grandparents

The legal definition of injury is when any harm is done to a person by the acts or omissions of another.

---

[1]   Version 13, 29 May 2015.

The rules are only for people who have been the victim of domestic violence during their probationary period of leave.

...

The rules are not intended to benefit people:

- whose relationship broke down because they were the perpetrator of domestic violence
- where the relationship broke down for reasons other than being a victim of domestic violence

The fact that the relationship broke down due to domestic violence during the very early stages of the probationary period is not an adverse factor in reaching a decision. If an applicant meets the requirements in the Immigration Rules, you must grant ILR regardless of how much of the probationary period is completed.

You can accept the relationship was subsisting when domestic violence occurred if evidence is provided that the couple were living at the same address when the incident took place.

The fact the couple are still living at the same address when the application is made must not be taken as an indicator the relationship has not broken down, as this could be due to a number of reasons.

IF AN APPLICANT CLAIMS TO BE DESTITUTE

This page explains how you decide if a victim of domestic violence claims to be destitute and exempt from the application fee.

A person who appears to be destitute will be exempt from paying the application fee for indefinite leave to remain (ILR) as a victim of domestic violence.

If the applicant claims to be destitute they must submit the SET(DV) application form as normal, but will not submit the specified fee. They must provide a letter which says why they are destitute and provide additional evidence to show they:

- do not have access to enough funds to pay the specified application fee
- have total and necessary reliance on a third party for essential living costs, such as basic accommodation and food

If a person shows they are totally reliant on third party support, you must consider them destitute.

Applicants are warned their application will be rejected if this evidence is not provided.

...

Evidence

Evidence to show they are unable to pay could include:

- bank statements
- savings account statements
- wage slips if employed
- other documents that indicate the applicant's financial position

Reliance on third parties

An applicant is deemed reliant on third party support if they can provide evidence to show the third party provides them with the means to live day-to-day.

A written statement from the supporting body is needed if the applicant claims they are totally reliant on a third party for essential housing and living costs, such as:

- a local authority
- a refuge
- friends
- relatives

This statement must confirm:

- the applicant's position
- they are providing housing and living costs support

If an applicant claims they are totally reliant on friends and relatives, they must provide evidence to show they receive this support. The Home Office does not expect that support to extend to paying an application fee. If they are assessed by a local authority or refuge as destitute, written confirmation of that assessment will be evidence to support the decision to waive the fee.

Decision to waive fee

If you decide the applicant is destitute you must waive the application fee.

No decision possible on the evidence supplied

You must not write out for further information when you assess destitution. Your decision must be made based on the evidence the applicant submitted with their application. If you cannot make a decision on the evidence supplied you must get authority from a senior caseworker to reject the application.

Evidence provided does not meet the definition of destitution

You must reject the application on the basis no fee has been paid if the evidence the applicant provides does not support their claim to be destitute. You must fully explain why the applicant does not appear to be destitute based on the evidence they have provided. Applicants will then be expected to pay the fee or resubmit their application and provide other evidence to prove they are destitute.

APPLICATIONS: OUT OF TIME

This page explains what to do with out of time applications on the grounds of domestic violence.

Paragraph 289A, Part 6 of Appendix Armed Forces and section DVILR.1.1 of Appendix FM of the Immigration Rules for indefinite leave to remain (ILR) as a victim of domestic violence do not require a person to have valid leave to remain in the UK. The rules only require a person to have or previously been admitted or granted as a:

- spouse
- civil partner
- un-married partner
- same-sex partner

If an application is received from a person without valid leave to remain in the UK, you must consider the reason they were out of time and must make a judgement on whether this affects the assessment of the evidence submitted in support of the application.

You must consider:

- the age of evidence being relied upon – this may impact verifying the evidence
- how the applicant has been financially supported
- when the relationship permanently broke down
- if there are any official reports, for example from the police that show passports and travel documents were withheld and the police had to retrieve them
- the time between the breakdown of the relationship and the application

CRIMINAL CONVICTIONS AND POLICE CAUTIONS

This page gives guidance about criminal convictions and police cautions as they relate to an application on the basis of domestic violence.

You must take the following types of evidence as proof of domestic violence, they do not need further consideration:

- a relevant court conviction against the sponsor
- full details of a relevant police caution issued against the sponsor

Criminal conviction

A criminal conviction which relates to domestic violence is indisputable evidence that domestic violence has occurred and proof of such a criminal conviction can automatically be used for the purposes of paragraph 289A, Part 6 of Appendix Armed Forces and section DVILR.1.1 of Appendix FM of the Immigration Rules.

Criminal conviction: case not yet heard

Where a criminal case is pending, you must ask the applicant for all relevant evidence from both parties if this has not been provided.

You must make a separate assessment of their application. You must remember the burden of proof in criminal cases is 'beyond reasonable doubt' but the standard of proof in immigration cases is 'on the balance of probabilities'.

If you decide it is not possible to make a decision until the criminal court case is heard, you must refer the case to a deputy chief caseworker.

Police cautions

The applicant will not be able to provide documentary evidence the police have either:

- issued a caution against the sponsor
- have decided to prosecute

Where the applicant alleges a caution has been issued you must ask them for details of the sponsor's:

- full name
- date of birth
- nationality
- address (both at the time of the incident and at the time of the application, if different)
- the date, time and place where the incident took place

Using these details, you must confirm with the criminal records office (CRO) of the police force covering the area where the incident took place. ...

If the police confirm a caution was issued to the sponsor for domestic violence against the applicant it can be used as evidence that domestic violence has occurred for the purposes of paragraph 289A, Part 6 of Appendix Armed Forces or section DVILR.1.1. This is because a police caution is an admission of guilt.

Court orders

This page gives further guidance about court orders as they relate to an application on the basis of domestic violence.

The applicant must submit the original, or a certified copy of, the court order (also known as an injunction).

Without notice (also called ex-parte) order

A without notice order is a type of interim order. Courts give these orders when they think it necessary to set out conditions of an injunction immediately even though the respondent (the alleged perpetrator of the violence) does not know an injunction is being sought.

An applicant usually provides the court with an affidavit (sworn statement) which sets out what has happened and why they feel an order should be made against the respondent.

The court will assess:

- any risk of significant harm to the applicant or a relevant child, because of the conduct of the respondent, if the order is not made immediately
- whether it is likely that the applicant will be deterred or prevented from pursuing the application if an order is not made immediately
- whether there is reason to believe that the respondent is aware of the proceedings but is deliberately avoiding service and that the applicant or a relevant child will be seriously prejudiced by the delay involved

Because a without notice order is given on the basis of a perceived risk rather than a finding of fact or admission of guilt, you cannot accept them as proof of domestic violence.

If not already provided you must request all the evidence submitted to the court, for example the affidavit, and make a decision based on all the evidence provided.

Interim order

An interim order is an order which sets out the conditions the respondent must meet until a final hearing. You must take these as proof domestic violence has occurred.

Final order

Final orders are made where there has been a full hearing and are made for a specified period or until a further order (indefinite) is issued.

The judge will give some final orders as a 'finding of fact'. You must take these as proof that domestic violence has occurred.

The court order will state if there is 'no finding of fact'. If this is the case, the giving of the non-molestation order is not evidence on its own domestic violence has occurred.

In such circumstances, if not already provided, you must request all the evidence submitted to the court and make a decision based on all the evidence provided.

You should reflect on what a judge considers when he or she gives an order, the consistency and credibility of evidence provided and the standard of proof required by immigration law when making a decision based on such evidence.

Delay in hearing

You can delay a decision on the application until the outcome of a hearing if you have:

- confirmation from the court the case is listed to be heard
- the date the case is due to be heard

Normally the court will hear a without notice application on the day of application and the date for the full hearing (the 'return date') should be within seven days. This depends on court availability. The court makes every effort to resolve the case on the return date set, but where the allegations are contested or the case is complicated, it may be re-listed.

The courts give priority to domestic violence cases but demands on court time mean it can take longer than seven days for a hearing to take place.

Terms used in court orders

Applicant's name: This should be the same name as the person who requests leave to remain on the basis of domestic violence.

Respondent's name: This person committed the offence and should be the applicant's partner's name or a member of their family. If the respondent's name does not come within the category of a family member or you are not sure you must consult your senior case worker. …

Layout of court orders

The orders generally follow this layout:

- district Judge's name and court address
- paragraph which indicates whether the order is made without notice (ex-parte)
- paragraph about any 'undertakings' if any are made – undertakings, by one or both parties, may be given to a court instead of proceeding to a full hearing for a final nonmolestation order, or together with the issue of a final non-molestation order where 'no finding of fact' is made – this means there is not necessarily a 'finding of fact' on the allegation(s) – an undertaking is not an admission of guilt unless it specifically says so
- 'Important notice to the respondent' 'it is ordered that:' followed by details of what the respondent 'must not do'
- detail about period for which the order is to remain in force
- 'Power of arrest' – reference to attachment
- 'No finding of fact' (on the allegations by the applicant) – may be detailed at the start or end of the order
- 'Notice of further hearing' (interim orders) – may be 'headed up' in this way, or may just provide details of time/date/place of further hearing
- costs

Formal documentary evidence

This page gives guidance about formal documentary evidence in relation to an application on the basis of domestic violence.

Some evidence may suggest domestic violence has occurred but the alleged perpetrator has not been found guilty by a court or admitted to guilt. You must treat this evidence with caution and consider it along with all evidence supplied. These include a:

- non-molestation order
- letter from the Chair of a multi-agency risk assessment conference (MARAC)

Non-molestation order

Under Section 33 and 42 of the Family Law Act 1996, a person can file for occupancy or a non-molestation order. A non-molestation order is usually the most relevant in domestic violence cases.

Court orders can be unclear and the applicant might present them in a misleading way. If you are unclear on the content of a court order, refer to the guide on layout and terms used in court orders (see related link: Court orders). If you still have doubts, you must refer to your senior caseworker.

A non-molestation order bans the respondent (usually the spouse or partner) from molesting a person associated with them (usually the applicant or a relevant child). When making a non-molestation order the court looks at all the circumstances including the need to secure the health, safety and well-being of the claimant and any relevant child.

Do not confuse non-molestation orders made under the Family Law Act 1996 with contact orders issued under the Children's Act 1989.

POWER OF ARREST

The Domestic Violence, Crime and Victims Act 2004 made breaching non-molestation orders an offence.

The power of arrest is a standard statement and can contradict what is in the main text of the order. You must only take what is written in the order as evidence of domestic violence, not what is written under the power of arrest.

Multi agency risk assessment conference (MARAC)

A MARAC is independent of any civil or criminal court proceeding and, because of this, there may not be any court involvement. The MARAC helps information sharing between a number of different agencies, both statutory and voluntary to contribute to a safety plan for each victim. Only the most high risk cases are referred to a MARAC.

If an applicant states they were referred to a MARAC, you must identify the chair person and send them a letter to ask them to confirm the applicant is the subject of a convened MARAC.

If confirmed this can be used as evidence domestic violence has occurred for the purposes of paragraph 289A, Part 6 of Appendix Armed Forces or section DVILR.1.1 of Appendix FM of the Immigration Rules.

FURTHER TYPES OF EVIDENCE

This page explains what other evidence can be submitted with an application on the basis of domestic violence.

Often victims do not have the official documentary evidence to prove domestic violence.

This may be because of an unwillingness or not enough evidence to take the matter to court or to a multi-agency risk assessment conference (MARAC).

You must always try to get any evidence the applicant has from the police, courts or MARACs. When this is not possible, you must ask the applicant to submit as much evidence as they can.

The list below details some evidence that might be available and would help prove domestic violence. It is not an exhaustive list:

- medical report from a doctor at a UK hospital which confirms the applicant has injuries consistent with being a victim of domestic violence – these may not be physical injuries – for a definition of injuries see Definition of domestic violence
- a letter from a General Medical Council (GMC) registered general practitioner which

confirms they examined the applicant and are satisfied the applicant had injuries consistent with being a victim of domestic violence

- a report or letter from a doctor employed by HM Forces confirming the applicant has injuries consistent with being a victim of domestic violence
- an undertaking given to a court that the perpetrator of the violence will not approach the applicant who is the victim of the violence – however many undertakings are given in order to resolve a non-molestation order proceeding without further costs and hearings:

    - an undertaking is not an admission of guilt and a power of arrest cannot be attached to it. There is equal chance the applicant has given an undertaking to court themselves – you must investigate whether this is the case by either consult with your senior caseworker or write out for further information

- police report which confirms attendance at an incident resulting from domestic violence
- letter from a social services department which confirms its involvement in connection with domestic violence
- if appropriate, letter from a welfare officer connected to HM Forces
- letter of support or a report from a domestic violence support organisation or, if appropriate, from an organisation providing support to family members of HM Forces

This evidence may relate to one incident or a number of incidents and must be used to build a case history, in order to make as thorough a decision as possible, when you make a judgement on whether domestic violence has taken place. You must thoroughly explain all decisions based on such evidence listed above.

Applicants must provide as much evidence as possible to prove they were the victim of domestic violence. Whilst an applicant provides just one piece of evidence from the list above may be able to prove their case, in general an applicant who submitted only one piece of evidence would not usually be considered to have proven their case.

You must treat with caution all witness statements from friends or family and letters from official sources that relay unfounded reports by the applicant but do not confirm the incident.

This type of evidence must be verified where possible and treated as additional evidence when you build the case background.

You must be satisfied the evidence provided is genuine. If you have doubts, you must seek advice from your senior caseworker and/or make enquires with the relevant bodies.

DOMESTIC VIOLENCE FROM A FAMILY MEMBER OTHER THAN THE PARTNER

This page explains what to do if the perpetrator of domestic violence is a family member.

For a definition of 'family member' in a domestic violence context see related link: Definition of domestic violence

If an applicant submits evidence to show they have been subjected to domestic violence from someone other than their partner, they can still qualify for settlement under the rule.

Evidence must clearly show the violence has been the reason for the breakdown of the relationship, for example where the person who abuses the applicant is a member of the sponsor's family and against whom the sponsor offers no protection.

Where this involves minors

If the perpetrator is under 18 in England and Wales or under 16 in Scotland, the law deals with them differently. Offenders may be given a reprimand or a final warning. Both of these are admissions of guilt and are evidence that domestic violence has occurred.

COUNTER CLAIMS

This page explains what to do when there is a counter claim of domestic violence.

You may receive counter claims from the alleged perpetrator, in some cases these claims may already be on the Home Office file.

You can consider counter claims as evidence alongside an application. However, you must disregard any counter claim where the applicant is able to produce evidence:

- of a court conviction
- of a police caution
- they are subject of a multi-agency risk assessment conference (MARAC)

If the applicant is relying on other evidence that domestic violence has occurred, you must consider the counter claims. You must weigh up the evidence presented by each side and make a judgement as to whether you are satisfied, on the balance of probabilities, domestic violence has occurred.

RIGHT OF APPEAL

An applicant who applied on or after 6 April 2015 will not have a right of appeal. Instead they may be able to have their decision reviewed under the administrative review process.

An applicant who applied before 6 April 2015 will have a right of appeal if they:

- applied for an extension of leave before their previous leave has run out
- will not have any leave left as a result of the decision to refuse

An applicant who applied before 6 April 2015 will not have a right of appeal if they have existing leave on the date you refuse the application or did not have any leave on the date they applied.

DESTITUTION DOMESTIC VIOLENCE (DDV) CONCESSION

This section tells you about the destitution domestic violence (DDV) concession effective from 1 April 2012.

A person who flees domestic violence and intends to make a claim for settlement (indefinite leave to remain) under paragraph 289A, Part 6 of Appendix Armed Forces or section DVILR of Appendix FM of the Immigration Rules who is:

- the migrant spouse
- partner of a person present and settled in the UK
- partner of a member of HM Forces who is British or has 4 years' reckonable service

can notify the Home Office if they wish to be considered for limited leave under the DDV concession. This is on the basis that they claim to be destitute.

You must grant under this concession three months limited leave to remain outside the rules with recourse to public funds. This will give the applicant access to temporary accommodation such as a refuge in order to leave their abusive partner and submit a settlement application under the domestic violence rules

The Home Office operates this policy outside of the Immigration Rules to allow eligible applicants, who intend to make an application for settlement under the domestic violence rule, to be granted leave outside the rules (LOTR) which permits them to access public funds and vital services.

LOTR will mean anyone who is eligible does not have to meet the habitual residence test they would otherwise have to meet with other types of leave under criteria set by the

Department of Work and Pensions (DWP). It is in the interest of the applicant the policy is operated as a concession outside of the Immigration Rules.

Eligibility and criteria for destitution domestic violence (DDV) concession

This page explains the eligibility and criteria for people who want to apply for destitution domestic violence (DDV) concession.

The DDV concession for leave outside the rules (LOTR) and the domestic violence provisions of the Immigration Rules (paragraph 289A, paragraph 40 of Appendix Armed Forces and section DVILR of Appendix FM) only apply only to applicants who have previously been granted leave to enter or remain as the:

- spouse
- civil partner
- unmarried or same-sex partner of a:
  - British citizen
  - settled person
  - member of HM Forces who has served for at least 4 years

To be eligible for the DDV concession, the applicant must have last been granted leave under one of the following paragraphs of the Immigration Rules:

- paragraphs, 276AD, 282(a), 282(c), 285, 295B(a), 295B(c) or 295E of the Immigration Rules
- paragraphs 23, 26, 28 or 32 of Appendix Armed Forces
- paragraphs D-ECP.1.1., D-LTRP.1.1., D-LTRP.1.2, or D-DVILR.1.2 of Appendix FM

You must refuse the application for those:

- whose partner is not a British citizen, settled in the UK, or a serving member of HM Forces, with 4 years' reckonable service
- whose last grant of leave was not under one of the paragraphs cited above

Criteria for DDV concession

From 1 April 2012 those who meet the DDV concession criteria are granted 3 months LOTR with a condition code that does not restrict access to public funds. The concession applies to those:

- who were last granted leave to enter or remain in the UK as the spouse, civil partner, unmarried or same-sex partner of a British citizen under paragraphs 276AD, 282(a), 282(c), 285, 295B(a), 295B(c) or 295E or D-ECP.1.1., D-LTRP.1.1., D- LTRP.1.2, or D-DVILR.1.2 of Appendix FM of the Immigration Rules
- from 4 December 2013 onwards, were lasted granted leave under paragraph 23, 26, 28 or 32 of Appendix Armed Forces and are the partner of a member of HM Forces who is British or has served for at least 4 years
- whose relationship with their spouse, civil partner, unmarried or same-sex partner has broken down as a result of domestic violence
- who claim to be destitute and to not have access to funds
- intend to apply for indefinite leave to remain as a victim of domestic violence under either paragraph 289A, paragraph 40 of Appendix Armed Forces or section DVILR of Appendix FM

From 9 July 2012 if you grant the applicant as a post-flight partner under Appendix FM the applicant will qualify under section DVILR only if their partner has settled status at the date of their original application for leave to enter.

Only those eligible to apply for leave under paragraph 289A, Section DVILR of Appendix FM or paragraph 40 of Appendix Armed Forces are eligible for the DDV concession.

Migrants with leave other than as a spouse or partner of a settled person or foreign or

Commonwealth member of HM Forces with 4 years' service

A victim of domestic violence with leave in any category other than as a partner, as defined above, cannot benefit under the DDV concession, as the purpose of the concession is to facilitate an application under the domestic violence provisions and therefore the same eligibility criteria apply.

It is open for migrants in other routes to submit an FLR(O) application if they wish to apply on the basis of Article 8 family life or private life.

Grants of leave under the concession

For people who meet the criteria of the concession, you must issue LOTR (DDV) for 3 months. You must send them a letter which confirms you have granted LOTR (DDV) and issue a status document.

Applicants must submit their SET(DV) application before their 3 months limited leave expires. The Home Office encourages those who are granted three months LOTR to submit a SET(DV) application within eight weeks of their initial grant to make sure their case is considered before their concession leave expires.

If an applicant fails to submit their SET(DV) application within the three months limited leave they become an overstayer and will become subject to removal. This means if you have not received the application within 28 days of their LOTR lapsing, you must refer their case for enforcement action.

Additional notes

To benefit under the DDV concession victims of domestic violence who need access to public funds, must complete and submit the LOTR (DDV) notification form to the Home Office using the email address Domestic.Violence@homeoffice.gsi.gov.uk where possible.

You can accept postal applications, although processing times will be longer. Postal applications can be submitted to the following address: DV Duty Officer Dept 81 UKBA PO Box 306 LIVERPOOL L2 0QN

As part of the notification form, the applicant must say they consent for you to disclose details of their case to any third parties to assist them in their application, such as a refuge, social services, legal representative or DWP.

You must confirm receipt of the notification by email where possible. The Home Office aims to process notifications within 5 working days of receipt.

Index

Advocacy
    legal aid 8.2.8
Age
    assessment 2.2.2
    challenging assessment 2.2.3
    relevance of 2.2.1
**Anti-Trafficking Legal Project
(ATLeP)** 6.2
Anxious scrutiny 2.9.2, 6.9.2
Appeals
    controlled legal representation 8.5.3
    deportation
      assessing public interest 4.4.1
      EEA deportation appeals 4.9
      Nexus cases 4.5
      non-suspensive appeals 4.4.2
      rights under the 2014 Act 4.4
    detained fast-track 2.2.2, 2.4
    fast-track 2.4
    victims of domestic violence 7.5
    victims of trafficking 6.9.1
    see also First-tier Tribunal; Upper
      Tribunal
**Application registration card
(ARC)** 2.1.1
Asylum claims 1.2, 2.1
    activities in the UK 1.6
    acts of persecution 1.10
    application registration card 2.1.1
    assessing risk: country evidence *see*
      Country evidence
    asylum interview 2.1.4
    Asylum Operating Model 2.1
    asylum seekers 1.2
    asylum support 2.1.6
      legal aid 8.2.6
    bad faith, activities conducted in 1.7
    best practice guides 1.1
    burden of proof 1.3.5, 1.3.7, 1.3.8
    children *see* Children
    civil war 1.10.3

'clearly unfounded' certificates 2.7
Convention reasons *see* Refugee
    Convention
country evidence *see* Country
    evidence
credibility *see* Credibility
decision 2.1.5
definition 2.1, **D1**
delays in claiming asylum 1.3.6
demeanour of claimant 1.4.2
different types of claim 1.3.1
discrepancies 1.3.11
documents 1.3.7, 1.3.8
entering the country 1.3.10
EU nationals 2.8, **D1**
evidence from victims of trauma 1.4
fee exemptions 3.7
fresh claims *see* Fresh claims
humanitarian protection *see*
    Humanitarian protection
Immigration Rules **D1**, **D2**
inconsistencies 1.3.11
information and language analysis
    1.3.9
initial steps 2.1.1
internal relocation 1.13, **D1**
journey risks 1.9
language analysis 1.3.9
legal aid 8.2.5
memory 1.3.4, 1.3.11
multiple countries of
    nationality/returnability 1.14
nationality 1.11.3
plausibility 1.4.2
political opinion 1.11.5
race 1.10.3, 1.11.1
refusal of application 1.2, **D1**
religion 1.5.2, 1.11.2
representative's role 2.1.3
risks arising from mode and reality
    of return 1.9

Asylum claims – *continued*
  route of return 1.9
  routing 2.1.2
  screening interview 1.3.11, 2.1.1
  sexuality, based on 1.3.11
  social group, membership of 1.11.4
  state protection 1.12
  stateless individuals 1.1, 1.14.2
  support *see* Asylum support
  sur place claims 1.6, **D1**
  third country cases *see* Third country
    cases
  trauma victims' evidence 1.4
  UNHCR mandated grants of status
    1.8
Asylum interview 2.1.4
Asylum Operating Model 2.1
**Asylum policy instructions
  (APIs)** 2.1
Asylum routing team (ART)
  2.1.2
Asylum seekers
  benefits and services, information
    on 2.1.1, **D2**
  children *see* Children
  definition 1.2
  gender *see* Gender
  local authority support 2.1.6
  well-founded fear *see* Well-founded
    fear
Asylum support 2.1.6
  legal aid 8.2.6

Bad faith
  activities conducted in 1.7
Bail 5.3, 5.4, 5.5
  access to 5.4.2.1
  application process 5.4.2.2
  Chief Immigration Officer bail (CIO
    bail) 5.4.1
  conditions 5.4.2.5
  guidance 5.4.2.3
  power to grant 5.4.2.1
  relevant factors 5.4.2.3
  repeat applications 5.4.2.1
  sureties/recognisance 5.4.2.4
  tribunal bail 5.4.2

Certificate of Travel 2.12.2
**Charter of Fundamental
  Rights of the European
  Union** 3.4

**Chief Immigration Officer bail
  (CIO bail)** 5.4.1
Children
  acts of persecution 1.10
  age assessment 2.2.2
    challenging 2.2.3
  age, relevance of 2.2.1
  as asylum seekers 2.2
  asylum support 2.1.6
  credibility 2.2.1
  domestic violence and 7.4.1
  inconsistencies in evidence 1.3.11,
    2.2.1
  interviewing 2.2.1
  social work records 2.2.1
  third country cases 2.6.1
  tracing parents 2.2.1
  travel documents 3.3.5
  unaccompanied children 2.1.6, 2.2.1,
    D1
    duty to refer 8.6.1
  victims of trafficking 6.3
Civil war 1.10.3
**'Clearly unfounded'
  certificates** 2.7
  human rights claims 2.6.1, 2.7
  judicial review 2.6.1
Compensation 3.1.3
**Convention Relating to the
  Status of Refugees 1951** *see*
  Refugee Convention
**Convention Travel Document
  (CTD)** 2.10.4
Corroboration 1.3.5
  country evidence 1.4.4
  documentary evidence 1.4.4
  evidence from victims of trauma
    1.4.4
  expert evidence 1.4.4
  media reports 1.4.4
  witnesses 1.4.4
**Council of Europe Convention
  on Action against Trafficking
  in Human Beings (CAT)** 6.1,
  6.2, **C5**
  assistance to victims 6.7.2
  definition of trafficking 6.4
Country evidence 1.5
  country guidelines cases 1.5.2
  country information 1.5.1
  expert evidence 1.4.4, 3.6.2
  generic risk cases 1.5.5
  Government reports 1.5.1

Home Office sources 1.5.1.1
inter-governmental reports 1.5.1
monitoring of returnees 1.5.1.1
non-governmental reports 1.5.1
objectivity 1.5.1
online sources 1.5.1
origins 1.5.1
press 1.5.1
relevance of past experiences to
    future risk 1.5.3
researching and presenting 1.5.2.1
specific individual risk 1.5.4
Credibility 1.3, 1.3.4
AITCA 2004 1.3.6, 1.5.4
burden of proof 1.3.5, 1.3.7, 1.3.8
children 2.2.1
delays in claiming asylum 1.3.6
demeanour of asylum seeker 1.4.2
dishonesty and 1.4.3
documents 1.3.7, 1.3.8
Immigration Rules 1.3.5
information and language analysis
    1.3.9
relevant factors 1.3.4
shared duty in establishing facts
    1.3.8
types of behaviour 1.3.6
victims of trafficking 6.3
well-founded fear 1.3
Crimes against humanity
1.15.2.1

Damages 3.1.3
immigration detention cases 3.2.9
judicial review 3.5.3
victims of trafficking 6.8
Degrading
  treatment/punishment
3.2.6.4
destitution in the UK 3.2.6.5
see also Torture
Deportation
appeals
  assessing public interest 4.4.1
  EEA deportation appeals 4.9
  Nexus cases 4.5
  non-suspensive appeals 4.4.2
  rights under the 2014 Act 4.4
automatic 4.2.1, 4.3
discretionary 4.2.2, 4.3
exempted persons 4.1.1
Immigration Rules 4.3.1, **D4**
leave to remain granted 4.6

national security cases 4.2.3
Nexus cases 4.5
procedure 4.3
public policy, public security and
    public health grounds 4.8
  impact of imprisonment 4.8.2
  imperative public security grounds
      4.8.3
  levels of protection 4.8.1
  relevant factors 4.8.4
regimes 4.2
revocation of order 4.7
statutory framework 4.1
'very compelling circumstances'
    4.3.2.1
Detained asylum casework 2.5
Detained fast-track (DFT)
2.2.2, 2.4
Detention
bail *see* Bail
challenging lawfulness 5.4.3
factors influencing decision 5.3.1
judicial review 5.4.3, 5.5
legal aid 8.2.3
persons unsuitable for 5.3.2
power to detain 5.1
  exercise of 5.3
processes 5.2
release 5.4
reviews 5.2
statutory framework 5.1
temporary admission 5.4.1
Discretionary leave 3.3
criminals 3.3.3
medical problems 3.3.1
modern discretionary leave 3.3.2
pre-July 2012 3.3.1
restricted leave 3.3.4
travel documents 3.3.5
victims of trafficking 6.7.3, **E1**
Discrimination, prohibition of
ECHR, Art.14 3.2.13
Dishonesty 1.4.3
evidence from victims of trauma
    1.4.3
Documents
allegations of forgery 1.3.7
approach to 1.3.7
burden of proof 1.3.7, 1.3.8
as corroboration 1.4.4
credibility and 1.3.7, 1.3.8
medical reports 1.3.8

Documents – *continued*
    shared duty in establishing facts
      1.3.8
    UNHCR 1.3.8
    unimpeachable sources 1.3.8
    verification 1.3.8
Domestic violence *see* Victims
  of domestic violence

**EEA nationals and family
members**
    deportation appeals 4.9
    victims of domestic violence 7.7
EU nationals
    asylum claims 2.8, **D1**
**European Convention for the
Protection of Human Rights
and Fundamental Freedoms
(ECHR)** 3.1, 3.2, **C3**
    categories of rights 3.2.2
    death penalty, prohibition on 3.2.5
    discrimination, prohibition of
      (Art.14) 3.2.13
    fair trial, right to (Art.6) 3.2.10
    Human Rights Act 1998 and 3.2.1
    immigration cases 3.2.4
    liberty and security, right to 3.2.9
    life, right to (Art.2) 1.10, 3.2.5,
      3.2.6.5
    non-derogable rights 1.10
    private and family life, right to
      respect for (Art.8) *see* Private and
      family life
    'real risk' 3.2.3
    slavery and forced labour, prohibition
      of (Art.4) 1.10, 3.2.7, 6.8
    standard of proof 3.2.3
    threshold for interference in foreign
      cases 3.2.8
    torture (Art.3) *see* Torture
    unavailability of medical treatment
      abroad 3.2.12
    victims of trafficking 6.8, 6.9.1
Expert evidence 3.6
    as corroboration 1.4.4
    country evidence 1.4.4, 3.6.2
    instructing experts 3.6.1
    medical evidence 3.6.3

Fair trial, right to
    ECHR, Art.6 3.2.10
    extra-territorial application to resist
      removal 3.2.10.2

    legal proceedings in UK 3.2.10.1
Family
    as social group 1.11.4
Family reunion 2.10.3, **D1**
    adult dependent relatives 2.10.3.2
    applications outside Rules 2.10.3.3
    humanitarian protection 2.12.2
    post-flight 2.10.3.2
    pre-existing family 2.10.3.1
Fast-track appeals 2.4
    detained fast-track (DFT) 2.2.2, 2.4
Fee exemptions 3.7
**Female genital mutilation
(FGM)** 1.11.4
First-tier Tribunal
    appeals 3.1.4, 3.5.1
      absence of party 3.5.1.5
      adjournments 3.5.1.5
      case management powers 3.5.1.5
      controlled legal representation
        8.5.3
      deadline 3.5.1.5
      disclosure of evidence 3.5.1.5
      documents provided by Home
        Office 3.5.1.5
      extension of time for lodging notice
        3.5.1.5
      family law proceedings 3.5.1.5
      grounds of appeal 3.5.1.4
      hearings 3.5.1.5
      lodging appeals 3.5.1.5
      onwards appeals to Upper Tribunal
        see Upper Tribunal
      Procedure Rules 3.5.1.5
      protection claims 3.5.1.3
      rejecting invalid notice 3.5.1.5
      rights of appeal 3.5.1.2
      victims of trafficking 6.9.1
    country guidelines cases 1.5.2, **B3**
    Practice Directions **B3**
    Practice Statements **B4**
Forced labour, prohibition of
    ECHR, Art.4 3.2.7
Forced marriage 7.3
Fresh claims 1.2, 2.9
    case law 2.9.2
    human rights claims 1.2, 2.9.2
    Immigration Rules **D3**
    test under 2.9.1
    judicial review 2.9
    previously unavailable evidence
      2.9.4
    sur place style arguments 2.9.5

Gender
    acts of persecution 1.10
    asylum and 2.3
    gender-based violence against
      males 1.4.1
Genocide 1.10.3
Guilt by association 1.15.4

Homosexuality
    persecution 1.10, 1.10.4
Human Rights Act 1998 3.1
    compensation 3.1.3
    damages 3.1.3, 3.2.9
    ECHR, Art.1 and 3.2.1
    effect on public authorities 3.1.2
    interpretation 3.1.1
    remedies and 3.1.4
Human rights claims
    'clearly unfounded' certificates 2.6.1,
      2.7
    fresh claims 1.2, 2.9.2
    third country cases 2.6.1
Humanitarian protection 1.2,
  1.16, **D1**
    benefits of 2.12
    Certificate of Travel 2.12.2
    exclusion 1.16.2, **D1**
    family reunion 2.12.2
    Immigration Rules 1.16.1
    immigration status 2.12.1
    internal relocation and 1.13
    refusal 1.13, **D1**
    revocation 1.16.2, **D1**
    serious harm 1.16.1
    travel documents 2.12.2
    work, benefits and education 2.11

Immigration and Asylum
  Accreditation Scheme
  (IAAS) 8.6.2
Immigration status
    humanitarian protection 2.12.1
    refugees 2.10.1
Inhumane
  treatment/punishment
  3.2.6.3
    destitution in the UK 3.2.6.5
    see also Torture
Internal relocation 1.13, **D1**
    fact-specific enquiries 1.13.2
    safe havens 1.13, 1.13.2
    vulnerable relocators 1.13.1
Istanbul Protocol 3.6.3.1

Journey risks 1.9
Judicial review 3.5.3
    age assessments 2.2.3
    'clearly unfounded' certificates 2.6.1
    damages 3.5.3
    detention 5.4.3, 5.5
    fresh claims 2.9
    further evidence 3.5.3
    human rights breaches 3.1.4
    legal aid 8.2.1, 8.5.5
    of social services 2.2.3
    time limit 3.5.3
    victims of domestic violence 7.5
    victims of trafficking 6.9, 6.9.2

Language analysis 1.3.9
Leave to remain
    application fees 3.7
    discretionary *see* Discretionary leave
    granted where deportation resisted
      4.6
    restricted leave 3.3.4
Legal aid 8.1
    advocacy 8.2.8
    asylum claims 8.2.5
    asylum support 8.2.6
    CW4 and provider obligations 8.5.6
    detention under immigration
      powers 8.2.3
    exceptional case funding 8.4
    full representation 8.5.5
    investigative representation 8.5.4
    judicial review 8.2.1, 8.5.5
    LASPO 2012 8.1
    Legal Help 8.5.1
    matters out of scope 8.3
    matters in scope 8.2
    Merits Regulations 8.5
    'prospects of success' test 8.5.2
    residence test 8.7
    SIAC cases 8.2.2
    victims of domestic violence 8.2.4
    victims of trafficking 8.2.7
Liberty, right to
    ECHR, Art.5 3.2.9

Medical evidence 3.6.3
    as corroboration 1.4.4
    Istanbul Protocol 3.6.3.1
    physical injuries/scarring 3.6.3.1
Medical problems
    discretionary leave 3.3.1

Medical problems – *continued*
  unavailability of medical treatment
    abroad 3.2.12
Memory 1.3.4, 1.3.11
Military action
  contrary to purposes/principles of
    UN 1.15.3
Military service
  acts of persecution 1.10.2
  conscientious objection 1.10.2
  evasion 1.3.1
  refusal to perform 1.10
**Multiple countries of
  nationality/returnability** 1.14
  entitlements to nationality based on
    discretion rather than right 1.14.1
  stateless individuals 1.14.2

**National Asylum Support
  Service (NASS)** 2.1.6, 8.2.6
  see also Asylum support
National security
  deportation 4.2.3
Nationality
  Convention reason 1.11.3
  definition 1.11.3
  deprivation of 1.10
  entitlements based on discretion
    1.14.1
Nexus cases
  special deportation category 4.5
Non-*refoulement* 1.15.6

Operation Nexus 4.5

Palestinians 1.15, 1.15.1
Persecution
  acts of 1.10
  civil war 1.10.3
  future activities 1.10.4
  gay individuals 1.10, 1.10.4
  internal relocation 1.13
  military service 1.10.2
  prosecution and 1.10.1
Plausibility 1.4.2
  evidence from victims of trauma
    1.4.2
Political opinion
  attributed 1.11.6
  Convention reason 1.11.5
  internal relocation 1.13

**Private and family life, right
  to respect for (Art.8)** 3.2.1,
  3.2.11
  deportation and 4.3.1
  discretionary leave 3.3.1
  unavailability of medical treatment
    abroad and 3.2.12, 3.2.12.2
Prosecution
  persecution and 1.10.1
  refusal to perform military service
    1.10
Public funding *see* Legal aid

Race
  Convention reason 1.10.3, 1.11.1
Refugee Convention 1.1, **C4**
  cessation **D1**
  civil war 1.10.3
  Convention reasons 1.11
    attributed 1.11.6
    membership of a particular social
      group 1.11.4
    nationality 1.11.3
    political opinion 1.11.5
    race 1.10.3, 1.11.1
    religion 1.11.2
    torture and 3.2.6.5
  Convention Travel Document
    (CTD) 2.10.4
  definition of a refugee 1.1, 1.11
  exclusions 1.15, **D1**
    activities contrary to
      purposes/principles of the UN
      1.15.3
    crimes against humanity 1.15.2.1
    crimes against international law
      1.15.2
    defences to criminal responsibility
      1.15.5
    evidence and procedure 1.15.5
    guilt by association 1.15.4
    no benefit of the doubt 1.15.5
    non-*refoulement* 1.15.6
    Palestinians 1.15, 1.15.1
    serious non-political crimes
      1.15.2.2
    torture and 3.2.6.5
    war crimes 1.15.2.1
    victims of trafficking 6.9.1
Refugees
  benefits of recognition as 2.10
  definition of a refugee 1.1, 1.11
  family reunion *see* Family reunion

immigration status 2.10.1
settlement protection 2.10.2, 2.12.1
travel documents 2.10.4
work, benefits and education 2.11
Religion
asylum claims 1.5.2
Convention reason 1.11.2
conversion 1.11.2
internal relocation 1.13
Residence permits D1
victims of trafficking 6.7.3
Restricted leave 3.3.4
Routes of return 1.9

Safe havens 1.13, 1.13.2
Screening interview 1.3.11,
2.1.1
Security, right to
ECHR, Art.5 3.2.9
Serious non-political crimes
1.15.2.2
Settlement protection 2.10.2,
2.12.1
Sexual violence
against males 1.4.1
domestic violence 7.3
Sexuality
asylum claims based on 1.3.11
persecution of gay individuals 1.10,
1.10.4
Slavery, prohibition of
ECHR, Art.4 1.10, 3.2.7, 6.8
see also Victims of trafficking
Social group
discrimination 1.11.4
membership of 1.11.4
Social work records 2.2.1
Sprakab reports 1.3.9
Standard civil contract 2013
Immigration and Asylum
Specification 8.6
duty to refer unaccompanied
asylum-seeking children 8.6.1
Immigration and asylum supervisor
legal competence standard 8.6.2
level of accreditation for contract
work 8.6.3
work restrictions 8.6.4
State protection 1.12
Stateless individuals 1.1, 1.14.2
Subsidiary protection *see*
Humanitarian protection

Sufficiency of protection
3.2.6.5
Sur place **claims** 1.6, **D1**
fresh claims 2.9.5

Temporary admission 5.1, 5.3,
5.4.1
Third country cases 2.6, **D1**
adults 2.6.1
Dublin III 2.6.1, 2.6.2
human rights claims 2.6.1
minors 2.6.1
substance of third country
challenges 2.6.3
vulnerability 2.6.2
Torture
absolute nature of prohibition 3.2.6.1
definition 3.2.6.2
degrading treatment/punishment
3.2.6.4
evidence from victims 1.4
inhumane treatment/punishment
3.2.6.3
Istanbul Protocol 3.6.3.1
medical evidence 3.6.3
physical injuries/scarring 3.6.3.1
prohibition of (ECHR, Art.3) 1.10,
3.2.1, 3.2.6
unavailability of medical treatment
abroad and 3.2.12, 3.2.12.1
Trafficking *see* Victims of
trafficking
Trauma victims
evidence from 1.4
Travel documents
Certificate of Travel 2.12.2
children 3.3.5
Convention Travel Document
(CTD) 2.10.4
discretionary leave 3.3.5
humanitarian protection 2.12.2
Immigration Rules **D1**

UNHCR mandated grants of
status 1.8
United Nations Committee
Against Torture (UNCAT)
1.3.11
United Nations Convention
Relating to the Status of
Refugees 1951 *see* Refugee
Convention
Upper Tribunal 1.3.8

Upper Tribunal – *continued*
    appeals from First-tier Tribunals
      3.5.2
      basis of application 3.5.2.1
      controlled legal representation
        8.5.3
      seeking permission to appeal
        3.5.2.2, 3.5.2.3
    country guidelines cases 1.5.2, **B3**
    judicial review 3.5.3
    Practice Directions **B3**
    Practice Statements **B4**

Victims of domestic violence
2.3, 7.1
    appeal right 7.5
    children 7.4.1
    definition of domestic violence 7.3
    destitution domestic violence (DDV)
      concession 7.2.2, 7.6
    EEA nationals and family members
      7.7
    eligibility 7.2.2
    evidencing the claim 7.4
    Home Office guidance **E3**
    Immigration Rules 7.2
    judicial review 7.5
    late applications 7.2.3
    legal aid 8.2.4
    refusals 7.2.1
    signs of domestic violence 7.3
Victims of trafficking
    assessment of claims 6.3
    assistance and support 6.7.2
    asylum appeals 6.9.1
    challenging decisions 6.9
    children 6.3

    competent authorities 6.6.1
    'conclusive grounds' decision 6.7.2
    Convention on Action against
      Trafficking in Human Beings 6.2
    credibility 6.3
    damages claims 6.8
    decision-making process 6.7
    definition of trafficking 6.4
    delayed disclosure 6.3
    discretionary leave 6.7.3, **E1**
    ECHR Article 4 duties 6.8
    EU law protection 6.7.5
    historic trafficking 6.5
    Home Office guidance **E2**
    identification of 6.8
    judicial review 6.9, 6.9.2
    legal aid 8.2.7
    National Referral Mechanism
      (NRM) 6.2
    needs of victims 6.1
    'reasonable grounds' stage 6.7.1
    referral process 6.6
    residence permits 6.7.3
    as social group 1.114

War crimes 1.15.2.1
Well-founded fear 1.3
    credibility 1.3
    different types of claim 1.3.1
    fear 1.3
    future risk 1.3.2
    historic fact 1.3.2
    shared duty in establishing the facts
      1.3.8
    standard of proof 1.3.3
    well-foundedness 1.3, 1.3.2